Intermediate C Programming

Revised for a new second edition, Intermediate C Programming provides a stepping-stone for intermediate-level students to go from writing short programs to writing real programs well. It shows students how to identify and eliminate bugs, write clean code, share code with others, and use standard Linux-based tools, such as ddd and valgrind.

This second edition provides expanded coverage of these topics with new material focused on software engineering, including version control and unit testing. The text enhances their programming skills by explaining programming concepts and comparing common mistakes with correct programs. It also discusses how to use debuggers and the strategies for debugging as well as studies the connection between programming and discrete mathematics.

Including additional student and instructor resources available online, this book is particularly appealing as a classroom resource.

Yung-Hsiang Lu is a professor in the School of Electrical and Computer Engineering of Purdue University, West Lafayette, Indiana USA. He is a fellow of the IEEE and distinguished scientist of the ACM. He is the first director of Purdue's John Martinson Entrepreneurial Center. His research areas include computer vision and embedded systems. He received the PhD. from Electrical Engineering of Stanford University, California, USA.

George K. Thiruvathukal is a professor of computer science and the department chairperson at Loyola University Chicago. He is also a visiting computer scientist at Argonne National Laboratory. He is a senior member of the IEEE. His research interests include high-performance computing, distributed systems, software engineering, machine learning, and computer vision. Thiruvathukal received his Ph.D. from the Illinois Institute of Technology.

Intermediate C Programming
Second Edition

Yung-Hsiang Lu and George K. Thiruvathukal

CRC Press
Taylor & Francis Group
Boca Raton London New York

CRC Press is an imprint of the
Taylor & Francis Group, an **informa** business

Second edition published 2024
by CRC Press
2385 NW Executive Center Drive, Suite 320, Boca Raton FL 33431

and by CRC Press
4 Park Square, Milton Park, Abingdon, Oxon, OX14 4RN

CRC Press is an imprint of Taylor & Francis Group, LLC

© 2024 Lu Yung-Hsiang and George K. Thiruvathukal

First edition published by CRC Press 2017

Library of Congress Cataloging-in-Publication Data

Names: Lu, Yung-Hsiang (Computer scientist), author. | Thiruvathukal, George K. (George Kuriakose), author.
Title: Intermediate C programming / Lu Yung-Hsiang and George K. Thiruvathukal.
Description: Second edition. | Boca Raton, FL : CRC Press, 2024. | Includes bibliographical references and index. | Summary: "Revised for a new second edition, Intermediate C Programming provides a stepping-stone for intermediate-level students to go from writing short programs to writing real programs well. It shows students how to identify and eliminate bugs, write clean code, share code with others, and use standard Linux-based tools, such as ddd and valgrind. This second edition provides expanded coverage of these topics with new material focused on software engineering, including version control and unit testing. The text enhances their programming skills by explaining programming concepts and comparing common mistakes with correct programs. It also discusses how to use debuggers and the strategies for debugging as well as studies the connection between programming and discrete mathematics. Including additional student and instructor resources available online, this book is particularly appealing as a classroom resource"-- Provided by publisher.
Identifiers: LCCN 2023035994 (print) | LCCN 2023035995 (ebook) | ISBN 9781032191744 (hbk) | ISBN 9781032189819 (pbk) | ISBN 9781003257981 (ebk)
Subjects: LCSH: C (Computer program language) | Computer programming.
Classification: LCC QA76.73.C15 L83 2024 (print) | LCC QA76.73.C15 (ebook) | DDC 005.13/3--dc23/eng/20231026
LC record available at https://lccn.loc.gov/2023035994
LC ebook record available at https://lccn.loc.gov/2023035995

ISBN: 978-1-032-19174-4 (hbk)
ISBN: 978-1-032-18981-9 (pbk)
ISBN: 978-1-003-25798-1 (ebk)

DOI: 10.1201/9781003257981

Typeset in CMR10 font
by KnowledgeWorks Global Ltd.

Publisher's note: This book has been prepared from camera-ready copy provided by the authors.

Access the Instructor Resources: https://www.routledge.com/Intermediate-C-Programming-2nd-edition/Lu/p/book/9781032191744

Contents

List of Figures

List of Tables

Foreword for the First Edition

Imagine you run a research or development group where writing software is the means to examine new physics or new designs. You look for students or employees who have a technical background in that specific physics or science, yet you also look for some software experience. You will typically find that students will have taken a programming class or have tinkered around with some small programs. But in general, they have never written software with any serious complexity, they have never worked in a team of people, and they are scared to dive into an existing piece of scientific software.

Well, that is my situation. My research group studies electron flow at the nanometer scale in the very transistors that power your future computer. As a faculty member, I have found that most of today's graduated bachelor students in engineering or physical sciences are used to writing small programs in scripting languages and are not even familiar with compiling, practical debugging, or good programming practices.

I believe my situation is not unique but quite common in academia and industry. How can you bring these novices up to speed? How can you give them the day-to-day practical insights fast, that I had to learn through years of slow-cut and try experiences?

Most advanced programming books explain complex or larger programs that are correct and beautiful. There is an analogy here between reading a well-written book and composing a new novel yourself. Literature analysis helps the reader to appreciate the content or the context of a novel. While many people can read a correctly formulated algorithm in C, few people would be able to write this code even if they were given the pseudocode (the storyline). This book provides an entry into writing your own real code in C.

I believe that this new book provides an excellent entry way into practical software development practices that will enable my beginning and even advanced students to be more productive in their day-to-day work, by avoiding typical mistakes and by writing cleaner code, since they understand the underlying implications better. This book will also facilitate the collaborations within the group through exemplary coding styles and practices.

This book explains the importance of detecting hidden problems. A common mistake among most students is that they pay attention to only the surface: the outputs of their programs. Their programs may have serious problems beneath the surface. If the programs generate correct outputs in a few cases, the students believe that the programs are correct. This is dangerous in this connected world: A small careless mistake may become a security threat to large complex systems. Creating a secure and reliable system starts from paying attention to details. This book certainly covers many details where careless mistakes may cause serious problems.

I wished I had this book some 20 years ago after I had read through Kernighan and Richie. Back then I began writing a large code basis in C after my coding experience in FORTRAN. Passing by reference, passing by value—simple concepts, but this book plays out these concepts in a pedagogically sound approach. I truly like the hands-on examples that are eye-opening.

I recommend this book to anyone who needs to write software beyond the tinkering level. You will learn how to program well. You will learn how to identify and eliminate bugs. You will learn how to write clean code, that cleans up after itself, so it can be called millions of times without crashing your own or someone else's computer. You will learn how to share code with others. All along you will begin to use standard LINUX-based tools such as ddd, valgrind, and others.

Gerhard Klimeck

Reilly Director of the Center for Predictive Materials and Devices (c-PRIMED) and the
NCN (Network for Computational Nanotechnology)
Professor of Electrical and Computer Engineering at Purdue.
Fellow of the Institute of Physics (IOP), the American Physical Society (APS), and
Institute of Electrical and Electronics Engineers (IEEE).

Recommendations for the First Edition

"Intermediate C Programming bridges that critical gap between beginner and expert with clear examples in key areas. This book covers important concepts we use every day in industry when developing and debugging code."

Harald Smit, Software Manager

"Higher-order cognition occurs when one can analyze disparate parts of problems and issues or perform complicated operations. But advanced, critical thinking requires an assessment of how negative consequences can be avoided. In computer programming education, the leap between beginner-level recognition of syntax and artful, efficient language authoring occurs only when a student can regularly identify and predict likely errors in authored code. Intermediate C Programming provides essential lessons and practice in error analysis. By prioritizing debugging into each lesson, the author compels learners to consider the consequences of coding choices, one block at a time."

David B. Nelson, Ph.D., Associate Director, Center for Instructional Excellence, Purdue University

"This well-written book provides the necessary tools and practical skills to turn students into seasoned programmers. It not only teaches students how to write good programs but, more uniquely, also teaches them how to avoid writing bad programs. The inclusion of Linux operations and Versioning control as well as the coverage of applications and IDE build students' confidence in taking control over large-scale software developments. At the end of this learning journey, students will possess the skills for helping others to debug their programs, an important step for building a new generation of programmers who are able to help one another in software development."

Siau Cheng Khoo, Ph.D., National University of Singapore

"This book is unique in that it covers the C programming language from a bottom-up perspective, which is rare in programming books. Instead of starting with the high-level concepts, which easily get dry and uninspiring for students, the book begins with practical problems and progressively introduces the C concepts necessary to solve those problems. This means that students immediately understand how the language works from a very practical and pragmatic perspective."

Niklas Elmqvist, Ph.D., Associate Professor and Program Director, Master of Science in Human–Computer Interaction, University of Maryland

All materials, contents, functions, information, products and services made available or accessed are provided "as is". The authors and the publisher make no warranties or representations of any kind whatsoever, express or implied, concerning the contents, materials, functions, and information or the information, materials, products, and services made available through or in connection with this book. The authors and the publisher make no warranties or representations that the materials, information, contents and services will be error-free, secure, meet your needs or be uninterrupted. The authors and the publisher make no warranties or representations as to the accuracy, reliability and completeness of any information contained in this book. The authors and the publisher disclaim any warranty that the information will be free of viruses, worms, or any other destructive codes. You agree to use and access the information at your own risk.

The authors and the publisher shall not be liable under any theory of contract, tort, strict liability, negligence or any other legal or equitable theory for any direct, indirect, compensatory, consequential, special, exemplary, punitive, or incidental damages arising out of or in any manner connected with the use of or access to the materials and information contained on the book.

Preface

Why Is This Book Needed?

There are hundreds of books about programming, many of them about C programming. Why do we write this book? Why should you spend time reading it? How is this book different from any other book? We write this book because we perceive a need for it. *We think the approach in this book is better.*

We divide existing programming books into two types: *introductory* and *advanced*. Introductory books assume readers have no background in programming and explain the basic concepts, sometimes starting with the "Hello World!" program. These books explain language features step-by-step: keywords, data types, control structures, file operations, and so on. Every program in these books is short, at most 100 lines of code. Each short program can explain one new concept about the programming language. If we think of learning a computer language as learning a natural language like English, Chinese, French, or Korean, these books teach us how to write sentences and short paragraphs. The second type of book is written for people comfortable with programming. These books describe programs solving real problems, such as computer games or networks. The examples in these books are usually quite long, sometimes thousands of lines of code. The source code can be downloaded from the Internet. These books focus mostly on algorithms, not on how to write programs. Readers won't find "Hello World!" examples in these books. Returning to the natural language analogy, these books teach us how to write short novels, maybe a twenty-page story.

It is difficult to jump from writing a paragraph to writing a novel.

A Book for Intermediate-Level Readers

To fill this need, we write this book for intermediate-level readers as a second book on programming. Very few books are written for intermediate-level readers. They know something about programming already and are not surprised when they see `if` or `while`. They know how to create functions and call functions. They can write short programs, perhaps dozens of lines of code. However, they are not ready to handle thousand-line programs. They make mistakes sometimes. Most books talk about how to write correct programs without much help with avoiding common mistakes. The readers are unfamiliar with many concepts and tools that can help them write better programs. These readers need a stepping stone to take them from being capable of writing short programs to writing real programs.

Emphasis on Preventing Mistakes ("Bugs") and Debugging

Most programming books talk about how to create correct programs. However, few books talk about common mistakes and why they are wrong. It is helpful to learn what is correct and also what is wrong. It is important to compare correct programs with incorrect programs. A careless mistake can make a program behave unexpectedly. Worse, the program may be correct in some scenarios and wrong in others. Such bugs (mistakes in computer programs are often called "bugs") are difficult to find. This book explains some common mistakes so that readers understand how to prevent these mistakes. Debugging is ignored in most books. Few books mention the word "debugger" and readers simply do not know the existence of such tools. Learning how to use a debugger can save precious time.

Integration of Programming and Discrete Mathematics

Programming and discrete mathematics are two important subjects in computing. However, most books treat these two topics independently. It is rare to see mathematical equations in programming books. It is rare to see code in books for discrete mathematics. We believe that readers can learn better if they see a closer connection between these two subjects.

Why Does This Book Use C?

IEEE (Institute of Electrical and Electronics Engineers) is a professional society. IEEE reports the most popular programming languages every year. In the 2022 report, the top five programming languages are (1) Python, (2) C, (3) C++, (4) C#, and (5) Java. Among these languages, C++ and C# are directly inspired by C. Java is inspired by C++. Thus, four of the top five programming languages are directly related to C.

Who Should Read this book?

If you are a student in computer science, computer engineering, or electrical engineering, you should read this book. This book covers many concepts essential for understanding how programs work inside computers. If your major is engineering, science, mathematics, or technology, you will very likely need to work with computers and this book will be helpful.

Improvements in the Second Edition

The first edition was published in 2015. We received many suggestions to improve the book. Here is a summary of the changes in the second edition:

- Many chapters have practice questions. If this book is used as a textbook, the questions may be used for homework assignments. Answers are available to the instructors.
- A chapter about computer security is added to Part I. The chapter provides an example of how to modify a program's behavior by using an invalid index of an array.
- A chapter about Unit Test is added to Part III.
- A chapter about solving Sudoku is added to Part IV. This chapter also explains how to transfer data over the Internet.
- The chapter on Huffman compression is revised for better clarity. The reference code is better organized to show how to test the program.
- Appendix A Linux is removed because many websites provide similar information.
- Appendix B Version Control is updated by using `github` and moved to a chapter in Part I.
- Appendix C Integrated Development Environment (IDE) is removed because many websites offer similar information.
- Some materials in the first edition were similar and appeared repetitive. The overlaps have been removed.
- In terms of representation, the source code and the Linux commands have light gray background for easier reading.
- Slides are available online.

Acknowledgments

The authors want to thank James Davis, Usman Chaudhary, and Dev Thakkar for their valuable suggestions.

Source Code

The book's source code is available at

`https://github.com/icptwo`

(`icptwo` means Intermediate C Programming, 2nd Edition.)

Author and Artist

Author

Yung-Hsiang Lu is a professor at the School of Electrical and Computer Engineering at Purdue University, West Lafayette, Indiana, USA. His research areas include computer vision and embedded systems. He is the inaugural director of Purdue John Martinson Engineering Entrepreneurial Center (2020–2022). In 2021, he was selected as a University Faculty Scholar of Purdue University. Dr. Lu is a Fellow of the IEEE (Institute of Electrical and Electronics Engineers), a Distinguished Visitor of the IEEE Computer Society, Distinguished Scientist and Distinguished Speaker of the ACM (Association for Computing Machinery). Dr. Lu received the Ph.D. degree from the Department of Electrical Engineering in Stanford University, California, USA and the BS. degree from the Department of Electrical Engineering at National Taiwan University, Taipei, Taiwan. He is one of the editors of the book "Low-Power Computer Vision: Improve the Efficiency of Artificial Intelligence" (ISBN 9780367744700, published by Chapman & Hall in 2022).

George K. Thiruvathukal is a professor and chairperson at the Department of Computer Science at Loyola University Chicago. He is also a visiting computer scientist at the Argonne National Laboratory in the Leadership Computing Facility. His primary research areas include high-performance computing, distributed systems, software engineering and energy-efficient computer vision. His interdisciplinary interests include computational science, data science, neuroscience, and digital humanities. He has co-authored multiple books: Software Engineering for Science (CRC Press), Codename Revolution: The Nintendo WII Platform (MIT Press), Web Programming: Techniques for Integrating Python, Linux, Apache, and MySQL (Prentice Hall PTR), and High Performance Java Computing: Multi-Threaded and Networked Programming (Prentice Hall PTR and Sun Microsystems Press Java Series). Dr. Thiruvathukal received the Ph.D. degree from the Department of Computer Science at Illinois Institute of Technology, Illinois, USA. He is one of the editors of the book "Low-Power Computer Vision: Improve the Efficiency of Artificial Intelligence" (ISBN 9780367744700, published by Chapman & Hall in 2022).

Artist

The book's cover is painted by Kyong Jo Yoon. Yoon is a Korean artist and he often places heroic figures in natural settings. He is an adviser of the Korean SongPa Arts Association.

Part I

Storage: Memory and File

Chapter 1

Program Execution

1.1 Compile

This chapter explains how to write, compile, and execute programs in Linux. We use a Linux terminal and explain the commands. The terminal is a flexible and convenient interface for working with a computer. Many cloud computing or web services offer terminal access. This is a natural method of providing computing resources, especially when working with many computers (like in a data center). A graphical user interface (GUI) is nice when working with one computer. However, when dealing with many computers, GUI can become a distraction. Start a terminal in Linux and type

```
$ cd
$ pwd
$ mkdir cprogram
$ cd cprogram
```

In this book, `$` is used as the terminal prompt. The first command `cd` means "change directory". If no argument is added after `cd`, as in the first command, then it will return to the home directory (also called "folder"). The second command `pwd` means "print the current working directory". It will be something like `/home/yourname/`. The third command `mkdir` means "make a directory". The command `mkdir cprogram` means "make a directory whose name is `cprogram`". Do not create a directory or a file whose name includes spaces. The international standard for directory names and file names (called *International Standard Organization* or *ISO* 9660) disallows spaces. If a name has spaces, then some programs may not work. The last command `cd cprogram` means "change directory to (i.e., enter) `cprogram`". This is the directory that was just created. In the terminal, use your favorite text editor (such as `vi`, `vim`, `gedit`, or `emacs`). Type the following code:

```c
// CH01:prog1.c
#include <stdio.h> // needed for printf
#include <stdlib.h> // needed for EXIT_SUCCESS
int main(int argc, char * * argv)
{
    int a = 5;
    int b = 17;
    printf("main: a = %d, b = %d, argc = %d\n", a, b, argc);
    return EXIT_SUCCESS;
}
```

Save the file. You can probably guess that this program prints something like

```
main: a = 5, b = 17, argc = 1
```

This is the first complete program shown in this book and requires some explanation. This program prints something by calling `printf`. This is a function provided by the C language. You need to include `stdio.h` before you can use this function; `stdio.h` is a *header file* for standard input and output functions. In a C program, the starting point is the `main` function. The program returns `EXIT_SUCCESS` after it successfully prints some numbers. As you can guess, this program returns `EXIT_SUCCESS` and another program may return `EXIT_FAILURE`. Why should a program return either `EXIT_SUCCESS` or `EXIT_FAILURE`? In today's complex computer systems, many programs are called by other computer programs. Thus, it is important that your programs inform the calling programs whether your programs have successfully accomplished what they are designed to do. This information allows the calling programs to decide what actions to take next. `EXIT_SUCCESS` and `EXIT_FAILURE` are symbols defined in `stdlib.h` so it is included.

Next, let us explain how to convert this program from a human-readable format to a computer-readable format. What is typed into an editor is a "C source file". The representations are readable to humans but computers do not understand this format. The source file needs to be converted into a computer-readable format called an *executable*. A *compiler* is the tool for this conversion; `gcc` is a popular compiler on Linux. In the terminal, type

```
$ gcc prog1.c -o prog
```

This command means the following:

- Execute the `gcc` command.
- Use `prog1.c` as the input for the `gcc` command.
- Set the output file name to be `prog` (`-o` specifies the name of the output file). The output file is an *executable* file, meaning that the computer can execute the file. If `-o prog` is not provided, `a.out` is the default name for the output executable file.

Do not do this:

```
$ gcc prog1.c -o prog1.c
```

This command erases the file `prog1.c` because it sets `gcc`'s output to `prog1.c`.

In Linux, the `file` command reports information about a file. Please type this in the terminal:

```
$ file prog
```

The output should be similar to the following but the details may depend on the computer:

```
ELF 64-bit LSB executable, x86-64, version 1 (SYSV), dynamically linked
(uses shared libs), for GNU/Linux 2.6.24,
```

The word "executable" means that the file "prog" is a program. By convention, executable files in Linux have no extension, unlike ".exe" used in Windows. To execute the program, type this command:

```
$ ./prog
```

Here, `prog` is the name of the program; `./` means the current directory. It is necessary to add `./` because it is possible to have files of the same name in different directories. By adding `./`, the terminal knows that the desired program is in this directory. The program's output is

```
main: a = 5, b = 17, argc = 1
```

The starting point of a C program is the `main` function. What is `argc`? It is easier to answer this question by running the program several times:

```
$ ./prog
main: a = 5, b = 17, argc = 1
$ ./prog abc
main: a = 5, b = 17, argc = 2
$ ./prog abc 123
main: a = 5, b = 17, argc = 3
$ ./prog abc 123 C Programs
main: a = 5, b = 17, argc = 5
```

Do you notice the changes in `argc`? When the program is executed without anything else, `argc` is 1. If some words are added after the program, then `argc` becomes larger. The more words (i.e., *arguments*) are added, the larger `argc` becomes. This illustrates that arguments can be given to the program. Arguments are separated by one or more spaces. The terminal tells your program (specifically, the `main` function) the number of arguments. Adding extra spaces between words makes no difference. One space has the same effect as several spaces. The program itself is always the first argument; thus, the value of `argc` is always at least one. The arguments themselves are strings and are stored in `argv`. Strings will be covered in Chapter 6.

1.2 Redirect Output

This program's output (by the `printf` function) appears in the terminal. In many cases, it is useful to *redirect* the information and save it to a file. Here are some reasons why redirection may be useful:

- A program prints too much information and the computer screen cannot display everything.
- You do not want to wait while the program runs; instead, you want to see the information later.
- You want to check whether the program produces the same information when it runs again. You can use the `diff` command to detect whether two files are identical.
- The program may need to be run on many computers simultaneously. It may be impossible to watch many screens at once.

To save the output to a file, add $>$ and a file name at the end. The output is saved in that file.

```
$ ./prog abc 123 C Programs > output
```

Nothing appears on the computer screen because the information is redirected to the file whose name is `output`. You can use a text editor to see the contents of this file. You can also use the Linux command `more` or `less` or `cat` to see the file's content. If you type `more output` in the terminal, this is what appears on the computer screen:

```
main: a = 5, b = 17, argc = 5
```

Since the output is saved in a file, you can use the `diff` command to check whether that output is the same as the correct output, assuming you have the correct output saved in another file. The `diff` command requires the names of two files and determines whether these files are the same or not. If they are different, the command shows the line-by-line differences. The `diff` program will compare the files exactly. It is often useful to ignore whitespace and this can be done by adding `-w` after `diff`. Adding `-q` after `diff` shows whether the files are different or not, without showing the line-by-line differences. Although the `diff` command is useful, sometimes we want to see the differences side-by-side. The `meld` program in Linux does precisely that.

1.3   Problems

These exercises ask you questions about Linux commands. You may find yourself needing to read the manual pages for these commands using the `man` command.

1.3.1   Replace String

Use the `sed` command to replace all "one" in a file by "two" (without the quotation marks). Please be aware that "one" may appear multiple times in a single line.

1.3.2   Keep Third Column

A file has several columns separated by space. Use a Linux command to keep only the third column in a file.

1.3.3   Find String in a File

Use `grep` to print the lines that contain the word "hello".

1.3.4   Sort by a Column

A file contains many names. The first column stores the first names and the second column stores the last names. Find the lines that contain "Jennifer" as the first names, and sort the lines by the last names.

1.3.5   gcc Warnings

If you add `-Wall` after `gcc`, what does it do?

1.3.6   du command

What does du -s do?

1.3.7   Show End of a File

Which command shows the last 10 lines of a file?

Chapter 2

Stack Memory

2.1 Values and Addresses

In a computer, programs and data must be kept in *storage*. Storage can be divided into *volatile* and *non-volatile*. Volatile storage requires electricity, and can keep data only when a computer is turned on. Volatile storage is usually called "memory". Non-volatile storage persists when a computer is turned off. Non-volatile storage usually uses flash memory or hard disks. Flash memory is also called a *solid-state disk* or *SSD*. A typical laptop computer today has several GB of memory. G means "giga" for one billion. B means "byte" and is a

TABLE 2.1: Memory is arranged into address-value pairs.

Address	Value
First	Zero
Second	Zero
Third	One

sequence of 8 bits. Each bit can store either 0 or 1. If a laptop has 8 GB of memory, the computer can store 64 billion bits in memory. As a reference, the world's population was about 7.8 billion in 2021.

A computer's memory is organized into *address-value* pairs. These pairs are analogous to street addresses and the families that live there. Consider the following scenario:

- The Jones family lives at One Silicon Street.
- The Smith family lives at Two Silicon Street.
- The Brown family lives at Three Silicon Street.

In a computer's memory, each location stores either a zero or a one, like the following, also shown in Table 2.1.

- Zero is stored at the first location.
- Zero is stored at the second location.
- One is stored at the third location.

Programmers usually consider more than one bit at a time. In other words, the unit of data is more than one bit (for example, 8 bits for `char`, 32 bits for `int`, or 64 bits for `double`). For the time being, let us ignore the *size* of the data. Instead, assume that each piece of data occupies one unit of memory. Operating systems guarantee that everything has a unique and positive address. The address is never zero or negative. The symbol `NULL` is defined as the zero as an invalid address. This symbol will be used frequently when we study memory management in Chapter 7. It would be difficult to remember the addresses of the billions of bits in a computer. Instead, programmers create *symbols*, such as `counter` or `sum` to refer to the relevant bits of memory. If the value stored corresponding to a symbol may change during the program's execution, this symbol is called a *variable*. The symbols have meanings to humans writing computer programs. Compilers (such as `gcc`) convert these symbols to addresses. The program reads and modifies the values stored in different

DOI: 10.1201/9781003257981-2

addresses, and does not see the symbols directly. Inside a computer's memory, there are only pairs of addresses and values.

The following figure shows the relationships between symbols and addresses:

source code .c or .h files human readable symbols	compiler (e.g., gcc) $\longrightarrow$	executable program computer readable addresses

Consider the following sample code:

```c
int a = 5;
double b = 6.7;
char z = 'c';
```

TABLE 2.2: Each symbol corresponds to an address and a value.

Symbol	Address	Value
a	100	5
b	108	6.7
z	124	'c'

The relationship between symbol, address, and value may look something like Table 2.2. A programmer has no control over the addresses: The operating systems (e.g., Linux) and the compilers determine the addresses. Programmers do not need to know the addresses of a, b, or z as long as the following rules are observed:

- Each piece of data has a unique address.
- The address cannot be zero (NULL) or negative.
- The compiler can convert symbols to addresses.

2.2 Stack

Computers organize memory into three types: (1) stack memory, (2) heap memory, and (3) program memory. The first two store data and the last stores computer programs. This chapter focuses on stack memory. Heap memory will be explained in Chapter 7. Program memory is managed by the operating systems and thus not discussed in this book. Before talking about stack memory, we must first introduce the concept of a *stack*.

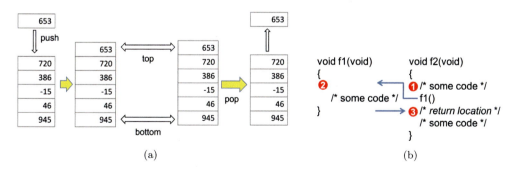

FIGURE 2.1: (a) Pushing and popping data on a stack. (b) The return location is the place where the program continues after the function f1 returns.

Figure 2.1 (a) shows a stack. Adding a number means placing it on the top. Removing a number takes the one from the top. This arrangement is called "last in, first out" (or "first in, last out"). Placing a number on the top is called *push*, and removing a number is called *pop*. The stack concept is used in everyday life. When a person puts on socks and shoes, the socks must go on before the shoes—push the socks, push the shoes. Then, to remove the socks and the shoes, the shoes come off before the socks—pop the shoes, pop the socks. The order is reversed and this is the characteristic of "last in, first out".

Stack memory follows *first in, last out*. New data enters the stack memory at the top, and data is always removed from the top. It would be equivalent to add and remove data from the bottom; however, by convention, we use the top instead of the bottom. Figure 2.1 (a) illustrates these two operations of stack memory. Originally the top of the stack stores the number 720. The number 653 is pushed onto the top of the stack. Later, the top of the stack is popped and 653 is removed. Although this figure illustrates the idea with integers, a stack is a general concept and can manage any type of data.

2.3 The Call Stack

2.3.1 The Return Location

How do computers use stack memory? Consider the following code snippet:

```
1  void f1(void)
2  // void before f1 means no returned value
3  // void in the parentheses means no argument
4  {
5    // ...
6  }
7  void f2(void)
8  {
9    f1();
10   // return location (RL): program continues from here after f1 finishes
11 }
```

The function `f2` calls `f1` at line 9. After `f1` finishes its work, the program continues running `f2` from the line after `f1`. Imagine that a mark is inserted right below the place where `f1` is called, as shown in Figure 2.1 (b). This mark tells the program where it should continue after `f1` finishes. It is called the "return location" (RL), meaning that this is the place where the program should continue after the function `f1` returns (i.e., after `f1` finishes its work). A function is finished when it executes the **return** statement—anything below this statement is ignored. Consider the following example:

```
1  void f(void)
2  {
3    if (...)
4      {
5        // ...
6        return;
7        // the program will never reach here
8      }
9    // else not needed
10   // more code
```

```
11    return;
12    // the program will never reach here
13    // ... code never executed, must be syntactically correct still
14  }
```

In this function, if the condition at line 3 is true, then the function will **return** at line 6. Anything at line 7 is ignored and the program continues from the return location of the function that calls **f**. If the condition at line 3 is false, the function will execute the code at line 9. It is not necessary to have an **else** at line 9 because **return** at line 6 skips everything else in the function completely. When the function reaches line 11, a **return** is executed, and the function stops (line 12 is ignored). Even though lines 7 and 12 are never executed, the code still needs to be correct syntactically. If the unreachable code has any syntax error, a compile cannot generate the executable.

Next, let's consider three functions:

```
1   void f1(void)
2   {
3     // ...
4   }
5   void f2(void)
6   {
7     f1();
8     // line after calling f1, return location B
9     // ...
10  }
11  void f3(void)
12  {
13    f2();
14    // line after calling f2, return location A
15    // ...
16  }
```

Function **f3** calls **f2** at line 13, and **f2** calls **f1** at line 7. When **f1** finishes, the program continues from the line after calling **f1** (line 8). When **f2** finishes, the program continues from the line after calling **f2** (line 14). When **f3** calls **f2**, line number 14 is pushed to the stack memory. Imagine that the line after each function call is marked as a return location (RL), as shown in Figure 2.2. This book uses line numbers as the return locations. The call stack in this book is a simplified conceptual model and does not reflect any specific processor. Real processors use *program counters* instead of line numbers.

The *last in, first out* nature of stack memory is important: The stack memory stores the *reverse order* of function calls. This is how the program knows that it should continue from RL B instead of RL A after **f1** finishes. The program uses the stack memory to remember the return locations. This *stack memory* is also called the *call stack* (or *call stack*).

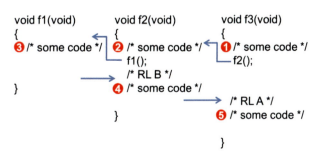

FIGURE 2.2: The return locations (RLs) are marked at the lines after calling **f2** (RL A) and **f1** (RL B).

Every C program has stack memory to control the flow of execution. Almost all computer programming languages employ this scheme.

As our three-function program executes, the *call stack* may appear as follows: When f3 calls f2, the line number after calling f2 (RL A) is pushed to the call stack.

line number (14) after calling f2, i.e., RL A

When f2 calls f1, the line number after calling f1 (RL B) is pushed to the call stack.

line number (8) after calling f1, i.e., RL B
line number (14) after calling f2, i.e., RL A

When f1 finishes, the line number 8 is popped and the program continues at this line number. The call stack now has line number 14.

line number (14) after calling f2, i.e., RL A

When f2 finishes, the line number 14 is popped and the program continues at this line number. Programmers do not need to worry about marking return locations; the compiler inserts appropriate code to do this. It is instructive to note why the stack must store the return locations. Consider this example:

```c
void f1(void)
{
    // ...
}
void f2(void)
{
    f1();
    // RL A
    // some statements ...
    f1();
    // RL B
    // ...
}
```

Function f1 is called in two different locations (line 7 and line 10). When f1 is called the first time, the program continues from line 8 (RL A) after f1 finishes. When f1 is called the second time, the program continues from line 11 (RL B) after f1 finishes. A call stack can manage the situation when the same function (f1) is called from multiple places.

2.3.2 Function Arguments

The Merriam-Webster Dictionary defines an argument as "*one of the independent variables upon whose value that of a function depends*". For a mathematical function, such as $f(x, y, z)$, the variables x, y, and z are the arguments of the function f. In C programs, functions have a similar syntax. Consider the following example:

```c
void f1(int a, char b, double c)
{
    // ...
}
```

```
5    void f2(void)
6    {
7      f1(5, 'm', 3.7);
8      // RL A
9      // ...
10   }
```

The inputs a, b, and c are the arguments for f1. When f2 calls f1, three arguments are provided and their values are pushed onto the call stack. The table shows the addresses and values: every value has a unique address. The arguments are stored in different addresses of the computer's memory managed by the operating system and the hardware. A programmer has no control over the exact addresses used. The addresses can vary widely

TABLE 2.3: A frame includes the return location (RL) and arguments

Frame	Symbol	Address	Value
	c	103	3.7
f1	b	102	'm'
	a	101	5
	RL	100	line 8

on different types of computers. This book uses 100, 101, ... for these addresses. By convention, the addresses start from a smaller number at the bottom and increase upward. The return location (RL) and the arguments together form a *frame* for the called function f1 (not f2). A frame occupies a contiguous chunk of memory. Table 2.3 shows a frame, with the symbols, addresses, and values.

What happens when there is another function call? Consider the following example:

```
1    void f1(int t, int u)
2    {
3      // ...
4    }
5    void f2(int a, int b)
6    {
7      f1(a - b, a + b);
8      // RL B
9      // ...
10   }
11   void f3(void)
12   {
13     f2(5, -17);
14     // RL A
15     // ...
16   }
```

Function f3 calls f2 so f2's frame is pushed to the call stack. Argument a's value is 5 because that is the value given to a when f3 calls f2 at line 13. Similarly, the argument b's value is −17 because that is the value given to b when f3 calls f2 at line 13. Function f2 calls f1 and f1's frame is pushed onto the call stack. Argument t's value is 22 because that is the value of a−b at line 7. Similarly, the argument u's value is −12 because that is the value of a + b at line 7. Table 2.4 shows the two frames.

TABLE 2.4: When f2 calls f1, f1's frame is pushed above f2's frame.

Frame	Symbol	Address	Value
	u	105	−12
f1	t	104	22
	RL B	103	line 8
	b	102	−17
f2	a	101	5
	RL A	100	line 14

2.3.3 Local Variables

If a function has local variables, then the local variables are stored in the call stack. Consider the following program:

```
1  void f1 (int k, int m, int p)
2  {
3    int t = k + m;
4    int u = m * p;
5  }
6  void f2 (void)
7  {
8    f2 (5, 11, -8);
9    // RL A
10 }
```

The arguments k, m, and p are stored in the same frame above the return location. The local variables t and u are stored on the call stack above the arguments. Local variables are always stored on the stack, where they reside for the duration of the function call. They exist in contrast to "global variables": global variables exist throughout the entire program's execution. Global variables can lead to subtle bugs. In 1973, William Wulf and Mary Shaw wrote an article, "Global Variables Considered Harmful". It explained why programmers should avoid global variables. The software community generally concurs, and the use of global variables has been strongly discouraged since then. Although C allows global variables, well-written software avoids global variables. The main problem is that global variables may be changed anywhere in a program. As the program becomes larger and more complex, it becomes increasingly harder to track the places where these global variables may change. Losing track of the changes can often lead to surprising behavior in the program. Although global variables are strongly discouraged, global constants are acceptable and commonly used because they cannot change.

2.3.4 Value Address

So far, all our functions' return types have been void, i.e., the functions return no values. Functions can return values. Consider this example:

```
1  int f1(int k, int m)
2  {
3    return (k + m);
4  }
5  void f2(void)
6  {
7    int u; // value unknown, must not assume it is zero
8    u = f1(7, 6);
9    // RL A
10 }
```

The local variable u is inside f2 so it is in f2's frame. The value of u is unknown before calling function f1. **C does not initialize variables**, so uninitialized variables could store any values (i.e., garbage). It is incorrect to assume that the value is zero. The address of u is stored in the call stack of f1's frame. This address is called the *value address* (VA) because it is the address where the return value of function f1 will be stored. When the frame for

TABLE 2.5: (a) Variable address (VA) stores the address of u from the caller f2. The symbol 𝔸 indicates that it is an address. (b) After f1 ends, the top frame for f1 is popped and 13 is written to the address marked by VA.

Frame	Symbol	Address	Value	Frame	Symbol	Address	Value
	m	104	6				
f1	k	103	7				
	VA	102	𝔸100				
	RL	101	RL 𝔸 (line 9)				
f2	u	100	garbage	f2	u	100	**13**
		(a)				(b)	

f1 is constructed, one more row is added for the value address, and its value is the address of u, shown in Table 2.5 (a). When function f1 executes, it adds the values of k and m and gets 13. The value 13 replaces the value at address 100 (original garbage). After f1 finishes and its frame has been popped, the call stack will appear as Table 2.5 (b).

These are the rules of the call stack:

- When a function is called, the line number after this call is pushed onto the call stack. This line number is the "return location" (RL). This is the place where the program will continue after the called function finishes (i.e., returns).
- If the same function is called from multiple lines, then each call has a corresponding return location (the line after each function call).
- When a function finishes, the program continues from the line number stored at the top of the call stack. The top of the call stack is then popped.
- If a function has arguments, the arguments are stored above the return location.
- A function's local variables are stored above the arguments.
- If a function returns a value, the value is written to a local variable in the caller's frame. This variable's address (called the "value address", VA) is stored in the call stack.
- The arguments, local variables, value address, and the return location together form the *frame* of the called function.

Note that the caller (f2) is not obliged to store the return value of the callee (f1), and line 8 in the example above can be written as:

```
f1(7, 2);
```

In this case, function f1 is called but the returned value is discarded. Since there is no need to store the return value, the value address is not pushed onto the call stack. The word return stops the function and the program continues from the return location; return can be used for two different purposes:

- If void is in front of the function's name, the function does not return any value.
- If the function is not void, the word return assigns a value to the variable given by the value address in the call stack.

2.3.5 Arrays

The following example creates an array of five elements. Each element contains one integer, and the value is uninitialized. Thus, the values are marked as "garbage".

```
int arr[5];
```

If an array has five elements, the valid indexes are 0, 1, 2, 3, and 4. The first index is 0, not 1; the last index is 4, not 5. In general, if an array has n elements, the valid indexes are 0, 1, 2, ..., $n - 1$. Please remember that n is not a valid index. The addresses of an array's elements are always contiguous. Suppose $0 \leq k < n$ (i.e., k is a valid index for an array with n elements). The following equation is always true:

TABLE 2.6: The addresses of an array's elements are contiguous. This example assumes each element has one byte.

Symbol	Address	Value
arr[4]	104	garbage
arr[3]	103	garbage
arr[2]	102	garbage
arr[1]	101	garbage
arr[0]	100	garbage

$$\text{address of } \texttt{arr[k]} = \text{address of } \texttt{arr[0]} + k \times \text{size of each element.}$$
(2.1)

Each element of an array has the same size. Different data types have different sizes; for example, **double** uses 8 bytes and **char** uses 1 byte. The size of **int** is usually 4 bytes but can be 2 bytes in some machines. If an array's elements are not initialized, then the values are garbage (not necessarily zero). The following example initializes all the elements to zero:

```
int arr[5] = {0}; // all elements are initialized to 0
```

The following line

```
int arr[] = {-31, 52, 65, 49, -18}; // no need to give size between []
```

creates an array without giving the size. In this case, the compiler automatically calculates the size as 5. Please be aware that the size of **arr** is 5 times the size of one **int**. If the size of **int** is 4 (on most machines), then the size of **arr** is 20.

2.3.6 Retrieving Addresses

It is possible to get a variable's address by adding **&** in front of the variable. This address can be printed with the **printf** function by using the "**%p**" format specifier. The following example prints the addresses of **a** and **c**.

```
1   // CH02:address.c
2   #include <stdio.h>
3   #include <stdlib.h>
4   int main(int argc, char * * argv)
5   {
6     int a = 5;
7     int c = 17;
8     printf("a's address is %p, c's address is %p\n", &a, &c);
9     return EXIT_SUCCESS;
10  }
```

Below is a sample output from this program:

```
a's address is 0x7fff2261aea8, c's address is 0x7fff2261aeac
```

The output will probably be different when the program runs again:

```
a's address is 0x7fffb8dad0b8, c's address is 0x7fffb8dad0bc
```

If you execute the same program several times, you will likely see different addresses. The addresses are assigned by operating systems.

2.4 Visibility

Every time a function is called, a new frame is pushed to the call stack. **A function can see only its own frame.** Consider these two examples:

```
1  int f1(int k, int m)
2  {
3      return (k + m);
4  }
5  void f2(void)
6  {
7      int a = 5;
8      int b = 6;
9      int u;
10     u = f1(a + 3, b - 4);
11     // some additional code
12 }
13 // version (1)
```

```
1  int f1(int a, int b)
2  {
3      return (a + b);
4  }
5  void f2(void)
6  {
7      int a = 5;
8      int b = 6;
9      int u;
10     u = f1(a + 3, b - 4);
11     // some additional code
12 }
13 // version (2)
```

TABLE 2.7: Renaming arguments has no impact on the call stack. This example assumes each `int` uses four bytes. Each address uses eight bytes.

Frame	Symbol	Address	Value	Symbol	Address	Value
f1	m	132	2	b	132	2
	k	128	8	a	128	8
	VA	120	A\108	VA	120	A\108
	RL	112	line 11	RL	112	line 11
f2	u	108	garbage	u	108	garbage
	b	104	6	b	104	6
	a	100	5	a	100	5
		Version (1)			Version (2)	

These two programs are identical. Renaming the arguments of `f1` from k and m to a and b has no effect on the program's behavior. The a and b in `f1` refer to different address–value pairs than the a and b in `f2`. Table 2.7 shows the call stacks of the two versions. In Version 2, the a in `f1`'s frame has nothing to do with the a in `f2`'s frame. They are unrelated because they occupy different locations in the call stack. The same rule applies to b. Remember that computers do not know about symbols. Computers only use addresses and values. Symbols are only useful for humans; symbols are discarded when a program is compiled into a machine-readable format.

The following example offers a further explanation.

```
1   int f1(int a, int b)
2   {
3       a = a + 9;
4       b = b * 2;
5       return (a + b);
6   }
7   void f2(void)
8   {
9       int a = 5;
10      int b = 6;
11      int u;
12      u = f1(a + 3, b - 4);
13      // some additional code
14  }
```

TABLE 2.8:   Changes in the call stack as the program makes progress.

Frame	Symbol	Address	Value	Value	Value	Value
f1	b	132	2	2	2 → 4	
	a	128	8	8 → 17	17	
	VA	120	A108	A108	A108	
	RL	112	line 13	line 13	line 13	
f2	u	108	garbage	garbage	garbage	21
	b	104	6	6	6	6
	a	100	5	5	5	5
			(a)	(b)	(c)	(d)

Table 2.8 (a) shows the call stack when the program has entered `f1` but has not yet executed line 3. After line 3 has been executed, the call stack will appear as in Table 2.8 (b). Note that function `f1` only modifies the variable a in its frame, since a function can only see arguments and variables in its own frame. Table 2.8 (c) shows the call stack after the program has executed line 4. The value address and the return location do not change as the program moves through the lines of `f1`.

Function `f1` returns a + b, which is $17 + 4 = 21$. The value 21 is written to the value at address A108 (i.e., the value address). After `f1` returns, the call stack is shown in Table 2.8 (d). Note that the values of a and b in `f2` have not changed.

Even though the same symbol may appear in different frames, the same name cannot be defined twice inside the same frame (as an argument or a local variable). The following program is invalid because a is used as both an argument and a local variable, in the same function:

```
1   int f1(int a, int b)
2   {
3     int k = 3;
4     int m = -5;
5     int a = k + 2; // cannot define 'a' twice
6     // a is already used for the name of an argument
7     // cannot use the same name a for a local variable
8     int b = m - 1;
9     return (k + m);
10  }
11  void f2(void)
12  {
13    int a = 5;
14    int b = 6;
15    int u;
16    u = f1(a + 3, b - 4);
17  }
18
```

2.5   Examine the Call Stack with DDD

Type the following program into an editor and save it under the name `ddd.c`

```
1   // CH02:ddd.c
2   #include <stdio.h>
3   #include <stdlib.h>
4   int g1(int a, int b)
5   {
6     int c = (a + b) * b;
7     printf("g1:   a = %d, b = %d, c = %d\n", a, b, c);
8     return c;
9   }
10  int g2(int a, int b)
11  {
12    int c = g1(a + 3, b - 11);
13    printf("g2:   a = %d, b = %d, c = %d\n", a, b, c);
14    return c - b;
15  }
16  int main(int argc, char * * argv)
17  {
18    int a = 5;
19    int b = 17;
20    int c = g2(a - 1, b * 2);
21    printf("main: a = %d, b = %d, c = %d\n", a, b, c);
22    return EXIT_SUCCESS;
23  }
```

Create the executable using the following command in a Linux terminal:

```
$ gcc -g -Wall -Wshadow ddd.c -o ddd
```

This uses `gcc` to convert the source file of the C program `ddd.c`, to an executable file. Adding `-g` enables debugging so that we can examine the call stack. Adding `-Wall` and `-Wshadow` enables warning messages. Shadow variables will be explained in Section 4.1. Warning messages usually indicate serious problems. It is good practice to always enable warning messages, and to act on `gcc`'s advice. The name of the output file (i.e., the executable file) is specified by `-o`. In this example, `ddd` is the output of the `gcc` command. To run this program in a terminal, type

```
$ ./ddd
```

The output should be the same as the following:

```
g1:   a = 7, b = 23, c = 690
g2:   a = 4, b = 34, c = 690
main: a = 5, b = 17, c = 656
```

To view the call stack, we will need to start the debugger. In this example, we will use DDD (Data Display Debugger). DDD is a graphical user interface for the GDB debugger. Start DDD, go to the menu and click `File - Open Program - select ddd - Open`. Please select the executable program, not the `.c` file. The debugger will automatically find the `.c` file based on information added by `gcc -g`.

Set breakpoints at the two functions g1 and g2 with the following commands after the `(gdb)` prompt in the bottom window:

```
(gdb) b g1
(gdb) b g2
```

The first command `b g1` sets a breakpoint when the function `g1` starts. When the program reaches the first line of `g1`, the program stops and you can check the status of the program. The command `b g2` similarly sets a breakpoint when the function `g2` starts. Execute the program by typing the following command at the `(gdb)` prompt:

```
(gdb) run
```

The program will start, and then pause at the breakpoint of function `g2`. Why does the program stop at `g2`, not `g1`? Because the main function `main` calls `g2` first, `g2` is encountered before `g1`. If several breakpoints are set, the program will pause at the breakpoints based on the order in which they are executed, not the order in which they are set. In this example, although the breakpoint at `g1` is set first, the program executes `g2` first. Thus, the program pauses at the breakpoint `g2` first. To continue the program, type the following command:

```
(gdb) continue
```

The program will continue executing and then pause at the next breakpoint, located at function `g1`. The call stack can be viewed by asking for the backtrace. This is done with the following command:

```
(gdb) bt
#0  g1 (a=7, b=23) at ddd.c:6
#1  0x00005555555551b7 in g2 (a=4, b=34) at ddd.c:12
#2  0x0000555555555217 in main (argc=1, argv=0x7fffffffdf78) at ddd.c:20
```

The values of a and b for calling g1 are shown in the top frame. The beginning of each line shows the frames (0, 1, and 2) of the call stack, corresponding to the functions g1, g2, and main. You can use the f command to see different frames: for example, type

```
(gdb) f 1
```

to go to frame 1, i.e., the frame of function g2. The values of a and b can be displayed again. The digits after 0x are likely different on your computer; these are the addresses. In g2's frame, the values of a and b are different from the values in the top frame. Figures 2.3 and 2.4 show some screenshots of DDD.

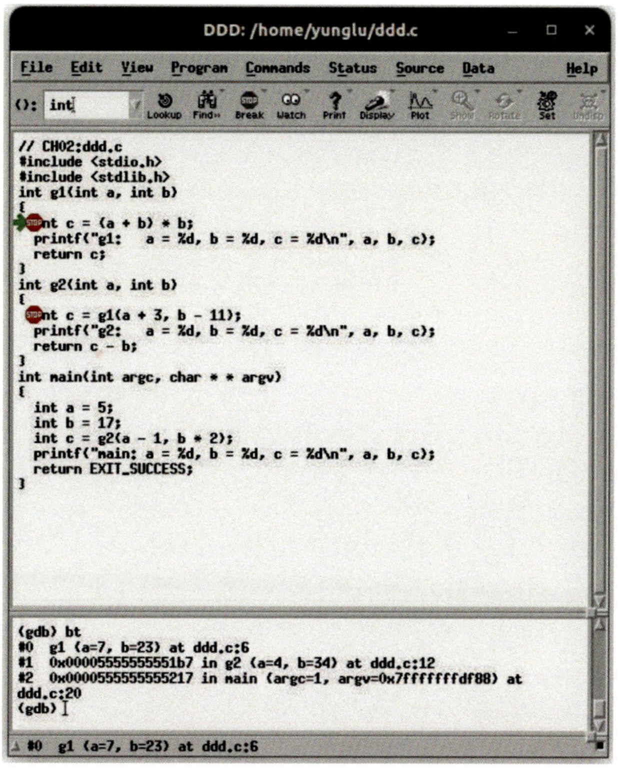

FIGURE 2.3: Use the bt command to show the stack memory.

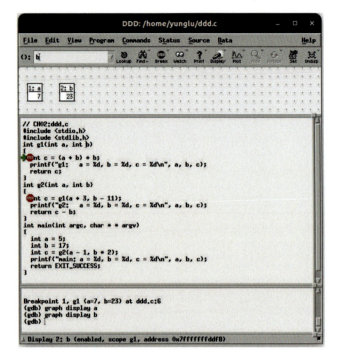

FIGURE 2.4: Display the values of a and b.

2.6 Problems

2.6.1 Draw Call Stack I

```
1   int f1(int k, int m)
2   {
3       int y;
4       y = k + m;
5       return y;
6   }
7   void f2(void)
8   {
9       int a = 83;
10      int c = -74;
11      c = f1(a, c);
12      /* RL */
13  }
```

Draw the call stack

- Before f1 is called.
- When the program has finished the line y = k + m;.
- When the program has finished f1 and the top frame has been popped.

2.6.2   Draw Call Stack II

```
1   void f1(int k, int m)
2   {
3     int y;
4     y = k;
5     k = m;
6     m = y;
7   }
8   void f2(void)
9   {
10    int a = 83;
11    int c = -74;
12    f1(a, c);
13    /* RL */
14  }
```

Draw the call stack

- When the program has entered f1 and finished the line y = k;, what are the values of k and m?
- When the program has finished the line m = y;, and before f1's frame is popped, what are the values of k and m?
- When the program has finished f1 and f1's frame has been popped, what are the values of a and c?

2.6.3   Addresses

- What information is always added to the stack memory when a function is called?
- What information may be added to the stack memory when a function is called?
- How can a programmer control the address of a variable?
- If the same program runs multiple times, will variables' addresses be the same?
- Are the addresses of an array's elements contiguous or scattered?

Chapter 3

Prevent, Detect, and Remove Bugs

Software errors can be expensive. Searching "cost of software error" on the Internet can easily discover dozens of examples where software errors cost millions or even billions of dollars. Some books suggest that software should be well-designed, carefully written, and never debugged. These books do not say anything about debugging. From our experience writing programs, working with students, and talking to people in the software industry, debugging is difficult to avoid completely, even when software is planned and written carefully. In some ways, debugging is like editing an article. It is very difficult to write a good article without any editing. Even though debugging is often necessary, experienced programmers carefully prevent bugs from happening and detect them as early as possible.

Many people learn software development by writing small programs (tens of lines for each program). This is good because learning should progress in stages. The problem is that many people hold onto habits acceptable for small programs when they attempt to write larger programs. Building a one-story house is different from building a skyscraper. Similarly, writing a program of 400 lines requires different strategies than writing a program of 40 lines. This book is written for people learning how to write programs that are several hundred to several thousand lines of code (LoC).

3.1 Rules in Software Development

- Understand that 99.9% success is a failure.
- Use the right tools.
- Spend time to save time.
- Understand that computers cannot tolerate small mistakes.
- Inspect the inside of programs.
- Develop strategies to prevent, detect, and correct mistakes.

Would you be satisfied if a bank lost 0.1% of your money due to a software mistake? Would you accept a wristwatch that lost 40 minutes every month? If you lead in a marathon but you stop several meters before the finish line, what medal do you get? All of these are cases of "99.9% success" but are nonetheless unacceptable. Computers are now being used in many applications, some of which could affect human safety. If your program works correctly 99.9% of the time, then your program could injure people the remaining 0.1% of the time. This is totally unacceptable, and such a program is a failure. Thus, *99.9% success is failure.*

If you live in Pasadena, California, and want to go to New York, which route should you take? Perhaps you could go to the Los Angeles Airport and take a flight. New York is at the east side of Pasadena but the airport is at the west side of Pasadena. Why don't you drive (or even walk) east from Pasadena right away? Why do you travel farther by going

DOI: 10.1201/9781003257981-3

west to the airport? If you drove east rather than waiting in lines at an airport, after one hour of travel you would be close to New York. Why don't you drive? The answer is simple: An airplane is a better tool than a car for long-distance travel. In program development, there are many tools (such as a debugger) designed for managing and improving programs. You need to learn these tools. Learning these tools takes time but you can save much more time when using the right tools.

Despite decades of effort, computers are still pretty "dumb". Computers cannot guess what is on your mind. If your programs tell a computer to do the wrong thing, then the computer will do the wrong thing. If your program is wrong, it is your fault. *Computers cannot read your mind.* There are many instances in which "small" mistakes in computer programs cause significant financial damages, injuries, or loss of lives. Missing a single semicolon (;) can make a C program unusable. Replacing . by , can also make a C program fail. *Computer programs cannot tolerate "small" mistakes.*

Passing test cases does not guarantee a program is correct. Testing can only tell you that a program is wrong. Testing cannot tell you that a program is correct. Why? Can test cases cover every possible scenario? Covering all possible scenarios is difficult and, in many cases, impossible. Problems can be hidden inside your programs. *Producing correct outputs does not mean a program is correct.* Would you consider a plane safe if the plane has taken off and landed without any injuries? If the plane leaks fuel, would you demand the airline fix the plane before boarding? Would you accept the airline's response "Nobody was hurt so this means that plane is safe."? If a driver runs a red light without hitting another car, does that mean running a red light is safe? A program that produces correct outputs is like a plane that lands without injury. There may be problems beneath the surface. Many tools are available to detect hidden problems in human health, for example, X-ray, MRI, and ultrasonic scan. To detect hidden problems in computer programs, we need good tools. We need to fix programs even though they produce correct outputs.

You have to assume that your programs will fail and develop a strategy to detect and correct mistakes. When writing a program, focus on one small part each time. Check it carefully and ensure that it is correct before working on other small parts. For most programs, you need to write additional code for testing these small parts. You will save a lot of time if you write additional testing code, even though the testing code is not included in the final program. Sometimes, the testing code is more than the programs themselves. Our own experience suggests 1:3 to 1:5 ratio—for every line in the final program, about three to five lines of testing code are needed.

No tools can replace a clear mind. Tools can help but cannot replace a deep and thorough understanding of the concepts. If you want to be a good software developer, then you need to fully understand every detail. Do not rely on tools to think for you: They cannot.

This is a general principle in writing good programs: Do not copy-paste code. Do not copy-paste-modify code. When a program has two (or more) pieces of identical or similar code, the program is called "WET" code: WET stands for "We Enjoy Typing". Instead, it is better to write DRY code. DRY stands for "Don't Repeat Yourself". If the two pieces of code are identical, then create a function and call it twice. If they are mostly similar but with a few differences, then the function's arguments can handle the differences. Spending some time fixing WET code usually helps tremendously in developing good programs. Consolidating similar code also helps debugging because a programmer can focus on the common code. WET code is difficult to debug because you have to keep track of several pieces of similar code.

3.2   Developing Software $\neq$ Coding

From the experience of writing small programs, some people have the habit of "coding → testing → debugging". Unfortunately, this is the wrong approach to developing complex software. Expert programmers use strategies to prevent, detect, and remove software bugs. Coding is not developing software, in the same way, laying bricks is not constructing a building. Coding is only one part of developing software. Before typing a single line of code, it is important to know why you are developing the software. Perhaps you are working on homework assignments for a programming class. In this case, you should ask the purposes of these assignments. In particular, there should be some learning objectives. Without knowing the purposes, it is impossible to understand how to evaluate software. This is increasingly important as software becomes more complex. Complex software has many parts and you need to understand why these parts are needed and how they affect each other. Developing software requires many steps before, during, and after coding. The following gives a few principles for you.

3.2.1   Before Coding

- Read the specification and understand the requirements.
- Consider possible inputs and expected outputs.
- Identify valid but unexpected inputs and the correct outputs. For example, when writing a sorting program, what would the program do if the input is already sorted? What would the program do if the same number occurs multiple times? Identifying unexpected inputs is a key concern for developing reliable software.
- Identify invalid inputs and the ways to detect them. Consider the sorting program as an example again. If the specification says valid inputs are positive integers. What would the program do if the input contains floating-point numbers? What would the program do if the input contains negative numbers? What would the program do if the input contains symbols (such as !@#&)? Even when the input is invalid, your program should never crash (for example, producing a segmentation fault).
- Think about the solution and sketch down an approach on paper.
- Draw block diagrams showing how information is exchanged among different parts.
- After you have a design, plan the implementation aspect of the program: How many functions should be created? What does each function do? How many files are needed? When you design a function, try to keep these two suggestions in mind: Each function should do only one thing, and should consist of no more than 40 lines of code. This number is not rigid: 45 lines are all right; 120 lines are too long for a function. A general rule is that the entire function should fit on your computer screen using a readable font size.
- Before writing code, write comments. The comments describe what the program should do and the flow of information. Many people have the habit of "writing code first, then writing comments". This approach will not work for complex programs. Would you like to move into a house that had been built before the blueprints were drawn?
- If you have a detailed design, you will save time on coding and debugging.

3.2.2 During Coding

- This may surprise you: If you want to finish the programs correctly and faster, write more code. Write code to test the program, even though the testing code is not used in the final program. Before you put the code for *one* requirement into a larger program, write a small program to test your solution for that requirement. This is called the *unit test*. If you cannot make one function work, you will be unable to make the entire program work after putting many functions together. After you have done some parts of the programs, make sure these parts work before continuing. You need to write additional code to test these parts since the other parts are not ready yet. This additional work helps you understand what you must do and helps you test what you have done.
- Use a text editor that automatically indents programs and highlights keywords. Such an editor can help you detect braces at wrong places and visually detect possible mistakes. Using the right tools can save you valuable time.
- Read your code line by line before running any test case. We have worked with many students in programming courses. Reading code is a very effective way of detecting problems. Reading code can help find problems that are difficult to find by testing. One example is:

```
if (a > 0); // adding ; is wrong
{
    ... // always runs, not controlled by the if condition
}
```

The semicolon ; ends the `if` condition. As a result, the code inside { and } is not controlled by the `if` condition and always runs. A similar mistake occurs when adding ; after `while` or `for`.

- Run some simple test cases in your head. If you do not understand what your program does, the computer will not be able to do what you want.
- Write code to test whether certain conditions are met. Suppose sorting is part of a program: Check whether the data has been sorted before the program uses the data.
- Avoid copying and pasting code; instead, *refactor* the code by creating a function and, thus, avoiding duplication. If you need to make slight changes to the copied code, use the function's argument(s) to handle the differences. This is a tried-and-true principle: Similar code invites mistakes. You will soon lose track of the number of copies and the differences among similar code. It is difficult to maintain the consistency of multiple copies of the code. You will likely find that your program is correct in some cases and wrong in others. Finding and removing this type of bug can be very time-consuming. It is better to debug a program that is *always* wrong than a program that is *sometimes* right. If it is always wrong, and the problems come from only a single place, you can focus on that place. If the problems appear sometimes and may come from many possible places, it is more difficult to identify and remove the mistakes.
- Use version control. Have you ever had an experience like this: "Some parts of the program worked yesterday. I made some changes and nothing works now. I don't remember exactly what I have changed."? Version control allows you to see the changes. Chapter 12 explains how to use version control.
- Resolve all compiler warnings. Warnings are likely to be serious errors, even though they are not syntax errors.

3.2.3   After Coding

Read your program after you think you have finished it. Check the common mistakes described below.

- *Uninitialized Variables.* One common mistake is uninitialized variables. C does not initialize variables; uninitialized variables store unknown values, not necessarily zero. This type of mistake is difficult to discover by testing. Sometimes, the values may happen to be zero and the program appears correct. When the values are not zero, the programs may have problems.
- *Wrong Array Indexes.* For an array of n elements, the valid indexes are 0, 1, 2, ..., $n - 1$; n is an invalid index. When a program has a wrong index, the program may *seem* to work on some occasions but may crash later.
- *Wrong Types.* Type mistakes are common when pointers are used. The next chapter explains pointers in detail. You can ride a bicycle. You can write with a pen. You cannot ride a pen. You cannot write with a bicycle. In a program, types specify what can be done. You need to understand and use types correctly. The trend of programming languages is to make types more restrictive and to prevent programmers from making accidental mistakes (such as intending to ride a pen). Often `gcc` can detect suspicious type problems as warnings.

3.3   Post-Execution and Interactive Debugging

To debug a program, you need a strategy. You need to divide the program into stages and *isolate the problems based on the stages*. Ensure the program is correct in each stage before integrating the stages. For example, consider a program with three stages: (i) reads some integers from a file, (ii) sorts the integers, and (iii) saves the sorted integers to another file. Testing each stage before integration is called *unit testing*. For unit tests, you often need to write additional code as the "drivers" of a stage. For example, to test whether sorting works without getting the data from a file, you need to write code that generates the data (maybe using a random number generator). Chapter 23 explains unit tests.

Debugging can be interactive or post-execution. Interactive debugging occurs when you inspect a program's behavior while it is running. This is often accomplished by using a debugger, such as `gdb` or DDD. If a program takes hours, you may not want to debug the program interactively. Instead, you may want the program to print debugging messages (this is called *logging*). The messages help you understand what occurs during the long execution. Another situation is debugging a program that communicates with another program that has timing requirements. For example, a program communicates with another program through networks. If you debug the program interactively and slow it down too much, the other program may think the network is disconnected and stop communicating with your program. Yet another scenario is that your program interfaces with the physical world (e.g., controlling a robot). The physical world does not wait for your program and it cannot slow down too much. Logging also slows down a program; thus, do not add excessive amounts of logging.

In some cases, you can slow down your programs and debug the programs interactively—run some parts of the programs, see the intermediate results, change the programs, run them again, and continue the process until you are convinced the programs are correct. For interactive debugging, printing debugging messages is usually ineffective and time-wasting. There are several problems with printing debugging messages for interactive debugging:

- Code needs to be inserted for printing debugging messages. This can be a considerable amount of effort. In most cases, the debugging messages must be removed later because debugging messages should not appear in the final code.
- If there are too few messages or too many messages, it is difficult to determine what is wrong. Getting the right amount of messages can be difficult.
- Worst of all, problems are likely to occur at unexpected places where no debugging messages have been inserted. As a result, more and more debugging messages must be added. This can be time-consuming and frustrating. Instead of using debugging messages in interactive debugging, `gdb` (or DDD) can be a better way for debugging.

3.4 Separate Testing Code from Production Code

You should write programs that can detect their own bugs. If you want to check whether an array is sorted, do not print the elements on the screen and check with your eyes. Write a function that checks whether an array is sorted. You should consider writing testing code *before* you write a program. This is a common practice called *test-driven development*. This section gives you some suggestions about writing tests. Consider the following two examples of testing your code. Suppose `func` is the function you want to test and `test_func` is the code for testing `func`.

```
func(arguments)
{
    /* do work to get result */
    /* test to check result */  // <== This is bad
}
test_func(arguments)
{
    /* create arguments */
    result = func(arguments);  // <== This is better
    /* check the result */
}
```

The first puts the testing code *inside* a function. In the second, the testing code is *outside* the program and the testing code calls `func`. This difference is important because the first mixes the testing code with the actual code needed for the program (called "production code"). As a result, it will be difficult to remove the testing code later when the code is ready for customers. The second separates the testing code from the production code and the testing code can be removed easily. The second is the correct approach for testing. Figure 3.1 illustrates how to separate testing code from production code.

Production Code	Testing Code
function 1	prepare data
...	call function 1
...	check function 1's output
function 2	
...	
...	

FIGURE 3.1: Separate production code from testing code.

3.5   Use assert Correctly

In a C program, the **assert** function evaluates a condition and stops the program immediately if the condition is false. For example,

```
func(int x, int y)
{
  assert(x == y); // stop if x and y are different
  // do more work if x equals to y
}
```

If x equals to y, the program continues and does more work after **assert**. If x and y are different, the program stops. If -DNDEBUG is added after gcc, **assert** is removed. Some books encourage readers to use **assert**. These books claim that stopping a program immediately after detecting a problem is a good strategy in debugging. Unfortunately, these books do not explain how to use **assert** correctly. Production code should *not* use **assert**; instead, **assert** should be used in testing code only. Here are the reasons:

- Some books claim that **assert** should be used when a programmer is "100% sure the condition must be true". This statement is self-contradictory. If a programmer is "100% certain" the condition is true, the programmer would not need to check. Programmers add **assert** when they have doubts. In other words, **assert** may fail.
- Checking the condition of **assert** takes time and slows down a program. Thus, **assert** should not be included in production code.
- It is critical that **assert** does only a simple evaluation, such as comparing two values in the example above. Consider the following example:

```
int * ptr;
assert((ptr = malloc(sizeof(int) * 10)) != NULL);
```

In this example, memory allocation occurs inside **assert**. If -DNDEBUG is added after gcc, then **assert** is removed and **malloc** is not called. As a result, the program will definitely fail. Yes, we have seen code like this.

3.6   How to Comment Code

Almost every programming class requires that students comment their code. Additionally, almost every programming book tells readers to comment their code. However, very few classes or books say how to comment code. Writing comments is like writing an article and it is difficult to grade comments. Comments are about communicating with the readers of the code: Style and clarity are important. If comments do not explain code, then they are not useful.

This book frequently lists the steps before writing a program. These steps should be written in the comments. Programs are written to solve problems: the programs *implement* the solutions. The solutions must be known *before* the first line of code is typed. Writing a program without a solution first is like laying bricks for a house before knowing how many rooms the house will have: this is surely terrible. It is good practice to think about the solution, write down the steps, and explain the thinking process in comments.

In addition to explaining the steps, comments are needed to explain specifics of how the program works: what is required of the function's arguments, and what the return result means. Linux manual pages are good examples. Consider the manual page for the `fgets` function:

---

char *fgets(char *s, int size, FILE *stream);

fgets() reads in at most one less than size characters from stream and stores them into the buffer pointed to by s. Reading stops after an EOF or a newline. If a newline is read, it is stored into the buffer. A terminating null byte ('\0') is stored after the last character in the buffer.

fgets() return s on success, and NULL on error or when end of file occurs while no characters have been read.

This explains the arguments, the behavior of the function, and the return value.

A common mistake is to repeat information that is obvious from the syntax. The following comment is unnecessary:

```
// This function has two arguments (integers).
// The function returns an integer.
int func(int a, int b);
```

In contrast, the following example shows comments with useful information unavailable by reading the code.

```
// The function returns
//    1  if a > b
//    0  if a == b
//   -1 if a < b
int func(int a, int b);
```

Comments should provide information unavailable from the syntax. Comments are important when explaining complex concepts. The following comment describes the steps:

```
// 1. open input file
// 2. count the number of lines
// 3. allocate memory
// 4. return to the beginning of the file
```

Writing good comments takes practice. It is helpful to read others' code and see what comments are useful, and what are merely distractions. This is also important for your own code. If you read a program written six months ago, can you understand it easily? If the meaning is not apparent, then the comments can be improved. With practice, comments become a good way to further understand your code by testing your ability to explain it. This, in turn, helps catch subtle problems, and also helps you generate good test cases. Good comments augment carefully chosen variable names and clear syntax. Doing this shows that you have thought deeply about the program.

This chapter provides some strategies for writing correct programs. With these strategies, you can have a systematic way to prevent, detect, and remove bugs.

Chapter 4

Pointers

4.1 Scope

Chapter 2 described several rules about the stack memory. One of those rules was that each function could see only its own frame. This is called *scope*. A new scope is created every time a pair of { and } is used. This could be inside of a function body, for example, an `if` statement, or a `while` loop. The following example shows two scopes:

```
void f(int a, int b)
{
    // this is a scope, call it X
    int i;
    for (i = 0; i < a + b; i ++)
      {
        // this is another scope, call it Y. a, b, i visible here
        int j; // j is visible only between the { ... } pair
        // some code
      }
    // j is not visible here
}
```

In the scope marked X (in the comments), a and b are arguments and i is a local variable. Another scope called Y is created inside of X. Variables from the outer scope are still accessible, so scope Y can see a, b, and i. A local variable j is created inside of scope Y and is accessible only inside scope Y, between the { and } of the for loop (lines 8 and 9). Line 11 is in scope X and outside Y; thus, j cannot be seen at line 11.

The following example has three scopes: X, Y, and Z. The arguments a and b in f1 have nothing to do with the arguments of a and b in f2 because they are in different and non-overlapping scopes: f1 is not nested in f2 or vice versa. They are in different frames in the stack memory.

```
void f1(int a, int b)
{
    // this is a scope, call it X
    int i;
    for (i = 0; i < a + b; i ++)
      {
        // this is another scope, call it Y
        int j;
      }
}
```

DOI: 10.1201/9781003257981-4

```
11    void f2(int a, int b)
12    {
13      // this is a scope, call it Z
14      f1(a + b, a - b);
15      /* RL A */
16    }
```

It is legal to create another variable of the same name in an inner scope, like u.

```
1    void f1(int u, int v)
2    {
3      int i; // scope X
4      for (i = 0; i < u + v; i ++)
5        {
6          // scope Y
7          int j;
8          int u; // shadow variable, notice int before u
9        }
10   }
```

In the inner scope Y, we create a new variable called u. Please note that Y already has an argument called u. By adding the type int in front of u, a new variable is created. This function now has two variables both called u in the overlapping scopes (Y is nested inside of X). This makes the u in Y a *shadow variable* of the u in X. These two variables have two different memory addresses. Modifying the u in scope Y does not change the u in scope X. Shadow variables are considered a bad programming style because they make programs difficult to understand, and can introduce subtle errors. Consider the following example:

```
1    void f1(int u, int v)
2    {
3      int i;
4      u = 27;
5      for (i = 0; i < u + v; i ++)
6        {
7          int u; // shadow variable because of int before u
8          u = 5;
9        }
10     // u is 27 even though it was assigned to 5 two lines earlier
11   }
```

The value of u is 5 just above the closing brace (line 9) that encloses scope Y. After leaving Y, the value of u is 27 because the outer u was never changed. This can make the program confusing, and confusing programs are error-prone. Fortunately, gcc can detect shadow variables by adding -Wshadow.

4.2 The Swap Function

A function can return only one value. The returned value can be used to modify one variable in the caller. For example,

```
1   int f1(int a, int b)
2   {
3     return (a + b);
4   }
5   void f2(void)
6   {
7     int s;
8     s = f1(2, 37);
9     /* RL A */
10  }
```

In the function f2, we see s becomes the sum of 2 and 37. By calling f1, we change one variable in the caller f2 (the value of s). What can we do if we want to change two or more variables in the caller? Suppose we want to write a *swap function*,

```
1   void swap(int x, int y)
2   {
3     /* do something to swap x and y */
4   }
5   void f2(void)
6   {
7     int a = 2;
8     int b = 37;
9     swap(a, b);
10    /* RL A */
11  }
```

Can this swap function work?

```
1   void swap(int x, int y)
2   {
3     int z = x;
4     x = y;
5     y = z;
6   }
```

When the swap function is called, the values of a and b are *copied* to the arguments x and y. The call stack is shown in Table 4.1.

The value of x is stored in a temporary variable z. Then y's value is assigned to x and z's value is assigned to y. After these three steps, x has y's old value and y has x's old value (through z). After finishing line 5 in swap.

Inside the swap function, the values of x and y have been swapped. As explained in Chapter 2, when swap finishes, the top frame is popped. The swap function was called and finished, and the values of a and b have not

TABLE 4.1: Calling swap copies the values of a and b to x and y.

Frame	Symbol	Address	Value
	z	120	-
swap	y	116	37
	x	112	2
	RL	108	RL A
f2	b	104	37
	a	100	2

changed. This `swap` function does not work. C programs use "call-by-value" when calling functions. That means that values are copied from the caller to the arguments of the called function (i.e., callee). This is the only way to call functions in C. Does this mean it is impossible to write a swap function?

4.3   Pointers

C solves this problem by creating the concept of *pointers*. A pointer is a variable whose value is a memory address. To create a pointer, add `*` after the type.

```
type * ptr; // ptr is a pointer, its value is a memory address
```

This creates a pointer called `ptr`. Its value is an address. At that address stores a value of the given type. This may seem abstract so let us see some examples:

```
int    * iptr;
char   * cptr;
double * dptr;
```

name	value	at that address
iptr	an address	an integer
cptr	an address	a character
dptr	an address	a double-precision floating-point number

In each case, the pointer stores a memory address. Chapter 2 said programmers cannot control addresses. That is still true: programmers cannot decide the addresses of variables. Programmers can *read* the addresses assigned to variables. C provides special syntax for this purpose: by adding an `&` in front of a variable. For example,

```
int a = -61;   // a is an integer
int * iptr;    // iptr is a pointer
iptr = & a;    // iptr's value is a's address
```

A programmer can change variables' values or read variables' addresses; a programmer cannot change variables' addresses. Section 2.3.6 prints the addresses of two variables a and c. It shows that the addresses change when the same program runs again. By using an ampersand (&)

Symbol	Address	Value
iptr	104	A100
a	100	−61

in front of a, iptr's value changes when a's address changes. You may want to ask why this example uses A100 for a's address; the prefix A means this is an address. The addresses in Section 2.3.6 are much larger values. In order to make the book easier to read, the book uses smaller values for addresses. Like any other variable type (such as `int` or `char`), two pointers can have the same value.

```
int a = 632;
int c;         // c's value is garbage now
c = a;         // c's value is the same as a's value (i.e., 632)
```

```
4   int * iptr1;    // iptr1's value is garbage now
5   int * iptr2;    // iptr2's value is garbage now
6   iptr1 = & a;    // iptr1's value is a's address
7   iptr2 = iptr1;  // iptr2 and iptr1 have the same value
```

After executing the first line, an integer called a has been created and its value is 632. The next line creates another integer variable called c and its value is not defined yet. The third line makes c's value the same as a's value. The fourth and fifth lines create two pointers. Their values are currently undefined. The seventh line assigns a's address to iptr1's value. Since a's address is A100, iptr1's value is A100. Please notice that iptr1's address is 108, not A100: 108 is iptr1's address and A100 is iptr1's value. The seventh line assigns iptr1's value to iptr2's value. The third and the seventh lines are similar: The third line assigns a's value to c's value; the seventh line assigns the value of iptr1 to the value of iptr2. Table 4.2 shows the result. This book assumes that each integer (i.e., int) uses four bytes; each pointer uses eight bytes. The actual sizes depend on the machines.

It is possible to use a pointer and retrieve the value stored at that address.

TABLE 4.2: Result of iptr2 = iptr1.

Symbol	Address	Value
iptr2	116	A100
iptr1	108	A100
c	104	632
a	100	632

```
1    int a = 632;
2    int * iptr;
3    int c;
4    iptr = & a;
5    c = * iptr;
6    // 1. read iptr's value as an address
7    // 2. go to that address
8    // 3. read the value at that address
9    // 4. assign the value to c
10   printf("%d", * iptr); // print 632
11   * iptr = -84; // this changes the value of a
```

The fifth line does the following things: (1) Takes iptr's value as an address. The value is A100. (2) Goes to address A100. (3) Reads the value at that address and it is 632. (4) Assigns 632 to c. After the fifth line, the value of c has the same value of a: Both store 632. Table 4.3 (a) shows the call stack.

If a program has something like the following:

```
= * iptr; // iptr is a pointer
```

TABLE 4.3: (a) The fifth line assigns a's value to c's value through pointer iptr. (b) The eleventh line modifies the value of a through the pointer iptr.

Symbol	Address	Value	Value
iptr	108	A100	A100
c	104	632	632
a	100	632	-84
		(a)	(b)

The program will

1. take `iptr`'s value as an address.
2. go to that address.
3. read the value at that address.
4. assign the value to the variable at the left of `=`.

This rule is applicable if `* iptr` is at the right-hand side (RHS) of the assignment sign (`=`). This is also called *dereferencing* a pointer. The assignment sign `=` is not strictly necessary. For example, the tenth line of the code above prints 632. The emphasis on the "right-hand side" is important.

When `* iptr` is on the left-hand side (LHS) as shown in the eleventh line, the pointer behaves differently. The last line of code does the following:

1. Takes `iptr`'s value as an address and it is A100.
2. Goes to that address (A100).
3. Modifies the value at address A100 to -84.

After the last line, the call stack is shown in Table 4.3 (b).

Pointers can be confusing because the same symbol `*` has different meanings. The symbol also means multiplication when it is between two numeric values (integer, float, double). Table 4.4 summarizes the different meanings:

TABLE 4.4: Different usages of `*` in C programs. Please notice that `ptr =` and `* ptr =` have different meanings.

Example	Meaning
1. `int * ptr;`	Create a pointer variable. `ptr`'s value is an address. An integer is stored at that address. `*` is after the type (`int` in this case)
2. `ptr = & val`	Assign `val`'s address to `ptr`'s value. This is how to assign a valid address to `ptr`; note that `*` is not used.
3. `= * ptr`	(right hand side of assignment, RHS) Take `ptr`'s value as an address and read the value at that address. `=` is not always necessary, for example, when printing or calling a function.
4. `* ptr =`	(left hand side of assignment, LHS) Take `ptr`'s value as an address and modify the value at that address.
5. `5 * 17`	Multiplication: `5 * 17` is 85. In this case, `*` is between two numbers.

4.4 Self Test: Pointers

It is time to test your understanding of the different usages of `*`. Draw the call stack for the following code snippet:

```
1   int a = 21;
2   int c = -4;
3   int * ptr;
```

```
4  ptr = & a; // assign a's address to ptr's value
5  * ptr = 7;  // modify a's value through ptr
6  c = * ptr;  // read a's value, assign to c's value
7  * ptr = a * c; // right side: multiplication, modify a's value
```

TABLE 4.5:   Progression of program. The changes are marked by boldface.

Symbol	Address	Value	Value	Value	Value	Value
ptr	108	garbage	A100	A100	A100	A100
c	104	−4	-4	-4	**7**	7
a	100	21	21	**7**	7	**49**
		(a)	(b)	(c)	(d)	(e)

After executing the first three lines, the call stack is shown in Table 4.5 (a). The fourth line assigns a's address to ptr's value. Table 4.5 (b) shows the change. The next line has * ptr at the left-hand side of the assignment sign. This assigns value 7 to the address A100, shown in Table 4.5 (c). The next line reads the value at address A100; the value is 7. This value is assigned to c. The call stack is shown in Table 4.5 (d). The next line reads the values of a and c; both are 7. The symbol * is used twice. On the right-hand side, * means multiplication and the result is 49. Then, 49 is assigned to the value at address A100. This changes a's value to 49, as shown in Table 4.5 (e).

4.5   The Swap Function Revisited

Section 4.2 explains that

```
1  void swap(int x, int y)
2  {
3    int z = x;
4    x = y;
5    y = z;
6  }
```

does not work because the changes to x and y are lost after the swap function finishes (i.e., returns) and the top frame is popped. How can we write a correct swap function? The swap function needs to change the values of both arguments and their addresses reside outside of the swap function's frame. To do so, swap must have their addresses.

```
1  void swap( /* the addresses of a and c */ )
2  {
3  }
4  void f(void)
5  {
```

```
6      int a = 83;
7      int c = -74;
8      swap( /* the addresses of a and c */ );
9      /* RL */
10   }
```

Since the function f must provide the addresses of a and c, the swap function's arguments must be pointers that store these addresses.

```
1    void swap(int * k, int * m)
2    {
3    }
4    void f(void)
5    {
6        int a = 83;
7        int c = -74;
8        swap(& a, & c);
9        /* RL */
10   }
```

The following code implements the swap function:

```
1    void swap (int * k, int * m) // notice *
2    {
3      int s = * k; // s is int, not int *
4      * k = * m;   // notice *
5      * m = s;     // no * in front of s
6    }
7    void f(void)
8    {
9        int a = 83;
10       int c = -74;
11       swap (& a, & c);
12       // RL. a is -74; c is 83
13   }
```

Table 4.6(a) shows the beginning of the swap function before the third line. The local variable s has not been created yet. The third line reads the value at the address of A100 and stores the value in s, based on the RHS rule. The fourth line reads the value stored at address A104; the value is −74. This value is written to the value at the address A100, shown in Table 4.6(b). The fifth line assigns 83 to the value at address A104 using the LHS rule, shown in Table 4.6(c). After the swap function finishes, the top frame is popped, as shown in Table 4.6(d). Note that the values of a and c have been changed.

Pointers are a central feature of C programming, and they must be handled carefully. The swap function should be understood thoroughly since it is an educational example of using pointers. You should understand how to call swap, how it is implemented, and why it is implemented in the way that it is.

Section 2.4 says a function can see only its own frame. However, the swap function modifies the values of a and c even though a and c are in a different frame. Does this mean

TABLE 4.6: Progression of `swap06`.

Frame	Symbol	Address	Value	Value	Value	Value
swap	s	132	-	83	83	-
	m	124	A104	A104	A104	-
	k	116	A100	A100	A100	-
	RL	108	RL	RL	RL	-
f	c	104	−74	-74	**83**	83
	a	100	83	**-74**	-74	74
			(a)	(b)	(c)	(d)

the rule in Section 2.4 is violated? The answer is no. The `swap` function still cannot access `a` or `c` directly. The `swap` function can access `a` or `c` *indirectly* because `k` and `m` store the addresses of `a` and `c`. Through pointers, the `swap` function can access (i.e., read or write) the values of variables in function `f`'s frame. Is it possible for `f` to use pointers to read or write variables in `swap`'s frame? We can illustrate this question with a simple example. Will the following code change `m`'s value from 0 to 7?

```
int * f1(void)
{
    int m = 0;
    return & m;
}
void f2(void)
{
    int * iptr = f1();
    /* RL */
    * iptr = 7;
}
```

The answer is no: `m` exists only inside of `f1`'s frame.

- Before `f2` calls `f1`, `m` does not exist.
- When running the code in `f1`, the program executes the statements in `f1`, not in `f2`.
- After `f1` finishes, the program continues from the return location (RL). The top frame has been popped and `m` no longer exists.

Hence, it is impossible for `f2` to modify `m`. In fact, `gcc` has a warning that the fourth line is likely a mistake. Using pointers to read or write only works in one direction. If `f2` calls `f1`, `f1` can read or write values in `f2`'s frame but `f2` cannot read or write values in `f1`'s frame. This rule can be generalized: Through pointers, a function can read or write values stored in the function's frame or the stack frames below it. It is impossible to read or write values in a frame that is above the function's frame.

4.6   Type Errors

The type of a pointer is important because the type specifies the number of bytes. One `char` has only one byte. On most machines, one `int` is four bytes. On some machines, one `int` may be only two bytes. The following is correct ways of using pointers.

```
1   char a = 'm';
2   char * cptr;     // a is char; cptr is char *; their types match
3   cptr = & a;      // cptr's value is a's address
4   * cptr = 't';    // change a to 't'
5   int b = 1999;
6   int * iptr;      // b is int; iptr is int *; their types match
7   iptr = & b;      // iptr's value is b's address
8   * iptr = 2022;   // change b to 2022
```

What happens if the types are mixed up? For example,

```
1   char a = 'm';    // space for only one byte
2   int * iptr;
3   iptr = & a;      // type error: a's type is char; iptr's type is int *
4   * iptr = 32;     // modifies more than one byte
5   int b = 1999;
6   char * cptr;
7   cptr = & b;      // type error: b's type is int; cptr's type is char *
8   * cptr = 't';    // modifies only one byte; the other bytes in b undefined
```

The type of a is char and iptr is a pointer to int. What will happen if they are mixed in the example above? The short answer is "*You don't need to know. Just don't do it.*" Mixing types is asking for trouble. In this case, the program will assume that there is an int variable at the address of a, but a stores only one char. The size of char is smaller than the size of int. The fourth line intends to assign 32 to the address pointed by iptr. This will modify four bytes as one integer. However, the third line makes iptr point to the address of a and it has space to store only char. The fourth line will change the bytes that do not belong to a. This is problematic. The sixth to the eighth lines are also wrong. The seventh line makes cptr points to b's address and the eighth line modifies the value at that address. The problem is that char is smaller than int and this line does not modify all bytes of b. Fortunately, adding -Wall added after gcc can usually detect type errors.

The next example is also problematic.

```
1   int a = 5;
2   int * iptr;
3   iptr = a;        // should be iptr = & a, gcc warning
4   * iptr = -12;    // intends to write -12 to address 5
```

The program stores a's value (5) instead of a's address in iptr. Thus, iptr's value is Å5. The fourth line intends to write -12 to the value at address Å5. However, programmers have no control over specific addresses. Address Å5 is almost certainly inaccessible to this program. Attempting to write to the value at this address will cause the operating system to stop the program, called *segmentation fault*. In an operating system, memory space is organized in units of segments. A segmentation fault occurs when a program intends to read from or write to a segment that does not belong to the program.

4.7 Arrays and Pointers

Arrays have a special relationship with pointers. Consider the following example:

```
int arr[5];
```

This line of code creates an array of 5 elements; each element is an integer. The elements have not been initialized so the values are garbage. The following example shows how to write to the array elements.

```
arr[0] = 6;      // assign 6 to the first element, index starts from 0
arr[1] = -11;    // assign -11 to the second element
arr[2] = 9;      // assign 9 to the third element
```

An array's indexes always start from zero, not one. We can illustrate this by explaining the specific meaning of the last line. This line does three things:

1. Interprets arr's value as a pointer and it's value is the address of the first element (i.e., arr is equivalent to &arr[0]).
2. Finds the address of two elements after the address of the first element to get a new address. For arr[2], the value 2 is used inside []. The value is called the address *offset*. Page 16 says, address of arr[2] = address of arr[0] + 2 × size of each element.
3. Modifies the value at that address to 9.

Next, consider the following example?

```
int c;       // create an integer variable called c
c = arr[1];  // read the value of the second element and assign it to c
```

The second line does four things:

1. Interprets arr's value as a pointer whose value is the address of the first element.
2. Finds the address of one element after that address to get a new address. Here, the value 1 is the address offset.
3. Reads the value at that address and it is −11.
4. Writes −11 to c's value.

If arr is a function's argument, the function can access the entire array's elements (for both reading and writing). We can use a pointer type as the argument for the array. The following example adds the elements in an array:

```
1   int sumarr(int * intarr, int len)
2   {
3     int ind;
4     int sum2 = 0; // remember to initialize to zero
5     for (ind = 0; ind < len; ind ++)
6       {
7         sum2 += intarr[ind];
8       }
9     return sum2;
10  }
11  void f(void)
12  {
13    int sum = 0;
14    int arr[5];
15    arr[0] = 4;
```

```
16    arr[1] = -7;
17    arr[2] = 2;
18    arr[3] = 3;
19    arr[4] = 9;
20    sum = sumarr(arr, 5);
21    /* RL */
22    printf("sum = %d\n", sum);
23  }
```

TABLE 4.7: Progress of `sumarr`.

Frame	Symbol	Address	Value	Value	Value	Value
	sum2	156	-	0	11	-
	ind	152	-	garbage	5	-
	len	148	-	5	5	-
sumarr	intarr	140	-	A104	A104	-
	VA	132	-	A100	A100	-
	RL	124	-	RL	RL	-
	arr[4]	120	9	9	9	9
	arr[3]	116	3	3	3	3
	arr[2]	112	2	2	2	2
f	arr[1]	108	-7	-7	-7	-7
	arr[0]	104	4	4	4	4
	sum	100	0	0	0	11
			(a)	(b)	(c)	(d)

The function `f` creates `arr`, an array of five elements and `sum`, an integer. Table 4.7(a) is the call stack before calling `sumarr`. The frame for `sumarr` has not been pushed to the stack yet. Function `f` calls function `sumarr` with two arguments: `arr` and 5. The former is the address of `arr[0]`. Table 4.7(b) is the call stack after starting the function `sumarr` before the fifth line. Please pay special attention to the value of `intarr` at address A140. The value is A104 because the address of the first element, i.e., & `arr[0]`, is A104. In a C program, an array itself does not provide information about the number of elements. In contrast, some other programming languages such as Java and Python, arrays are objects and know their sizes. As a result, when calling `sumarr` in this C program, another argument (`len`) is needed for the number of elements. Because `intarr` has the address of the array's first element, function `sumarr` can read the array's elements even though the array is stored in a different frame. The `for` loop adds the elements' values and stores the result in `sum2`. Table 4.7(c) is the call stack after finishing the `for` block. The value of `sum2` is then written to the value at address A100 (`sum`'s address). Table 4.7(d) is the call stack after function `sumarr` has finished and the top frame has been popped.

Because an array is passed as a pointer to the first element, a function can modify the values of an array in another frame. Consider this example:

```
1  void incrarr(int * intarr, int len)
2  {
3    int ind;
4    for (ind = 0; ind < len; ind ++)
5      {
6        intarr[ind] ++;
7      }
8  }
```

```
9    void f(void)
10   {
11     int arr[5];
12     arr[0] = 4;
13     arr[1] = -7;
14     arr[2] = 2;
15     arr[3] = 3;
16     arr[4] = 9;
17     incrarr(arr, 5);
18     // RL
19     // arr[] is {5, -6, 3, 4, 10} now
20   }
```

What is the difference between the following two statements?

```
// assume a and intarr[ind] are integers
a ++;              // assign a + 1 to a
intarr[ind] ++; // assign intarr[ind] + 1 to  intarr[ind]
```

The first line executes the following steps:

1. Reads a's value.
2. Increments the value by one.
3. Writes the incremented value back to a.

The second statement does something similar:

1. Reads intarr[ind]'s value.
2. Increments the value by one.
3. Writes the incremented value back to intarr[ind].

Because intarr is the address of the array's first element, the function incrarr can read and modify the array's elements even though the array is stored in a different frame.

4.8 Type Rules

Here are some rules about types:

- If var's type is $\mathbb{T}$, then & var's type is $\mathbb{T}$ *.
- If ptr's type is $\mathbb{T}$ *, then * ptr's type is $\mathbb{T}$ (both LHS and RHS).
- If arr is an array of type $\mathbb{T}$, then each element (such as arr[1]) stores a value of type $\mathbb{T}$. Please notice the presence of an index.
- If arr is an array of type $\mathbb{T}$, then arr's type is $\mathbb{T}$ *. Please notice the lack of an index. Please remember that arr is equivalent to & arr[0].
- An array's name is always a pointer. If arr is an array of type $\mathbb{T}$ and $\mathbb{T}$ * ptr is a pointer of type $\mathbb{T}$, then ptr = arr is a valid assignment. It is equivalent to ptr = & arr[0], namely assigning the address of the first element to ptr.
- Pointers are not necessarily arrays. For example, $\mathbb{T}$ * ptr creates a pointer of type $\mathbb{T}$ and it may not be related to any array. A statement like ptr[1] = may write to an invalid address and cause segmentation fault.

4.9   Pointer Arithmetic

Pointers can be used to visit the elements of an array. This is called *pointer arithmetic*. Consider the following example.

```
// CH04:arithmetic01.c
#include <stdio.h>
#include <stdlib.h>
int main (int argc ,char * * argv)
{
   int    arr1[] = {7, 2, 5, 3, 1, 6, -8, 16, 4};
   char   arr2[] = {'m', 'q', 'k', 'z', '%', '>'};
   double arr3[] = {3.14, -2.718, 6.626, 0.529};
   int len1 = sizeof(arr1) / sizeof(int); // get the array's size
   // This method works only for an array created on the stack memory.
   // This method does not work if the array is created by calling malloc.
   int len2 = sizeof(arr2) / sizeof(char);
   int len3 = sizeof(arr3) / sizeof(double);
   printf("lengths = %d, %d, %d\n", len1, len2, len3);
   int    * iptr = arr1; // same as iptr = & arr[0]
   char   * cptr = arr2;
   double * dptr = arr3;
   printf("values = %d, %c, %f\n", * iptr, * cptr, * dptr); // notice *
   iptr ++;
   cptr ++;
   dptr ++;
   printf("values = %d, %c, %f\n", * iptr, * cptr, * dptr);
   iptr ++;
   cptr ++;
   dptr ++;
   printf("values = %d, %c, %f\n", * iptr, * cptr, * dptr);
   iptr ++;
   cptr ++;
   dptr ++;
   printf("values = %d, %c, %f\n", * iptr, * cptr, * dptr);
   return EXIT_SUCCESS;
}
```

This is the output of this program:

```
lengths = 9, 6, 4
values = 7, m, 3.140000
values = 2, q, -2.718000
values = 5, k, 6.626000
values = 3, z, 0.529000
```

Lines 6 to 8 create three arrays, one of integers, one of characters, and one of double-precision floating point numbers. A C program can create a constant array without giving the size, by putting nothing between [and]. The compiler will automatically calculate the array's size. Lines 9 to 13 calculate the lengths of the three arrays. Different data types take different amounts of memory, and therefore have different sizes (reported by `sizeof`). These lines divide the array sizes by the types' sizes in order to get the numbers of the elements. Line 14 prints the lengths. As you can see, the program prints the correct lengths. This method for calculating an array's size is valid only for constant arrays. If an array is created using `malloc` (explained in Chapter 7), this method to calculate an array's length will not work. Lines 15 to 17 assign the addresses of the first element in each array to the pointers.

Do not mix the pointer types. For example, the following statements are wrong:

```
int * iptr = arr2;      // arr2 is an array of char
int * iptr = arr1[1];   // arr[1] is int, not int *
```

Line 18 prints the values stored at the corresponding addresses. The printed values are the first elements. Lines 19 to 21 are called *pointer arithmetic*. Each pointer is advanced by one array element and points to the next element of the array. Line 22 prints the values stored at the corresponding addresses. The printed values are the second elements of these arrays. Lines 23 to 25 make each pointer point to the next element. Line 26 prints the values stored at the corresponding addresses. The printed values are the third elements. Even though different types have different sizes in memory, the compiler will automatically move the pointers to correctly point to the next array elements.

4.10   Sizes of Data Types

The sizes of different types are different as shown by the following program.

```
1   // CH04:arithmetic02.c
2   #include <stdio.h>
3   #include <stdlib.h>
4   int main (int argc ,char * * argv)
5   {
6     int    arr1[] = {7, 2, 5, 3, 1, 6, -8, 16, 4};
7     char   arr2[] = {'m', 'q', 'k', 'z', '%', '>'};
8     double arr3[] = {3.14, -2.718, 6.626, 0.529};
9     long int addr10 = (long int) (& arr1[0]);
10    long int addr11 = (long int) (& arr1[1]);
11    long int addr12 = (long int) (& arr1[2]);
12    printf("%ld, %ld, %ld\n", addr12, addr11, addr10);
13    printf("%ld, %ld\n", addr12 - addr11, addr11 - addr10);
14    long int addr20 = (long int) (& arr2[0]);
15    long int addr21 = (long int) (& arr2[1]);
16    long int addr22 = (long int) (& arr2[2]);
17    printf("%ld, %ld, %ld\n", addr22, addr21, addr20);
18    printf("%ld, %ld\n", addr22 - addr21, addr21 - addr20);
19    long int addr30 = (long int) (& arr3[0]);
20    long int addr31 = (long int) (& arr3[1]);
21    long int addr32 = (long int) (& arr3[2]);
22    printf("%ld, %ld, %ld\n", addr32, addr31, addr30);
```

```
23    printf("%ld, %ld\n", addr32 - addr31, addr31 - addr30);
24    return EXIT_SUCCESS;
25    }
```

The output of the program is:

```
140735471859144, 140735471859140, 140735471859136
4, 4
140735471859186, 140735471859185, 140735471859184
1, 1
140735471859120, 140735471859112, 140735471859104
8, 8
```

This program shows that the sizes of different types can be different. What do lines 9 to 11 do? At the right side of the assignment, `& arr1[0]` gets the address of the first element of `arr1`. This address is assigned to `addr10`. Because this code is compiled on a 64-bit computer (i.e., 8 bytes), the memory addresses use 64 bits, and require the `long int` type to store the addresses. We need to use some special syntax (called *type cast*) to tell the compiler to store the memory address inside an integer. This is why we have `(long int)` after `=`. In general, storing memory addresses in integers is bad, because doing so can lead to subtle problems when the code is compiled under different circumstances. Using `(long int)` tells the compiler "I know this is bad, but let me do it."

Lines 10 and 11 get the addresses of the second, and the third elements of the array. Line 12 prints the values of these long integers. In `printf`, `%ld` is used to print a longer integer. The value changes if you execute the program again. However, line 13 always prints `4, 4` meaning that the addresses of two adjacent elements differ by 4. This means each integer uses 4 bytes of memory. Line 17 prints some addresses and they change when the program is executed again. Line 18 always prints `1, 1` meaning that the addresses of two adjacent elements differ by 1. In other words, each character needs 1 byte of memory. Line 23 always prints `8, 8` meaning that the addresses of two adjacent elements differ by 8. Each `double` needs 8 bytes of memory.

The next example combines these two programs.

```
1   // CH04:arithmetic03.c
2   #include <stdio.h>
3   #include <stdlib.h>
4   int main (int argc ,char * * argv)
5   {
6     int     arr1[] = {7, 2, 5, 3, 1, 6, -8, 16, 4};
7     char    arr2[] = {'m', 'q', 'k', 'z', '%', '>'};
8     double arr3[] = {3.14, -2.718, 6.626, 0.529};
9     int    * iptr = & arr1[3]; // iptr starts from & arr1[3]
10    printf("%d\n", * iptr);
11    long int addr13 = (long int) iptr;
12    iptr --;
13    printf("%d\n", * iptr);
14    long int addr12 = (long int) iptr;
15    printf("addr13 - addr12 = %ld\n", addr13 - addr12);
16    printf("===================================\n");
```

```
17    char   * cptr = & arr2[1];
18    printf("%c\n", * cptr);
19    long int addr21 = (long int) cptr;
20    cptr ++;
21    printf("%c\n", * cptr);
22    long int addr22 = (long int) cptr;
23    printf("addr22 - addr21 = %ld\n", addr22 - addr21);
24    printf("=====================================\n");
25    double * dptr = & arr3[2];
26    printf("%f\n", * dptr);
27    long int addr32 = (long int) dptr;
28    dptr --;
29    printf("%f\n", * dptr);
30    long int addr31 = (long int) dptr;
31    printf("addr32 - addr31 = %ld\n", addr32 - addr31);
32    return EXIT_SUCCESS;
33  }
```

This is the output of the program:

```
3
5
addr13 - addr12 = 4
=====================================
q
k
addr22 - addr21 = 1
=====================================
6.626000
-2.718000
addr32 - addr31 = 8
```

Line 9 assigns the address of `arr1[3]` to `iptr` and line 10 prints the value stored at that address. As you can see in this example, `iptr` does not have to start from the first element of the array. Line 11 stores `iptr`'s value in `addr13`. Please remember that `iptr`'s value is an address. Line 12 decrements `iptr`'s value and line 13 prints the value at the address. The value is 5, the same as `arr1[2]`. Line 14 stores `iptr`'s value in `addr12`. Line 15 shows the differences of the two addresses stored in `addr13` and `addr12` and the difference is 4, not 1. Even though line 12 decrements `iptr` by one, the compiler actually decreases `iptr`'s value by 4 *because the size of an integer is 4*. In other words, the specific change in `iptr`'s value depends on the size of the type being pointed to. The outputs for the other two arrays further illustrate this point. Line 23 prints 1 and line 31 prints 8 because of the sizes of the types being pointed to. This explains why mixing types can be problematic. Programs have odd behavior when the types are mixed like this.

```
int * iptr = arr2; // arr2 is a char array, iptr is a pointer of int
int * iptr = arr3; // arr3 is a double array
```

When the types are mixed, the compiler is confused and the program's behavior is difficult to predict.

4.11 Problems

4.11.1 Swap Function 1

Does this program have any syntax problems because of wrong types (such as assigning an integer to a pointer's value)? Will this function actually swap the values of u and t? What is the program's output? Please draw the call stack and explain.

```c
// CH04:swapex1.c
#include <stdio.h>
#include <stdlib.h>
void swap1 (int a , int b)
{
  int k = a;
  a = b;
  b = k;
}
int main (int argc ,char * * argv)
{
  int u;
  int t;
  u = 17;
  t = -96;
  printf ("before swap1: u = %d , t = %d \n" , u , t);
  swap1 (u , t);
  // RL
  printf ("after  swap1: u = %d , t = %d \n" , u , t);
  return EXIT_SUCCESS;
}
```

4.11.2 Swap Function 2

How about this program?

```c
// CH04:swapex2.c
#include <stdio.h>
#include <stdlib.h>
void swap2 (int * a , int * b)
{
  int * k = a;
  a = b;
  b = k;
}
int main (int argc ,char * * argv)
{
  int u;
  int t;
  u = 17;
```

```
15    t = -96;
16    printf ("before swap2: u = %d , t = %d \n" , u , t);
17    swap2 (& u , & t);
18    // RL
19    printf ("after  swap2: u = %d , t = %d \n" , u , t);
20    return EXIT_SUCCESS;
21  }
```

4.11.3   Swap Function 3

How about this program?

```
1   // CH04:swapex3.c
2   #include <stdio.h>
3   #include <stdlib.h>
4   void swap3 (int * a, int * b)
5   {
6     int k = * a;
7     a = b;
8     * b = k;
9   }
10  int main (int argc ,char * * argv)
11  {
12    int u;
13    int t;
14    u = 17;
15    t = -96;
16    printf ("before swap3: u = %d , t = %d \n" , u , t);
17    swap3 (& u , & t);
18    // RL
19    printf ("after  swap3: u = %d , t = %d \n" , u , t);
20    return EXIT_SUCCESS;
21  }
```

4.11.4   Swap Function 4

How about this program?

```
1   // CH04:swapex4.c
2   #include <stdio.h>
3   #include <stdlib.h>
4   void swap4 (int * a, int * b)
5   {
6     int k = * a;
7     * a = * b;
8     * b = * k;
9   }
```

```
10   int main (int argc ,char * * argv)
11   {
12     int u;
13     int t;
14     u = 17;
15     t = -96;
16     printf ("before swap4: u = %d , t = %d \n" , u , t);
17     swap4 (& u , & t);
18     // RL
19     printf ("after  swap4: u = %d , t = %d \n" , u , t);
20     return EXIT_SUCCESS;
21   }
```

4.11.5 Swap Function 5

How about this program?

```
1    // CH04:swap5ex.c
2    #include <stdio.h>
3    #include <stdlib.h>
4    void swap5 (int * a, int * b)
5    {
6      int k = a;
7      a = b;
8      b = k;
9    }
10   int main (int argc ,char * * argv)
11   {
12     int u;
13     int t;
14     u = 17;
15     t = -96;
16     printf ("before swap5: u = %d , t = %d \n" , u , t);
17     swap5 (& u , * t);
18     // RL
19     printf ("after  swap5: u = %d , t = %d \n" , u , t);
20     return EXIT_SUCCESS;
21   }
```

4.11.6 15,552 Variations

There are many variations of the **swap** function. To be specific, there are 15,552 variations and only one of them is correct. Some variations have syntax errors (wrong types) and some of them do not swap the values in the **main** function. Let me explain why there are so many variations. First, this is the correct **swap** function and the correct way to call it:

```
1   void swap (int * k, int * m)
2   {
3     int s;
4     s = * k;
5     * k = * m;
6     * m = s;
7   }
8   void f(void)
9   {
10    int a = 83;
11    int c = -74;
12    swap (& a, & c);
13  }
```

How do we get 15,552 variations? In the first line, there are two options for k:

1. int k
2. int * k

int & k is illegal so it is not considered.

Similarly, there are two options for m and two options for s. So far, there are 8 variations of the function up to the third line. Next, consider the number of options for s = k at the fourth line; there are six options:

1. s = * k;
2. s = & k;
3. s = k;
4. * s = * k;
5. * s = & k;
6. * s = k;

& s = is illegal so it is not considered.

Similarly, there are also six options for k = m and another six options for m = s. So far there are $8 \times 6 \times 6 \times 6 = 1,728$ variations for swap function.

From the main function, calling swap has three options for using a in the thirteenth line:

1. a
2. & a
3. * a

Similarly, there are another three options in using c. Thus, in total, there are $1,728 \times 3 \times 3 = 15,552$ variations.

Among all these variations, if the swap function is called without using addresses, the changes are lost when the swap function finishes. In other words, regardless of what happens inside swap, calling swap in this way,

```
12  swap (a, c); // wrong, should have & before and and c
```

is always wrong.

4.11.7 Pointer and Array

What is the output of this program?

```c
// CH04:array08.c
#include <stdio.h>
#include <stdlib.h>
void incrarr(int * arr, int len)
{
  int ind;
  int * ptr = arr;
  for (ind = 0; ind < len; ind ++)
    {
      (* ptr) ++;
      ptr ++;
    }
}
void printarr(int * arr, int len)
{
  int ind;
  for (ind = 0; ind < len; ind ++) { printf("%d ", arr[ind]); }
  printf("\n");
}
int main(int argc, char * * argv)
{
  int arr[] = {1, 2, 3, 4, 5, 6, 7, 8, 9, 10, 11, 12, 13};
  int arrlen = sizeof(arr) / sizeof(arr[0]);
  printarr(arr, arrlen);
  printf("-------------\n");
  incrarr(& arr[arrlen / 3], arrlen / 2);
  // please notice /3 and /2
  printarr(arr, arrlen);
  return EXIT_SUCCESS;
}
```

Explain whether line 10 is the same as

```c
* ptr = (* ptr) + 1;
```

or

```c
* (ptr + 1);
```

or neither. Explain the meaning.

Chapter 5

Writing and Testing Programs

This chapter uses programming problems to illustrate how to use pointers and how to use tools for testing programs. This chapter teaches the following important concepts:

- Understand the differences between function declarations and definitions.
- Write programs with multiple files, compile them separately and link them together to create an executable.
- Use the `make` command in Linux to build and test programs.
- Detect memory errors using `gcc -fsanitize` and `valgrind`.
- Use `gcov` to detect untested lines.

5.1 Distinct Array Elements

This program has a function with two arguments: an array of integers and the number of array elements. The function returns 1 if the array elements are distinct, and the function returns 0 if two or more elements store the same value.

```
int areDistinct(int * arr, int len)
// returns 1 if the elements are distinct; otherwise, return 0
// arr stores the address of the first element
// len is the number of elements
// If len is zero, the function returns 1.
```

5.1.1 `main` Function

Consider the `main` function of this program:

```
1   // CH05:main.c
2   #include <stdio.h>
3   #include <stdlib.h>
4   #include <string.h>
5   int areDistinct(int * arr, int len);
6   int main(int argc, char * * argv)
7   {
8     if (argc != 2)
9       {
10        return EXIT_FAILURE;
11      }
12    FILE * fptr = fopen(argv[1], "r");
```

```
13    if (fptr == NULL)
14      {
15        return EXIT_FAILURE;
16      }
17    int length = 0;
18    int value;
19    while (fscanf(fptr, "%d", & value) == 1)
20      {
21        length ++;
22      }
23    fseek (fptr, 0, SEEK_SET);
24    int * arr = malloc(length * sizeof(int));
25    length = 0;
26    while (fscanf(fptr, "%d", & (arr[length])) == 1)
27      {
28        length ++;
29      }
30    fclose (fptr);
31    int dist = areDistinct(arr, length);
32    printf("The elements are");
33    if (dist == 0)
34      {
35        printf(" not");
36      }
37    printf(" distinct.\n");
38    free (arr);
39    return EXIT_SUCCESS;
40  }
```

The `main` function has two input arguments. The names of the arguments are `argc` and `argv` by convention. The prefix `arg` means arguments. The first is an integer (`int`) called `argc`. Section 1.1 explains that the value of `argc` means the count of arguments that are passed to the program. The second is a pointer to pointers of characters (`char * *`) called `argv`. Do not worry about the second argument `argv` for now. We will explain `argv` in Chapter 6 about strings.

The condition at line 8 is used to ensure that the program has two arguments. The first argument is always the name of this program. By requiring two arguments, one additional argument can specify the name of a file that contains the data. If the program does not have exactly two arguments, the program stops by returning `EXIT_FAILURE`. This symbol is defined in `stdlib.h`. When the `main` function returns, this program terminates. `EXIT_FAILURE` means that the program failed to accomplish what the program is supposed to do. For now, we can ignore the program between lines 12 and line 30 and also line 38. This part of the program is about reading data from a file, and will be explained in detail in Chapter 9. Line 31 calls the `areDistinct` function. Dependent on the result of line 31, this program prints either "The elements are distinct." or "The elements are not distinct." Finally, the program returns `EXIT_SUCCESS` because it successfully determines whether or not the values are distinct.

The fifth line *declares* the `areDistinct` function so that `main` knows about it. This declaration says that the `areDistinct` function returns an integer and takes two arguments. The first argument is a pointer to an integer, and the second argument is an integer. Without this declaration, the `gcc` compiler would not know anything about `areDistinct`. If the fifth line is removed, then `gcc` will give the following warning message

```
warning: implicit declaration of function 'areDistinct'
```

To summarize the `main` function:

- The program checks the value of `argc` to determine whether or not an additional input argument is given.
- If the program cannot accomplish what it is supposed to do, the `main` function returns `EXIT_FAILURE`.
- The `main` function must include `stdlib.h` because `EXIT_FAILURE` and `EXIT_SUCCESS` are defined in `stdlib.h`.
- The program terminates when the `main` function uses `return`.
- The `main` function returns `EXIT_SUCCESS` after it accomplishes its work.

5.1.2   areDistinct **Function**

The fifth line in `main.c` declares the `areDistinct` function; however, the function has not been *defined* yet. A function declaration informs `gcc` that this function exists, the number and types of arguments, and the type of the returned value. A function's definition *implements* the function. This implementation may be in the same file or another file. Some people also call a function's definition the function's *body*. A function's definition must have a pair of { and } enclosing the body. In contrast, a function's declaration replaces the body (i.e., everything between { and }) by a semicolon.

```
// declaration: has ; after ), no { }
int areDistinct(int * arr, int len);
// definition: no ; after ), has { }
int areDistinct(int * arr, int len)
{
  // code
}
```

Below is the definition of the `areDistinct` function. It goes through the elements in the input array one by one, and checks whether any element after this current one has the same value. Checking the elements before the current element is unnecessary, because they have already been checked in earlier iterations. If two elements have the same value, the function returns 0. If no match is found after going through all elements, then this function returns 1. If `len` is zero, the function does not enter the for-loop at the sixth line, goes directly to line 18, and then returns 1.

```
1   // CH05:aredistinct.c
2   int areDistinct(int * arr, int len)
3   {
4     int ind1;
5     int ind2;
6     for (ind1 = 0; ind1 < len; ind1 ++)
7       {
8         for (ind2 = ind1 + 1; ind2 < len; ind2 ++)
9           {
10            if (arr[ind1] == arr[ind2])
```

```
11              {
12                      // found two elements with the same value
13                      return 0;
14              }
15          }
16      }
17      // have not found two elements of the same value
18      return 1;
19  }
```

This program returns 0 means the array's elements are not distinct; 1 means the elements are distinct. It is also possible to use the `bool` type in C and return `true` or `false`.

5.1.3 Compiling and Linking

The functions `main` and `areDistinct` are in two different files. Large programs use multiple files—perhaps dozens or hundreds. There are many reasons for using multiple files when writing large programs. For example,

- Large programs require teams of people. It is easier for different people to work on different files.
- A large program is developed in many phases, and more files are added gradually.
- In good software design, each file should implement a set of closely related features. If two features are sufficiently different, then they should reside in two different files. This approach makes it easy to manage and navigate large amounts of code.

Attempting to write a large program in a single file would be equivalent to putting everything into a single drawer: It is messy and creates problems every time someone wants to find, add, or remove anything in the drawer. Section 1.1 explained how to use `gcc` to convert a source file into an executable file. It can also be used to convert two or more source files into one executable. Section 2.5 suggests that `gcc` should always be run with `-Wall -Wshadow`. Furthermore, if you want to run gdb or ddd, then you must also add `-g` after `gcc`. This is the command to type in a Linux Terminal:

```
$ gcc -g -Wall -Wshadow aredistinct.c main.c -o prog
```

This command creates an executable file called `prog`. This example has only two source files (files ending with .c). As a program becomes larger and more files are added, this command becomes too long to type. Moreover, running `gcc` may take a rather long time because every source (.c) file is recompiled every time. This seems acceptable for two files, but becomes a serious problem for larger projects with many files.

Fortunately, it is possible to *compile* individual files separately. When a source file is compiled, an intermediate file is created. This intermediate file is called an *object* file and it has the .o extension. Once an object file has been created for the corresponding source file, `gcc` has a special procedure, called *linking*, for creating an executable file. The following shows the commands.

```
$ gcc -g -Wall -Wshadow -c aredistinct.c
$ gcc -g -Wall -Wshadow -c main.c
$ gcc -g -Wall -Wshadow ardistinct.o main.o -o prog
```

The first `gcc` command compiles `aredistinct.c` and creates the object file called `aredistinct.o`. Adding `-c` after `gcc` tells `gcc` to create an object file. The object file has the same name as the source file, except the extension is changed from `.c` to `.o`. Similarly, the second command compiles `main.c` and creates `main.o`. The third command takes the two object files and creates the executable file. This command *links* the two files because the input files are object files and uses `-o` for the name of the executable output file. Please notice that the last command has no `-c`.

This approach can save time. If only `aredistinct.c` is changed, only `aredistinct.o` only needs to be updated. If `main.c` is changed, only `main.o` needs to be updated. This is called *separate compilation*. If either of the object files changes, then the link command (the third command above) needs to be rerun to generate the updated executable. Even if the advantages of separate compilation are compelling, typing the three commands is even more awkward and tedious than typing one command. It certainly is inefficient to type

```
$ gcc -g -Wall -Wshadow -c main.c
$ gcc -g -Wall -Wshadow ardistinct.o main.o -o prog
```

whenever `main.c` changes. These commands are too long to type over and over again. Moreover, it is necessary to keep track of which files have been changed and need recompilation. Fortunately, tools have been developed to take care of these issues. The `make` program in Linux is one popular tool for this purpose.

5.2   Build and Test Program with Multiple Files

5.2.1   make and Makefile

The `make` program in Linux can build and test a program with multiple files. The `make` program takes a special input file called `Makefile`. `Makefile` can instruct `make` which `.c` files need to be recompiled. `Makefile` is the default name for `make`. You can tell `make` to use another file by adding `-f name` after `make`:

```
$ make -f name
```

In this case, the `make` program uses `name` as the input, not `Makefile`.

Let's read an example of `Makefile`. This chapter will show several examples. The first is called `Makefile1`.

```
1   # CH05:Makefile1
2   # This is a comment
3   # to run it:
4   # make -f Makefile1
5   # make test -f Makefile1
6   # make clean -f Makefile1
7
8   GCC = gcc
9   CFLAGS = -g -Wall -Wshadow
10  SRCS = aredistinct.c main.c
11  OBJS = $(SRCS:%.c=%.o) # OBJS = aredistinct.o main.o
12
```

```
13   program: $(OBJS)
14           $(GCC) $(CFLAGS) $(OBJS) -o program # link, no -c
15
16   .c.o:
17           $(GCC) $(CFLAGS) -c $*.c # compile .c to .o, notice -c
18
19   test: program
20           for case in 0 1 2 3 4; do \
21           echo input$$case; \
22           ./program inputs/input$$case > output$$case; \
23           diff output$$case expected/expected$$case; \
24           done
25
26   clean:
27           /bin/rm -f *.o program *~ *bak output*
```

This file is a little long and some symbols make it look mysterious. Do not worry. We will explain the file step by step. The top of this file is comments. In `Makefile`, anything after `#` is a comment, similar to `//` in a C file.

After the comments, the file defines some symbols: `GCC`, `CFLAGS`, `SRC`, and `OBJS`. This book uses `gcc` as the compiler and linker. If another compiler is used, only one change is needed: replacing `gcc` by the preferred compiler. The next line defines the flags after `gcc`. The symbol `SRCS` lists the source `.c` files. For `OBJS`, we can simply define it as

```
OBJS = aredistinct.o main.o
```

Another way to define `OBJS` replaces `.c` by `.o` using the line in this `Makefile`:

```
OBJS = $(SRCS:%.c=%.o)
```

Replacing `.c` by `.o` has an advantage: If more `.c` files are added to the list of `SRCS`, `OBJS` is updated automatically. After defining these symbols, the next section is

```
program: $(OBJS)
        $(GCC) $(CFLAGS) $(OBJS) -o program
```

These two lines include three parts:

```
target: dependence
        action
```

In this part of `Makefile`, `program` is the target. We want to build an executable called `program`. This target depends on the list of files specified by `$(OBJS)`, namely `aredistinct.o` and `main.o`. If these two files are available, `make` will take the action

```
        $(GCC) $(CFLAGS) $(OBJS) -o program
```

This line is equivalent to

```
        gcc -g -Wall -Wshadow aredistinct.o main.o -o program
```

after replacing the symbols by their definitions. Please be aware that `$(GCC)` is after a TAB key, not space.

The next two lines may appear mysterious due to the symbols.

```
.c.o:
        $(GCC) $(CFLAGS) -c $*.c
```

The first line .c.o: means "converting a .c source file to a .o object file". The second line specifies how to convert the file, by using $(GCC) $(CFLAGS) -c. The ending $*.c refers to the .c source file.

Earlier, we saw that the **program** depends on $(OBJS). $(OBJS) means the two object files, aredistinct.o and main.o. Thus, to build the program, two object files are needed. To obtain the two object files, we use the $(GCC) command with -c; adding -c after gcc produces the object file. Using these two lines has an advantage: If $(SRCS) changes (for example, adding more source files), then $(OBJS) is updated automatically and these two lines need no change. The Makefile up to this point can build the executable program. To run **make** and build the program, type

```
$  make program -f Makefile1
```

Since **program** is the first target, it is not necessary to type **program**. Instead, it is sufficient to type

```
$  make -f Makefile1
```

This is the output on a terminal:

```
gcc -g -Wall -Wshadow -c aredistinct.c # compile .c to .o, notice -c
gcc -g -Wall -Wshadow -c main.c # compile .c to .o, notice -c
gcc -g -Wall -Wshadow aredistinct.o main.o  -o program # link, no -c
```

Suppose main.c is modified. Typing the **make** command will produce this output:

```
gcc -g -Wall -Wshadow -c main.c # compile .c to .o, notice -c
gcc -g -Wall -Wshadow aredistinct.o main.o  -o program # link, no -c
```

As you can see, it is not necessary to compile aredistinct.c because aredistinct.o already exists. How does **make** know which source files have been modified? The decisions are based on the modification time of the object files and the relevant .c files. If an object file is newer than the corresponding source file, then it is unnecessary to recompile the source file. If an object file is older than the corresponding source file, then **make** recompiles the source file.

Before explaining the section about **test**, let's go to the bottom and consider the **clean** section first.

```
clean:
        /bin/rm -f *.o program *~ *bak output*
```

This section deletes computer-generated files, including the object files, the executable, and the backup files (usually ending with ∼ or bak). The **test** section produces some output files. The **clean** section also deletes these files. To delete these computer-generated files, type

```
$  make clean -f Makefile1
```

This is the output on the terminal:

```
/bin/rm -f *.o program *~ *bak output*
```

5.2.2 Test using make

Now, let's example the **test** section. First, let's examine the depenence:

```
test: program
```

This means **test** needs **program**. This ensures that the executable is built (or rebuilt if one of the .c file has been changed) before running the **test** section.

The action for **test** is actually a shell program. This shell program needs **$$** to use the value of **case**; this is the syntax for the shell program. If you ignore **$$**, then the program becomes easier to read.

```
for case in 0 1 2 3 4; do \
echo input$$case; \
./program inputs/input$$case > output$$case; \
diff output$$case expected/expected$$case; \
done
```

The shell program tests `./program` using five test cases `inputs/input0` to `inputs/input4`. These files reside in the directory called `inputs`. The results are saved in files called `output0` to `output4`. These output files are compared with the expected outputs stored in `expected/expected0` to `expected/expected4`. The `diff` compares two files. If the two files have the same content, `diff` provides no output. If the two files have different content, `diff` shows the differences.

To test the program, please type

```
$ make test -f Makefile1
```

This is the output in the terminal:

```
1   gcc -g -Wall -Wshadow -c aredistinct.c # compile .c to .o, notice -c
2   gcc -g -Wall -Wshadow -c main.c # compile .c to .o, notice -c
3   gcc -g -Wall -Wshadow aredistinct.o main.o  -o program # link, no -c
4   for case in 0 1 2 3 4; do \
5   echo input$case; \
6   ./program inputs/input$case > output$case; \
7   diff output$case expected/expected$case; \
8   done
9   input0
10  input1
11  input2
12  input3
13  input4
```

As you can see, **make** has done many things. Lines 1–2 compile the .c files and create the object .o files. The third line links the two object files into the executable called **program**. Lines 4–8 run the shell program to test the program using five test cases. Lines 9–13 print the names of the test cases. Nothing is printed by the **diff** command; thus, the program's outputs (stored in **output0** to **output4**) are the same as the expected outputs.

5.2.3   Generate Test Cases

To test a program, we need test cases. To test `areDistinct`, we need different test cases, for example,

- `len` is zero or not.
- `arr` either contains distinct elements or not.

At least three test cases are needed:

1. an empty file making `len` zero
2. a file with distinct numbers
3. a file with duplicate numbers

Creating the first test case is easy: Make an empty file. The `touch` command in Linux can create an empty file.

```
$ touch case1
```

This generates an empty file called `case1`. The second and the third test cases can be created by typing in a text editor. Alternatively, test cases can be created using an on-line random number generator, saving the results to a file. The `shuf` command in Linux can do that.

```
$ shuf -i 1-10
$ shuf -i 1-100 -n 20
$ shuf -i 1-100 -r -n 20
$ shuf -i 1-100 -n 20 -r > case2
```

The first `shuf` command shuffles numbers between 1 and 10; `-i` specifies the range of the numbers. In this case, `-i 1-10` means the command shuffles numbers between 1 and 10. Running this command multiple times can produce different orders of these numbers. The second first `shuf` command shuffles numbers between 1 and 100 and then keeps only the first 20 numbers; `-n` specifies how many numbers are kept. The third command adds `-r` to repeat some numbers. For these three commands, the outputs are shown on the computer screen. The fourth command saves the output to a file called `case2`. Section 1.2 explained how to redirect a program's output using > and save the output to a file.

How do we know whether the numbers are distinct? We can read the file by eyes and decide. Alternatively, we can use tools in Linux to do that. The `sort` command in Linux can order (i.e., sort) numbers. Another command `uniq` can tell whether the sorted numbers are unique or not. If we add `-d` after `uniq`, the command displays which numbers duplicate. We can put the two commands together using a *pipe* (the vertical line |). The pipe takes the output of the `sort` command, and makes it the input to the `uniq` command. In a Linux Terminal:

```
$ sort case2 | uniq -d
```

here `case2` is the name of the file that stores the shuffled numbers. If the numbers in this file are distinct, nothing appears. If some numbers duplicate, then the duplicate numbers are shown on the screen.

5.3   Detect Invalid Memory Access

Section 2.3.5 said "if an array has n elements, the valid indexes are 0, 1, 2, ..., $n-1$."
What happens if we use an invalid index? The program's behavior is undefined. If the index
is incorrect, the program will access a memory address that does not belong to the array.
Programmers have no control over memory addresses and do not know what is stored at a
particular address outside the range of the array. Consider this program:

```c
// CH05:wrongindex.c
#include <stdio.h>
#include <stdlib.h>
#include <string.h>
int main(int argc, char * * argv)
{
    int x = -2;
    int arr[] = {0, 1, 2, 3, 4};
    int y = 15;
    printf("& x     = %p, & y     = %p\n", (void*) & x, (void*) & y);
    printf("& arr[0] = %p, & arr[4] = %p\n", (void*) & arr[0],
           (void*) & arr[4]);
    printf("x = %d, y = %d\n", x, y);
    arr[-1] = 7;
    arr[5]  = -23;
    printf("x = %d, y = %d\n", x, y);
    arr[6]  = 108;
    printf("x = %d, y = %d\n", x, y);
    arr[7]  = -353;
    printf("x = %d, y = %d\n", x, y);
    return EXIT_SUCCESS;
}
```

An array is created at line 8 and it has 5 elements. The valid indexes are 0, 1, 2, 3,
and 4. Lines 10 and 11 print the addresses of x, y, and the array. In `printf`, `%p` shows an
address and its type is `void *`. Thus, it is necessary adding `(void *)` before `& x`. Lines 14,
15, 17, and 19 use incorrect indexes. The values of x or y are changed:

```
& x      = 0x7fffcabf4e68, & y      = 0x7fffcabf4e6c
& arr[0] = 0x7fffcabf4e50, & arr[4] = 0x7fffcabf4e60
x = -2, y = 15
x = -2, y = 15
x = 108, y = 15
x = 108, y = -353
```

As we can see, x has changed because of this assignment:

```
arr[6]  = 108;
```

Similarly, y is changed because of this assignment:

```
arr[7]  = -353;
```

In this example, the gcc compiler has reordered the local variables in the call stack. The addresses of x and y are larger than the addresses of the array elements. Thus, x and y are changed when the indexes are 6 and 7 respectively. If we run the above program again, we may see different addresses for x and y. It is possible that neither x nor y, but something else, is changed due to using the invalid indexes.

The real problem is that the program's behavior is undefined. The effects of wrong indexes may change when the program runs on different machines, or runs multiple times on the same machine. Sometimes, the program seems correct and nothing obviously wrong occurs. Sometimes, the values of x or y may be changed. Sometimes, the program stops with the message "*Segmentation fault (core dumped)*." This means that the program intends to read from or write to a memory address that does not belong to the program. Modern computers usually run many programs. Each program is given parts of the memory. If one program tries to read from or write to the wrong address, the operating system may stop the program. This protects the other programs running on the same computer.

It is possible to use gcc -fsanitize to detect memory errors. To enable this detection, use this gcc command:

```
$ gcc -g -fsanitize=address -static-libasan wrongindex.c
```

Running this program produces the following output:

```
WRITE of size 4 at 0x7fff4535ebac thread T0
#0 0x5582c354f99b in main wrongindex.c:14
```

The output clearly marks line 14 as problematic. This Makefile shows how to add -fsanitize=address -static-libasan after gcc:

```
1   # CH05:Makefile2
2
3   GCC = gcc
4   CFLAGS = -g -Wall -Wshadow
5   CFLAGS += -fsanitize=address -static-libasan
6
7   wrongindex: wrongindex.c
8           $(GCC) $(CFLAGS) $(FLAGS2) wrongindex.c -o wrongindex
9           ./wrongindex
10
11  clean:
12          /bin/rm -f *.o wrongindex *~ *bak output*
```

The line

```
CFLAGS += -fsanitize=address -static-libasan
```

adds more flags for gcc.

5.4 Test Coverage

If some lines of a program are not tested, these lines may contain mistakes not revealed by testing. This may occur because the tests overlook the possible scenarios. It is also possible that the program has a defect in its logic and the code can never be tested. Consider this example:

```c
if ((x < 0) && (x > 400)) // x is horizontal location
{
    vx = -vx; // vx is  the velocity in the horizontal direction
}
```

This example is from a homework assignment for a computer game of a bouncing ball. The court's width is 400. The intent is to change the horizontal velocity vx when the ball hits the left wall as x < 0 or hits the right wall as x > 400. What is wrong with this code? The intention is

```c
if ((x < 0) || (x > 400))
{
    vx = -vx;
}
```

However, the mistake is using && (and) instead of || (or). Since it is impossible for x to be smaller than zero and at the same time greater than 400, the if condition is never true. It is possible to find such problems using a tool called *test coverage*. The tool determines whether a particular line of code has been executed for a particular test input. Here is an example:

```c
1   // CH05:coverage.c
2   #include <stdio.h>
3   #include <stdlib.h>
4   int main(int argc, char * argv[])
5   {
6       int x;
7       int vx = 10;
8       for (x = -100; x < 1000; x ++)
9           {
10              if ((x < 0) && (x > 400))
11                  {
12                      vx = -vx;
13                      printf("change direction\n");
14                  }
15          }
16      return EXIT_SUCCESS;
17  }
```

The tool **gcov** finds that the two lines

```c
vx = -vx;
printf("change direction\n");
```

are never executed. This tool works in collaboration with `gcc`, and additional arguments are required when running `gcc`:

```
-fprofile-arcs -ftest-coverage
```

If the executable file is called `coverge`, run the program and two output files are generated: `coverage.gcda` and `coverage.gcno`. We can now run the `gcov` command.

```
$ gcov coverage.c
```

The output is

```
File 'coverage.c'
Lines executed:71.43% of 7
coverage.c:creating 'coverage.c.gcov'
```

A new file called `coverage.c.gcov` is generated. Here is the content of this file:

```
 1        -:    0:Source:coverage.c
 2        -:    0:Graph:coverage.gcno
 3        -:    0:Data:coverage.gcda
 4        -:    0:Runs:1
 5        -:    1:// CH05:coverage.c
 6        -:    2:#include <stdio.h>
 7        -:    3:#include <stdlib.h>
 8        1:    4:int main(int argc, char * argv[])
 9        -:    5:{
10        -:    6:  int x;
11        1:    7:  int vx = 10;
12     1101:    8:  for (x = -100; x < 1000; x ++)
13        -:    9:    {
14     1100:   10:      if ((x < 0) && (x > 400))
15        -:   11:        {
16    #####:   12:          vx = -vx;
17    #####:   13:          printf("change direction\n");
18        -:   14:        }
19        -:   15:    }
20        1:   16:  return EXIT_SUCCESS;
21        -:   17:}
```

Two lines are marked by `#####` because these two lines have not been tested. This tool can be used with complex programs to determine whether particular lines are never executed. If the same program runs several times, `gcov` reports the union of the coverage. Typing these commands is too much work and it is better to write the `Makefile` such that everything is handled by `make` every time the program is modified.

```
1  # CH05:Makefile3
2  GCC = gcc -g -Wall -Wshadow -fprofile-arcs -ftest-coverage
3  coverge: coverage.c
4          $(GCC) coverage.c -o coverage
5          ./coverage
6          gcov coverage.c
```

```
7              grep "##" coverage.c.gcov
8     clean:
9              rm -f *.gcno coverage *gcda
```

This `Makefile` also has an option called `clean`. Typing `make clean` deletes the file generated by `gcov`. If `gcov` reports that some lines are never tested, then the problem may come from the program, as shown in this case. Sometimes, the problem comes from the test inputs. Designing good test inputs is not easy and some books discuss in details on how to design test inputs.

It is important to understand the limitations of test coverage. Low coverage means that the test inputs need improvement, or the program has a problem, or both. However, high coverage is not necessarily better. Good tests aim to detect problems. A simple program like the following can get 100% coverage:

```
1    // CH05:donothing.c
2    #include <stdio.h>
3    #include <stdlib.h>
4    int main(int argc, char * argv[])
5    {
6      return EXIT_SUCCESS;
7    }
```

However, this program does nothing. Pursuing high coverage should not be a goal in itself. The goal should be detecting and fixing problems.

5.5   Limit Core Size

In some cases, invalid memory accesses will cause a "core dumped" message. The core file is a way to debug programs. A core file can occupy a lot of space on your disk. Use the following command to find whether a core file exists.

```
$ cd
$ find . -name "core"
```

The first command returns to your home directory. The second command finds any core file. The core file can be deleted by using the following command:

```
$ rm `find . -name "core"`
```

The command `rm` means remove. The earlier command `find . -name "core"` is now enclosed by single back-quotes. This is the quote mark ' sharing the key with ~ (for a common keyboard layout, your keyboard may have a different layout). This is not the single quote ' sharing the same key with the double quote ". The system settings can be modified to eliminate cores. If you use the C shell, you can type

```
$ limit coredumpsize 0
```

to prevent the generation of a core file. This does not prevent programs from making invalid memory accesses and having segmentation faults. We still have to correct our programs and remove invalid memory accesses.

5.6   Remove Large Files

If a program has an infinite loop (i.e., a loop that will never end) and the program prints something inside of the loop, then redirecting output to a file will create an infinitely large file. Here is an example of an infinite loop:

```
#define MAX_VALUE 100
int count = 0;
while (count < MAX_VALUE)
{
    printf("some information\n");
}
```

This `while` loop will not end because `count` is zero and never changes. The program will print forever. When this occurs, use `Ctrl-c` to stop the program. This means pressing the `Ctrl` key (usually at the left lower corner of keyboard) and the `c` key at the same time. If you suspect that your program generates exceptionally large files, you can find the existence of these large files by using the following command in the Terminal:

```
$ cd
$ du -s * | sort -n
```

The first command returns to the home directory. The second line has two commands: `du -s *` displays the space occupied by each directory. The output is then sorted by treating the values as numbers (not strings). When sorting by numbers (adding `-n`), 10 comes after 9. When sorting by strings (without `-n`), 10 comes before 9. The vertical bar is *pipe* as explained on Page 62. It takes the output from the first program and makes it the input to the second program. You can see which directories occupy a lot of space. Enter these directories and run the `du` command again to find large files. Then, you can delete the large files.

5.7   Problems

5.7.1   Array Index

Write a program that has an array of 10 elements. The program uses −1, 10, and 100 as the array indexes. Run the program and observe what happens.

5.7.2   gcov

Write a program that has several `if` conditions. Use `gcov` to observe the coverage of tests.

5.7.3   Test Coverage

If `gcov` reports 100% coverage, does that mean all possible scenarios have been tested?

Chapter 6

Strings

C does not have a specific data type for strings. Instead, in C programs, strings are arrays of characters (`char`). A string can include alphabet characters, digits, spaces, and symbols. Strings can be created by putting characters between double quotations. For example,

- "Hello"
- "The C language"
- "write 2 programs"
- "symbols $%# can be part of a string"

The examples are string constants: their data cannot be edited. Often *string variables* are preferable to store strings whose values may change. For example, a program may ask a user to enter a name. The programmer does not know the user's name in advance, and thus cannot use any constant. From the program's point of view, the name is a string variable that receives the name from the keyboard input.

6.1 Array of Characters

In C programs, every string is an array of characters but an array of characters is not necessarily a string. To be a string, one array element must be the special character '\0'. Please notice that this is different from '0'. This character terminates the string, and is called the *null terminator*. If an array has characters after the null terminator, those characters are not part of the string. Below are four arrays of characters but only `arr3` and `arr4` are strings because only those two arrays contain '\0'.

```c
char arr1[] = {'T', 'h', 'i', 's', ' ', 'n', 'v', 't'};
char arr2[] = {'T', 'h', 'i', 's', ' ', 's', 't', 'r', '0'};
char arr3[] = {'2', 'n', 'd', ' ', 's', 't', '\0', 'M'};
char arr4[] = {'C', ' ', 'P', ' ', '@', '-', '\0', '1', '8'};
```

The string in `arr3` is "2nd st". The character 'M' is an array element but it is not part of the string because it is after '\0'. Similarly, for `arr4`, the string is "C P @-". The trailing characters '1' and '8' are elements of the array but they are not part of the string. We do not need to put any number between [and] because gcc calculates the size for each array.

Single quotations enclose a single letter, such as 'M' and '@', and represent a character type. Double quotations enclose a string and the null terminator, '\0', is automatically added to the end of the string. Thus, the string stored in `arr3` is "2nd st" (no '\0') but it actually contains the element '\0'. Note that "W" is different from 'W'. The former uses double quotes and means a string, ending with a null terminator even though it is not shown. Hence, "W" actually means two characters. In contrast, 'W' is a character without

DOI: 10.1201/9781003257981-6

a null terminator. When storing a string of n characters, the array needs space for $n + 1$ characters. The additional character is used to store the terminating '\0'. For example, to store the string "Hello" (5 characters), we need to create an array of 6 elements:

```
char arr[6];          // create an array with 6 characters
arr[0] = 'H';
arr[1] = 'e';
arr[2] = 'l';
arr[3] = 'l';
arr[4] = 'o';
arr[5] = '\0';        // remember to add '\0'
```

Forgetting the null terminator '\0' is a common mistake. The null terminator is important because it indicates the end of the string. In the earlier examples, arr3 and arr4 were two arrays; arr3 had 8 elements and arr4 had 10 elements. However, if they are treated as strings, the length of each is only 6. The null terminator is not counted at part of the length. C provides a function strlen for calculating the length of strings. Before calling strlen, the program needs to include the file string.h because strlen and many string-related functions are declared in string.h.

```
1   // CH06:strlen.c
2   #include <stdio.h>
3   #include <stdlib.h>
4   #include <string.h>
5   int main(int argc, char * * argv)
6   {
7     char str1[] = {'T','h','i','s',' ','n','v','t'};
8     char str2[] = {'T','h','i','s',' ','s','t','r','0'};
9     char str3[] = {'2','n','d',' ','s','t','\0','M'};
10    char str4[] = {'C',' ','P',' ','@','-','\0','1','8','k'};
11    char str5[6];
12    int len3, len4, len5;
13    str5[0] = 'H';
14    str5[1] = 'e';
15    str5[2] = 'l';
16    str5[3] = 'l';
17    str5[4] = 'o';
18    str5[5] = '\0';
19    len3 = strlen(str3);
20    len4 = strlen(str4);
21    len5 = strlen(str5);
22    printf("len3 = %d,len4 = %d,len5 = %d\n",len3,len4,len5);
23    return EXIT_SUCCESS;
24  }
```

The output for this program is

```
len3 = 6, len4 = 6, len5 = 5
```

The following is one possible way to implement `strlen`:

```c
int strlen(char *str)
{
    int length = 0;
    while ((* str) != '\0')
      {
        length ++; // length does not include '\0'
        str ++;
      }
    return(length);
}
```

Section 4.7 explains that when calling a function, the argument `str` stores the address of the first array element. The sixth line increments an integer. The seventh line uses pointer arithmetic, as explained in Section 4.9. The `strlen` function ignores everything after '\0'. If the input `str` does not include '\0', `while` does not end. The program keeps increasing `str` (line 7) until it is no longer a valid memory address. As a result, the program's behavior is undefined.

6.2 String Functions in C

In addition to `strlen`, C provides many functions for processing strings. All functions assume that '\0' is an element in the array. Below we introduce a few of these functions.

6.2.1 Copy: strcpy

This function copies a string into a pre-allocated memory region. This function takes two arguments: The first is the destination and the second is the source. Here is an example:

```c
char src[] = {'H', 'e', 'l', 'l', 'o', '\0'}; // must contain '\0'
char dest[6]; // must be 6 or larger
strcpy(dest, src);
```

There are five characters in "Hello" but one element is needed for the null terminator '\0'—the destination's size needs to be six or larger. The `strcpy` function does not check whether the destination has enough space. You must ensure that there is enough space at the destination. If the destination does not have enough space, then the program has a serious security problem and may be vulnerable to "buffer overflow attacks". The function `strcpy` has this format:

```c
char *strcpy(char *restrict dest, const char *src);
```

Here `restrict` means `dest` is the only way to access the piece of memory because `src` and `dest` refer to two pieces of non-overlapping memory. Adding `restrict` allows the compiler to improve performance. The word `const` in front of `src` means that the `strcpy` function must not change the content through the pointer `src`.

6.2.2   Copy: `strdup`

The function `strcpy` assumes that the destination has enough memory space. The function `strdup` combines two functions: (1) calling `malloc` to allocate enough space for the destination and (2) copying the content of a string, including '\0'.

```
// src is the source string
char * dest; // destination of copy
dest = malloc(sizeof(char) * (strlen(src) + 1)); // + 1 for '\0'
strcpy(dest, src);
```

The function `strdup` is equivalent to the two functions, `malloc` and `strcpy` combined.

```
char * dest = strdup(src); // src is the source string
```

Since `malloc` is used, the memory needs to be released by **free** later. The functions `malloc` and **free** will be explained in Chapter 7.

6.2.3   Compare: `strcmp`

This function can be used to compare two strings. It takes two arguments:

```
strcmp(str1, str2);
```

The function returns a negative integer, a zero, or a positive integer depending on whether `str1` is less than, equal to, or greater than `str2`. The order of two strings is defined in the same way as the order of words in a dictionary—also known as lexicographical order. For example, "about" is smaller than "forever" because the letter a is before the letter f in a dictionary. "Education" is after "Change". The order is determined by the ASCII (American Standard Code for Information Interchange) values. ASCII assigns an integer value to each character, symbol, or digit. For example, the values for 'A' 'a', '#', and '7' are 65, 97, 35, and 55 respectively.

The last one may sound strange. Why does the value of digit '7' have a value of 55? The answer is that character values are treated differently from integer values. This can be shown using the following example:

```
1   // CH06:charint.c
2   #include <stdio.h>
3   #include <stdlib.h>
4   int main(int argc, char * * argv)
5   {
6     int v = 55;
7     printf("%d\n", v); // 55 as integer
8     printf("%c\n", v); // '7' as character
9     return EXIT_SUCCESS;
10  }
```

The output is 55 7. The first `printf` treats v as an integer by using `%d` and the value is 55. The second `printf` treats v as a character by using `%c` and the character '7'.

6.2.4   Find Substrings: `strstr`

If string `str1` is part of another string `str2`, `str1` is a *substring* of `str2`. For example, "str" is a substring of "structure" and "ure" is also a substring of "structure". "W" is a substring of "Welcome" but "sea" is not a substring of "sightseeing". If we want to determine whether one string is part of another string, we can use the `strstr` function. This function takes two arguments: `haystack` and `needle`. The function attempts to locate `needle` within `haystack`. If `needle` is a substring of `haystack`, `strstr(haystack, needle)` returns the address where the `needle` starts within `haystack`. This address must not be NULL. If `needle` is not a substring of `haystack`, `strstr(haystack, needle)` returns NULL. Please notice the order of the two arguments: The first is the longer one. Here are two examples:

```
char haystack[] = {'H', 'e', 'l', 'l', 'o', '\0'};
char * chptr; // a pointer
chptr = strstr(haystack, "llo"); // chptr's value is & haystack[2]
chptr = strstr(haystack, "XY");  // chptr's value is NULL
```

In the first call of `strstr`, "llo" is part of "Hello" and the "llo" starts at the third element (index is 2). Thus, `strstr` returns `& haystack[2]`. In the second call of `strstr`, "XY" is not part of "Hello" and `chptr`'s value is NULL. The ending character '\0' is not considered when finding `needle`.

6.2.5   Find Characters: `strchr`

The function `strchr` searches a string for a specific character. It returns the address of the first occurrence of the character within the string. If this string does not contain the character, then `strchr` returns NULL. Here are some examples:

```
char str[] = {'H', 'e', 'l', 'l', 'o', '\0'};
char * chptr; // a pointer
chptr = strchr(str, 'H'); // chptr's value is & str[0]
chptr = strchr(str, 'l'); // chptr's value is & str[2]
chptr = strchr(str, 'o'); // chptr's value is & str[4]
chptr = strchr(str, 't'); // chptr's value is NULL
```

6.3   Understand `argv`

Section 1.1 says that every C program starts at the special `main` function

```
int main(int argc, char * * argv)
```

Adding spaces between `*`, or in front of `argv` makes no difference (i.e., `char * * argv` is the same as `char ** argv`). What is `argv`? As explained in the previous chapter and summarized in Table 4.4, adding an asterisk after a type makes the type into a pointer. What does it mean if there are two asterisks?

C uses arrays of characters for strings. An array is a pointer. Let's imagine that C had the `string` type, this type would need to be equivalent to `char *` in real C programs. If string were a type, then what would be the type for an array of strings? That would be string *. Since string is actually char *, the type of string * is char * *.

The argument argv is an array of strings. The first element of this array argv[0] is a string and its type is char *. The first letter of the first string is argv[0][0]. The type of argv[0][0] is char. Please review Section 4.8 for the type rules. When calling the main function, the arguments are provided by the operating system, more precisely, by the shell program in the Terminal. Since main is also a function, the arguments are stored on the call stack. This is how to execute a program called prog with "some arguments":

```
$ ./prog some arguments
```

When running this program, "some" and "arguments" are called the *command-line arguments*. There are three arguments so argc is 3, including ./prog itself. The value of argv is the address of the first element, i.e., & argv[0]. Table 6.1 shows the call stack. Assume char is one byte; int is four bytes; and a pointer is eight bytes. We can use argv[0] to get the first string. The value of argv is the address of argv[0]. As with all arrays, the addresses of argv[0], argv[1], and argv[2] are contiguous. Since argv[0], argv[1], and argv[2] are strings, each of them is also a pointer storing the starting address of the first letter in each of those strings. The value of argv[0] is the address of argv[0][0]. To make it clearer a horizontal line separates the strings. Everything still belongs to the same frame.

TABLE 6.1:   Call stack of the main function with command-line arguments.

Frame	Symbol	Address	Value
	argv[2][9]	157	'\0'
	argv[2][8]	156	s
	argv[2][7]	155	t
	argv[2][6]	154	n
	argv[2][5]	153	e
	argv[2][4]	152	m
	argv[2][3]	151	u
	argv[2][2]	150	g
	argv[2][1]	149	r
main	argv[2][0]	148	a
	argv[1][4]	147	'\0'
	argv[1][3]	146	e
	argv[1][2]	145	m
	argv[1][1]	144	o
	argv[1][0]	143	s
	argv[0][6]	142	'\0'
	argv[0][5]	141	g
	argv[0][4]	140	o
	argv[0][3]	139	r
	argv[0][2]	138	p
	argv[0][1]	137	/
	argv[0][0]	136	.
	argv[2]	128	A148
	argv[1]	120	A143
	argv[0]	112	A136
	argv	104	A112
	argc	100	3

6.4   Count Substrings

How can we count the occurrences of a substring? For example, "ice" is a substring of "nice" and it occurs only once. In the string, "This is his history book", the substring "is" occurs 4 times: "Th*is* *is* h*is* h*is*tory book". The following program combines what we have learned about strstr and argv to count the occurrences of a substring.

```
1  // CH06:countsubstr.c
2  // count the occurrence of a substring
3  // argv[1] is the longer string
4  // argv[2] is the shorter string
5  // argv[1] may contain space if it is enclosed by " "
```

```
6    #include <stdio.h>
7    #include <stdlib.h>
8    #include <string.h>
9    int main(int argc, char * argv[])
10   {
11     int count = 0;
12     char * ptr;
13     if (argc < 3)
14       {
15         printf("Please enter two strings.\n");
16         return EXIT_FAILURE;
17       }
18     printf("argv[1] = %s, strlen = %d\n", argv[1], (int) strlen(argv[1]));
19     printf("argv[2] = %s, strlen = %d\n", argv[2], (int) strlen(argv[2]));
20     ptr = argv[1];
21     do
22       {
23         ptr = strstr(ptr, argv[2]);
24         if (ptr != NULL)
25           {
26             printf("%s\n", ptr);
27             count ++;
28             ptr ++;
29           }
30       } while (ptr != NULL);
31     if (count == 0)
32       { printf("argv[2] is not a substring of argv[1].\n"); }
33     else
34       { printf("argv[2] occurs %d times in argv[1].\n", count); }
35     return EXIT_SUCCESS;
36   }
```

This program is compiled and executed as follows:

```
$ gcc -g -Wall -Wshadow countsubstr.c -o countsubstr
$ ./countsubstr "This is his history book." is
```

Earlier we noted that spaces separate the command line arguments. If we enclose a sentence in double quotation marks, the whole sentence is treated as a single argument, as shown in this example. The output of the program is:

```
argv[1] = This is his history book., strlen = 25
argv[2] = is, strlen = 2
is is his history book.
is his history book.
is history book.
istory book.
argv[2] occurs 4 times in argv[1].
```

C provides many more functions for processing strings. You can find a list of the C's string processing functions by typing into the Terminal:

```
$ man string
```

man stands for "manual". The manual displays a list of functions related to processing strings, for example `strcat`.

6.5   Problems

6.5.1   Compare Strings

The manual of `strcmp` says that it returns a negative value if the first string is less than the second. Does that mean `strcmp` returns -1 when the first string is less than the second?

6.5.2   Count Substring-1

Consider the program on page 74. What is the output when the inputs: `argv[1]` is "ECECECECE" and `argv[2]` is "ECE"?

6.5.3   Count Substring-2

What change is needed so that each match of `argv[2]` consumes as many characters as `argv[2]` and a character in `argv[1]` cannot be counted multiple times? Using the previous example Consider `argv[1]` is "ECECECECE" and `argv[2]` is "ECE". The first three letters are used for the first match. Thus, the second match should be found in "CECECE".

Chapter 7

Heap Memory

Chapter 2 describes one type of memory: stack memory (also called the call stack). Stack memory follows a simple rule: first in, last out. The call stack is managed by the code generated by the compiler. Every time a function is called, a new frame is pushed. Every time a function ends, the frame is popped. Programmers have no direct control over this process. One consequence is that a function may read from or write to memory addresses in lower frames; however, a function can never "look upward" into memory above its frame. This is because whenever a function is actively executing, there are no valid memory addresses "above" the current function's frame. Sometimes programmers need more control over memory. They want to be able to *allocate* memory when necessary and *release* memory when the allocated memory is no longer needed. For this purpose, computers have another type of memory: *heap memory*.

7.1 Allocate Memory using `malloc`

If a called function can access the frame of the calling (lower) function through pointers, would this be sufficient? No. At the bottom of the call stack is the frame of the `main` function. Can a program store all of its data in the `main` function, since this data can be accessed by all the other functions? This would make the `main` function rather complex for even a simple program. We would need to consider every possible way the data could be read or written and the `main` would have to manage space for all of the data. Even if we are willing to do this analysis and write this `main` function, we still have problems. Most programs take some form of input, such as reading a file from a disk. At the time the program is written, we cannot know what input will be given to the program. We do not know the size of the input. We cannot write a program that can handle the inputs whose size is greater than our expectation. This is a severe limitation. We need a way to allocate memory as needed while the program is running.

Before talking about how to use heap memory, let's review how to create a fixed-size array. The following example creates an array of six integers and assigns the first three elements to 11, −29, and 74.

```
int arr1[6];
arr1[0] = 11;
arr1[1] = -29;
arr1[2] = 74;
// the values of arr1[3], arr1[4], arr1[5] are undefined
```

This array is stored inside a frame in the call stack. The values of the other three elements (`arr[3]`, `arr[4]`, and `arr[5]`) are still garbage. To create a fixed-size array, the array's size

DOI: 10.1201/9781003257981-7

must be specified in the source code. This is problematic because the size may be unknown at the time the code is written. For example,

```c
int num;
printf("Please enter a number: ");
scanf("%d", & num);
```

Note that the number is given *after* the program starts running. We can use this number to create an integer array with `num` elements. The program uses `malloc` to create the array:

```c
int * arr2;
arr2 = malloc(num * sizeof(int)); // no * inside sizeof
// old style: arr2 = (int *) malloc(num * sizeof(int));
// num must be a positive number
```

Notice `*` in front of `arr2`. The value of `num` is entered by a user. To create an array of integers, an integer pointer is needed. This allocation must use `sizeof(int)` because the size of an integer can be different on different machines. If `sizeof(int)` is 4 (most computers), then the program allocates `num * 4` bytes of memory. If `sizeof(int)` is 2 (common in some microcontrollers), then the program allocates `num * 2` bytes of memory. The type of the pointer must match what is in `sizeof(...)`. The following example is wrong.

```c
int * arr3;
arr3 = malloc(length * sizeof(char)); /* WRONG */
// types do not match, one is int, the other is char
int * arr4;
arr4 = malloc(length * sizeof(double)); /* WRONG */
// types do not match, one is int, the other is double
```

The program will behave strangely when types do not match. Programs should check whether `malloc` succeeds. If it fails, then it returns `NULL`. Programs should handle this problem before doing anything else. Calling `malloc` may fail when the system cannot provide the requested memory (usually because the requested amount is too large). C uses `NULL` to indicate an invalid memory address.

```c
int * arr5;
arr5 = malloc(length * sizeof(int));
if (arr5 == NULL)
{
    // malloc has failed, handle the problem here.
}
```

If a program allocates memory successfully, then the program can assign values to the elements in the same way as an array:

```c
arr2[0] = 11;
arr2[1] = -29;
arr2[2] = 74;
```

When using `malloc` to allocate an array, the memory addresses of the elements are contiguous. When the memory is no longer needed, the program must release (also called free) the memory by calling:

```
free(arr2); // no information about the size
```

It is impossible to release only one part of the memory. All the memory allocated in a given call to `malloc` must be freed at once. Each `malloc` should have exactly one `free`. Calling `free` does not change `arr2`'s value (`free` does not change `arr2`'s value to NULL). The `malloc` and `free` functions work together, and `free` knows how much memory should be freed. If a program calls `malloc` without calling `free`, then the program has a *memory leak*. Memory leaks are serious problems because a program has a limited amount of memory. The limit depends on the hardware and also the operating systems. Later in this chapter, we will explain how to use `valgrind` to detect memory leaks.

7.2 Stack and Heap Memory

When a program declares a pointer, the pointer is stored in the call stack.

```
int * arr2;
```

Suppose `arr2`'s address is 200 as shown in Table 7.1. Next, allocates memory for an array of 6 integers:

```
arr2 = malloc(6 * sizeof(int));
```

TABLE 7.1: The pointer `arr2` is in the call stack. The allocated memory (using `malloc`) is in the heap.

Symbol	Address	Value	Address	Value	Value	Value
arr2	200	A10000	10020	?		
			10016	?		
			10012	?		
			10008	?		$\rightarrow$ 74
			10004	?		
			10000	?	$\rightarrow$ 11	
				(a)	(b)	(c)
	Stack Memory			Heap Memory		

Section 4.9 mentioned that different types have different sizes. That is the reason why `malloc` is used in conjunction with `sizeof`. From now on, let us assume that each integer requires 4 bytes; thus, the addresses of two adjacent array elements are different by 4. Calling `malloc` returns a valid heap address to a piece of memory large enough to store 6 integers, and `arr2`'s value stores that address. In this example, we use A10000 for the heap address. The memory is uninitialized, so we use "?" for each integer's value, as shown in Table 7.1(a). You may use `calloc` to allocate memory and also set the values to zero.

The following assignment changes the first element of the array:

```
arr2[0] = 11;
```

This causes the heap memory at 𝔸10000 to change, as shown in Table 7.1(b).

```
arr2[2] = 74;
```

This changes the heap memory at 𝔸10008, as shown in Table 7.1(c). This is what happens when the program executes this line:

1. Takes `arr2`'s value as an address. In this example the value is 𝔸10000.
2. The index is 2, so `sizeof(int)` $\times 2 = 4 \times 2 = 8$ is added to 𝔸10000 and the new address is 𝔸10008.
3. This is at the left side of the assignment, the value at the address is changed to 74.

The following example creates an array whose length is determined by `argc`. The program uses `strtol` to convert the command line arguments (elements of `argv`) into integers. This is necessary because each element of `argv` is a string. Then, the program adds up the integers' values and prints the sum.

```
1    // CH07:malloc.c
2    // create an array whose size is specified at run time.  The array's
3    // elements are the command line arguments.  The program adds the
4    // elements and prints the sum.
5    #include <stdio.h>
6    #include <stdlib.h>
7    int main(int argc, char * argv[])
8    {
9      int * arr2;
10     int iter;
11     int sum = 0;
12     if (argc < 2)
13       {
14         printf("Need to provide some integers.\n");
15         return EXIT_FAILURE;
16       }
17     arr2 = malloc(argc * sizeof(int));
18     if (arr2 == NULL)
19       {
20         printf("malloc fails.\n");
21         return EXIT_FAILURE;
22       }
23     // iter starts at 1 because argv[0] is the program's name
24     for (iter = 1; iter < argc; iter ++)
25       { arr2[iter] = (int) strtol(argv[iter], NULL, 10);  }
26     printf("The sum of ");
27     for (iter = 1; iter < argc; iter ++)
28       {
29         printf("%d ", arr2[iter]);
30         sum += arr2[iter];
31       }
32     printf("is %d.\n", sum);
33     free (arr2);
34     return EXIT_SUCCESS;
35   }
```

The program uses `strtol` to convert the strings into integers. Some books suggest using `atoi` but `strtol` is preferred for two reasons: (i) `strtol` is more general because it is not limited to decimal bases. For example, `strtol` can be used to convert binary numbers or hexadecimal (base 16) numbers. (ii) More important, `strtol` allows the calling program to check whether the conversion fails. The conversion fails when the string contains no number. In contrast, `atoi` provides no information on whether the conversion fails. Use `gcc` to convert the program into an executable file called malloc:

```
$ gcc -Wall -Wshadow malloc.c -o malloc
```

The following shows examples running this program. If an argument is not an integer ("hello" and "C" in the second example), then the value of that argument is zero.

```
$ ./malloc 5 8 -11 4 3 27
The sum of 5 8 -11 4 3 27 is 36.
$ ./malloc 7 9 hello 1 6 C 2 4 8
The sum of 7 9 0 1 6 0 2 4 8 is 37.
$ ./malloc 7 9 123hello 1 6 C 2 4 8
The sum of 7 9 123 1 6 0 2 4 8 is 160.
```

In the second example, "hello" and "C" are not valid numbers. Thus, `strtol` converts them to zeros. In the third example, "123hello" is converted to 123.

7.3   Functions that Return a Heap Address

A function may return the address of heap memory. For example,

```
1   int * f1(int n)
2   {
3     int * ptr;
4     ptr = malloc (n * sizeof(int));
5     return ptr;
6   }
7   void f2(void)
8   {
9     int * arr;
10    arr = f1(6);
11    // RL
12    arr[4] = 7;
13    free (arr);
14  }
```

Let's consider the call stack just before `f1` returns `ptr`:

Symbol	Address	Value		Address	Value
n	132	6			
ptr	124	A10000		10020	?
value address	116	A100		10016	?
return location	108	RL		10012	?
arr	100	?		10008	?
				10004	?
				10000	?
	Stack Memory			Heap Memory	

After `f1` returns, the address A10000 is written to the value of `arr`. The allocated heap memory is still available because the program has not called `free` yet. The stack variable `ptr`, declared on line 3, is destroyed when `f1` returns because `ptr` is on the stack. However, the allocated heap memory is available until it is freed. This is a fundamental difference between stack and heap memory. Heap memory is more flexible. The statement,

```
arr[4] = 7;
```

changes an element in the array. Now the stack and heap memory look as follows:

Symbol	Address	Value		Address	Value
arr	100	A10000		10020	?
				10016	7
				10012	?
				10008	?
				10004	?
				10000	?
	Stack Memory			Heap Memory	

Before `f2` finishes, it must call `free`. Otherwise, the program leaks memory. This example shows that memory allocated by `malloc` can be passed between functions. We have used A10000 as the memory address returned by `malloc`. In a real computer, the address can change every time the program runs and the address will likely be a very large number.

Please notice the difference between this program and the program on page 40. The program on page 40 intends to return the address of a variable on the call stack. The program here returns the address in the heap memory.

7.4   Two-Dimensional Arrays in C

We have seen two-dimensional arrays already. In Section 6.3, `argv` is an array of strings. Each string is an array of characters. Thus, `argv` is a two-dimensional array. The strings may have different sizes. The characters in each string are stored contiguously, and the string pointers are stored contiguously. C programs may create a fixed-size two-dimensional array in the following way:

```
int arr2d[8][3]; // an array with 8 rows and 3 columns
arr2d[0][2] = 4; // assign 4 to the 3rd column of the 1st row
arr2d[3][1] = 6; // assign 6 to the 2nd column of the 4th row
```

A two-dimensional array is like a matrix. The elements are organized into rows and columns. In this example, the first dimension has eight rows and the indexes are between zero and seven (inclusively). The second dimension has three columns; the indexes are between zero and two. As explained earlier, the elements in an array occupy contiguous memory. Thus, `arr2d[0][1]` and `arr2d[0][2]` are adjacent to each other inside memory.

It is more complicated to creat a two-dimensional array whose size is known only at run time. To create this array, we will allocate memory one dimension at a time. First, imagine a new type called `one_d_array`. A two-dimensional array would be an array of this new type `one_d_array`. To create this two-dimensional array, `malloc` is used:

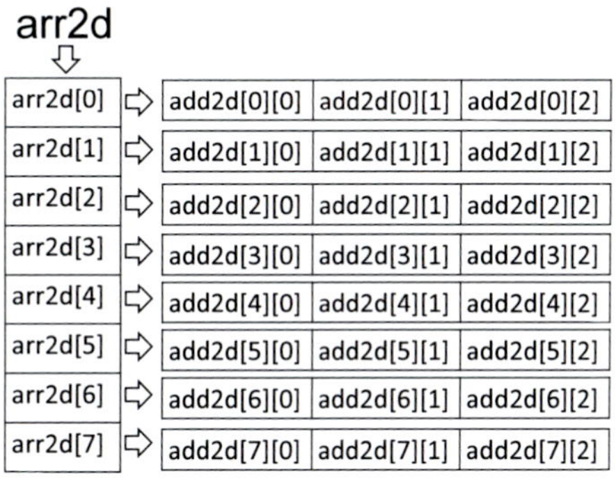

FIGURE 7.1: A two-dimensional array has an array of pointers as the first dimension.

```
one_d_array * arr2d;
arr2d = malloc(numrow * sizeof(one_d_array));
```

This allocates the first dimension shown in Figure 7.1: `arr2d[0]`, `arr2d[1]`, ... This allocates space for `arr2d[i]` and each is a pointer. There is no space for the integers yet. It is necessary to allocate the memory for the second dimension (the columns) that can store integers. Each row is an array; thus, each element `arr2d[i]` is a pointer to integers, i.e., `int *`. Next, let's examine the type `one_d_array`. If each element's (e.g., arr2d[0]) type is `int *`, what is the type of `one_d_array`? It is `int *`. We can replace `one_d_array` by `int *` and the type of `arr2d` is `int * *`.

This is how to allocate the memory for the first dimension:

```
int * * arr2d;
arr2d = malloc(numrow * sizeof(int *));
```

Please notice `int *` inside `sizeof`. After allocating the first dimension, we can allocate the memory for each row:

```
for (row = 0; row < NUMROW; row ++)
{ arr2d[row] = malloc(NUMCOLUMN * sizeof (int)); }
// no * inside sizeof()
```

Please notice `int` inside `sizeof`. Later in the program, these arrays must be freed later in the program. Calling `free` must follow the reverse order of `malloc`.

```
for (row = 0; row < NUMROW; row ++)
{ free(arr2d[row]); }
free(arr2d); // must be after free(arr2d[row])
```

If we freed `arr2d` before freeing the individual rows, then attempting to free the rows would be an error. Thus, `malloc` and `free` are always in the reverse order: the memory allocated first is released later. This is an example using a two-dimensional array:

```
1   // CH07:twodarray.c
2   // purpose: show how to create a two-dimensional array.  The size of
3   // the array is 8 rows x 3 columns
4   #include <stdio.h>
5   #include <stdlib.h>
6   #define NUMROW 8
7   #define NUMCOLUMN 3
8   int main(int argc, char * argv[])
9   {
10      int * * arr2d;
11      int row;
12      // step 1: create an array of integer pointers
13      arr2d = malloc(NUMROW * sizeof (int *));
14      for (row = 0; row < NUMROW; row ++)
15        {
16          // step 2: for each row,  create an integer array
17          arr2d[row] = malloc(NUMCOLUMN * sizeof (int));
18        }
19      // now, the two-dimensional array can be used
20      arr2d[4][1] = 6;    // first index can be 0 to 7 (inclusive)
21      arr2d[6][0] = 19;   // second index can be 0 to 2 (inclusive)
22      // memory must be released in the reverse order of malloc
23      for (row = 0; row < NUMROW; row ++)
24        {
25          free (arr2d[row]); // release the memory for each row
26        }
27      free (arr2d); // release the array of integer pointers
28      return EXIT_SUCCESS;
29   }
```

After creating the two-dimensional array, the elements can be used as integers (shown in lines 20 and 21). Before the program ends, the allocated memory must be freed, in the reverse order of allocations.

In the above example, it is worth noting that the allocated data for each row are not guaranteed to be allocated contiguously. That is, each row's `malloc()` is not guaranteed to be nearby in memory. In fact there is no guarantee that two `malloc()` calls return addresses that are ordered in any predictable way by memory address.

In many applications, it is desirable to allocate the underlying array data contiguously, which can improve caching performance as well. That is, all of the data for the 2D array are allocated as a 1D array of dimension `NUMROW` times `NUMCOLUMN`. Then we initialize each of the rows to point to the appropriate offset in a one-dimensional array. These offsets ensure that each row begins at a memory address where the previous row ended. The following shows how to make a slight revision to the previous example so it can accommodate contiguous data, organized in row-major order:

```
1   // CH07:twodarraycontiguous.c
2   // purpose: show how to create a two-dimensional array.  The size of
3   // the array is 8 rows x 3 columns
4   // This version ensures that the allocation is contiguous.
5   // That is, all of the "rows" are located in a single allocated block of memory
6   #include <stdio.h>
7   #include <stdlib.h>
8   #define NUMROW 8
9   #define NUMCOLUMN 3
10  int main(int argc, char * argv[])
11  {
12    int * * arr2d;
13    int * arr2d_data;
14    int row;
15    // step 1: create an array of integer pointers
16    arr2d = malloc(NUMROW * sizeof (int *));
17    // step 1a: create an array of NUMROWS * NUMCOLUMN integers
18    // all row data is allocated as a single block of data
19    arr2d_data = malloc(NUMROW * NUMCOLUMN * sizeof(int));
20    for (row = 0; row < NUMROW; row ++)
21      {
22        // step 2: for each row, initialize to an offset of the underlying 1d array
23        arr2d[row] = arr2d_data + row * NUMCOLUMN;
24      }
25    // now, the two-dimensional array can be used
26    arr2d[4][1] = 6;    // first index can be 0 to 7 (inclusive)
27    arr2d[6][0] = 19;   // second index can be 0 to 2 (inclusive)
28    // memory must be released in the reverse order of malloc
29    free (arr2d); // release the array of integer pointers
30    free (arr2d_data); // release the array for 1d array of integer
31    return EXIT_SUCCESS;
32  }
```

Does this mean we need `int * * *` if we want to allocate a three-dimensional array of integers? Yes. Even though two-dimensional arrays are very common in programs, higher dimensions are less common. The data is probably managed differently using *structures*, not arrays. Part III will explain how to create structures.

7.5   Pointers and Function Arguments

A function argument can be a pointer that stores the address in either stack memory or heap memory. The following example passes an address in the heap memory to a function:

```
1   // CH07:heaparg.c
2   // pass the address of heap memory as a function argument
3   #include <stdio.h>
4   #include <stdlib.h>
5   int sum(int * array, int length)
6   {
```

```
7      int iter;
8      int answer = 0;
9      for (iter = 0; iter < length; iter ++)
10        { answer += array[iter]; }
11     return answer;
12   }
13   int main(int argc, char * argv[])
14   {
15     int * arr;
16     int iter;
17     int length = 12;
18     int total;
19     arr = malloc(length * sizeof(int));
20     if (arr == NULL)
21       {
22         printf("malloc fails.\n");
23         return EXIT_FAILURE;
24       }
25     for (iter = 0; iter < length; iter ++)
26       { arr[iter] = iter; }
27     total = sum(arr, length);
28     // RL
29     printf("Total is %d.\n", total);
30     free (arr); // remember to call free after malloc
31     return EXIT_SUCCESS;
32   }
```

In this example, `arr` is passed to function `sum` as an argument. The `sum` function itself does not need to know whether the value in the `array` is an address in stack memory or heap memory. The function only needs to know that the `array` contains a valid address somewhere in memory. The address is copied when it is passed as the argument `array` in the function called `sum`. The call stack and the heap memory look like the following inside the `sum` function, just before the `for` block starts:

Frame	Symbol	Address	Value		Address	Value
	answer	332	0		10044	11
	iter	328	-		10040	10
sum	length	324	12		10036	9
	array	316	A10000		10032	8
	value address	308	A228		10028	7
	return location	300	RL		10024	6
	total	228	?		10020	5
	length	224	12		10016	4
main	iter	220	13		10012	3
	arr	212	A10000		10008	2
	argv	204	-		10004	1
	argc	200	-		10000	0

(a) Stack Memory	(b) Heap Memory

Inside `sum`, `array[0]` refers to the value stored at 10000 and it is 0. Similarly, `array[7]` refers to the value stored at 10028 (10000 + 7 × `sizeof(int)`) and it is 7. The `sum` function adds the elements' values and stores the result in the `answer`. This is a local variable. Before the `sum` function ends, the value in `answer` is returned. The value address is A228. Thus, this value is stored in the `main` function local variable `total`.

7.6 Problems

7.6.1 free

What occurs if the argument to `free` is NULL?

7.6.2 malloc

What occurs if the argument to `malloc` is negative?

7.6.3 Address of Stack Memory

The following program has a warning message from `gcc`. Please explain why `gcc` thinks this program is likely wrong.

```
1  // CH07:returnaddr.c
2  #include <stdio.h>
3  #include <stdlib.h>
4  int * f1(void)
5  {
6    int val;
7    return & val;
8  }
9  int main(int argc, char * * argv)
10 {
11   int * ptr = f1();
12   * ptr = 10;
13   return EXIT_SUCCESS;
14 }
```

Chapter 8

Programming Problems Using Heap Memory

8.1 Sort an Array

This problem asks you to write a program that reads integers from a file, sorts the numbers, and writes the sorted numbers to another file.

8.1.1 Generate Test Input and Expected Output

A common problem for many software developers is to create versatile test cases. If a developer types test cases by hand, only small test cases can be created. Without good test cases, it is difficult to test whether a sorting program is correct. Without a correct sorting program, it is difficult to generate large test cases. Fortunately, for sorting integers, two Linux commands can solve this problem easily: (1) The shuf command can shuffle numbers. (2) The sort command can sort numbers. Section 5.2.3 explained how to use the shuf and sort. This section is a review. For the shuf command, -i specifies the range of the numbers; -n specifies how many numbers are selected. The output can be saved in a file by using >. The following command shuffles numbers between 1 and 100, selects 30 of them, and saves them to a file called tetst1. This is the input file for a test case.

```
shuf -i 1-100 -n 30 > test1
```

The sort command can read inputs from a file and sort the numbers:

```
sort -n test1 > expected1
```

Adding -n after sort treats the input values as numbers, not strings. This is the expected output of the test case.

8.1.2 Sort Integers

The header file declares the sort function:

```c
// CH08:sort/mysort.h
#ifndef MYSORT_H
#define MYSORT_H
void mysort(int * arr, int len);
#endif
```

DOI: 10.1201/9781003257981-8

A header file has the `.h` extension and can be used to define constants, for example,

```
1  #define MATH_PI 3.14159265
2  #define MATH_E  2.71828183
```

These are two widely used mathematical constants. A header file can create new data types as explained in Part III. A header file can *declare* functions. The declaration provides the following information: (1) return data type, (2) name of the function, (3) input arguments and their types are shown in the following format:

```
1  return_type function_name(type1 arg1, type2 arg2, ...);
```

The declaration ends with a semicolon; after the parentheses. The function's body (i.e., definition or implementation) is not provided in the header file. Instead, the body is in a `.c` file. The structure of a header should follow this format:

```
1  #ifndef NAME_H
2  #define NAME_H
3      // definition of constants
4      // definition of new data types
5      // declaration of functions
6  #endif
```

The top two lines of a head file has `#ifndef` ... and `#define` .... The purpose is to prevent this header file from being included multiple times. If it is included multiple times, the compiler `gcc` may be confused. Before explaining how to write the `mysort` function, let us explain the `main` function. The `main` function has a few places that require explanation:

- This `main` function stores the data in an array. The array's size is `argv[1]`. Section 10.1 will explain how to write a program that can automatically calculate the amount of data.
- Before using `argv[1]`, the program must check that `argc` is 2. If `argc` is 1, then `argv[1]` does not exist and attempting to access `argv[1]` will fail.
- The program uses `strtol` to convert `argv[1]` from a string to an integer.
- The `main` function must call `malloc` to allocate heap memory for the array before reading data from the file.
- The `main` function calls `free` to release the heap memory before the program ends.

Section 1.2 describes how to use redirection for program outputs. This program uses redirection for inputs. When a program calls `scanf`, the program waits for the user to enter data from the keyboard. If we execute the program by adding `<` and a file name, the program reads data from the file, not from the keyboard. The fifth line includes the header file. If a header file is provided by the C language, such as `stdio.h` or `string.h`, then the file's name is enclosed by `<` and `>`, as shown in lines 2-4. If the header file is created by the programmer, the file's name is enclosed by `"` and `"` as shown by the fifth line.

```
1  // CH08:sort/main.c
2  #include <stdio.h>
3  #include <stdlib.h>
4  #include <string.h>
5  #include "mysort.h"
6  int main(int argc, char * * argv)
7  {
8      if (argc != 2) { return EXIT_FAILURE; }
```

```
9    int number = strtol(argv[1], NULL, 10);
10   int * arr;
11   arr = malloc(sizeof(int) * number);
12   if (arr == NULL) { return EXIT_FAILURE; }
13   int ind;
14   for (ind = 0; ind < number; ind ++)
15     { scanf("%d", & arr[ind]); } // read from keyboard, or a file by <
16   mysort(arr, number);
17   for (ind = 0; ind < number; ind ++)
18     { printf("%d\n", arr[ind]); }
19   free (arr);
20   return EXIT_SUCCESS;
21 }
```

This program uses *selection sort*. It selects the smallest value among the array elements and then puts it at the beginning of the array. Then, it selects the second smallest value and puts it as the second element of the array. This process continues until reaching the end of the array.

```
1    // CH08:sort/mysort.c
2    #include <stdio.h>
3    static void swap(int * a, int * b)
4    {
5      // printf("swap called, %d %d\n", *a, *b);
6      int t = * a;
7      * a = * b;
8      * b = t;
9    }
10   void mysort(int * arr, int len) // use selection sort algorithm
11   {
12     // In each iteration, find the smallest value and put it at the
13     // beginning of the unsorted array
14     int ind1;
15     int ind2;
16     for (ind1 = 0; ind1 < len; ind1 ++)
17       {
18         int minind = ind1;
19         for (ind2 = ind1 + 1; ind2 < len; ind2 ++)
20           {
21             if (arr[minind] > arr[ind2])
22               {
23                 minind = ind2; // index of the smallest value
24               }
25           }
26         if (minind != ind1)
27           {
28             // move the smallest value to the correct location
29             swap(& arr[ind1], & arr[minind]);
30           }
31       }
32   }
```

In `mysort`, `ind1` is the counter for each iteration. When `ind1` is zero, the smallest element is moved to the beginning of the array. When `ind1` is one, the second smallest element is moved to the second element of the array. The value `ind1` separates the array into two parts: the part before `ind1` has been sorted and the part after `ind1` has not been sorted. To sort the second part, we select the smallest inside this part and move it to the beginning of the second part. As `ind1` increases, the second part shrinks.

Line 18 initializes `minind` to `ind1`. This stores the index of the smallest element seen so far in the second part of the array. Then, lines 19 to 25 find the index of the smallest element in the second part of the array. Lines 26 to 30 move the smallest value to the correct place in the array. This is achieved by swapping the smallest value from its current location to the correct location. The number of comparisons (line 21) depends on the number of elements and is independent of the actual values of the elements. This program uses the same `swap` function described in Section 4.5. The `swap` function is marked *static*. A static function can be called by functions in the same file only. A static function is invisible outside this file.

Consider the following example: The input values are 1694, 8137, 609, 7118, 5614, and 8848. The smallest value is the third element (index is 2). The first iteration of `ind1` swaps the first (index is 0) and the third elements and now the array's elements are 609, 8137, 1694, 7118, 5614, and 8848. The following table shows the array's elements in each iteration, just before calling `swap`:

ind1	minind	Sorted	Unsorted
0	2		1694 8137 **609** 7118 5614 8848
1	2	609	8137 **1694** 7118 5614 8848
2	4	609 1694	8137 7118 **5614** 8848
3	3	609 1694 5614	7118 8137 8848
4	4	609 1694 5614 7118	8137 8848
5	5	609 1694 5614 7118 8137	8848

This is the sorted array: 609 1694 5614 7118 8137 8848.

8.1.3 Makefile

The `Makefile` has a section for testing. It runs the program for the four test cases and compares the outputs with the expected results.

```
1   # CH08:sort/Makefile
2   # build and test mysort function
3   GCC = gcc
4   CFLAGS = -g -Wall -Wshadow
5   VALGRIND = valgrind --tool=memcheck --leak-check=full
6   VALGRIND += --verbose --log-file=valog
7   OBJS = mysort.o main.o
8   HDRS = mysort.h
9   test: inputgen mysort
10          ./mysort 16   < input16   > output16
11          diff output16   expected16
12  inputgen:
13          shuf -i 1-1000 -n 16 > input16
14          sort -n input16   > expected16
15  mysort: $(OBJS) $(HDRS)
16          $(GCC) $(CFLAGS) $(OBJS) -o $@
```

```
17   .c.o:
18           $(GCC) $(CFLAGS) -c $*.c
19   memory: inputgen mysort
20           $(VALGRIND) ./mysort 16    < input16    > output16
21           grep "ERROR" valog
22   clean:
23           /bin/rm -f mysort *.o *~ output16 input16 expected16 valog
```

This `Makefile` has several parts: test, inputgen, mysort, and clean. Section 5.2.1 already explained the purpose of `clean`. The `test` section is the first target in the file. Thus,

```
$ make
```

is equivalent to typing

```
$ make test
```

Before taking the action, `test` needs `inputgen` and `mysort`. The section `inputgen` uses `shuf` to generate a file with 16 numbers between 1 and 1000. This is the input of the test case. These numbers are sorted by using `sort -n` and the result is the expected output. The section `mysort` builds the executable. After `inputgen` and `mysort` sections complete, the `test` section executes the program and compares the result with the expected output. This is the result of the Terminal:

```
shuf -i 1-1000 -n 16 > input16
sort -n input16    > expected16
gcc -g -Wall -Wshadow  -c mysort.c
gcc -g -Wall -Wshadow  -c main.c
gcc -g -Wall -Wshadow  mysort.o main.o -o mysort
./mysort 16    < input16    > output16
diff output16   expected16
```

The program's output is correct (matching the content stored in `expected16`); hence `diff` command shows nothing.

8.1.4   Use `valgrind` to Detect Memory Leaks

If a program calls `malloc` without calling `free`, the program *leaks memory*. We can use `valgrind` to detect memory leaks. This `Makefile` has a section called `memory` and it checks memory leaks:

If we remove

```
free(arr);
```

near the end of `main`, then the program will leak memory. The log files generated by `valgrind` will show something like:

```
ERROR SUMMARY: 1 errors from 1 contexts (suppressed: 2 from 2)
```

at the bottom. If we look backward in the log file, we will something similar to:

```
==4645== 64 bytes in 1 blocks are definitely lost in loss record 1 of 1
==4645==     by 0x1092EE: main (main.c:11)
==4645==
==4645== LEAK SUMMARY:
==4645==    definitely lost: 64 bytes in 1 blocks
```

The program leaks 64 bytes of memory, and the memory was allocated at line 11 in main.c. Why does the program leak 64 bytes? The program allocates space for 16 integers by calling `malloc`. Each integer occupies 4 bytes so the program leaks 64 bytes. (i.e., `sizeof(int)` $\times$ 16 = 64.) If we put the `free` statement back, `valgrind` reports

```
All heap blocks were freed -- no leaks are possible
ERROR SUMMARY: 0 errors from 0 contexts
```

We should always check `valgrind`'s reports when writing programs that use `malloc` and `free`. Remember that if `valgrind` reports problems then the program has problems. If `valgrind` reports no problems, then the program may still have problems but `valgrind` failed to detect them because the test cases may not trigger the problems.

8.1.5   Use `gcc -fsanitize` to Detect Memory Leaks

Next, consider this program with a memory leak:

```c
// CH08:sort/memoryleak.c
#include <stdio.h>
#include <stdlib.h>
int main(int argc, char * * argv)
{
  char * cptr;
  cptr = malloc(sizeof(char) * 100);
  if (cptr == NULL)
    {
      return EXIT_FAILURE;
    }
  // free (cptr); // leak memory
  return EXIT_SUCCESS;
}
```

Use this `gcc` command to create the executable:

```
$ gcc -g -fsanitize=address -static-libasan memoryleak.c
```

Running this program produces the following message:

```
Direct leak of 100 byte(s) in 1 object(s) allocated from:
    #1 0x56410937c67a in main memoryleak.c:7
SUMMARY: AddressSanitizer: 100 byte(s) leaked in 1 allocation(s).
```

It shows line 7 allocates 100 bytes of memory and it is not freed. If `free(cptr);` is added before `return EXIT_SUCCESS;` there is no error message.

8.2 Sort Using `qsort`

The previous problem asks you to write a program that sorts an array of integers. The program uses *selection sort*. Even though the algorithm is easy to understand and implement, it is inefficient for large arrays. The inefficiency occurs because the algorithm does not use the *transitivity* of integers. What is transitivity? Consider three integers x, y, and z. If x > y and y > z, then x > z. C provides a function called `qsort` and it uses the *quick sort* algorithm. It is a much faster sorting algorithm than selection sort for large arrays because `qsort` uses transitivity to reduce the number of comparisons.

8.2.1 qsort

The `qsort` function is provided by C and needs four arguments:

```
void qsort(void * base, size_t nmemb, size_t size,
           int (* compar)(const void *, const void *));
```

The four arguments are

1. `base`: the address of the first element of an array. This should be `& arr[0]` if we want to sort an array called `arr`. The `qsort` function can accept an array of any type. The type `void *` means that the argument is a pointer (its value is a memory address).
2. `nmemb`: the number of elements in the array.
3. `size`: the size of each element in bytes. This is how `qsort` handles different data types.
4. `compar`: a function that tells `qsort` how to compare two elements in the array.

Among the four arguments, the last one introduces a new concept: passing a function as an argument to another function. Let's understand this argument step-by-step. First, `int (* compar)(const void *, const void *)` means that this argument is the name of a function. It is a function because of the parenthesis around `(* compar)`. Why is there an asterisk? Because the name of a function is a pointer to the function. Second, the `int` before `(* compar)` means that the function must return an integer.

The specification of `qsort` says, "*The comparison function must return an integer less than, equal to, or greater than zero if the first argument is considered to be respectively less than, equal to, or greater than the second. If two members compare as equal, their order in the sorted array is undefined.*" What does "undefined" mean here? Consider an array with two elements of the same value. If `compar` returns 0, then `qsort` may or may not swap these two elements. Consider the situation when a program sorts students' records. Each element in an array is a record of a student. These students' records may be sorted by last names. If the comparison function compares the last names, `qsort` does not guarantee the order of the first names. For example, suppose two students' names are "Amy Smith" and "Bob Smith". The comparison function returns zero when comparing these two names because they have the same last names. These two names will appear adjacent because they have the same last names. There is no guarantee whether "Amy Smith" appears before or after "Bob Smith".

The comparison function takes two input arguments. Each argument stores an address. Again, `void *` means that the address can be of any type. Page 6.2.1 explained the meaning of `const`: this function can read the value but cannot change the value stored at the address.

8.2.2   The Comparison Function

The goal of qsort is to sort arrays of any type. This means that qsort needs to know how to compare two elements in an array without knowing the type. This requires the comparison function provided by programmers. When we talk about programmer-defined structures later in this book, one structure may contain multiple attributes (such as first names, last names, and dates of birth). To make qsort work, programmers have to tell qsort how to compare the elements. The comparison function can decide ascending or descending order. The comparison function must have the following structure:

```
1   int comparefunc(const void * arg1, const void * arg2)
2   {
3     // convert void * to a known type (int, char, double ...)
4     const type * ptr1 = (const type *) arg1;
5     const type * ptr2 = (const type *) arg2;
6     // get the value from the address
7     const type val1 = * ptr1;
8     const type val2 = * ptr2;
9     // compare the value
10    if (val1 < val2)  { return -1; }
11    if (val1 == val2) { return 0; }
12    return 1; // must be val1 > val2
13  }
```

The comparison function has three steps:

1. The arguments **arg1** and **arg2** point to two distinct elements in the array. The first step in the comparison function is to convert them into the correct types, as shown in lines 4 and 5. This is called *type casting*. If we are sorting an array of integers, then the array elements are of type **int**. The pointers to those elements must be **int ***.
2. After type casting, **ptr1** and **ptr2** have the addresses of two elements of the array. The comparison function can now access the data at those memory locations. Lines 7 and 8 retrieve the values at those addresses, using the RHS rule of pointers. The values are stored in **val1** and **val2**.
3. Lines 10 to 12 return a negative, zero, or positive value based on whether **val1** is less than, equal to, or greater than **val2**. This comparison function will cause the array elements to be sorted in ascending order. If we want the elements to be sorted in descending order, then we can change lines 10 to 12 so that the function returns positive, zero, or negative if **val1** is less than, equal to, or greater than **val2**.

The following shows a program that uses qsort to sort an array of integers:

```
1   // CH08:qsort/compareint.c
2   #include <stdio.h>
3   int compareint(const void * arg1, const void * arg2)
4   {
5     const int * ptr1 = (const int *) arg1;
6     const int * ptr2 = (const int *) arg2;
7     int val1 = * ptr1;
8     int val2 = * ptr2;
9     printf("comparefunc %d %d\n", val1, val2);
10    if (val1 < val2)  { return -1; }
```

```
11      if (val1 == val2) { return 0; }
12      return 1;
13    }
```

Here is the `main` function:

```
1   // CH08:qsort/main.c
2   #include <time.h>
3   #include <stdio.h>
4   #include <stdlib.h>
5   #include <string.h>
6   #define RANGE 10000
7   int compareint(const void * arg1, const void * arg2);
8   void printArray(int * arr, int size)
9   {
10    int ind;
11    for (ind = 0; ind < size; ind ++) { printf("%d ", arr[ind]); }
12    printf("\n");
13  }
14  int main(int argc, char * * argv)
15  {
16    if (argc != 2) { return EXIT_FAILURE; }
17    int size = strtol(argv[1], NULL, 10);
18    if (size <= 0) { return EXIT_FAILURE; }
19    int * arr;
20    arr = malloc(sizeof(int) * size);
21    if (arr == NULL) { return EXIT_FAILURE; }
22    int ind;
23    srand(time(NULL)); // set the seed
24    for (ind = 0; ind < size; ind ++) // create a test case
25      { arr[ind] = rand() % RANGE; }
26    printArray(arr, size);
27    qsort(& arr[0], size, sizeof(int), compareint);
28    printArray(arr, size);
29    free (arr);
30    return EXIT_SUCCESS;
31  }
```

This `main` function needs a number (`argv[1]`) for the length of the array. Lines 24–25 generate random numbers between 0 and 9999 for the array's elements. The program uses the `rand` function to generate random numbers. Line 23 sets the seed for the random number generator. The same seed will produce the same sequence of random numbers. By using the current time as the seed, as shown in Line 23, the sequences will vary. The program prints the array before (Line 26) and after (Line 28) the array is sorted. Line 27 shows an example calling the `qsort` function.

8.2.3   Execution Examples

The following shows an example of running the program for an array with eight integers:

```
 1  5045 3603 7935 2430 1019 3445 6339 9545
 2  comparefunc: 5045 3603
 3  comparefunc: 7935 2430
 4  comparefunc: 3603 2430
 5  comparefunc: 3603 7935
 6  comparefunc: 5045 7935
 7  comparefunc: 1019 3445
 8  comparefunc: 6339 9545
 9  comparefunc: 1019 6339
10  comparefunc: 3445 6339
11  comparefunc: 2430 1019
12  comparefunc: 2430 3445
13  comparefunc: 3603 3445
14  comparefunc: 3603 6339
15  comparefunc: 5045 6339
16  comparefunc: 7935 6339
17  comparefunc: 7935 9545
18  1019 2430 3445 3603 5045 6339 7935 9545
```

These outputs have been generated by printing `val1` and `val2` in the comparison function. The outputs tell us some information about using `qsort`: (1) The comparison function `compareint` is called 16 times. Using the selection sort for an array of 8 elements, the comparison will be called

$$\sum_{\text{ind}=0}^{7} \sum_{\text{ind2} = \text{ind1} +1}^{7} 1 = 28 \text{ times.} \tag{8.1}$$

The number of comparisons depends on the original order of the input data. Section 16.2 will explain the reasons. (2) Some pairs of numbers are not compared, for example, 1019 and 7935. As mentioned earlier, `qsort` uses transitivity to reduce the number of comparisons.

8.2.4 Sort Strings

The next example uses `qsort` to sort strings. Consider a program called `sortstr` printing the command-line arguments in the ascending order. If we execute this program with the following arguments:

```
$ ./sortstr there are several arguments in the command line
```

the output is

```
./sortstr
are
arguments
command
in
line
several
the
there
```

Below is the `main` function.

```
// CH08:qsort/mainqsortstring.c
#include <stdio.h>
#include <stdlib.h>
#include <string.h>
int comparestring(const void *arg1, const void *arg2);
int main(int argc, char * *argv)
{
  int ar;
  if (argc < 2)
    {
      fprintf(stderr, "Usage: %s <string>...\n", argv[0]);
      return EXIT_FAILURE;
    }
  qsort(&argv[0], argc, sizeof(char *), comparestring);
  for (ar = 0; ar < argc; ar++)
    {
      printf("%s\n", argv[ar]);
    }
  return EXIT_SUCCESS;
}
```

Let us examine line 14 more carefully:

1. The first argument is the address of the first element of the array, i.e., `& argv[0]`.
2. The second argument is the number of strings in the array and it is `argc`.
3. The third argument is the size of each element. Since each element is a string, the argument should be `sizeof(string)`. C does not actually have the `string` type; instead, a string is an array of `char`. Thus, the argument is `sizeof(char *)`.
4. The last argument is the comparison function.

The comparison function is similar to the one for an array of integers but the types are different: `arg1` and `arg2` are the addresses of strings. Thus, their types are `string *`. Again, C does not have the `string` type; `string` means `char *` and `arg1` and `arg2` are of type `char * *`. After casting the types of `arg1` and `arg2`, the program then needs to get the strings from the addresses by adding `*` to retrieve the values stored at the addresses. Finally, the program uses `strcmp` to compare the two strings.

```
// CH08:qsort/comparestring.c
#include <string.h>
int comparestring(const void *arg1, const void *arg2)
{
  // ptr1 and ptr2 are string *
  // string is char *, thus ptr1 and ptr2 are char * *
  const char * const * ptr1 = (const char * *) arg1;
  const char * const * ptr2 = (const char * *) arg2;
  const char * str1 = * ptr1; // type: string
  const char * str2 = * ptr2;
  return strcmp(str1, str2);
}
```

Quick sort is faster than selection sort because quick sort uses transitivity. When the number of elements increases, the execution time increases for both quick sort and selection sort. However, the execution time for selection sort increases much faster. The speed advantage of quick sort becomes more apparent for very large arrays.

8.3   Problems

8.3.1   Bubble Sort

Bubble Sort is another sorting algorithm. In this algorithm, the smaller numbers gradually move to the beginning of the array, like bubbles floating upwards. The following is an implementation of the algorithm:

```c
// CH08:qsort/bubblesort.c
#include <stdio.h>
#include <stdlib.h>
#include <stdbool.h>
#define ARRAY_SIZE 15
static void swap(int * a, int * b)
{
  int t = * a;
  * a = * b;
  * b = t;
}
void bubble(int * arr, int len)
{
  // find the smallest value and move it to the beginning of the array
  int ind1, ind2;
  int count = 0;
  for (ind1 = 0; ind1 < (len - 1); ind1++)
    {
      for (ind2 = ind1 + 1; ind2 < len ; ind2 ++)
        {
          if (arr[ind1] > arr[ind2])
            {
              swap(& arr[ind1], & arr[ind2]);
              count ++;
            }
        }
    }
  printf("swap is called %d times\n", count);
}
void printArray(int * array, int len)
{
  int ind;
  for (ind = 0; ind < len; ind ++)
    { printf("%d ", array[ind]); }
  printf("\n");
```

```
36  }
37  int main(int argc, char * * argv)
38  {
39    int arr[ARRAY_SIZE];
40    int ind;
41    for (ind = 0; ind < ARRAY_SIZE; ind ++)
42      {
43        arr[ind] = ARRAY_SIZE - ind;
44      }
45    printArray(arr, ARRAY_SIZE);
46    bubble(arr, ARRAY_SIZE);
47    printArray(arr, ARRAY_SIZE);
48    return EXIT_SUCCESS;
49  }
```

Consider an input file with 15 numbers in the descending order. How many times is the swap function called for sorting the array into the ascending order?

8.3.2   Selection Sort

Consider an input file with 15 numbers in the descending order. How many times is the swap function called by selection sort for sorting the array into ascending order?

8.3.3   Comparison in qsort

Consider the comparison function for qsort. If the input array has 100 elements, how many times is the comparison function called? Does the answer depend on the relative order of the elements? Consider two cases: (1) The original array is already sorted in ascending order. (2) The original array is already sorted in descending order. How many times is the comparison executed?

Chapter 9

Reading and Writing Files

We have already taken advantage of redirection to use files as inputs and outputs. This chapter explains how to use C functions to read from or write to files.

9.1 Read from Files

A program has many ways to obtain input data, for example:

1. Use scanf to get data from a user through the keyboard.
2. Use scanf and redirection to get data from a file.
3. Use argc and argv to get data from the command line.
4. Use argv[1] as the name of an input file and read the data stored on a disk.

The first three methods have been explained in earlier chapters. This chapter explains the fourth method. After getting the file's name from argv[1], we need to *open* the file for reading. This is accomplished by calling the fopen function. The function requires two arguments. The first is the name of the file, and the second specifies the mode—for reading or for writing. They are two different ways of opening the same file. In this example, we want to read the file, and this mode is specified by "r" in the second argument.

```
1   // CH09:countchar.c
2   #include <stdio.h>
3   #include <stdlib.h>
4   int main(int argc, char * argv[])
5   {
6     FILE * fptr;
7     int ch; // must be int. cannot be char or unsigned char
8     int counter = 0;
9     if (argc < 2)
10       {
11         printf("Need to provide the file's name.\n");
12         return EXIT_FAILURE;
13       }
14     fptr = fopen(argv[1], "r");
15     if (fptr == NULL)
16       {
17         printf("fopen fail.\n");
18         // do not fclose (fptr) because fptr is NULL
19         return EXIT_FAILURE;
20       }
```

DOI: 10.1201/9781003257981-9

```
21    printf("The name of the file is %s.\n", argv[1]);
22    do
23      {
24        ch = fgetc(fptr);
25        if (ch != EOF)
26          {
27            counter ++;
28          }
29      } while (ch != EOF);
30    fclose(fptr);
31    printf("The file has %d characters.\n", counter);
32    return EXIT_SUCCESS;
33  }
```

Calling `fopen` does not always succeed. There are many reasons why `fopen` can fail. For example, the file may not exist, or the user running the program may not have the permission to open the file. When `fopen` fails, it returns `NULL`. It is important to check whether `fopen` returns `NULL` before reading or writing. After opening a file, `fgetc` can be used to read the characters one by one. A file is a *stream*. After calling `fopen`, the stream starts from the first character of the file and ends with `EOF` (End Of File). `EOF` is a special character that does not actually exist in the file. Each time `fgetc` is called, one character is taken out of the stream. After calling `fgetc` enough times, all the characters have been read. Finally, the end of file character `EOF` is reached.

This program counts the number of characters. A character may be a character ('a' to 'z' or 'A' to 'Z'), a digit ('0' to '9'), a punctuation mark (such as ',' and ';'), space, or an invisible character. At the end of each line, a new line character ('\n') is also counted. When the program attempts to read beyond the end of the file, `fgetc` returns `EOF` defined in `stdio.h`. If we search `EOF` using Linux' `grep` command:

```
$ grep EOF /usr/include/stdio.h
# define EOF (-1)
```

The value of `EOF` is -1. If `fgetc` gets one character, why does line 7 use `int` for `ch`? Should it be `char ch;`? The manual for `fgetc` says, "*fgetc() reads the next character from stream and returns it as an unsigned char cast to an int, or EOF on end of file or error.*" The `fgetc` function reads one character from a file. This character is treated as an unsigned character because ASCII (American Standard Code for Information Interchange) has only positive values. Unsigned characters can have values between 0 and 255 inclusively. The function then casts the character to an integer. This is necessary because `EOF` is negative and is not an unsigned character. Thus `fgetc` returns -1, or 0 to 255. This guarantees that `EOF` can be distinguished from the valid characters that are actually in the file. At line 7 `ch` must be `int`. Both `char` and `unsigned char` are wrong.

Another way to detect the end of file is by calling the function `feof`. This function returns a non-zero value if the end of file has been reached. Thus we can replace line 22 by:

```
while (! feof(fptr))
```

and remove `while (ch != EOF );` at line 29.

This program reports the number of characters in the file. Suppose that the source for this program is in the file `file2.c` and we compile and execute it like so:

```
$ gcc -Wall -Wshadow countchar.c -o countchar
$ ./countchar countchar.c
The name of the file is countchar.c.
The file has 713 characters.
```

Linux has a program called `wc` and it reports the number of lines, words, and characters in a file. The program reports that the file has 33 lines, 105 words, and 713 characters.

Operating systems usually restrict the number of files that a program can open at once to ensure that one program does not use too many resources. Thus programs should call `fclose` when a previously opened file is no longer needed. The pair `fopen` and `fclose` should be used together, similar to the pair of `malloc` and `free`. In fact, `fopen` will allocate memory in the program. If a program does not call `fclose`, then the program has memory leak. When `fopen` fails, it returns `NULL`. Do not write `fclose(NULL)`. Also, it is an error to close the same file twice.

In addition to `fgetc`, C provides many functions for reading data from a file. One of them is `fscanf`. It is very similar to `scanf`, except that it requires one more argument: the first argument is a `FILE` pointer. The following program adds the numbers in a file.

```c
// CH09:fscanf.c
#include <stdio.h>
#include <stdlib.h>
int main(int argc, char * argv[])
{
  FILE * fptr;
  int val;
  int sum = 0;
  if (argc < 2)
    {
      printf("Need to provide the file's name.\n");
      return EXIT_FAILURE;
    }
  fptr = fopen(argv[1], "r");
  if (fptr == NULL)
    {
      printf("fopen fail.\n");
      return EXIT_FAILURE;
    }
  printf("The name of the file is %s.\n", argv[1]);
  while (fscanf(fptr, "%d", & val) == 1) // %d means integer
    {
      printf("%d ", val);
      sum += val;
    }
  fclose(fptr);
  printf("\nThe sum is %d.\n", sum);
  return EXIT_SUCCESS;
}
```

This program keeps reading until no more integers can be read. Each call of the `fscanf` function returns the number of value(s) successfully read. This example reads only one integer at a time. The returned value will be either 1 if a single value is successfully read, or 0 if no value can be successfully read. Line 21 keeps reading as long as `fscanf` can still find another integer in the file. Please be aware that `fscanf` does not return the value from file; instead, `fscanf` returns how many values are read from the file. The pattern `"%d"` indicates that we only attempt to read one integer. Every time `fscanf` is called, the file stream moves forward and eventually reaches the end of the file. Suppose we have a file called `intfile` that stores some integers:

```
4 7 8
32
71
6 -2 5 8
```

Below is the output when we run the program with `intfile` as the command-line argument:

```
The name of the file is intfile.
4 7 8 32 71 6 -2 5 8
The sum is 139.
```

Compared with `fgetc`, `fscanf` has several advantages:

- When using `%d`, `fscanf` skips characters (such as space and new line `'\n'`) that are not digits.
- When `fgetc` reads the first character, it is not the integer 4, but the character `'4'`. A character can be converted to an integer using the ASCII table. The character `'4'` has a decimal value 52.
- If a number is greater than 9, the number has two or more digits. Using `fgetc`, only one digit is read at a time. If the number is 123, then we need to call `fgetc` three times in order to get the three digits. Moreover, we need to change the three characters `'1'`, `'2'`, and `'3'` (ASCII values 49, 50, 51) to the integer value 123 (one hundred and twenty three). This is done by `fscanf` automatically.

Due to the above reasons, if a program reads integers from a file, `fscanf` is a better choice than `fgetc`.

9.2   Write to Files

We can use `fprintf` to write information to a file. It is very similar to `printf`; the difference is that `fprintf` writes information to a file and `printf` writes information to the computer screen. The following example shows how to write a program that reads integers from two input files, adds the values, and stores the sum (another integer) into the output file, one integer per line. This program takes three command-line arguments:

- `argv[1]`: Name of the first input file.
- `argv[2]`: Name of the second input file.
- `argv[3]`: Name of the output file.

Each input file contains some integers. It is possible that several integers are in the same line separated by spaces. It is also possible that the two files contain different numbers of integers. If this happens, after running out of the integers from the shorter file, the program copies the remaining integers from the longer input file to the output file. The program does not know how many integers are stored in either file. The program ignores space in each line and it also ignores empty lines. For simplicity, the program does not consider overflow or underflow of integers. The following program solves this problem:

```c
// CH09:addint.c
#include <stdio.h>
#include <stdlib.h>
int main(int argc, char * argv[])
{
  if (argc < 4) { return EXIT_FAILURE; } // need two inputs + one output
  FILE * fin1;
  FILE * fin2;
  fin1 = fopen(argv[1], "r");
  if (fin1 == NULL) { return EXIT_FAILURE; } // fail to open
  fin2 = fopen(argv[2], "r");
  if (fin2 == NULL)
    {
      fclose (fin1); // need to close opened file
      return EXIT_FAILURE;
    }
  // open the output file
  FILE * fout;
  fout = fopen(argv[3], "w");
  if (fout == NULL)
    {
      fclose (fin1);
      fclose (fin2);
      return EXIT_FAILURE;
    }
  int val1;
  int val2;
  int in1ok = 1; // can still read input file 1
  int in2ok = 1; // can still read input file 2
  // continue as long as one file still has numbers
  while ((in1ok == 1) || (in2ok == 1))
    {
      val1 = 0; // reset the values before reading from files
      val2 = 0;
      if (fscanf(fin1, "%d", & val1) != 1) // do not use == 0
        {
          in1ok = 0; // cannot read input file 1 any more
        }
      if (fscanf(fin2, "%d", & val2) != 1)
        {
          in2ok = 0; // cannot read input file 1 any more
        }
      if ((in1ok == 1) || (in2ok == 1))
        {
          fprintf(fout, "%d\n", val1 + val2); // save the sum
```

```
46          }
47        }
48      /* close the files */
49      fclose (fin1);
50      fclose (fin2);
51      fclose (fout);
52      return EXIT_SUCCESS;
53    }
```

Line 6 checks whether enough arguments have been provided. Lines 9 and 11 open the input files. For `fopen`, the first argument is the name of the file (`argv[1]` or `argv[2]`). The second argument indicates whether the file is for reading or writing: "r" means reading; "w" means writing; "a" means appending. If `fopen` fails, then the program returns `EXIT_FAILURE`. Please remember to close all successfully opened files; otherwise, the program leaks memory allocated by `fopen`. At line 12, the program has failed to open the second file, and thus needs to close the first opened file before returning. Line 19 opens the file for writing because the second argument is "w". Please be careful when using "w". If the file already exists, this `fopen` will erase the content of the file. The condition at line 31 means "continue if one (or both) of the files still has numbers". This handles the situation when the two files have different numbers of integers. The variables `in1ok` and `in2ok` are updated at lines 35 and 39.

Note that when a file reaches its end, `fscanf` returns EOF, and not zero. A common mistake at lines 35 and 39 is using `== 0`. Since EOF is −1, if we replace `!= 1` by `== 0` at these two lines, the `if` conditions will not be satisfied. Thus, `in1ok` and `in2ok` will never become zero and the program will not stop. If the program reads successfully from at least one of the two files, the program writes the sum to the output file. Lines 33 and 34 reset the values to zero. This is necessary because one file may have already reached the end and calling `fscanf` will not update one of `val1` and `val2`.

This program does not consider overflowing or underflowing of integers. What does this mean? When a program creates an integer variable, the size of the variable is fixed (dependent on the machine). Suppose an integer has 4 bytes, i.e., `sizeof(int)` is 4. One byte is 8 bits and each bit can hold either 0 or 1. Thus, a 4-byte integer can hold 32 bits, namely 2^{32} possible values. The possible values include both positive and negative integers. An integer can hold a value between $2^{31} - 1$ (2147483647) and -2^{31} (−2147483648). If a file contains a number greater than 2147483647 or smaller than −2147483648, this program does not work. Thus the behavior of the program is unspecified if the input numbers are too large or too small.

9.3   Read and Write Strings

How can a program read a string, for example, someone's name? There are several solutions. One solution uses `fgetc` reading one character at a time. Another solution uses `fscanf` with `%s`.

```
1    // CH09:fscanfstr.c
2    #include <stdio.h>
```

```
3    #include <stdlib.h>
4    #define MAXSIZE 6
5    int main(int argc, char * argv[])
6    {
7      FILE * fptr;
8      if (argc < 2)
9        {
10         printf("Need to provide the file's name.\n");
11         return EXIT_FAILURE;
12       }
13     fptr = fopen(argv[1], "r");
14     if (fptr == NULL)
15       {
16         printf("fopen fail.\n");
17         return EXIT_FAILURE;
18       }
19     char buffer[MAXSIZE];
20     while (fscanf(fptr, "%5s", buffer) == 1)
21       {
22         printf("%s\n", buffer);
23       }
24     fclose(fptr);
25     return EXIT_SUCCESS;
26   }
```

Line 20 reads one word at a time by using `%s` in `fscanf`. The function distinguishes words by looking for spaces and new line characters ('\n'). Adding a number between `%` and `s` tells `fscanf` to limit the number of characters in a word. This line limits the length of the word to 5 characters. A string ends with '\0'. Thus, the length of the buffer (line 19) must be at least one larger than the number between `%` and `s` to accommodate '\0'. If there is no number between `%` and `s` and a word in the file is long, then the program will use up the memory space in `buffer`, and write past the end. When this occurs, the program's behavior is undefined due to invalid memory accesses. It is important to make sure that the programs cannot have invalid memory accesses regardless of the input data. Otherwise, a malicious user may be able to cause an invalid memory access, called the "buffer overflow attack"— a common form of security attacks.

C provides another way to read data from a file: `fgets` can read across space. In contrast, `fscanf` stops reading when it encounters space. The `fgets` function takes three arguments:

1. The starting address of an array of characters to store the data.
2. The number of characters to read.
3. A `FILE *` to read from.

If the second argument is `n`, the function reads as many as `n - 1` characters from the file. The `fgets` function adds the ending character '\0' automatically. The function may read fewer characters if (1) a new line character occurs before reading `n - 1` characters or (2) the file has reached its end. Please note that `fgets` does not stop when it reads a space. It can read multiple words in the same line even though these words are separated by one or more spaces. For `fscanf`, the size between `%` and `s` is optional. For `fgets`, the size is a required argument. If `fgets` succeeds in reading anything from the file, it returns the value of the first argument, i.e., the starting address to store the data. If **fgets** fails to read anything from the file, it returns NULL.

The following program reads a file line by line and counts the number of lines. We assume that the maximum length of each line is 80 characters, i.e., at least one '\n' occurs within every 80 characters.

```c
// CH09:fgets.c
#include <stdio.h>
#include <string.h>
#include <stdlib.h>
#define MAX_LINE_LENGTH 81
// assume that the maximum length of each line is 81
int main(int argc, char * argv[])
{
  FILE * fptr;
  int numLine = 0; // must initialize to zero
  char oneLine[MAX_LINE_LENGTH];
  if (argc < 2)
    // must check argc before using argv[1]
    {
      printf("Need to provide the file's name.\n");
      return EXIT_FAILURE;
    }
  fptr = fopen(argv[1], "r");
  if (fptr == NULL)
    {
      printf("fopen fail.\n");
      // do not call fclose (fptr) here
      return EXIT_FAILURE;
    }
  printf("The name of the file is %s.\n", argv[1]);
  while (fgets(oneLine, MAX_LINE_LENGTH, fptr) != NULL)
    {
      numLine ++;
    }
  fclose(fptr);
  printf("The file has %d lines.\n", numLine);
  return EXIT_SUCCESS;
}
```

When the program cannot read from the file anymore, **fgets** returns NULL. This means that the end of the file has been reached. The C library has a function called **getline** and it can be used to read a line of any size. The following is an example using **getline**:

```c
// modified from Linux Programmers' Manual
FILE * stream;
char * line = NULL; // must initialize to NULL
size_t len = 0;
ssize_t nread;
if (argc != 2)
```

```
7   {
8       fprintf(stderr, "Usage: %s <file>\n", argv[0]);
9       return EXIT_FAILURE;
10  }
11  stream = fopen(argv[1], "r");
12  if (stream == NULL)
13  {
14      return EXIT_FAILURE;
15  }
16  while ((nread = getline(&line, &len, stream)) != -1)
17  {
18      printf("Retrieved line of length %zu:\n", nread);
19      fwrite(line, nread, 1, stdout);
20  }
21  free(line); // getline allocates memory; need to free the memory
22  fclose(stream);
23  return EXIT_SUCCESS;
```

The first argument for `getline` is the address of a pointer of `char`. If `line`'s value is NULL (line 3), then `getline` allocates sufficient space for the line. If `line`'s value is not NULL (i.e., space has already been allocated) but the space is insufficient, `getline` will resize—releases the memory first, then allocates space large enough. After calling `getline`, `len` stores the length of the string read. The memory allocated by `getline` needs to be released by `free`, as shown in line 21. Section 18.3 will explain `fwrite`.

Chapter 10

Programming Problems Using File

10.1 Sort a File of Integers

This program reads integers from a file, sorts them, and stores the sorted integers into another file. We have already learned how to read integers from a file in Section 9.1. Chapter 8 explains how to sort arrays. Here we put these two things together. Before sorting the numbers, these are the steps: (1) Check whether there are arguments for the input and the output file names. (2) Open the input file. (3) Read integers from the file and count the number of integers in the file. (4) Allocate memory to store the integers.

As explained earlier, a file is a stream. Every time something is read from the file, the stream moves forward. After counting the number of integers, the stream has reached its end. To fill the array, it is necessary to read the file from the beginning again. We can do this in several ways. One way is to close the file and open it again. Another way is to use `fseek`. It goes to a particular position in a file. This is how to go to the beginning of a file: `fseek(fptr, 0, SEEK_SET)`. The first argument `fptr` is a `FILE` pointer and its value is set by `fopen` before calling `fseek`. The second argument specifies the distance from the reference point. The third argument is the reference point: `SEEK_SET` means the beginning of the file. The second and third arguments together make `fptr` return to the beginning of the file. A related function is `ftell`. This function reports the current position (measured in bytes) of the file stream. These two functions are often used together. For example, to find the length of a file, a program can use `fseek(fptr, 0, SEEK_END)` to reach the end of the file and then use `ftell(fptr)` to know the length.

The remaining steps are: (5) Use `fseek` to go to the beginning of the file. (6) Read the file again and fill the array. (7) Sort the array. (8) Close the input file. (9) Open the output file. (10) Write the sorted array to the output file. (11) Close the output file. (12) Free the memory for the array. The order of some of these steps may be changed. For example, the program may free the array memory before or after closing the output file (steps 11 and 12). The orders of steps 8 and 9 can also be exchanged. However, the order of some steps cannot be changed. For example, step 9 (opening the output file) must precede step 10 (writing to the output file). Below is a sample solution for this program.

```c
// CH10:sortint.c
#include <stdio.h>
#include <stdlib.h>
int comparefunc(const void * arg1, const void * arg2)
{
    const int * ptr1 = (const int *) arg1; // cast type
    const int * ptr2 = (const int *) arg2;
    const int val1 = * ptr1; // get the value from the address
    const int val2 = * ptr2;
    if (val1 < val2)  { return -1; }
```

```
11    if (val1 == val2) { return 0; }
12    return 1;
13  }
14  int main(int argc, char * argv[])
15  {
16    if (argc < 3)    // need two file names: input and output
17      { return EXIT_FAILURE; }
18    FILE * infptr;
19    infptr = fopen(argv[1], "r");    // open the input file
20    if (infptr == NULL)  { return EXIT_FAILURE;  }
21    // count the number of integers in the file
22    int count = 0;
23    int val;
24    while (fscanf(infptr, "%d", & val) == 1) { count ++; }
25    int * arr;
26    arr = malloc(sizeof(int) * count); // allocate memory for the array
27    if (arr == NULL)
28      {
29        fclose (infptr);
30        return EXIT_FAILURE;
31      }
32    fseek(infptr, 0, SEEK_SET); // go to the beginning of the file
33    int ind = 0; // array index
34    while (fscanf(infptr, "%d", & val) == 1) // fill the array
35      {
36        arr[ind] = val;
37        ind ++;
38      }
39    qsort(& arr[0], count, sizeof(int), comparefunc);    // sort the array
40    fclose (infptr);    // close the input file
41    FILE * outfptr;
42    outfptr = fopen(argv[2], "w"); // open the output file
43    if (outfptr == NULL)
44      {
45        free (arr); // do not forget to release memory
46        return EXIT_FAILURE;
47      }
48    // write the sorted array to the output file
49    for (ind = 0; ind < count; ind ++)
50      { fprintf(outfptr, "%d\n", arr[ind]);  }
51    fclose (outfptr);    // close outupt file
52    free (arr);    // release the array's memory
53    return EXIT_SUCCESS;
54  }
```

10.2   Count the Occurrences of Characters

The program reads characters from a file and counts their occurrences. The program does not distinguish between uppercase characters and lowercase characters. Only the 26 letters ('A' - 'Z' or 'a'-'z') used in English are counted. If a character is not a letter, the character is ignored. The program then saves the occurrences into an output file.

The program has the following steps: (1) Check whether there are command-line arguments for the input and the output files. (2) Create an array of 26 integers. The elements' values are set to zero. A fixed size array is preferred because the array's size is known in advance. This means that the array can be placed on the stack, and we do not need to call `malloc` and `free`. (3) Open the input file. (4) Read the characters from the file. If the character is a letter, increment the corresponding array element. (5) Close the input file. (6) Open the output file. (7) Write the array's elements to the output file. (8) Close the output file. These steps are similar to the steps for the previous program, except the parts for counting the characters. Below is a sample implementation of the above steps:

```
1   // CH10:countchar.c
2   #include <stdio.h>
3   #include <stdlib.h>
4   #include <ctype.h>
5   #define NUM_CHAR 26
6   int main(int argc, char * argv[])
7   {
8       if (argc < 3) { return EXIT_FAILURE; } // need input and output
9       char charcount[NUM_CHAR] = {0}; // initialize all elements to zeros
10      // open the input file
11      FILE * infptr;
12      infptr = fopen(argv[1], "r");
13      if (infptr == NULL) { return EXIT_FAILURE; }
14      // count the occurrences of the characters
15      int onechar;
16      do
17        {
18          onechar = fgetc(infptr);
19          if (isupper(onechar)) { charcount[onechar - 'A'] ++; }
20          if (islower(onechar)) { charcount[onechar - 'a'] ++; }
21        } while (onechar != EOF);
22      fclose (infptr);    // close the input file
23      FILE * outfptr;
24      outfptr = fopen(argv[2], "w");    // open the output file
25      if (outfptr == NULL)  { return EXIT_FAILURE; }
26      int ind;
27      for (ind = 0; ind < NUM_CHAR; ind ++)
28        { fprintf(outfptr, "%c: %d\n", ind  + 'A', charcount[ind]); }
29      fclose (outfptr);   // close outupt file
30      return EXIT_SUCCESS;
31  }
```

Line 19 uses the function `isupper` to determine whether the character is an uppercase letter. This function is declared in `ctype.h` so the program needs to include this header file at line 4. Calling `isupper` is equivalent to checking whether `onechar` is between 'A' and 'Z'. The ASCII value for 'A' is 65 and the ASCII value for 'Z' is 90. However, you should not check whether `onechar` is between numbers 65 and 90. There are a few reasons for this suggestion. First, if you accidentally type 89 instead of 90, it is not easy to detect the mistake. It is difficult remembering that 'Z' is 90, not 89. By contrast, if you type 'Y' instead 'Z', it is easier to detect the mistake. This brings us to the main reason for preferring 'A' and 'Z' to 64 and 90: It is clear and easy to read. Clarity is important for well-written code. Did you notice that we incorrectly wrote 64, not 65? If you missed that mistake of 64, it is likely that you would miss similar mistakes in your programs.

How about converting uppercase letters to lowercase? Many people write

```
if ((onechar >= 65) && (onechar <= 90))
{
   onechar += 32;
}
```

This is bad. Why? It is difficult to understand the meaning of 65, 90, and 32. What happens if we accidentally type 31 instead of 32? It is much clearer to write:

```
if ((onechar >= 'A') && (onechar <= 'Z'))
{
   onechar = (onechar - 'A') + 'a'; // convert to lower case
}
```

These details are important. A few "small" mistakes can make programs difficult to understand and debug. In a complex program, the problems from these details can easily take hours to detect and correct. Good programmers know this well and can save time by making things as simple and as clear as possible. Clarity allows programmers to write sophisticated computer programs more easily. Actually, C provides two functions for conversion: `tolower` and `toupper`. They can make programmers even easier to understand.

Lines 19 and 20 use the values in the ASCII table to calculate the corresponding index for the array `charcount`. If the character is 'A', then `onechar - 'A'` is 0. If the character is 'B', then `onechar - 'A'` is 1. If the character is 'c', `onechar - 'a'` is 2.

Please do not write anything like: (Yes, we have seen such code.)

```
1    if (onechar == 'A')    charcount[0] ++;
2    if (onechar == 'B')    charcount[1] ++;
3    if (onechar == 'C')    charcount[2] ++;
4    if (onechar == 'D');   charcount[2] ++;
5    if (onechar == 'E')    charcount[3] ++;
```

Fifty-two conditions are needed. It is easy to make mistakes. If fact, there are several mistakes in the code above. Can you detect them easily? The first mistake is that line 4 should be `charcount[3] ++;`, not `charcount[2] ++;`. The second mistake is that line 5 should be `charcount[4] ++;`. Also, there should be only one semicolon at line 4, after `++`. There should be no semicolon after `== 'D')`. As you can see, three mistakes exist in these five lines and they are not easy to detect.

This code is bad for another reason: they look similar. There are many reasons to avoid copy-paste code. If you copy-paste code, then you increase the chances of mistakes. This is especially true when the code is modified after it is written. Once you have two (or more) pieces of similar code, testing, debugging and improving the code becomes more difficult. You need to remember to change all places with identical or similar code. If you forget to change some places, then the program will surprise you: In some situations, the program is correct, but in others it fails.

10.3   Count the Occurrences of a Word

This program counts the occurrences of a word in an input file. This program takes three arguments:

1. `argv[1]`: The name of the input file.
2. `argv[2]`: The name of the output file.
3. `argv[3]`: A word to be searched for.

If a line in the input file includes the word, the program writes that line to the output file. After checking all lines in the input file, the program writes the total count to the output file. We must first think about how words are counted. If the search word is "eye" and a line in the input file contains "eyeye", do we count 1 or 2? The difference is whether the center 'e' can be used only once or twice. If it can be used only once, after matching "eyeye", then only "ye" is left. If the center 'e' can be counted twice, then we can find two "eye": "eyeye" and "eyeye". Both definitions are acceptable and we need to decide which definition to use. We will explain how to handle the differences in this example. For simplicity, each line in the input file contains at most 80 characters (and thus needs memory for 81 characters). The program does not count a word that spans two or more lines. The program uses `strstr` to search a word within a line.

```c
// CH10:countstr.c
#include <stdio.h>
#include <stdlib.h>
#include <string.h>
#define LINE_LENGTH 81
int main(int argc, char * argv[])
{
  if (argc < 4) { return EXIT_FAILURE; } // input word output
  FILE * infptr;
  infptr = fopen(argv[1], "r");    // open the input file
  if (infptr == NULL) { return EXIT_FAILURE; }
  FILE * outfptr;
  outfptr = fopen(argv[2], "w");     // open the output file
  if (outfptr == NULL)
    {
      fclose (infptr);
      return EXIT_FAILURE;
    }
  int count = 0;
  char oneline[LINE_LENGTH];
  while (fgets(oneline, LINE_LENGTH, infptr) != NULL)
    {
      if (strstr(oneline, argv[3]) != NULL)
        { fprintf(outfptr, "%s", oneline); }
```

```
25      char * chptr = oneline;
26      while (chptr != NULL)
27        {
28          chptr = strstr(chptr, argv[3]);
29          if (chptr != NULL)
30            {
31              count ++;
32              chptr ++;   // if "eyeye" counts as two "eye"
33              // if "eyeye" counts as one "eye", use
34              // chptr += strlen(argv[3]);
35            }
36        }
37    }
38    fprintf(outfptr, "%d\n", count);
39    fclose (infptr);     // close the input file
40    fclose (outfptr);    // close outuput file
41    return EXIT_SUCCESS;
42 }
```

Line 32 shows one definition: after finding one occurrence, the pointer `chptr` increments by only one. As a result, the center 'e' is still available to be used again. Line 34 (inside a comment) shows the other definition. After a match, the pointer `chptr` increments by the length of the string and the center 'e' is no longer available.

10.4 Problems

10.4.1 Determine Palindrome

A *palindrome* is a word, phrase, number, or other sequence of characters which reads the same backward as forward, such as `madam` or `racecar`. Here are some more examples of palindrome: `neveroddoreven`, `madamImadam`, `madam I madam`, `neve roddor even`. This question asks you to write a function that determines whether a file's content is a palindrome.

10.4.2 Compare Two Files

Write a program to compare two files line by line, i.e., the n-th line of the first file is compared with the n-th line of the second file. If the lines in the two files are identical, this line is ignored. If the lines in the two files are different, the program prints the two lines. You can assume that each line has at most 80 characters. Two lines are separated by the '\n' character.

10.4.3 fscanf and ftell

Consider the following input file.

```
264 2011 9 17 3.11 6.82
```

What is the program's output? Please notice that the input contains numbers with decimal points.

```c
// CH10:fscanf.c
#include <stdio.h>
#include <stdlib.h>
int main(int argc, char * * argv)
{
  if (argc != 2) { return EXIT_FAILURE; }
  FILE * fptr = fopen(argv[1], "r");
  if (fptr == NULL) { return EXIT_FAILURE; }
  int ind;
  // call fgetc five times
  for (ind = 0; ind < 5; ind ++)   { int ch = fgetc(fptr); }
  printf("ftell = %ld\n", ftell(fptr));
  fseek(fptr, 0, SEEK_SET); // return to the beginning of the file
  // call fscanf %d five times
  for (ind = 0; ind < 5; ind ++)
    {
      int val;
      if (fscanf(fptr, "%d", & val) == 1)
        {
          // printf("val = %d\n", val);
        }
    }
  printf("ftell = %ld\n", ftell(fptr));
  int ch = fgetc(fptr);
  printf("ch = %d, '%c'\n", ch, ch);
  fseek(fptr, 0, SEEK_SET); // return to the beginning of the file
  // call fscanf %lf five times
  for (ind = 0; ind < 5; ind ++)
    {
      double val;
      if (fscanf(fptr, "%lf", & val) == 1)
        {
          // printf("val = %lf\n", val);
        }
    }
  printf("ftell = %ld\n", ftell(fptr));
  ch = fgetc(fptr);
  printf("ch = %d, '%c'\n", ch, ch);
  fclose (fptr);
  return EXIT_SUCCESS;
}
```

Chapter 11

Array Index, Security, and Trends

When the C language was designed in the 1970s, computers were expensive. People needed several years of training before they could use computers. At that time, C's design principle was "If a programmer does not explicitly request something, don't do it." The purpose is to give programmers as much control as possible and allow C programs to run as fast as possible. Over the decades, the costs of computers drop significantly and meanwhile computers become much faster. Three things happened: (1) Computers are used widely from controlling washing machines to airplanes, from factory robots to mobile phones; (2) Many more people write computer software for these applications; (3) Computers can solve very complex problems such as translating speeches and controlling autonomous vehicles. Some design decisions of the C language were considered appropriate in the 1970s and insufficient today. One of the most discussed issues is that C does not check whether a program uses invalid memory addresses. Programmers are responsible for ensuring only valid addresses are used. Consider the description of the `strcpy` function: "*The strings may not overlap, and the destination string dest must be large enough to receive the copy. If the destination string of a strcpy() is not large enough, then anything might happen.*" This clearly puts the responsibility of ensuring programs' correctness on programmers.

11.1   Array Index

If an array has n elements, the valid indexes are 0, 1, 2, ... $n - 1$. Please notice that n is an invalid index. However, C does not check whether an index is valid or not. Consider the following example:

```c
// CH11:security1.c
#include <stdio.h>
#include <stdlib.h>
#include <string.h>
int main(int argc, char * * argv)
{
  char dest[5];
  dest[-3] = 'M';
  dest[0] = 'C';
  dest[1] = '-';
  dest[2] = 'P';
  dest[3] = 'R';
  dest[4] = 'O';
  dest[5] = '\0';
  printf("%s\n", dest);
```

DOI: 10.1201/9781003257981-11

```
16    return EXIT_SUCCESS;
17  }
```

Please remember a string ends with the special '\0' character. Thus, if a character array has 5 elements, the array can hold only 4 characters, excluding the ending '\0' character. This program has two places using invalid indexes: -3 and 5. These problems are not detected by gcc even when warning messages are turned on (i.e., adding -Wall -Wshadow -pedantic -Wvla -Werror after gcc). Running the program produces output

```
C-PRO
```

It appears that the program has no problem. In fact, some people may even think this program is great because line 7 creates an array of five elements and the program uses nine elements (indexes from -3 to 5). Is it really true that this program is harmless? Let's consider a slightly more complex program:

```
1   // CH11:security2.c
2   #include <stdio.h>
3   #include <stdlib.h>
4   #include <string.h>
5   int main(int argc, char * * argv)
6   {
7     char str1[5];
8     char str2[5];
9     char dest[5];
10    strcpy(str1, "ABC\n");
11    strcpy(str2, "XYZ\n");
12    printf("%s", str1);
13    printf("%s", str2);
14    dest[-3] = 'M';
15    dest[0] = 'C';
16    dest[1] = '-';
17    dest[2] = 'P';
18    dest[3] = 'R';
19    dest[4] = 'O';
20    dest[5] = '\0';
21    printf("=============\n");
22    printf("%s\n", dest);
23    printf("%s", str1);
24    printf("%s", str2);
25    return EXIT_SUCCESS;
26  }
```

The output of this program is

```
ABC
XYZ
=============
C-PRO
```

```
ABC
XYM
```

In this program, Lines 10 and 11 assign "ABC\n" and "XYZ\n" to str1 and str2. The new line character, '\n', is one character. Thus, each of str1 and str2 has four characters, excluding '\0'. Including '\0', each string has five array elements. Lines 7 and 8 provide sufficient space for each string. Lines 12-13 print these two strings. Things appear normal so far. Lines 14 and 20 use invalid indexes (-3 and 5) respectively. Lines 21 to 23 print the three strings. Line 22 appears "normal": Even though dest has space for only five elements (thus, space for only four characters after excluding '\0'), line 22 prints five letters. The next line also appears normal. Line 24 shows a problem: dest[-3] modifies str2 from "XYZ\n" to "XYM\n". This suggests that the memory for str2 is immediately before dest. Line 14 assigns '\M' to dest[5]. This is actually the third element of str2. As a result, line 24 prints "XYM\n".

By using incorrect indexes, it is possible for a function to modify variables even though these variables are not the function's arguments. Consider this example:

```
1   // CH11:security3.c
2   #include <stdio.h>
3   #include <stdlib.h>
4   #include <string.h>
5   void f1(int * arr)
6   {
7       arr[-2]   = 2016;
8       arr[-1]   = -12;
9   }
10
11  int main(int argc, char * * argv)
12  {
13      int x = -2;
14      int arr[] = {0, 1, 2, 3, 4};
15      int y = 15;
16      int z = 128;
17      printf("x = %d, y = %d, z = %d\n", x, y, z);
18      f1(arr);
19      printf("x = %d, y = %d, z = %d\n", x, y, z);
20      return EXIT_SUCCESS;
21  }
```

The program's output is

```
x = -2, y = 15, z = 128
x = -2, y = 2016, z = -12
```

Even though y and z are not the arguments of function f1, the values of y and z are modified by f1. Please notice that the value of x is unchanged. If, for any reason, this program never checks the values of y or z, the program may appear acceptable, even though the invalid indexes have modified y and z.

11.2 Modify Program Behavior

It is possible to change a program's behavior by using a wrong index. Consider this example

```
1   // CH11:security4.c
2   #include <stdio.h>
3   #include <stdlib.h>
4   void f0()
5   {
6   }
7   void f1(void)
8   {
9     char name[10] = {9, 8, 7, 6, 5, 4, 3, 2, 1, 27};
10    name[24] = 0x73;
11    f0();
12  }
13  void f2(void)
14  {
15    printf("f2 has done terrible things\n");
16  }
17  int main(int argc, char * * argv)
18  {
19    f1();
20    return EXIT_SUCCESS;
21  }
```

In this program, `main` calls `f1` and `f1` calls `f0`. The function `f2` is not called. This is the output of the program on some machines:

```
f2 has done terrible things
Segmentation fault (core dumped)
```

Even though `f2` is not called by `main` nor by `f1`, line 15 prints the message. How can this happen? Please be aware that this behavior depends on the hardware. It is possible "f2 has done terrible things" does not appear on your machine. The program's problem comes from

```
name[24] = 0x73;
```

This index (24) is too large for the array with only 10 elements (created at line 9). This particular index (24) is chosen based on the structure of the processor, in particular the stack memory. The value (0x73) depends on the structure of the program. The following two commands provide information about a computer:

```
$ more /proc/cpuinfo
vendor_id    : GenuineIntel
cpu family  : 6
model       : 44
```

```
model name   : Intel(R) Xeon(R) CPU X5675  @ 3.07GHz
stepping     : 2
microcode    : 0x1f
$ gcc --version
gcc (GCC) 4.8.5 20150623 (Red Hat 4.8.5-44)
```

The first command (`more /proc/cpuinfo`) shows the processor: it is Intel(R) Xeon(R). The second command shows the `gcc` version. If your computer has a different processor or a different version of `gcc`, you may need to modify line 10 to see the same problem. The explanation why line 10 causes `f2` to be called is beyond the scope of this book. The purpose of this example is to show that when a wrong index is used, a program may behave in an unexpected way. This example shows that it is possible to modify a program's behavior by using a wrong index. Line 10 modifies the stack memory (more specifically, the return location) and makes the program execute line 15. This simple example does not make all the necessary changes to the stack memory. As a result the operating system detects a problem and stops the program with `Segmentation fault`. However, it is too late because `f2` has already done something terrible (by printing the message). Imagine that line 15 could do something much worse and cause significant damage to a computer.

11.3   Trends in Programming Languages

Speed is often considered a major advantage of the C language. C gives programmers greater degrees of control and does not do anything more than what the programs explicitly request. C does not check whether array indexes are valid; this is the responsibility of programmers. Since the first programming language was invented in the late 1940s, the principles of designing programming languages have changed dramatically over the decades. Many programming languages were invented and never became popular. Some languages became popular and then gradually disappeared. C is one of few languages that stay widely used for decades. C is still one of the most popular programming languages.

Over the decades, compiler technologies have improved dramatically and it is possible to make other programming languages "fast enough". As hardware becomes faster and cheaper, many people write computer programs for a wide range of applications. Many applications do not need to be extremely fast. Many studies have shown that only small fractions of code affect programs' execution time. The general rule of thumb is "10% of code accounts for 90% of execution time." In other words, 90% of code has negligible effects on execution time. To make a program faster, programmers should identify and improve that 10% of the code. Choosing better algorithms can have a much larger impact on performance than programming languages. Over the years, many efficient algorithms have been invented and implemented in libraries. Programmers can use these libraries to improve speed. Nevertheless, knowing the most important algorithms and data structures is helpful to take advantage of built-in libraries.

The most important features of programming languages are changing due to the needs of specific applications, such as networking, human interfaces, artificial intelligence, and robots. Many people move to newer languages such as C++, Java, or Python because they have features convenient for some applications. Java and Python check array indexes and raise exceptions when invalid indexes are used. Checking indexes does slow down programs but the designers of Java and Python believe these features are needed. Additionally, Java and Python do not provide direct support for pointers and programmers cannot circumvent index checking by using pointers without utilizing the native interface support (e.g. Java Native Interface for Java or using tools such as SWIG to create Python wrappers for C code). Java and Python also have built-in support for strings and eliminate the need for the '\0' in C programs.

The choice of a programming language depends on the applications. Different applications need different features. We will likely see different languages for meeting different needs. At the time of writing, Go and Rust are both emerging as serious systems programming languages with Rust even being approved for use in Linux kernel programming. That said, the vast majority of kernel and systems programming continues to be done in C and C++, and we expect this to continue, owing to the great legacy of C code in computer science, engineering, and scientific computing domains. Debating whether C is better than Java or Python–or any language, for that matter–is equivalent to debating whether a sedan is better than a truck: They serve different purposes. We take the view that everyone should learn about C programming, which will help you to appreciate other languages you learn in the future.

Chapter 12

Version Control

12.1 Version Control Overview

Writing software is a process: features are added gradually and software goes through multiple *versions*. Each new version contains new features or bug fixes. A *version control* system manages these versions and supports many activities related to versions, for example

- Create a snapshot. After a feature is completed or a bug is fixed, a software developer takes a snapshot by creating a new version.
- Compare different versions. Version control tools can compare different versions line-by-line. This is helpful when a feature works in an earlier version and breaks in a later version. The comparison can show what has been changed between the two versions.
- Roll back to an earlier version. Sometimes, too many changes are made between versions and it is difficult to identify which changes break the program. Version control allows developers to roll back to an earlier version and start from there.
- Share versions with collaborators. Multiple developers can work on the same program simultaneously. Each developer has a copy of the program (not shared with the other developers) and improves different parts of the program (such as adding new features). When the parts are ready (the feature is completed and tested), a developer creates a new version and shares it with the other developers.

Version control is critical for anyone learning to write computer programs. Mistakes are common in programming. Version control can help manage mistakes. Both authors of this book have many years of experience hearing students saying, "Parts of my program worked yesterday. Now, nothing works. I have made many changes and I do not know which breaks the program." If these students use version control, they can easily compare the versions and determine which changes break the program. Version control is essential in creating open-source software. Many open-source programs are developed by people that are distributed globally. They can collaborate because they use version control systems.

12.2 `git` and `github.com`

Version control systems have been through many generations, such as CVS (concurrent version system) and SVN (subversion). One of the most popular version control systems now is *git*. The *git* project describes itself as "*Git is a free and open source distributed version control system designed to handle everything from small to very large projects with speed and efficiency.*" This one sentence means many things about `git`:

- Free: Anyone can use `git` for any purpose at no cost.

DOI: 10.1201/9781003257981-12

- Open Source: The source code is available for anyone to inspect the details. For open-source software, "free" can mean two different things: freedom of use and no cost. These two things are usually, but not always, together. It is possible that an open-source program costs no money but users may not modify it (limited freedom). It is also possible that users may modify the program (freedom) but have to pay (cost). For `git`, "free" means both no cost and freedom.
- Distributed: `git` does not require a central server. Instead, it can run on different network configurations.
- Small to Very Large Projects: `git` is designed for small projects like students' homework assignments, as well as large projects like Linux. The source code of this book (the C programs and the Latex file for the book's text) is managed by `git`.
- Speed and Efficiency: Compared with other version control systems, `git` improves the internal structure and methods to track different versions. As a result, `git` is faster in many tasks. Also, `git` separates creating versions from sharing versions: a developer can create new versions even when this developer is disconnected from the Internet. Later, when this developer is connected to the Internet, the developer can share the newly created versions with other developers.

Each software project in `git` is called a *repository*. A repository is like a directory (also called a folder) for storing files of source code. A repository also keeps the history of different versions. If a repository is open-source, it is called a *public* repository: everyone can read the content of this repository. Most public repositories restrict who can modify the content. A close-source repository is called a *private* repository: only selected people can see the content.

Because `git` is open-source and free, anyone can set up a version control system using `git`. Many cloud vendors provide `git` as a service. Among these services, `github.com` is widely used. This book uses `github` because it provides many good features, including

- No cost for education organizations or classroom use.
- No cost for open-source software (i.e., a public repository), even though the software is not for education. It is also possible to use `github.com` for close-source software (i.e., private repository) by paying `github.com` monthly fees.
- Fully compatible with `git`.
- Strong emphasis on social coding practices: In addition to code, `github` can also host web pages and wikis. Users can take advantage of many social networking functions with other developers.
- Good security features, such as using ssh keys.

It is important to distinguish `git` and `github.com`. The former (`git`) is an open-source tool that can be freely used. Software developers may create their own version control systems using `git`. The latter (`github`) is a cloud service supporting the `git` version control system, with additional features.

12.3 Create a Repository on `github`

A new repository can be created in several different ways. This book creates a new repository from `github.com`. After creating an account at `github.com` and logging in, you can see a + sign in the upper right corner. Click this sign and select "New Repository".

The `github` website will ask several questions, such as the repository's name, and whether this repository is public or private. The purpose of `.gitignore` is to ignore some computer-generated files, such as object files (ending with `.o`). These files should not be tracked by version control as shown in Figure 12.1 (a). Figure 12.1 (b) shows an example of the information for a new repository.

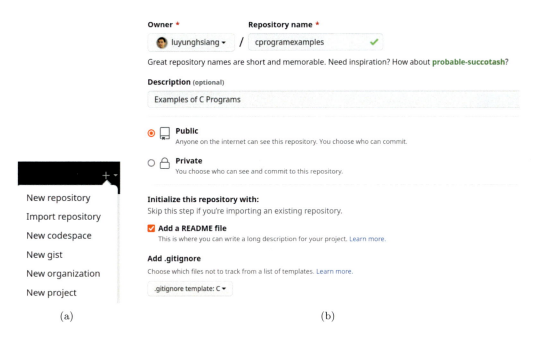

(a)   (b)

FIGURE 12.1: (a) At the upper right corner of the website of `github.com`, select "New Repository". (b) Enter information about the repository.

This repository has two files right now: `.gitignore` and `README.md`. It is possible to add, remove, or modify files at `github.com` directly. However, it is usually more convenient to have a copy of the repository on a local computer. At the right corner, a green button says "Code" and it shows three options to bring the files from `github.com` to a local computer. This book uses SSH (also `ssh`, secure shell).

It is necessary to set up an `ssh key` on your local computer so that your computer and `github.com` can trust each other. Communication over the Internet in general is not encrypted. In contrast, `ssh` encrypts the messages. Please create an *ssh key* using the `ssh-keygen` command. For added security, we recommend that you protect your SSH key with a passphrase where you see `<ENTER PASSPHRASE HERE>` below.

```
$ ssh-keygen -t rsa -b 2
Generating public/private rsa key pair.
Enter file in which to save the key (/Users/you/.ssh/id_rsa): you-temp-rsa
Enter passphrase (empty for no passphrase):
Enter same passphrase again: <ENTER PASSPHRASE HERE>
Your identification has been saved in you-temp-rsa
Your public key has been saved in you-temp-rsa.pub
The key fingerprint is:
SHA256:DiFcRMO3Z4Pp11BqEgxcsyaBZmTItoAyNvA8k you@coltrane.local
```

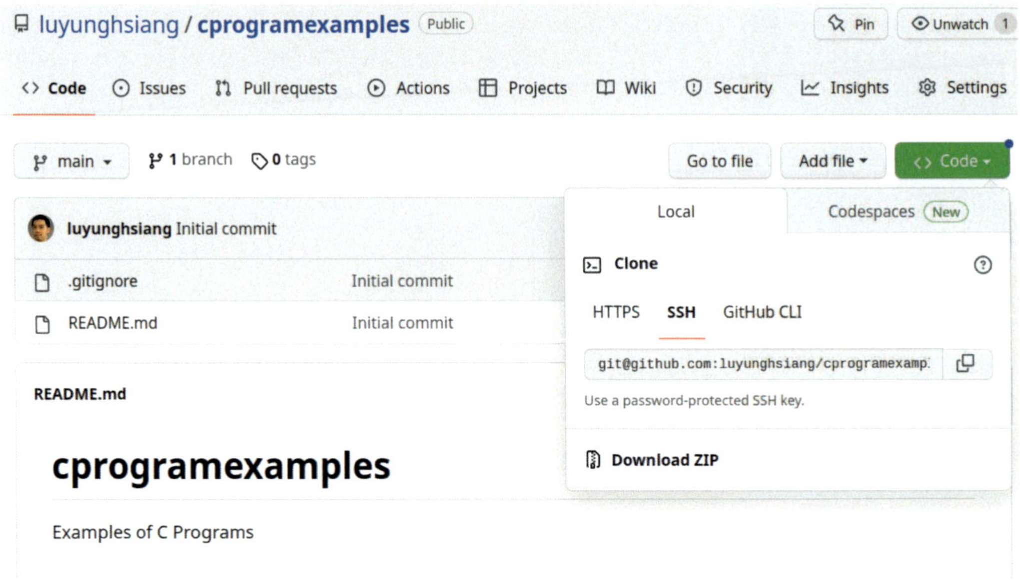

FIGURE 12.2: The repository contains two files. Clone the repository to a local computer.

```
The key's randomart image is:
+---[RSA 2]----+
|+.o  o++O*=oooo |
|.E + o =Oo.+o..o |
|  + * oB.+ . ... |
| . o o..+ o   . |
|     . S. .   . |
|       o + . . |
|        . * .  |
|         . o   |
|               |
+----[SHA256]-----+
```

```
$ cat ~/.ssh/you-temp-rsa.pub
ssh-rsa AAAAB3NzaC1yc2EAAAAQABAAABAQDC1c/6vnZLgLo1iMYKJLGXS
RN1vAhmfYaR/Efa+LK5O+TPnOOSMltwLGNq23ZG+91Lb/UnJW+NPtZns/2hvUIL
EhoJ146qmD8cI1ZOASvkjxQQhwHz2ic9OuDfC9NCgEmv3NXJrM+L3FhRV48x
vEUATs5TVOjzHyAqmWG5wAcS2TcZYjCf8R5cwHHyZkUOzMZ9zFmkg83cqHIGzFc
VNGPJTFBQaWOYeek5SY2Hehcu1+ZDOSEOwbPZJQiVchhIkPlOEo9k3MTWkHz
yvQnieMQwzjHdsXLKBOFDhtLrdbEffPueF8ett5ZmMvR316LXk5r+iABX3K41D
you@coltrane.local
```

An ssh key has been created. You can use the **cat** command to see it. Just in case you are curious, this is not the real ssh key of the authors. All ssh keys shown in this book are invalid keys.

Starting from August 2021, `github.com` no longer supports passwords for cloning a repository to a local computer. It is necessary to use ssh keys. You will need to copy the ssh key to `github.com`. To do that, click the upper right corner of the website and select "Settings" (under "Your profile"), as shown in Figure 12.3 (a). The next step selects "SSH and GPG keys", as shown in Figure 12.3 (b). Create a new SSH key by giving a name (probably the name of your computer) and copy-paste the ssh key created earlier. Now, you can use the `git clone` command to create a copy of the repository on your computer. This command must include the location of the repository. The location can be found in Figure 12.2 under `SSH`. For this example, the location is `git@github.com:yourname/cprogramexamples.git`. Enter that information after the `git clone` command:

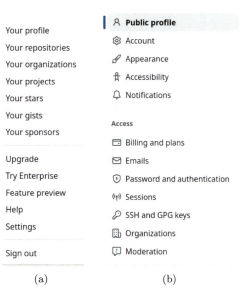

FIGURE 12.3: (a) Select "Settings". (b) Select "SSH and GPG keys".

```
$ git clone git@github.com:yourname/cprogramexamples.git
Cloning into 'cprogramexamples'...
remote: Enumerating objects: 4, done.
remote: Counting objects: 100% (4/4), done.
remote: Compressing objects: 100% (3/3), done.
remote: Total 4 (delta 0), reused 0 (delta 0), pack-reused 0
Receiving objects: 100% (4/4), done.
```

This retrieves (i.e., clones) the repository to your local computer. Next, enter the directory:

```
$ cd cprogramexamples/
```

Check the files and directories:

```
$ ls -a
.  ..  .git  .gitignore  README.md
$ more .git/config
[core]
        repositoryformatversion = 0
        filemode = true
        bare = false
        logallrefupdates = true
[remote "origin"]
        url = git@github.com:yourname/cprogramexamples.git
        fetch = +refs/heads/*:refs/remotes/origin/*
[branch "main"]
        remote = origin
        merge = refs/heads/main
```

A directory called .git contains files needed to communicate with github.com. A particular file, called config in the .git directory, shows that this repository is connected to git@github.com:yourname/cprogramexamples.git.

12.4   Sample Repository

This section will explain some git commands. For this purpose, a simple C project at https://github.com/gkthiruvathukal/intermediate-c-cmake-template is used. The project can be adapted for larger C programs by adding more files. Please use the git clone command to create a copy on your computer.

```
$ git clone git@github.com:gkthiruvathukal/book-demo-repo.git
Cloning into 'book-demo-repo'...
remote: Enumerating objects: 13, done.
remote: Counting objects: 100% (13/13), done.
remote: Compressing objects: 100% (13/13), done.
Receiving objects: 100% (13/13), done.
remote: Total 13 (delta 0), reused 12 (delta 0), pack-reused 0
```

We can use the ls -a command to list all files and directories; the option -a shows hidden files.

```
$ ls -al
total 32
drwxr-xr-x    9 gkt   staff   288 Sep 24 11:55 .
drwxrwxr-x@ 160 gkt   staff  5120 Sep 20 21:44 ..
drwxr-xr-x   12 gkt   staff   384 Sep 20 21:44 .git
-rw-r--r--    1 gkt   staff   932 Sep 20 21:44 .gitignore
-rw-r--r--    1 gkt   staff   668 Sep 20 21:44 CMakeLists.txt
-rw-r--r--    1 gkt   staff  1080 Sep 20 21:44 LICENSE
-rw-r--r--    1 gkt   staff    59 Sep 20 21:44 README.md
drwxr-xr-x    4 gkt   staff   128 Sep 20 21:44 hello-exe
drwxr-xr-x    5 gkt   staff   160 Sep 20 21:44 hello-lib
```

The directory .git means this entire directory is managed by version control. A file called .gitignore indicates which files should be ignored by version control. The version control system is designed to manage text files with versions. Version control cannot compare two binary files (such as an image, a video, an object file, or an executable) line by line. Thus, binary files are usually excluded from version control. Adding these files to .gitignore can prevent these binary files from being accidentally added to version control. This repository has .gitignore and its content is shown below.

```
# Ignore rules for CMake
CMakeLists.txt.user
CMakeCache.txt
CMakeFiles
_deps
# Ignore the directory
```

```
build/
# Ignore rules for C
# Object files
*.o
# Libraries
*.lib
*.a
*.la
*.lo
# backup files
*.bak
*~
# Shared objects (Windows DLLs)
*.dll
*.so
*.so.*
*.dylib
```

This is a "typical" .gitignore for a repository for C programs. Different programming languages will likely need different contents in .gitignore. In .gitignore, anything after # is treated as a comment. This file uses *glob patterns* and *regular expressions*. For example, * can replace any string. This .gitignore ignores all files stored in the build directory. Some text editors automatically save a backup file when a file is modified. The backup file's name may end with bak or ~. It is unnecessary adding backup files to version control because version control already takes snapshots of the files (by using the git commit command). This .gitignore also includes some computer-generated files for Windows.

The tree command can show the structure of the repository:

```
$ cd book-demo-repo
$ tree --charset=ascii
.
|-- CMakeLists.txt
|-- LICENSE
|-- README.md
|-- hello-exe
|   |-- CMakeLists.txt
|   `-- demo.c
`-- hello-lib
    |-- CMakeLists.txt
    |-- hello.c
    `-- hello.h
```

If your computer does not have the tree command already, you can install it using this command:

```
$ sudo apt install tree
```

The tree command is useful for seeing the structure of a directory hierarchy: the subdirectories and files. The following shows how to build the example project using cmake. The first step is to generate the Makefile by calling cmake:

```
$ cmake -S . -B build
-- The C compiler identification is AppleClang 14.0.0.14000029
-- The CXX compiler identification is AppleClang 14.0.0.14000029
-- Detecting C compiler ABI info
-- Detecting C compiler ABI info - done
-- Check for working C compiler: /Library/Developer/CommandLineTools
   /usr/bin/cc - skipped
-- Detecting C compile features
-- Detecting C compile features - done
-- Detecting CXX compiler ABI info
-- Detecting CXX compiler ABI info - done
-- Check for working CXX compiler: /Library/Developer/CommandLineTools
   /usr/bin/c++ - skipped
-- Detecting CXX compile features
-- Detecting CXX compile features - done
-- Found Python: /opt/homebrew/Frameworks/Python.framework/Versions/3.10
   /bin/python3.10 (found version "3.10.6") found components: Interpreter
-- Performing Test CMAKE_HAVE_LIBC_PTHREAD
-- Performing Test CMAKE_HAVE_LIBC_PTHREAD - Success
-- Found Threads: TRUE
-- Configuring done
-- Generating done
```

The command line option -S indicates where to find the source code (the current working directory, marked by .). The -B option indicates where to build the target executable and the object files (a directory called build). This option uses a different directory to store the generated files so that the directory for the source code will not be filled by object files or the executable file. You can remove the build directory when it is no longer needed without accidentally deleting the source code. These computer-generated files should not be added to the repository (build/ is in .gitignore). The next step builds the actual project, also using cmake:

```
1   $ cmake --build build
2   [  8%] Building CXX object _deps/googletest-build/googletest/CMakeFiles/
3          gtest.dir/src/gtest-all.cc.o
4   [ 16%] Linking CXX static library ../../../lib/libgtest.a
5   [ 16%] Built target gtest
6   [ 25%] Building CXX object _deps/googletest-build/googlemock/CMakeFiles/
7          gmock.dir/src/gmock-all.cc.o
8   [ 33%] Linking CXX static library ../../../lib/libgmock.a
9   [ 33%] Built target gmock
10  [ 41%] Building CXX object _deps/googletest-build/googlemock/CMakeFiles/
11         gmock_main.dir/src/gmock_main.cc.o
12  [ 50%] Linking CXX static library ../../../lib/libgmock_main.a
13  [ 50%] Built target gmock_main
14  [ 58%] Building CXX object _deps/googletest-build/googletest/CMakeFiles/
15         gtest_main.dir/src/gtest_main.cc.o
16  [ 66%] Linking CXX static library ../../../lib/libgtest_main.a
17  [ 66%] Built target gtest_main
18  [ 75%] Building C object hello-lib/CMakeFiles/hello-lib.dir/hello.c.o
19  [ 83%] Linking C static library libhello-lib.a
```

```
20   [ 83%] Built target hello-lib
21   [ 91%] Building C object hello-exe/CMakeFiles/hello-world.dir/demo.c.o
22   [100%] Linking C executable ../bin/hello-world
23   [100%] Built target hello-world
```

The output of the `cmake` command may vary based on your platform, e.g., Linux, Windows, or OS X. Please notice the following:

- The `GoogleTest` unit testing framework is downloaded (line 2) and built as part of the process, even if `GoogleTest` is not already installed on your computer.
- A library, `hello-lib`, is built for use with the `hello-world` application (line 19).
- An executable, `hello-world`, is installed in the `./bin` subdirectory (line 23).

You can run the executable and see the output as follows:

```
$ ./build/bin/hello-world
Hello, George
```

If you see "Hello, George", everything is set up correctly.

This book has explained **make** in multiple chapters. Even though **make** is very useful, it has limitations. It is not always easy to use the same `Makefile` on different types of computers. Different platforms may have different configurations and thus need different `Makefile`'s. Maintaining these `Makefile`'s can become a challenge. To solve this problem, `cmake` (meaning "Cross-Platform Make") is created and it can generate `Makefile`. A complete description of `cmake` is beyond the scope of this book.

12.5   Use `git` and `github.com`

The last two sections accomplish several things: (1) sets up a repository at `github.com`; (2) clones the sample repository on your computer; (3) builds the executable. This section explains how to use `git` to manage source code. Here are typical activities when developing a software project:

- Adding directories (folders) to the project. For example, adding an `src` folder. As the project becomes more complex, it needs to have better organization using folders.
- Adding or removing files in a directory.
- Changing the content of a file. This is the most common type of changes. Version control is designed to track the changes. For text files, the unit of changes is a line. Version control compares the program files line by line. If any line is changed, added, or removed, version control records the differences.
- Sharing files with collaborators. This is applicable to the situation when you are the only person using the repository and you have multiple computers (for example, one in the office and another at home). You can use the repository to transfer files between these computers.
- Retrieving files shared by a collaborator.

This process is summarized in Figure 12.4. We focus on the part on the local computer first. After a new file is added to a folder, this file is in the *untracked* state. This file can be added to version control and moves to the **stages** state by using the `git add`

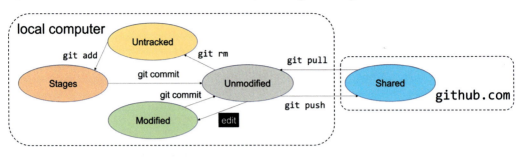

FIGURE 12.4: The states of a file in a repository. All transitions, except "edit" are `git` commands.

command. Please do not type `git add *` because doing so will likely add unnecessary files to version control. These unnecessary files (especially large files such as images and videos) can slow down version control dramatically. The command `git commit` takes a snapshot of the current content of the file and this file moves to the *unmodified* state. Here, "unmodified" means the version control has the latest version of the file and the file has not been modified. From the unmodified state, the file may be modified by any text editor. Here "edit" is not a `git` command so it is marked differently. The *modified* state means the latest version is different from the snapshot taken by the version control system. The `git commit` command can move to the unmodified state again. This file may be removed from the version control by using the `git rm` command. Please be aware that `git rm` also deletes the file. In typical scenarios, a software developer uses the `git commit` commands many times as a file is gradually improved with more and more features.

Earlier, we mentioned that `git` is a distributed version control system. This allows multiple versions of the same file to be stored on different machines. This is actually intentional. When one person modifies a file, this file may be unstable (i.e., "buggy"). At this moment, the person does not want to share this file with the collaborators. When this developer is ready to share the file, the `git push` command moves the file to the *Shared* state in `github.com`. If someone else has shared a file, the `git pull` command can retrieve this file from `github.com`. The `git` version control system has many functions but these four commands are used most frequently: (1) `git add`, (2) `git commit`, (3) `git push`, and (4) `git pull`. Usually, a developer should not `git push` a file before this file is ready for sharing. Sometimes, a developer may `git push` and share an incomplete file because this file needs to be completed by a collaborator. Of course, it is necessary to communicate with all collaborators so that they are not surprised seeing an incomplete file after they `git pull`. The `git status` command can inspect the states of the files.

```
$ git status
On branch main
Your branch is up to date with 'origin/main'.

nothing to commit, working tree clean
```

This output indicates that all files are up-to-date (i.e., in the unmodified state) with respect to the repository on the local computer. If any file is in the modified state (i.e., changed since the last `git commit`), this command will show the word "modified" in front of the file's name. It is advisable to run `git status` often and check the current condition of the repository. Sometimes, you may see output like this:

```
$ git status
On branch main
Your branch is up to date with 'origin/main'.

Changes not staged for commit:
  (use "git add <file>..." to update what will be committed)
  (use "git restore <file>..." to discard changes in working directory)
        modified:   hello-exe/demo.c

no changes added to commit (use "git add" and/or "git commit -a")
```

The output provides valuable information: (1) It indicates that the file `hello-exe/demo.c` is in the modified state. (2) You have not staged the changes to `git commit`. You should `git add` the file first, followed by `git commit`. You can also merge these two steps by using `git commit -a`. The following command adds the file to version control. Please be aware that a file should be added only once.

```
$ git add hello-exe/demo.c
```

The next command, `git remote -v`, shows the repository at `github.com`:

```
$ git remote -v
origin          git@github.com:gkthiruvathukal/book-demo-repo.git (fetch)
origin          git@github.com:gkthiruvathukal/book-demo-repo.git (push)
```

The `git diff` command shows the line-by-line differences of the files that have been modified since the last `git commit` command. Adding `--stat` after `git diff` shows only the summary of the changes:

```
$ git diff --stat
 hello-exe/demo.c | 1 +
 1 file changed, 1 insertion(+)
```

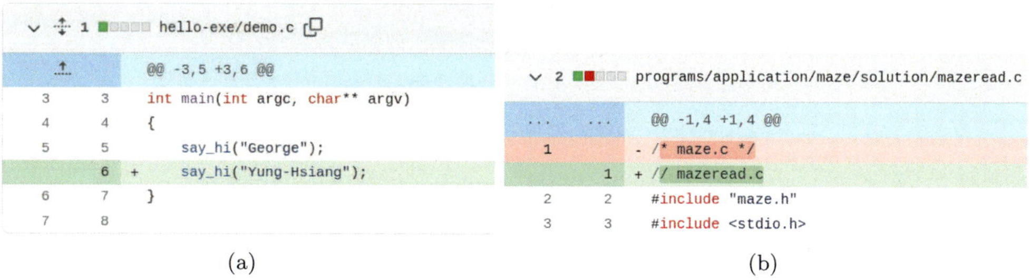

(a)   (b)

FIGURE 12.5: The change is recorded in `github.com`.

This information can be useful when you want to know which files have changed and how many changes are made. When using version control, it is better to have a plan before making any change, make the change, and then commit the changes. The concept is called *nanocommit*. The word nano means 10^{-9}. The general principle in version control is "Do one thing at a time. Complete it and commit it." After `git push`, this change is recorded in `github.com` as shown in Figure 12.5 (a). If a line is added to the file: a + symbol appears at the beginning of the line. If we test the program, this is the result:

```
$ cmake -build build
$ ./build/bin/hello-exe
Hello, George
Hello, Yung-Hsiang
```

Figure 12.5 (b) shows another example.
If the line

```
1   /* maze.c */
```

is replaced by

```
1   // mazeread.c
```

Figure 12.5 (b) shows one line is A removed line has (- in front of /* maze.c */) and
one line is added (+ in front of // mazeread.c).

The `git log` command shows the history:

```
$ git log
commit 0db495b8f7143eb74e2f56cf84b5978fb32e981c (HEAD -> main, origin/main,
origin/HEAD)
Author: George K. Thiruvathukal <gthiruvathukal@luc.edu>
Date:   Tue Sep 20 21:41:41 2022 -0500

    Initial commit
```

This initial commit shows that the only commit so far is the one creating the repository
from the template. Let's go ahead and commit the changes:

```
$ git commit -m "say hello to Yung-Hsiang"
[main f7d619e] say hello to Yung-Hsiang
 1 file changed, 1 insertion(+)
```

The words after `-m` is the commit message. It describes the purpose of this commit. As
more changes are committed, the messages can help find when a particular change is made.
The commit messages describe the progression of the software. Thus, it is advisable using
meaningful messages. Next, observe the output of `git log`:

```
$ git log
commit f7d619ee3f0458e6ef9185d360a057251e8b66 (HEAD -> main)
Author: George K. Thiruvathukal <gthiruvathukal@luc.edu>
Date:   Sat Sep 24 13:28:14 2022 -0500

    say hello to Yung-Hsiang

commit 0db495b8f7143eb74e2f56cf84b5978fb32e981c (origin/main, origin/HEAD)
Author: George K. Thiruvathukal <gthiruvathukal@luc.edu>
Date:   Tue Sep 20 21:41:41 2022 -0500

    Initial commit
```

Let's examine what information is presented here. Each commit has a unique signature
(known as a *hash*), such as `f7d619ee3f0458e6ef9185d360a057251e8b66`. The hash is

unique to the commits within a repository. The commit information shows the author, the time and the date. The time zone "-0500" means it is the Eastern Time of the United States because it is 5 hours behind the Greenwich Mean Time (GMT). The commit messages are also shown here: the first message is "Initial commit" and the second message is "say hello to Yung-Hsiang".

The `git commit` command takes a snapshot of a file and this snapshot is stored on the local computer. This is helpful because it is possible to roll back to an earlier version. However, this snapshot is not shared with collaborators. As shown in Figure 12.4, the `git push` command modifies the file at `github.com` and now this snapshot can be seen by collaborators.

```
$ git push
Enumerating objects: 7, done.
Counting objects: 100% (7/7), done.
Delta compression using up to 8 threads
Compressing objects: 100% (4/4), done.
Writing objects: 100% (4/4), 451 bytes | 451.00 KiB/s, done.
Total 4 (delta 1), reused 0 (delta 0), pack-reused 0
remote: Resolving deltas: 100% (1/1), completed with 1 local object.
To github.com:gkthiruvathukal/book-demo-repo.git
   0db495b..f7d619e  main -> main
```

The output contains a lot of information. In most cases, you do not need to worry about the details. The latest content of the file is stored on both the local computer and at `github.com`. If the local computer is damaged or stolen, it is easy to retrieve the files from `github.com`. If you have a brand new computer, you will `git clone` the entire repository from `github.com`. If you accidentally delete a file in your computer, you can `git checkout` that particular file from `github.com`. You can `git checkout` only if you have done `git commit` before. Without `git commit`, it is not possible to retrieve the file. It is recommended that you do `git commit` often. If you delete a file (using `git rm`) and change your mind, you can use `git reset` before `git checkout` to retrieve the most recent file.

This chapter has provided some commonly used `git` commands. Many more commands allow `git` to perform complex tasks needed for creating complex software projects developed by hundreds of people. Readers are encouraged to learn more features needed for their software projects.

12.6 Problems

12.6.1 `git commit` and `git push`

Explain the differences between `git commit` and `git push`.

12.6.2 Revert to an earlier version

The output of the `git command` on page 134 has "[main f7d619e]". How can it be used to revert to this version? Please show the `git command`.

12.6.3   When to commit?

How often should a developer use `git commit`?

12.6.4   When to clone?

How often should a developer use `git clone`?

12.6.5   Recover deleted file

A developer accidentally deleted a file. What command can recover this file?

Part II

Recursion

Chapter 13

Concept

Recursion is everywhere in our daily lives. For example, every person has parents and grandparents; they have their parents and grandparents. Take two mirrors and make them face each other: An object between the two mirrors appears over and over again, smaller and smaller. A tree's trunk is divided into main branches. Each branch is further divided into smaller branches. Smaller branches are divided into twigs and eventually leaves. Recursion is everywhere around us and is also part of every person. Recursion is one of nature's ways for solving many complex problems.

Recursion has three essential properties: (1) *Recurring patterns.* The examples above describe some recurring patterns: a person, the person's parents, and their parents. (2) *Changes.* Recursion does not merely mean repeating. A person is younger than their parents and they are younger than their parents. In the two mirrors, images become smaller. For a tree, branches become thinner. Each step of a recursive pattern has a characteristic change. (3) *Terminating condition (or conditions).* The recurring pattern eventually stops. A family tree stops at the youngest member that has no child. The images in the facing mirrors will become smaller and eventually invisible. When a branch eventually becomes leaves, the pattern stops.

Recursion can be a strategy for solving problems using a concept called *divide and conquer*: Divide a complex problem into smaller problems and solve (conquer) the smaller problems. This works when the smaller problems are related to the larger problem. Recursion uses the following steps: (1) Identify the argument (or arguments) of a problem; (2) Express the solution based on the arguments; (3) Determine the simple case (or cases) when the problem becomes easy enough and can be solved; (4) Derive the relationships between the complex case (or cases) and the simpler case (or cases).

Many introductory books treat recursion superficially, giving one or two examples without explaining why recursion can be useful and how to use recursion to solve problems. As a result, many people feel recursion mysterious. To fill this gap, this book gives many examples that explain how to use recursion to solve problems.

13.1 Select Balls with Restrictions

13.1.1 Balls of Two Colors

There are unlimited red ($\mathbb{R}$) and blue ($\mathbb{B}$) balls in a bag. A game selects n balls under the restriction that two adjacent balls must not be both red. The order matters: The selections $\mathbb{R}\mathbb{B}$ and $\mathbb{B}\mathbb{R}$ are considered different. The question is how many different ways can the balls be selected? This problem can be solved recursively by applying the four steps: (1) *Identify the argument of the problem:* For this problem, the number of balls, n, is the argument. (2) *Express the solution based on the arguments:* Let $f(n)$ be

DOI: 10.1201/9781003257981-13

the answer: the number of ways to select the n balls under the restriction. (3) *Determine the simple case when the problem is easy:* If only one ball is selected, there are two options: $\mathbb{R}$ or $\mathbb{B}$. Thus, $f(1)$ is 2. If only two balls are selected, there are three options: $\mathbb{R}\mathbb{B}$, $\mathbb{B}\mathbb{R}$, and $\mathbb{B}\mathbb{B}$. Therefore, $f(2)$ is 3. Please notice that $\mathbb{R}\mathbb{R}$ is not allowed. (4) *Derive the relationships between the complex cases and the simpler cases:* If there are n balls ($n > 2$), the first ball can be $\mathbb{R}$ or $\mathbb{B}$. There are exactly two choices for the first ball. Figure 13.1 (a) shows the two different scenarios in the selection of the second ball. If it is $\mathbb{B}$, the remaining $n - 1$ balls have $f(n - 1)$ options because a blue ball does not impose any restriction on the second ball. If the first ball is $\mathbb{R}$, then the second ball must be $\mathbb{B}$ and the remaining $n - 2$ balls have $f(n - 2)$ options. Based on this analysis, $f(n) = f(n - 1) + f(n - 2)$.

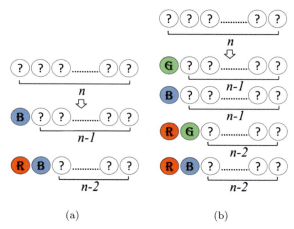

FIGURE 13.1: To decide $f(n)$, consider the options for the first ball. (a) Two colors. (b) Three colors.

13.1.2 Balls of Three Colors

The problem can be extended to balls of three colors. There are unlimited red ($\mathbb{R}$), green ($\mathbb{G}$), and blue ($\mathbb{B}$) balls. Two adjacent balls cannot be both red. The orders matter: $\mathbb{R}\mathbb{B}$ and $\mathbb{B}\mathbb{R}$ are different selections. How many options can n balls be selected? If the first ball is $\mathbb{G}$ or $\mathbb{B}$, the remaining $n - 1$ balls have $f(n - 1)$ options. If it is $\mathbb{R}$, the second ball must be $\mathbb{G}$ or $\mathbb{B}$ and the remaining $n - 2$ balls have $f(n - 2)$ options. When n is one, there are three options: (1) $\mathbb{R}$, (2) $\mathbb{G}$, and (3) $\mathbb{B}$. When n is two, there are eight options. (1) $\mathbb{R}\,\mathbb{G}$, (2) $\mathbb{R}\,\mathbb{B}$, (3) $\mathbb{G}\,\mathbb{R}$, (4) $\mathbb{G}\,\mathbb{G}$, (5) $\mathbb{G}\,\mathbb{B}$, (6) $\mathbb{B}\,\mathbb{R}$, (7) $\mathbb{B}\,\mathbb{G}$, and (8) $\mathbb{B}\,\mathbb{B}$; $\mathbb{R}\,\mathbb{R}$ is an invalid option.

What is the number of options for n balls when $n > 2$? To solve this problem, let $f(n)$ be the answer. We already know that $f(1) = 3$ and $f(2) = 8$. When $n > 2$, consider the options for the first ball. Figure 13.1 (b) shows three scenarios:

1. If the first ball is $\mathbb{G}$, then the second ball can be any of the three colors. There is no further restriction for the remaining $n - 1$ balls. Thus, there are $f(n - 1)$ options for the remaining $n - 1$ balls.
2. Likewise, if the first ball is $\mathbb{B}$, then the second ball can be any of the three colors. There is no further restriction for the remaining $n-1$ balls. There are $f(n-1)$ options for the remaining $n - 1$ balls.
3. If the first ball is $\mathbb{R}$, then there are two scenarios:
   (a) If the second ball is $\mathbb{G}$, then the third ball can be any of the three colors. There is no further restriction for the remaining $n - 2$ balls. Thus, there are $f(n - 2)$ possible sequences for the remaining $n - 2$ balls.
   (b) If the second ball is $\mathbb{B}$, then the third ball can be any of the three colors. There is no further restriction for the remaining $n - 2$ balls. Thus, there are $f(n - 2)$ options for the remaining $n - 2$ balls.

Thus, the relationships are:

$$f(n) = 2f(n - 1) + 2f(n - 2), \text{ if } n > 2. \tag{13.1}$$

13.2   One-Way Streets

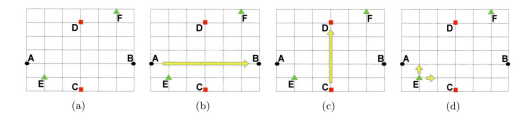

(a)   (b)   (c)   (d)

FIGURE 13.2: (a) A city's streets form a grid. (b) and (c) Only one way from A to B (East) or from C to D (North). (d) There are some turning options when traversing from E to F.

A city has severe traffic congestion during rush hours so the city government considers adopting a rule: During rush hours, cars can move only east or north. All streets run either East–West or North–South, forming a grid, as shown in Figure 13.2. A car can move only east or north. Assume we have the location of a car's origin and destination. How many ways can the destination be reached? This example may seem artificial but it is actually a reasonable simplification of the one-way streets in the downtown of many cities. These cities often have one-way streets. The simplification is useful for analyzing traffic patterns.

Figure 13.2 marks three pairs of origins and destinations: A → B (west to east), C → D (south to north), and E → F. For the first two pairs A → B and C → D, the driver has only one option: not to turn at all. This is shown in Figure 13.2 (b) and (c). There are more options for E → F. At E, the driver can go eastbound (left to right) first or northbound first (bottom to top), as indicated by the two arrows in Figure 13.2 (d). The question is the number of different paths a driver can make between the origin and the destination. This question can be answered using the four steps for solving the recursive problem: (1) *Identify the arguments of a problem.* Suppose E is at the intersection of $(x1, y1)$ and F is at the intersection of $(x2, y2)$. The distance between them can be expressed as $(\Delta x, \Delta y) = (x2 - x1, y2 - y1)$. (2) *Express the solution based on the arguments.* Let $f(\Delta x, \Delta y)$ express the number of unique paths. (3) *Determine the simple cases when the problem is easy.* If $\Delta x < 0$, the destination is at the west side of the origin and there is no solution. Similarly, there is no solution if $\Delta y < 0$. If $\Delta x > 0$ and $\Delta y = 0$ (the case A → B), then there is precisely one solution. Likewise, if $\Delta x = 0$ and $\Delta y > 0$ (the case C → D), there is also precisely one solution. These are the simple cases whose answers can be found easily. A special case occurs when $\Delta x = \Delta y = 0$. This means that the destination is the same as the origin. It can be defined as no solution or one solution depending on what the reader prefers. Our method considers that there is one solution for $\Delta x = \Delta y = 0$. (4) *Derive the relationships between the complex cases and the simpler cases.* When $\Delta x > 0$ and $\Delta y > 0$ (the case E → F), then the driver has two options at the origin (i.e., E): Either the driver goes north first or east first. If the driver heads north, then the new origin is at $(x1, y1 + 1)$. There are $f(\Delta x, \Delta y - 1)$ possible paths from this point. If the driver goes east first, then the new origin is at $(x1 + 1, y1)$. Similarly, there are $f(\Delta x - 1, \Delta y)$ possible paths from this point. These are the only two possible options at position E and they are exclusive. Therefore, when $\Delta x > 0$

and $\Delta y > 0$, the solution can expressed as $f(\Delta x, \Delta y) = f(\Delta x, \Delta y - 1) + f(\Delta x - 1, \Delta y)$.

$$f(\Delta x, \Delta y) = \begin{cases} 0 & \text{if } \Delta x < 0 \text{ or } \Delta y < 0 \\ 1 & \text{if } \Delta x = 0 \text{ and } \Delta y \geq 0 \\ 1 & \text{if } \Delta x \geq 0 \text{ and } \Delta y = 0 \\ f(\Delta x, \Delta y - 1) + f(\Delta x - 1, \Delta y) & \text{if } \Delta x > 0 \text{ and } \Delta y > 0 \end{cases} \quad (13.2)$$

13.3 The Tower of Hanoi

Several disks of different sizes are stacked on a single pole. The disks are arranged so that smaller disks are above larger disks. The problem is to move the disks from one pole to another pole. Only one disk can be moved each time. A larger disk cannot be placed above a smaller disk. The third pole can be used for temporary storage. Figure 13.3 (a) illustrates the problem with three disks. If there are n disks, how many steps are needed to move them? First, con-

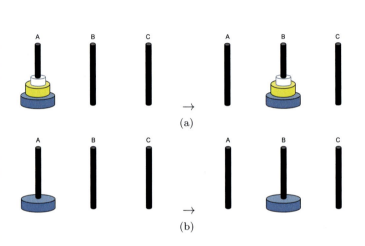

FIGURE 13.3: (a) Move three disks. (b) Moving one disk requires only one step.

sider moving only one disk from A to B. This is the simplest case and that disk can be moved directly from A to B as shown in Figure 13.3 (b). Moving two disks requires more work. It is necessary to move the smaller disk to C before moving the larger disk to B. Then, move the larger disk from A to B and move the smaller disk from C to B. Moving two disks needs three steps. This is the general strategy for moving n disks: If there is only one disk (i.e., $n = 1$), the problem takes only one step. Otherwise, the solution is divided into three parts: (1) Move the first $n - 1$ disks from A to C; (2) Move the largest disk from A to B; (3) Move the first $n - 1$ disks from C to B.

Now we put the steps together to solve the problem using recursion. The four-step approach for solving this problem is listed below: (1) *Identify the argument of a problem:* The number n is naturally the argument for the problem. (2) *Express the solution based on the argument:* Let $f(n)$ be the answer: how many steps are needed to move n disks from A to B. (3) *Determine the simple case when the problem is easy:* If n is one, only one step is sufficient; thus, $f(1)$ is 1. (4) *Derive the relationships between the complex case and the simpler case:* When n is greater than one, the problem can be divided into three parts: (a) Move $n - 1$ disks from pole A to pole C and this requires $f(n - 1)$ steps. (b) Move the largest disk from pole A to pole B and this requires 1 step. (c) Move $n - 1$ disks from pole

C to pole B and requires $f(n-1)$ steps. The following formula expresses the steps:

$$f(n) = \begin{cases} 1 & \text{if } n \text{ is } 1 \\ f(n-1)+1+f(n-1) = 2f(n-1)+1 & \text{if } n \geq 2 \end{cases} \quad (13.3)$$

It possible to find a *closed form* formula: $f(n)$ is expressed without $f(n-1)$ appearing on the right side of the = sign.

$$\begin{aligned} f(n) &= 2f(n-1)+1 \\ &= 4f(n-2)+2+1 \\ &= 2^k f(n-k) + 2^{k-1} + 2^{k-2} + ... + 4 + 2 + 1 \\ &= 2^{n-1}f(1) + 2^{n-2} + 2^{n-3} + ... + 4 + 2 + 1, \quad \text{when } k = n-1 \\ &= 2^{n-1} + 2^{n-2} + 2^{n-3} + ... + 4 + 2 + 1, \quad \text{because } f(1) = 1 \\ &= 2^n - 1 \end{aligned} \quad (13.4)$$

13.4 Calculate Integer Partitions

TABLE 13.1: Partition integers 1 - 4.

$1 = 1$	$2 = 1 + 1$	$3 = 1 + 1 + 1$	$4 = 1 + 1 + 1 + 1$
	$= 2$	$= 1 + 2$	$= 1 + 1 + 2$
		$= 2 + 1$	$= 1 + 2 + 1$
		$= 3$	$= 1 + 3$
			$= 2 + 1 + 1$
			$= 2 + 2$
			$= 3 + 1$
			$= 4$

A positive integer can be expressed as the sum of a sequence of positive integers. An *integer partition* creates such a sequence of integers. For example, 5 can be broken into the sum of $1 + 2 + 2$ or $2 + 3$. These two partitions use different numbers and thus are considered distinct partitions. The order of the numbers in the partition is also important. Thus, $1 + 2 + 2$ and $2 + 1 + 2$ are considered different partitions because 1 appears in different positions. Table 13.1 shows integer partition of one to four.

This question is the number of different partitions for a positive integer n. Let $f(n)$ be the number of different partitions for integer n. When n is 1, there is only one way to partition it: the number 1. Thus, $f(1) = 1$. When n is larger than 2, the solution selects the first number. It must be an integer between 1 and n inclusively. After selecting the first number, we have to partition the remaining number. Thus for each of the n options for the first number, we need to consider the number of options for the remaining partition. The relationship can be expressed in Table 13.2.

TABLE 13.2: To partition n, the first number can be 1, 2, ..., n. The remaining number is $n-1$, $n-2$, ..., 0.

First Number	Remaining Value
1	$n-1$
2	$n-2$
$\vdots$	$\vdots$
$n-1$	1
n	0

If the first number is 1, then the remaining value to be partitioned is $n-1$. By definition, there are $f(n-1)$ ways to partition the remaining $n-1$. If the first number is 2, there are $f(n-2)$ ways to partition the remaining $n-2$. The first number can be 1, or 2, or 3, ..., The value of $f(n)$ is therefore the sum of all the different cases when the first number is 1, 2, 3, ..., $n-1$, or n, i.e.,

$$f(n) = f(n-1) + f(n-2) + \ldots f(1) + 1 = 1 + \sum_{i=1}^{n-1} f(i), \text{ if } n > 1. \tag{13.5}$$

There is a convenient closed form solution to $f(n)$:

$$
\begin{array}{rll}
f(n) & = f(n-1) & +f(n-2) + f(n-3) + \ldots + 1 \\
-\quad f(n-1) & = & +f(n-2) + f(n-3) + \ldots + 1 \\
\hline
f(n) - f(n-1) & = f(n-1) & \\
f(n) & = 2f(n-1) &
\end{array}
\tag{13.6}
$$

There are 2^{n-1} ways to partition the integer n.

13.4.1 Count the Number of "1"s

The partition problem has many variations. In this variation, we count how many "1"s are used for partitioning n. Suppose $g(n)$ is the answer. First observe that $g(1) = 1$ and $g(2) = 2$. The more complicated cases can be related to the simpler cases with the following logic. Observe that there are 2^{n-2} partitions of n that begin with the digit "1". There may be "1"s in the partitions of the remaining value, $n-1$. Thus, when the first number is "1", we use $2^{n-2} + g(n-1)$ "1"s. We do not need to worry about the value of $g(n-1)$; instead, we just use it. When the first number is "2", "1" is not used for the first number but "1" may be used

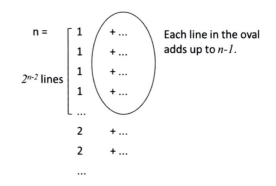

FIGURE 13.4: Count the occurrences of "1" when partitioning n.

for partitioning the remaining value of $n-2$. By definition, "1" is used $g(n-2)$ times when partitioning $n-2$. The value of $g(n)$ can be calculated

$$g(n) = 2^{n-2} + g(n-1) + g(n-2) + \ldots g(1), \text{ when } n > 1 \tag{13.7}$$

To obtain the closed form, first find the relationship between $g(n)$ and $g(n-1)$:

$$
\begin{array}{rll}
g(n) & = 2^{n-2} + g(n-1) & +g(n-2) + g(n-3) + \ldots + g(1) \\
-\quad g(n-1) & = 2^{n-3} & +g(n-2) + g(n-3) + \ldots + g(1) \\
\hline
g(n) - g(n-1) & = 2^{n-3} + g(n-1) & \\
g(n) & = 2^{n-3} + 2g(n-1) &
\end{array}
\tag{13.8}
$$

This relationship can be expanded for $g(n-2)$, $g(n-3)$, ..., $g(1)$.

$$
\begin{aligned}
g(n) &= 2^{n-3} + 2g(n-1) \\
g(n-1) &= 2^{n-4} + 2g(n-2) \\
g(n-2) &= 2^{n-5} + 2g(n-3) \\
&\ \ \vdots \\
g(n-k) &= 2^{n-k-3} + 2g(n-k-1) \\
g(3) &= 2^0 + 2g(2) \qquad \text{when } k = n-3
\end{aligned}
\tag{13.9}
$$

In (13.9), the coefficient for $g(n-1)$ on the right side is two. In order to cancel $g(n-1)$, the coefficient on the left size has to increase accordingly as shown below:

$$
\begin{aligned}
g(n) &= 2^{n-3} + 2g(n-1) \\
2g(n-1) &= 2^{n-3} + 4g(n-2) \\
4g(n-2) &= 2^{n-3} + 8g(n-3) \\
&\ \ \vdots \\
2^k g(n-k) &= 2^{n-3} + 2^{k+1}g(n-k-1) \\
+ \quad 2^{n-3}g(3) &= 2^{n-3} + 2^{n-2}g(2) \\
\hline
g(n) + \sum_{i=3}^{n-1} 2^{n-i}g(i) &= (n-2)2^{n-3} + 2^{n-2}g(2) + \sum_{i=3}^{n-1} 2^{n-i}g(i) \\
g(n) &= (n-2)2^{n-3} + 2^{n-2}g(2) \\
g(n) &= (n-2)2^{n-3} + 2^{n-1} \\
g(n) &= (n+2)2^{n-3}
\end{aligned}
\tag{13.10}
$$

Table 13.3 shows the value of $g(n)$ for $1 \le n < 10$.

13.4.2 Odd Numbers Only

We want to find the number of ways n can be partitioned using only odd numbers. It is helpful to review how Equation (13.5) is derived. What does $f(n-1)$ mean in this equation? It means the number of partitions using "1" as the first number. Similarly, what does $f(n-2)$ mean in this equation? It means the number of partitions using "2" as the first number. To restrict the partitions to odd numbers only, all partitions using even numbers must be discarded. Thus, $f(n-2)$, $f(n-4)$, $f(n-6)$, etc., must be excluded. Suppose $h(n)$ is the number of partitions for n using odd numbers only. Apparently, $h(1) = 1$ because there is one way to partition 1.

TABLE 13.3: Numbers of "1" used in partitions.

n	1	2	3	4	5	6	7	8	9
$g(n)$	1	2	5	12	28	64	144	320	704

$$
h(n) = h(n-1) + h(n-3) + h(n-5)... \text{ when } n > 1
\tag{13.11}
$$

The last few terms will be different depending on whether n itself is odd or even. If n is odd, $n-1$ is even so $h(1)$ is excluded. Also $n-3$ is an even number and $h(3)$ is excluded. The complete equation is shown below:

$$
h(n) = h(n-1) + h(n-3) + h(n-5)... + h(2) + 1, \text{ when } n > 1 \text{ and } n \text{ is odd.}
\tag{13.12}
$$

If n is even, $n - 1$ is odd so $h(1)$ is included. Also $n - 3$ is an odd number and $h(3)$ is included. Therefore the complete equation is shown below:

$$h(n) = \begin{cases} 1 & \text{when } n \text{ is 1} \\ h(n-1) + h(n-3) + h(n-5)... + h(2) + 1 & \text{when } n > 1 \text{ and } n \text{ is odd} \\ h(n-1) + h(n-3) + h(n-5)... + h(1) & \text{when } n \text{ is even} \end{cases}$$

(13.13)

13.4.3 Increasing Values

How many ways can the positive integer n be partitioned using increasing values or the number n itself? Suppose n is partitioned into the sum of k numbers:

$$n = a_1 + a_2 + a_3 + ... + a_k \tag{13.14}$$

while meeting the following conditions: (1) a_i ($1 \le i \le k$) are positive integers; (2) $a_i < a_{i+1}$ ($1 \le i < k$). Consider the first few cases of n shown in Table 13.4.

TABLE 13.4: Valid partitions using increasing numbers.

n	Valid Partitions			Number of Partitions
1	1			1
2	2			1
3	$1 + 2$	3		2
4	$1 + 3$	4		2
5	$1 + 4$	$2 + 3$	4	3

To solve this problem, two arguments are needed for the equation. We define $p(n, m)$ to be the number of ways to partition n where m is the smallest number used. If 1 is used as the first number, then 2 is the smallest allowed number to partition $n - 1$. There are $p(n - 1, 2)$ ways to partition $n - 1$ using 2 as the smallest number. Based on this reasoning,

$$\begin{aligned} p(n, 1) &= p(n-1, 2) + p(n-2, 3) + ... + p(n-k, k+1) + ... + p(1, n) + 1 \\ &= 1 + \sum_{i=1}^{n-1} p(n-i, i+1) \end{aligned} \tag{13.15}$$

Obviously, $p(n, n) = 1$ because there is only one way to partition n using n as the smallest number. Also, $p(n, m) = 0$ if $n < m$ because it is impossible to partition an integer using a larger integer.

13.4.4 Alternating Odd and Even Numbers

We want to find partitions that alternate between odd and even numbers. If an odd number is used, then the next must be an even number. If an even number is used, then the next must be an odd number. If only one number is used (i.e., the number to be partitioned itself), it is always a valid partition. This problem can be solved by defining two functions as follows: (1) $s(n)$ is the number of ways to partition n using an odd number as the first number. (2) $t(n)$ is the number of ways to partition n using an even number as the first number. By observation, we can create Table 13.5. To calculate $s(n)$, the first number can be 1, 3,

TABLE 13.5: The number of solutions is the sum of $s(n)$ and $t(n)$.

n	1	2	3	4	5
$s(n)$	1	0	2	1	3
$t(n)$	0	1	1	1	3
sum	1	1	3	2	6

5, ... and the second number must be an even number. For example, when 1 is used for the first number, then the remaining $n-1$ must start with an even number. By definition, there are $t(n-1)$ ways to partition $n-1$ starting with an even number. When 3 is used for the first number, then there are $t(n-3)$ ways to partition $n-3$ starting with an even number. Based on this reasoning, $s(n)$ is defined as:

$$s(n) = t(n-1) + t(n-3) + t(n-5)... \tag{13.16}$$

By definition, $s(n)$ must not start with an even number; thus, $t(n-2)$, $t(n-4)$, ... must not be included. It is necessary to distinguish whether n is odd or even while writing down the last few terms in this equation. If n is an even number then:

- $n-3$ is an odd number. This means that there are $t(n-(n-3)) = t(3)$ ways to partition n with $n-3$ as the first number. For example, if $n = 10$, there are $t(3)$ ways to partition 10 with 7 as the first number. Note that $t(3) = 1$, because the only valid partition of 3 that starts with an even number is: $3 = 2 + 1$.
- $n-2$ is an even number. We skip this case because $s(n)$ is only concerned with the number of ways to partition n using an odd number as the first number.
- $n-1$ is an odd number, so $t(n-(n-1)) = t(1)$ is included in the calculation of $s(n)$. Note, however, that $t(1) = 0$.
- n is an even number. We skip this case because $s(n)$ only concerns itself with partitions that begin with odd numbers.

Hence, when n is an even number:

$$s(n) = t(n-1) + t(n-3) + t(n-5)... + t(3) + t(1) \tag{13.17}$$

When n is an odd number:

- $n-3$ is an even number and this case is discarded when computing $s(n)$.
- $n-2$ is an odd number leaving the remainder 2 to be partitioned. Thus we add $t(2)$.
- $n-1$ is an even number and this case is discarded when computing $s(n)$.
- n is an odd number and it is a valid partition for $s(n)$. This means we add 1 to the end of the equation.

When n is an odd number, $s(n)$ can be written as:

$$s(n) = t(n-1) + t(n-3) + t(n-5)... + t(2) + 1 \tag{13.18}$$

Combining these two cases together, we get:

$$s(n) = \begin{cases} t(n-1) + t(n-3) + t(n-5)... + t(1) & \text{when } n \text{ is even} \\ t(n-1) + t(n-3) + t(n-5)... + t(2) + 1 & \text{when } n \text{ is odd} \end{cases} \tag{13.19}$$

Using similar reasoning, $t(n)$ can be written as follows:

$$t(n) = \begin{cases} s(n-2) + s(n-4) + s(n-6)... + s(4) + s(2) + 1 & \text{when } n \text{ is even} \\ s(n-2) + s(n-4) + s(n-6)... + s(3) + s(1) & \text{when } n \text{ is odd} \end{cases} \tag{13.20}$$

Since a partition may start with an odd number or an even number, $f(n) = s(n) + t(n)$ and it is the answer to the question. This is the number of ways to partition n using alternating odd and even numbers.

13.5   Problems

13.5.1   Parentheses

An arithmetic expression may include one or multiple pairs of parentheses, for example

```
(3 + 5) * 4
(3 + (5 + 4) * 6) * 2
3 + (5 + 4) * (6 + 2)
(3 + (5 + 4)) * (6 + 2)
```

The parentheses must be arranged by following these rules: (1) The number of left parentheses (must be the same as the number of right parentheses). (2) The left parentheses must appear first. (3) From left to right, the number of right parentheses) must not exceed the number of left parentheses (that have already been seen. The following are valid arrangements of one, two, or three pairs:

```
()
(())
()()
((()))
(()())
(())()
()(())
()()()
```

The following are invalid arrangements:

```
)(
())(
))((
)()()(
```

This question asks you to determine the number of valid arrangements for 4, 5, and 6 pairs. Next, generalize the problem to consider n pairs. Consider creating a function $f(n)$ as the number of valid arrangements when n pairs of (and) are used. Since this problem considers (and), $f(n)$ is further expressed by a function with two arguments: $f(n) = g(n, n)$: $g(n, m)$ is defined as the number of valid arrangements to use n (and m) while satisfying the rules described above. Consider arranging three pairs of (and). The first must be (. Then, two (and three) are left. Thus, $f(3) = g(3, 3) = g(2, 3)$. The second can be (or). These two options can be analyzed as (1) If (is used, one (and three) are left. There are $g(1, 3)$ arrangements. (2) If) is used, two (and two) are left. There are $g(2, 2)$ arrangements.

Please answer the following questions.

1. What is $g(0, m)$ when $m > 0$?
2. What is $g(n, m)$ when $n > m$?
3. What is $f(4) = g(4, 4)$?
4. What is $f(5) = g(5, 5)$?
5. What is $f(6) = g(6, 6)$?

13.5.2   Ball Selection

Select balls from three possible colors: $\mathbb{R}$, $\mathbb{G}$, $\mathbb{B}$. Two adjacent balls cannot be both red or green. Two adjacent balls can both be blue. How many options are there to select n balls?

13.5.3   Partition using Odd and Even Numbers

Section 13.4.2 explains how to find the number of partitions using odd numbers only. The answer is expressed as $h(n)$. A similar procedure can be used to find the number of partitions using even numbers only. Let's call it $u(n)$. Section 13.4.4 defines $s(n)$ and $t(n)$. Is $s(n) + t(n)$ equal to $h(n) + u(n)$? Please explain your answer.

Chapter 14

Recursive C Functions

This chapter converts the mathematical formulas from the previous chapter into C programs. A recursive function usually has the following structure:

```
return_type func(arguments)
{
  if (this is the base case) // by checking the arguments
  {
    solve the problem
  }
  else // Recursive case
  {
    return func(simplified arguments) // function calls itself
  }
}
```

A recursive function should first check whether the arguments satisfy a stop condition (also called *terminating condition* or *base case*) and the function can return the answer. When the condition is true, the problem is simple enough and recursive calls are unnecessary. If the problem is not simple, then the function enters the recursive case and the function calls itself with simplified versions of the arguments. The following sections implement the recursive equations in the previous chapter.

14.1   Select Balls with Restrictions

```
1  // CH14:balls.c
2  // f(1) = 2, f(2) = 3, f(n) = f(n-1) + f(n-2)
3  #include <stdio.h>
4  #include <stdlib.h>
5  int f(int m)
6  // use m instead of n to distinguish m in f and n in main
7  {
8    if (m <= 0)    // Base cases
9      {
10        printf("Invalid Number %d, must be positive.\n", m);
11        return -1;
12      }
13    if (m == 1) { return 2; } // f(1) = 2
14    if (m == 2) { return 3; } // f(2) = 3
```

```
15    // Recursive case
16    int a;
17    int b;
18    a = f(m - 1);
19    b = f(m - 2);
20    return (a + b);
21  }
22  int main(int argc, char * argv[])
23  {
24    int c;
25    int n;
26    if (argc < 2)
27      {
28        printf("need 1 integer.\n");
29        return EXIT_FAILURE;
30      }
31    n = (int) strtol(argv[1], NULL, 10);
32    c = f(n);
33    printf("f(%d) = %d.\n", n, c);
34    return EXIT_SUCCESS;
35  }
```

Lines 16–17 create two local variables a and b. Their values are f(m - 1) and f(m - 2) respectively. The sum are returned (line 20). Lines 16–20 can be written in a single line:

```
return (f(m - 1) + f(m - 2));
```

The compiler will automatically create temporary local variables (like a and b) to hold the values from f(m - 1) and f(m - 2).

14.2   One-Way Streets

```
1   // CH14:streets.c
2   // implement the recursive relation for calculating the number of
3   // routes in a city where cars can only move northbound or eastbound
4   #include <stdio.h>
5   #include <stdlib.h>
6   int f(int dx, int dy)
7   // No need to worry about dx < 0 or dy < 0,  already handled in main.
8   {
9     if ((dx == 0) || (dy == 0)) { return 1; } // Base case
10    // Recursive case
11    int a, b;
12    a = f(dx - 1, dy);
13    b = f(dx, dy - 1);
14    return (a + b);
```

```
15   }
16   int main(int argc, char * argv[])
17   {
18     int deltax, deltay;
19     int c;
20     if (argc < 3)
21       {
22         printf("need 2 positive integers.\n");
23         return EXIT_FAILURE;
24       }
25     deltax = (int) strtol(argv[1], NULL, 10);
26     deltay = (int) strtol(argv[2], NULL, 10);
27     if ((deltax < 0) || (deltay < 0))
28       {
29         printf("need 2 positive integers.\n");
30         return EXIT_FAILURE;
31       }
32     c = f(deltax, deltay);
33     printf("f(%d, %d) = %d.\n", deltax, deltay, c);
34     return EXIT_SUCCESS;
35   }
```

This program uses local variables to store the values returned from recursive calls:

```
a = f(dx - 1, dy);
b = f(dx, dy - 1);
return (a + b);
```

The local variables in lines 11–13 are unnecessary. Instead, lines 11–14 can be rewritten as follows:

```
return (f(dx - 1, dy) + f(dx, dy - 1));
```

14.3   The Tower of Hanoi

The listing below shows how to calculate the number of steps required to move n disks in the Tower of Hanoi problem:

```
1   // CH14:hanoi1.c
2   // calculate the number of moves needed to move n disks
3   #include <stdio.h>
4   #include <stdlib.h>
5   int f(int n)
6   {
7     if (n == 1) { return 1; }  // Base case
8     // Recursive case
9     return (2 * f(n - 1) + 1);
```

```
10    }
11    int main(int argc, char * argv[])
12    {
13      int n;
14      if (argc < 2)
15        {
16          printf("need one positive integer.\n");
17          return EXIT_FAILURE;
18        }
19      n = (int) strtol(argv[1], NULL, 10);
20      if (n <= 0)
21        {
22          printf("need one positive integer.\n");
23          return EXIT_FAILURE;
24        }
25      printf("f(%d) = %d.\n", n, f(n));
26      return EXIT_SUCCESS;
27    }
```

A more interesting program prints the solution—the sequence of disk moves that solves the problem. To do this, we create a function called `move` that takes four arguments:

1. The disks to move. The disks are represented by positive integers, where 1 is the smallest disk and 2 is the second smallest disk, etc.
2. The source pole.
3. The destination pole.
4. The additional pole.

This program follows the procedure in Section 13.3: Move the top $n-1$ disks to the additional pole (i.e., C), then move the nth disk from A to B, and then move the top $n-1$ disk from C to B.

```
1    // CH14:hanoi2.c
2    // print the steps moving n disks
3    #include <stdio.h>
4    #include <stdlib.h>
5    void move(int disk, char src, char dest, char additional)
6    {
7      /* Base case */
8      if (disk == 1)
9        {
10          printf("move disk 1 from %c to %c\n", src, dest);
11          return;
12        }
13      /* Recursive case */
14      move(disk - 1, src, additional, dest);
15      printf("move disk %d from %c to %c\n", disk, src, dest);
16      move(disk - 1, additional, dest, src);
17    }
18    int main(int argc, char * argv[])
```

```
19   {
20     int n;
21     if (argc < 2)
22       {
23         printf("need one positive integer.\n");
24         return EXIT_FAILURE;
25       }
26     n = (int) strtol(argv[1], NULL, 10);
27     if (n <= 0)
28       {
29         printf("need one positive integer.\n");
30         return EXIT_FAILURE;
31       }
32     move(n, 'A', 'B', 'C');
33     return EXIT_SUCCESS;
34   }
```

When the input is 3, the program's output is:

```
move disk 1 from A to B
move disk 2 from A to C
move disk 1 from B to C
move disk 3 from A to B
move disk 1 from C to A
move disk 2 from C to B
move disk 1 from A to B
```

14.4 Integer Partition

The implementation of formula (13.5) in C is shown below. Notice the nearly one-to-one mapping from the mathematical expression to the C code.

```
1    // CH14:partition.c
2    // implement the recursive relation for calculating
3    // the number of partitions for a positive integer
4    #include <stdio.h>
5    #include <stdlib.h>
6    int f(int n)
7    {
8      int i;
9      int sum = 0;
10     if (n == 1) { return 1; } // Base case: only one way to partition 1
11     // Recursive case
12     for (i = 1; i < n; i ++)
13       { sum += f(n - i); }
14     sum ++; // partition n itself
```

```
15      return sum;
16    }
17    int main(int argc, char * argv[])
18    {
19      int n;
20      if (argc < 2)
21        {
22          printf("need one positive integer.\n");
23          return EXIT_FAILURE;
24        }
25      n = (int) strtol(argv[1], NULL, 10);
26      if (n <= 0)
27        {
28          printf("need one positive integer.\n");
29          return EXIT_FAILURE;
30        }
31      printf("f(%d) = %d.\n", n, f(n));
32      return EXIT_SUCCESS;
33    }
```

14.5 Factorial

Many books use factorials and Fibonacci numbers to motivate the need of recursion. These are actually poor examples. This book does not start with these two popular examples for good reasons, as explained below. The definition of factorials is:

$$f(n) = \begin{cases} 1 & \text{when } n \text{ is } 0 \\ n \times f(n-1) & \text{when } n > 0 \end{cases} \tag{14.1}$$

The implementation should be straightforward:

```
1    // CH14:factorial1.c
2    #include <stdio.h>
3    #include <stdlib.h>
4    #define MAXN 20
5    long int fac(int n)
6    {
7      if (n < 0)
8        {
9          printf("n cannot be negative\n");
10         return 0;
11       }
12     if (n == 0) { return 1; } // Base case
13     /* Recursive case */
14     return n * fac(n - 1);
15   }
16   int main(int argc, char * argv[])
```

```
17  {
18    int nval;
19    for (nval = 0; nval <= MAXN; nval ++)
20      {
21        long int fval = fac(nval);
22        printf("fac(%2d) = %ld\n", nval, fval);
23      }
24    return EXIT_SUCCESS;
25  }
```

The function `fac` returns `long int` because the values quickly get too large for `int` (when n is greater than 12). The function `fac` is quite straightforward—a direct translation of the mathematical definition. Why is this a bad example for introducing recursion? The reason is that recursion is not necessary. It is possible to implement the same function *without* using recursion.

```
1   // CH14:factorial2.c
2   #include <stdio.h>
3   #include <stdlib.h>
4   #define MAXN 20
5   long int fac2(int n)
6   {
7     if (n < 0)
8       {
9         printf("n cannot be negative\n");
10        return 0;
11      }
12    if (n == 0) { return 1; }
13    long int result = 1;
14    while (n > 0)
15      {
16        result *= n;
17        n --;
18      }
19    return result;
20  }
21  int main(int argc, char * argv[])
22  {
23    int nval;
24    for (nval = 0; nval <= MAXN; nval ++)
25      {
26        long int fval = fac2(nval);
27        printf("fac2(%2d) = %ld\n", nval, fval);
28      }
29    return EXIT_SUCCESS;
30  }
```

This function uses `while` and stores the result in a local variable called `result`. The recursive solution is inefficient compared with the iterative solution and the recursive solution is slower. Recursive functions must push and pop frames on the call stack. Pushing and popping frames takes time. We compared the execution times of both functions. The iterative solution (using `while`) is slightly faster than the recursive solution. In the next example (Fibonacci numbers), we will see a remarkable performance difference between recursive and non-recursive functions.

14.6 Fibonacci Numbers

Calculating Fibonacci numbers is another popular example used in teaching recursion. The numbers are defined as follows:

$$f(n) = \begin{cases} 1 & \text{if } n \text{ is 1 or 2} \\ f(n-1) + f(n-2) & \text{if } n > 2. \end{cases} \tag{14.2}$$

This formula is similar to the ball selection problem in Section 13.1. The difference is the starting values of $f(1)$ and $f(2)$. Below is a straightforward implementation of the definition:

```
1   // CH14:fibonacci1.c
2   long int fib1(int n)
3   {
4       if ((n == 1) || (n == 2)) // base case
5           { return 1; }
6       return (fib1(n - 1) + fib1(n - 2)); // recursive case
7   }
```

This is a "top-down" approach. It computes $f(n)$ by using the values of $f(n-1)$ and $f(n-2)$. If n is greater than 2, then the function computes $f(n-1)$ by using the values of $f(n-2)$ and $f(n-3)$. This process continues until n is either 1 or 2.

The following implementation does not use recursion. Because the definition itself is recursive, the iterative solution must take a different approach:

```
1    // CH14:fibonacci2.c
2    long int fib2(int n)
3    {
4        if ((n == 1) || (n == 2))
5            { return 1; }
6        long int fna = 1; // fib(1)
7        long int fnb = 1; // fib(2)
8        long int fnc;      // to hold the latest value of fib
9        while (n > 2)
10           {
11               fnc = fnb + fna; // the new value
12               fna = fnb;
13               fnb = fnc;
14               n --;
15           }
16       return fnc;
17   }
```

This may seem a little complex, but it calculates the Fibonacci numbers "bottom-up". It knows $f(1)$ and $f(2)$ first and stores the values in **fna** and **fnb** respectively. Then, the function computes $f(3)$ by using the sum of $f(1)$ and $f(2)$. This value is stored in **fnc** in line 11. After computing $f(3)$, the value in **fnb** is stored in **fna** (line 12); the value in **fnc** is stored in **fnb** (line 13). Please be aware that the order of these two lines cannot change. At this point **fnb** stores $f(3)$ and **fna** stores $f(2)$. The next iteration computes $f(4)$ and stores the value in **fnc**. This process repeats until we get $f(n)$. The Fibonacci sequence is built up from 1 and 2 to n.

Why do we even bother to consider the bottom-up function? Isn't the recursive function good enough? It certainly looks simple since it is a direct translation from the mathematical definition. The problem is that the recursive function does a lot of unnecessary work, and is rather slow. Figure 14.1 (a) shows the ratio of the execution time for the first (recursive, top-down) and the second (non-recursive, bottom-up) functions. It is apparent that the first function is slower than the second. Moreover, the ratio keeps rising. Please notice that the vertical axis is in the logarithmic scale. The first function takes as much as 2,000 times longer than the second when n is 20. The data in Figure 14.1 (a) were generated by using the following program:

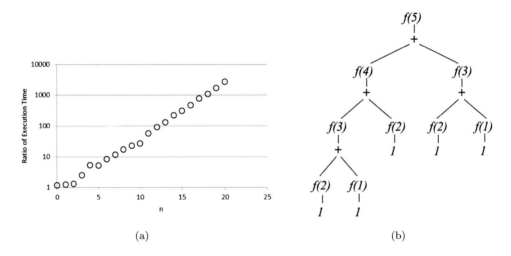

(a)   (b)

FIGURE 14.1: (a) Ratio of the execution times of the recursive and the non-recursive methods. (b) Procedure to computer $f(5)$: computing each $f(n)$ value requires the sum of $f(n-1)$ and $f(n-2)$.

```c
1   // CH14:fibtime.c
2   #include <stdio.h>
3   #include <stdlib.h>
4   #include <sys/time.h>
5   #define MAXN 25
6   #define REPEAT 100000
7   long int fib1(int n);
8   long int fib2(int n);
9   int main(int argc, char * argv[])
10  {
11      int nval, rept;
12      struct timeval time1;
```

```
13    struct timeval time2;
14    float intv1, intv2;
15    for (nval = 1; nval <= MAXN; nval ++)
16      {
17        long int fval;
18        gettimeofday(& time1, NULL);
19        for (rept = 0; rept < REPEAT; rept ++)
20          { fval = fib1(nval); }
21        gettimeofday(& time2, NULL);
22        intv1 = (time2.tv_sec - time1.tv_sec) +
23          1e-6 * (time2.tv_usec - time1.tv_usec);
24        printf("fib1 (%2d) = %ld, time = %f\n", nval, fval, intv1);
25        gettimeofday(& time1, NULL);
26        for (rept = 0; rept < REPEAT; rept ++)
27          { fval = fib2(nval); }
28        gettimeofday(& time2, NULL);
29        intv2 = (time2.tv_sec - time1.tv_sec) +
30          1e-6 * (time2.tv_usec - time1.tv_usec);
31        printf("fib2(%2d) = %ld, time = %f\n", nval, fval, intv2);
32        printf("ratio = %f\n", intv1/intv2);
33      }
34    return EXIT_SUCCESS;
35  }
```

This program uses `gettimeofday` to measure the execution time of the two functions. The function `gettimeofday` returns the time, expressed in seconds and microseconds, since 1970-01-01 00:00:00 (UTC). The two values are stored in a *structure* called `struct` in C programs. Structures will be discussed in great detail later in this book. This program measures the difference of the time before and after calculating Fibonacci numbers. The method for measuring a function's execution time is (1) get the current time, call it $t1$, (2) call the function, and (3) get the current time, call it $t2$. The execution time of this function is $t2 - t1$. This method of measuring execution time has limitations. The time $t1$ and $t2$ have finite precision. If this function's execution time is too short, $t2 - t1$ will be too small (possibly zero). To obtain acceptable accuracy, the execution time needs to be much longer than the precision. For `gettimeofday`, the precision is microseconds; thus, the execution time should be much longer than one microsecond. This is the reason why the program calls the functions calculating Fibonacci numbers multiple times between calling `gettimeofday`. The values may be slightly different when the program is run multiple times because the computer also runs many other programs. This is the last few lines of the program's output:

```
fib (18) = 2584, time = 5.678572
fib2(18) = 2584, time = 0.005474
ratio = 1037.371704
fib (19) = 4181, time = 9.399386
fib2(19) = 4181, time = 0.005677
ratio = 1655.696045
fib (20) = 6765, time = 15.530513
fib2(20) = 6765, time = 0.007862
ratio = 1975.389648
```

As you can see, the ratios of the execution time grow from 1037 to 1975 when **n** grows from 18 to 20. Why is there such a large difference in the execution time? Figure 14.1 (b) illustrates the sequence of computation. For the first function, to compute $f(5)$, it is necessary to compute $f(4)$ and $f(3)$. To compute $f(4)$, it is necessary to compute $f(3)$ and $f(2)$. Computing each value requires the sum of two values, until reaching the base cases. By definition,

$$\begin{cases} f(n) = f(n-1) + f(n-2) \\ f(n-1) = f(n-2) + f(n-3) \end{cases} \tag{14.3}$$

Therefore,

$$\begin{aligned} f(n) &= f(n-1) & + & \quad f(n-2) \\ &= 2f(n-2) & + & \quad f(n-3) \\ &= 2(f(n-3) & + & \quad f(n-4)) & + & \quad f(n-3) \\ &= 3f(n-3) & + & \quad 2f(n-4) \\ &= 3(f(n-4) & + & \quad f(n-5)) & + & \quad 2f(n-4) \\ &= 5f(n-4) & + & \quad 3f(n-5) \\ &= 5(f(n-5) & + & \quad f(n-6)) & + & \quad 3f(n-5) \\ &= 8f(n-5) & + & \quad 5f(n-6) \\ &= 8(f(n-6) & + & \quad f(n-7)) & + & \quad 5f(n-6) \\ &= 13f(n-6) & + & \quad 8f(n-7). \end{aligned} \tag{14.4}$$

Table 14.1 lists the coefficients for computing $f(n)$. The coefficient of $f(n-k)$ is actually $f(k+1)$. Table 14.1 and Figure 14.1 (b) both express similar concepts. Figure 14.1 computes $f(5)$ so n is 5 and $f(2)$ is $f(n-3)$. The coefficient for $f(n-3)$ is 3. If we count the occurrences of $f(2)$ in Figure 14.1 (b), we find that it is called three times.

The recursive method for calculating Fibonacci numbers is slower because it computes the same value over and over again. When computing $f(n-1)$, it has to compute $f(n-2)$. However, the recursive function does not remember the value for $f(n-2)$ and then computes the value again later. As n becomes larger, the function performs more and more redundant computation and becomes slower and slower.

Does this mean recursion is bad? Does this mean that recursion is slow? Why should we even bother to learn recursion? The problem is not recursion, but the example. Recursion can be fast in some efficient algorithms explained later in this book (such as quick sort). If you have a nail and a knife, you will find that hitting the nail with a knife is difficult. Does this mean a knife is bad? If you need to hit a nail, you need a hammer. A knife is a bad tool for hitting a nail. If you want to cut paper, a knife is better than a hammer. A hammer is not better than a knife and a knife is not better than a hammer. They are different. One is better than the other in some scenarios. Some books do not explain that *this particular* top-down method is slower than *this* bottom-up method. As a result some people mistakenly think recursion is slow by generalizing this example. Some other books mention that this top-down method is slower than the bottom-up method without further explanation. These books give readers the impression that recursion is slow.

TABLE 14.1: Coefficients for computing $f(n-k)$.

function	coefficient	
f(n - 1)	1	$f(2)$
f(n - 2)	2	$f(3)$
f(n - 3)	3	$f(4)$
f(n - 4)	5	$f(5)$
f(n - 5)	8	$f(6)$
f(n - 6)	13	$f(7)$

The truth is that recursion is a good approach for *some* problems, not all.

Let's go back to the Fibonacci numbers. Equation (14.4) suggests the following:

$$f(n) \quad = f(x+1)f(n-x) + f(x)f(n-x-1) \tag{14.5}$$

Suppose n is an even number: $n = 2m$ and set x to m. The equation is rewritten as

$$\begin{aligned} f(2m) &= f(m+1)f(2m-m) + f(m)f(2m-m-1) \\ &= f(m+1)f(m) + f(m)f(m-1) \end{aligned} \tag{14.6}$$

This means that $f(2m)$ can be calculated by using $f(m+1)$, $f(m)$, and $f(m-1)$ without going through $f(2m-1)$, $f(2m-2)$, and so on. This method can calculate the Fibonacci numbers much faster. Similarly, suppose n is an odd number: $n = 2m+1$ and set x to m, Equation (14.5) can be rewritten as

$$\begin{aligned} f(2m+1) &= f(m+1)f(2m+1-m) + f(m)f(2m+1-m-1) \\ &= f(m+1)f(m+1) + f(m)f(m) \end{aligned} \tag{14.7}$$

This recursive equation can be much faster because the argument drops fast: from $2m$ to $m+1$ and m, without going through $2m-1$, $2m-2$ ...

14.7 Performance Profiling with `gprof`

Many studies on software performance find that performance is generally dominated by just a few places. A general rule is "10% of the code consumes 90% of the time". Improving the correct 10% of code will have a noticeable impact on performance. Improving the other 90% of code will have negligible impact. The question is how to find the 10% of code. Guessing is not a good approach. Good tools can help identify that 10% of the code. A tool called `gprof` is designed specifically for this purpose. To use `gprof`, add `-pg` after `gcc` and execute the program as usual. For example:

```
$ gcc -Wall -Wshadow -pg fibonacci1.c fibonacci2.c fibmain.c  -o fibprog
```

Consider the Fibonacci functions referenced earlier. After running the program, a special file called `gmon.out` is generated. This file stores the profiling information for running the program and it is not readable using a text editor. Please use the `gprof` program to view the content in `gmon.out`. The command is:

```
$ gprof fibprog
```

The output is something like this:

```
index % time    self  children     called      name
                                                <spontaneous>
[1]     100.0    0.00    3.96                   main [1]
                 3.93    0.00 2000000/2000000       fib1 [2]
                 0.03    0.00 2000000/2000000       fib2 [3]
-----------------------------------------------------
                              3538000000               fib1 [2]
                 3.93    0.00 2000000/2000000       main [1]
[2]      99.2    3.93    0.00 2000000+3538000000 fib1 [2]
                              3538000000               fib1 [2]
-----------------------------------------------------
                 0.03    0.00 2000000/2000000       main [1]
[3]       0.8    0.03    0.00 2000000           fib2 [3]
-----------------------------------------------------
```

This output says that 99.2% of the time is spent on the function `fib1` and only 0.8% time is spent on the function `fib2`. The `main` function calls `fib1` 2,000,000 times (`REPEAT` × `MAXN`). In [2], the report says that `fib1` calls itself 3,538,000,000 times. In contrast, [4] says that `fib2` is called 2,000,000 times and it does not call itself. How can we use this information to help identify opportunities for improving performance? First, the report says more than 99% time is spent on `fib1`. This suggests that the function should be carefully inspected for better performance. Second, the report says that `main` calls `fib1` 2,000,000 and `fib1` calls itself 3,538,000,000 times, much more than the 2,000,000 invocations by `main`. This also suggests that `fib1` calls itself excessively and is a candidate for performance improvement.

14.8 Problems

14.8.1 Count Number of Calls: Original Definition

Write a program that counts how many times `fib1` is called when n is between 2 and 40 when using the definition in (14.2).

```c
// CH14:countfib1.c
#include <stdio.h>
#include <stdlib.h>
long int fib(int n, long int * count)
{
  (* count) ++;
  if (n == 1) { return 1; }
  if (n == 2) { return 1; }
  long int a = fib(n - 1, count);
  long int b = fib(n - 2, count);
  return (a + b);
}
int main(int argc, char * * argv)
{
  int n;
  for (n = 2; n <= 40; n ++)
    {
      long int count = 0;
      long int result = fib(n, & count);
      printf("n = %d, result = %ld, count = %ld\n", n, result, count);
    }
  return EXIT_SUCCESS;
}
```

14.8.2 Count Number of Calls: Efficient Recursion

Write a program that counts how many times `fib2` is called when n is between 2 and 30 when using the definition in (14.6) and (14.7).

```
1   // CH14:countfib2.c
2   #include <stdio.h>
3   #include <stdlib.h>
4   long int fib(int n, long int * count)
5   {
6     (* count) ++;
7     if (n == 1) { return 1; }
8     if (n == 2) { return 1; }
9     long int a;
10    long int b;
11    int m = n / 2;
12    if ((n % 2) == 0) // n is even number
13      {
14        // a = fib(m + 1, count); // no need to call fib
15        b = fib(m, count);
16        long int c = fib(m - 1, count);
17        a = b + c; // compute a from b and c
18        return (a * b + b * c);
19      }
20    // n is odd number
21    a = fib(m + 1, count);
22    b = fib(m, count);
23    return (a * a + b * b);
24  }
25  int main(int argc, char * * argv)
26  {
27    int n;
28    for (n = 2; n <= 30; n ++)
29      {
30        long int count = 0;
31        long int result = fib(n, & count);
32        printf("n = %d, result = %ld, count = %ld\n", n, result, count);
33      }
34    return EXIT_SUCCESS;
35  }
```

14.8.3 Parentheses

Write a program that can generate all possible orders of parentheses based on the rules described on page 148.

```
1   // CH14:parentheses.c
2   #include <stdio.h>
3   #include <stdlib.h>
4   void generate(char * parentheses, int num, int left, int right)
5   {
6     // num: total number of pairs
7     // left: how many left parentheses have been used
8     // right: how many right parentheses have been used
9     int ind = left + right;
```

```
10    if (left == num)    // use up all '('
11      {
12        for (int i = 0; i < ind; i ++) { printf("%c", parentheses[i]); }
13        // use all remaining ')'
14        for (int i = right; i < num; i ++) { printf(")");          }
15        printf("\n");
16        return;
17      }
18    // case 1: add '('. always possible because left < num
19    parentheses[ind] = '(';
20    generate(parentheses, num, left + 1, right);
21    // case 2: check whether ')' can be added
22    // allowed only if left > right
23    if (left > right)
24      {
25        parentheses[ind] = ')';
26        generate(parentheses, num, left, right + 1);
27      }
28  }
29  int main(int argc, char * * argv)
30  {
31    if (argc < 2) { return EXIT_FAILURE; }
32    int num = (int) strtol(argv[1], NULL, 10);   // num: how many pairs
33    if (num < 1)  { return EXIT_FAILURE; }
34    char * parentheses = malloc(sizeof (* parentheses) * num * 2);
35    generate(parentheses, num, 0, 0);
36    free (parentheses);
37    return EXIT_SUCCESS;
38  }
```

14.8.4   Fibonacci Numbers

Prove Equation(14.5) is true.

Chapter 15

Integer Partition

The previous two chapters explained how to obtain the formula for partitioning integers and also how to write a C program that implements the formula. This chapter explains how to print the partitions and also introduces some variations on the problem.

15.1 Print Partitions

The following program prints the partitions for an integer that is specified on the command line (`argv[1]`).

```
1   // CH15:printpartition.c
2   #include <stdio.h>
3   #include <stdlib.h>
4   #include <string.h>
5   void printPartition(int * arr, int length)
6   {
7     int ind;
8     for (ind = 0; ind < length - 1; ind ++)
9       { printf("%d + ", arr[ind]); }
10    printf("%d\n", arr[length - 1]);
11  }
12  void partition(int * arr, int ind, int left)
13  {
14    int val;
15    if (left == 0)
16      {
17        printPartition(arr, ind);
18        return; // not necessary
19      }
20    for (val = 1; val <= left; val ++) // start at 1, not 0
21      {
22        arr[ind] = val;
23        partition(arr, ind + 1, left - val);
24        // RL1 (return location 1)
25      }
26  }
27  int main(int argc, char * argv[])
28  {
29    if (argc != 2) { return EXIT_FAILURE; }
```

DOI: 10.1201/9781003257981-15

```
30    int n = (int) strtol(argv[1], NULL, 10);
31    if (n <= 0) { return EXIT_FAILURE; }
32    int * arr;
33    arr = malloc(sizeof(int) * n);
34    partition(arr, 0, n);
35    // RL2 (return location 2)
36    free (arr);
37    return EXIT_SUCCESS;
38  }
```

This is the program's output when given 4 as the argument:

```
1 + 1 + 1 + 1
1 + 1 + 2
1 + 2 + 1
1 + 3
2 + 1 + 1
2 + 2
3 + 1
4
```

The partition function is the core of this program. This function takes three arguments:

1. arr is an array storing the numbers used in a given partition.
2. ind is an integer. It is an index of the array. The value indicates where the next element will be written. It also gives the length of the partition so far.
3. left is an integer. It is the remaining value to be partitioned.

The terminating condition is when the value to partition (i.e., left as the third argument) is zero (line 15). When this condition is met, the program prints the partition. Please notice that ind (line 17) indicates how many array elements are used. The printPartition function prints only the used elements. The return statement at line 18 is unnecessary. When left is zero, the function will not enter the for loop of line 20 because this loop starts at one. Adding this return makes the program easier to read. This for loop chooses a number between 1 and left as the number to use. The remaining number is left - val and this value is sent to the partition function again. Since val is at least one, left - val is smaller than left. Thus, the third argument of the recursive call becomes smaller and eventually reaches zero.

15.2   Stack and Heap Memory

Understanding the stack memory is essential for understanding recursion. Even though this program is short, it reviews many important concepts explained earlier. Thus, it is worth explaining in detail. When main calls partition, ind is zero—the index of the first element of the array. The value left is the remaining value to be partitioned.

Table 15.1 is the call stack and the heap memory after entering the function partition, at line 13. The table assumes that each integer occupies 4 bytes (sizeof(int) is 4). Each pointer (such as `arr` and the return location) occupies 8 bytes. To make the frames easier to read, each frame starts at an address that is a multiple of 100.

TABLE 15.1: Call stack and heap memory after entering `partition` at line 13.

Frame	Symbol	Address	Value	Symbol	Address	Value
	val	224	garbage			
	left	220	4	arr[3]	10012	garbage
partition	ind	216	0	arr[2]	10008	garbage
	arr	208	A10000	arr[1]	10004	garbage
	RL	200	RL2	arr[0]	10000	garbage
main	arr	104	A10000			
	n	100	4			

Stack Memory Heap Memory

TABLE 15.2: Memory after finishing line 22.

Frame	Symbol	Address	Value	Symbol	Address	Value
	val	224	1			
	left	220	4	arr[3]	10012	garbage
partition	ind	216	0	arr[2]	10008	garbage
	arr	208	A10000	arr[1]	10004	garbage
	RL	200	RL2	arr[0]	10000	→ 1
main	arr	104	A10000			
	n	100	4			

Stack Memory Heap Memory

Suppose the value of `n` is 4. The value of `left` is not zero and the terminating condition at line 15 is false. The function continues to the `for` loop at lines 20–25. In this `for` loop, `val` iterates from 1 to `left`. The value of `val` starts at 1. Thus line 22 first assigns 1 to `arr[0]`. Table 15.2 shows the call stack and the heap memory after finishing line 22. The function then calls itself at line 23. Please notice the values of `ind` and `left`. The index has changed from 0 to 1 because line 23 uses `ind + 1`. This is the next position in `arr` for the next value. In the recursive call, the function needs to partition 3 because `left - val` is 3. Please pay attention to the top frame of the call stack. Table 15.3 shows two frames of `partition`. One is called by `main` (please notice the return location RL2). The other is called by `partition` (please notice the return location RL1).

The value of `left` decreases in each call and eventually reaches 0. The terminating condition at line 15 is true. This means that we have reached the base case. Line 17 calls `printPartition` and prints the 4 elements in the array. Four elements are printed because `ind` is 4. Remember, `ind` gives the next position to write an element into `arr`, and it also gives the length of the partition so far. Therefore, we can pass `ind` as the length of the array to `printPartition`. The program now prints:

```
1 + 1 + 1 + 1
```

The function then returns because of line 18. After meeting the terminating condition, the top frame of the call stack is popped, and the program continues at RL1.

For the next iteration, `val` increments to two, as shown in Table 15.4. This violates the condition `val <= left` and the `for` loop exists. Since the function has nothing else to do after the `for` loop, the top frame is popped. The program now continues at line 23. The `for`

TABLE 15.3: Line 23 calls `partition` itself. The second and third arguments (`ind` and `left`) have changed.

Frame	Symbol	Address	Value	Symbol	Address	Value
	val	324	garbage			
	left	320	→ **3**			
partition	ind	316	→ **1**			
	arr	308	A10000			
	RL	300	RL1			
	val	224	1			
	left	220	4	arr[3]	10012	garbage
partition	ind	216	0	arr[2]	10008	garbage
	arr	208	A10000	arr[1]	10004	garbage
	RL	200	RL2	arr[0]	10000	1
main	arr	104	10000			
	n	100	4			

Stack Memory.

loop enters the next iteration: `val` becomes 2 and the condition `val <= left` is satisfied. Line 22 assigns 2 to `arr[2]` and line 23 calls the function itself again. Because `left` is zero, the terminating condition at line 15 is true. The program prints the first 3 elements (because `ind` is 3) in `arr`. The program prints:

```
1 + 1 + 2
```

Line 18 returns and the top frame is popped. The next iteration increments `val` to 3 but the condition `val <= left` is not satisfied. The function exits the `for` loop. Since the function has nothing else to do after the `for` loop, the function returns and the top frame is popped. For the next iteration, `val` becomes 2 and assigns 2 to `arr[1]`.

Please follow the changes in the stack and heap memory closely and ensure that you fully understand. Our experience suggests that some people do not understand recursion because they do not understand how recursion modifies memory.

15.3 Trace Recursive Function Calls

One way to understand a program is to draw its *call tree*. A call tree is a graphical representation of the relationship between function calls. Figure 14.1 (b) already shows an example of a call tree. This tree is drawn "inverted" with the root at the top, and the leaves at the bottom. Consider the following example; Figure 15.1(a) illustrates the calling relation of the two functions.

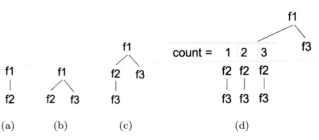

FIGURE 15.1: Call trees.

TABLE 15.4: After printing 1 + 1 + 1 + 1, the top frame is popped. Each element in the array (in heap memory) stores 1.

Frame	Symbol	Address	Value	Symbol	Address	Value
	val	524	→ **2**			
	left	520	1			
partition	ind	516	3			
	arr	508	A10000			
	RL	500	RL1			
	val	424	1			
	left	420	2			
partition	ind	416	2			
	arr	408	A10000			
	RL	400	RL1			
	val	324	1			
	left	320	3			
partition	ind	316	1			
	arr	308	A10000			
	RL	300	RL1			
	val	224	1			
	left	220	4	arr[3]	10012	1
partition	ind	216	0	arr[2]	10008	1
	arr	208	A10000	arr[1]	10004	1
	RL	200	RL2	arr[0]	10000	1
main	arr	104	10000			
	n	100	4			

Stack Memory.

```
void f1()
{
    f2();
}
```

Figure 15.1 (b) shows the calling relations:

```
void f1()
{
    f2();
    f3();
}
```

The third example is shown in Figure 15.1(c).

```
1  void f1()
2  {
3      f2();
4      f3();
5  }
6  void f2()
7  {
8      f3();
9  }
```

Figure 15.1 (d) adds a `for` loop to the function `f1`.

```
1   void f1()
2   {
3     int count;
4     for (count = 1; count < 4; count ++)
5     {
6         f2();
7     }
8     f3();
9   }
10  void f2()
11  {
12    f3();
13  }
```

Next, let's consider the the `partition` function:

```
12  void partition(int * arr, int ind, int left)
13  {
14    int val;
15    if (left == 0)
16      {
17        printPartition(arr, ind);
18        return; // not necessary
19      }
20    for (val = 1; val <= left; val ++) // start at 1, not 0
21      {
22        arr[ind] = val;
23        partition(arr, ind + 1, left - val);
24        // RL1 (return location 1)
25      }
26  }
```

When `left` is 3, then `val` can be 1, 2, or 3.

1. When `val` is 1, `left - val` is 2. Thus, `partition(arr, 1, 2)` is called.
2. When `val` is 2, `left - val` is 1. Thus, `partition(arr, 1, 1)` is called.
3. When `val` is 3, `left - val` is 0. Thus, `partition(arr, 1, 0)` is called.

When `left` is 2, `val` can be 1 or 2. The calling relationship is illustrated in Figure 15.2. The call tree is a different way to help understand the calling relation. It is a higher-level representation than the call stack because each call is represented by arguments and we do not need to examine all of the addresses and values used in each call.

15.4   Generate Partitions with Restrictions

The program at the beginning of this chapter prints all possible partitions. This section explains how to change the program such that it generates partitions with restrictions, for

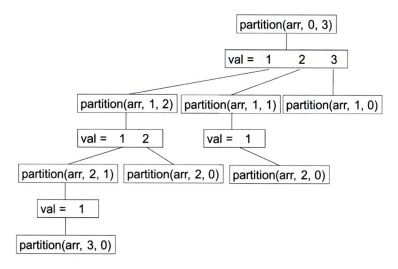

FIGURE 15.2: Graphical illustration of `partition` when the value of `left` starts at 3.

example, partitioning with odd numbers or using sequences of increasing numbers. One simple solution is to check whether the restrictions have been satisfied before printing. Before printing anything, the function checks whether this partition is valid satisfying the restriction. For example, if we are partitioning with odd numbers only, `printPartition` can be modified as follows:

```
void printPartition(int * arr, int length)
{
    // if an even number is used, do not print anything
    int ind;
    for (ind = 0; ind < length; ind ++)
      {
         if ((arr[ind] % 2) == 0) // even number is used
           { return; }
      }
    for (ind = 0; ind < length - 1; ind ++)
       { printf("%d + ", arr[ind]); }
    printf("%d\n", arr[length - 1]);
}
```

If the number to be partitioned is large, the method may generate a sequence like 2 + 1 + 1 ... and discard the sequence before it is printed.

To check whether the numbers form an increasing sequence:

```
void printPartition(int * arr, int length)
{
    int ind;
    for (ind = 0; ind < length - 1; ind ++)
      {
         if (arr[ind] >= arr[ind + 1]) // not increasing
           { return; }
      }
```

```
  for (ind = 0; ind < length - 1; ind ++)
    { printf("%d + ", arr[ind]); }
  printf("%d\n", arr[length - 1]);
}
```

However, checking before printing is inefficient because many invalid partitions have already been generated. Instead, a more efficient solution generates only valid partitions *before* calling `printPartition`. This section explains how to generate valid partitions satisfying one of the following restrictions: (1) using odd numbers only, (2) using increasing numbers, and (3) using alternating odd and even numbers.

15.4.1 Using Odd Numbers Only

It is more efficient if the function `partition` generates only partitions that meet the criteria. If only odd numbers are used, `val` can be an odd number only.

```
void partition(int * arr, int ind, int left)
{
  int val;
  if (left == 0)
    {
      printPartition(arr, ind);
      return;
    }
  for (val = 1; val <= left; val += 2) // odd numbers only
    {
      arr[ind] = val;
      partition(arr, ind + 1, left - val);
    }
}
```

This will generate only valid partitions. This is much more efficient than the earlier method.

15.4.2 Using Sequences of Increasing Numbers

To generate partitions using increasing numbers, the smallest value of `val` must be greater than the most recently used value stored in `arr`. If `ind` is zero, then no previously used value is stored in `arr`, and `val` can start from one.

```
void partition(int * arr, int ind, int left)
{
  int val;
  if (left == 0)
    {
      printPartition(arr, ind);
      return;
    }
  int min = 1;
  if (ind != 0)
```

```
        {
          min = arr[ind - 1] + 1;
        }
      for (val = min; val <= left; val ++)
        {
          arr[ind] = val;
          partition(arr, ind + 1, left - val);
        }
}
```

15.4.3 Using Alternating Odd and Even Numbers

To generate alternating odd and even numbers, the function must check whether `ind` is zero. If `ind` is zero, `val` can be either odd or even. If `ind` is greater than zero, then the function needs to check `arr[ind - 1]`. If `arr[ind - 1]` is odd, then `val` must be an even number. If `arr[ind - 1]` is even, then `val` must be an odd number.

```
void partition(int * arr, int ind, int left)
{
  int val;
  if (left == 0)
    {
      printPartition(arr, ind);
      return;
    }
  for (val = 1; val <= left; val ++)
    {
      int valid = 0;
      if (ind == 0)
        { valid = 1; } // no restriction for the first number
      else
        {
          // if arr[ind - 1] % 2) == (val % 2): both even or both odd
          valid = (arr[ind - 1] % 2) != (val % 2);
        }
      if (valid == 1)
        {
          arr[ind] = val;
          partition(arr, ind + 1, left - val);
        }
    }
}
```

As you can see, with only a few small changes, the program can print the solutions for the integer partition problem under different restrictions.

15.5 Problems

15.5.1 Even Numbers Only

Write a program that prints the partitions of an integer using only even numbers.

15.5.2 Decreasing Values

Write a program that prints the partitions of an integer using decreasing values.

15.5.3 Error in `partition`

Replace `<=` in

```
20  for (val = 1; val <= left; val ++) // start at 1, not 0
```

on Page 166 by

```
20  for (val = 1; val < left; val ++)  // <, not <=
```

How many partitions will be printed when n is 10 in `main`? Explain the reason.

15.5.4 Error in `partition`

Replace `val = 1` in

```
20  for (val = 1; val <= left; val ++) // start at 1, not 0
```

on Page 166 by

```
20  for (val = 0; val <= left; val ++)  // start at 0
```

How many partitions will be printed when n is 10 in `main`? Explain the reason.

15.5.5 Error in `partition`

Can `ind + 1` in

```
23  partition(arr, ind + 1, left - val);
```

on page 166 be replaced by

```
23  partition(arr, ++ind , left - val); // replace ind + 1 by ++ ind
```

Explain the reason.

Chapter 16

Programming Problems Using Recursion

This chapter describes several problems that can be solved using recursion.

16.1 Binary Search

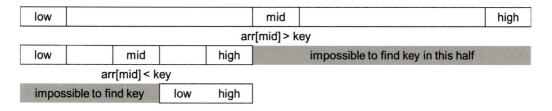

FIGURE 16.1: Steps of Binary Search.

A binary search is an efficient way to search for a value in a sorted array. The function `search` returns the index of the `key` within `arr`. If `arr` does not contain this `key`, then the function returns −1. The arguments mean the following:

- `arr`: an array of integers. The elements are distinct and sorted in the ascending order.
- `len`: the length of the array, i.e., the number of elements in the array.
- `key`: the value to search for. Think of `key` as the proverbial needle in the haystack.

Since the array is already sorted, it is possible to quickly discard many elements (nearly half) by comparing `key` with the element at the center of the array. If `key` is larger than that element, we do not need to search the lower part of the array, i.e., the part before the center element. If `key` is smaller than that element, we do not need to search the upper part of the array. These steps continue until either the index is found or it is impossible to find a match. Figure 16.1 is a graphical view of the steps: In each step, the binary search reduces the number of elements to search by half.

```c
// CH16:binarysearch.c
#include <stdio.h>
#include <stdlib.h>
#include <time.h>
#include <string.h>
#define RANGE 1000
int * arrGen(int size); // generate a sorted array of integers
static int binarySearchHelp(int * arr, int low, int high, int key)
{
```

```
10    if (low > high) // array has no element
11      { return -1; }
12    int ind = (low + high) / 2;
13    if (arr[ind] == key) // found
14      { return ind; }
15    if (arr[ind] > key) // discard arr[ind] to arr[high]
16      { return binarySearchHelp(arr, low, ind - 1, key); }
17    return binarySearchHelp(arr, ind + 1, high, key);
18 }
19 int binarySearch(int * arr, int len, int key)
20 {
21    return binarySearchHelp(arr, 0, len - 1, key);
22 }
23 void printArray(int * arr, int len);
24 int main(int argc, char * * argv)
25 {
26    if (argc < 2)
27      {
28        printf("need a positive integer\n");
29        return EXIT_FAILURE;
30      }
31    int num = strtol(argv[1], NULL, 10);
32    if (num <= 0)
33      {
34        printf("need a positive integer\n");
35        return EXIT_FAILURE;
36      }
37    int * arr = arrGen(num);
38    printArray(arr, num);
39    int count;
40    for (count = 0; count < 10; count ++)
41      {
42        int key;
43        if ((count % 2) == 0)
44          { key = arr[rand() % num]; }
45        else
46          { key = rand() % 100000; }
47        printf("search(%d), result = %d\n", key,
48               binarySearch(arr, num, key));
49      }
50    free (arr);
51    return EXIT_SUCCESS;
52 }
53 int * arrGen(int size)
54 {
55    if (size <= 0) { return NULL; }
56    int * arr = malloc(sizeof(int) * size);
57    if (arr == NULL) { return NULL; }
58    srand(time(NULL)); // set the seed
59    int ind;
```

```
60    arr[0] = rand() % RANGE;
61    for (ind = 1; ind < size; ind ++) // increasing values
62      { arr[ind] = arr[ind - 1] + (rand() % RANGE) + 1; }
63    return arr;
64  }
65  void printArray(int * arr, int len)
66  {
67    int ind;
68    for (ind = 0; ind < len; ind ++) { printf("%d ", arr[ind]); }
69    printf("\n\n");
70  }
```

This program introduces the concept of *helper* functions. Helper functions are common in recursion for organizing the arguments. In this example, `binarySearch` has three arguments: (1) the array's starting address, (2) the length, and (3) the key. The recursive function requires four arguments. Instead of passing the array's length, two arguments indicate the contiguous part of the array that remains to be searched. The range is expressed with two arguments: `low` and `high`. Adding `static` in front of `binarySearchHelp` means that this function can be called within the same file; this function is invisible outside this file.

Please pay attention to how the range changes in recursive calls: The range must shrink in each call. This ensures that the recursive calls eventually reach a stop condition. Line 12 uses integer division: If `low + high` is an odd number, then the remainder is discarded because `ind` is an integer. Line 16 uses `ind - 1` for the new high index, not `ind`, because `ind - 1` ensures that the range shrinks. When `low` is the same as `high`, `ind` is also the same. If line 16 uses `ind`, then the next recursive call still has `low` and `high` unchanged and the recursion will not end. Similarly, in line 17 the low index must be `ind + 1`, not `ind`. Another common mistake is using `if (low >= high)` for the condition at line 10. When the array has only one element, `low` is the same as `high`. This function returns −1 without checking whether this single element is the same as `key` (line 13).

16.2   Quick Sort

Section 8.2 explained how to use the `qsort` function. This section explains the algorithm of quick sort. Quick sort uses transitivity: If $x > y$ and $y > z$, then $x > z$. The algorithm first selects one element from the array as a reference. This element is called the *pivot*. It can be any element in the array. Some implementations use the first or last element; some implementations use a randomly selected element. After selecting the pivot, the algorithm divides the array into three parts: (1) elements smaller than the pivot, (2) equal to the pivot, and (3) greater than the pivot. The values in (1) and (3) will not be compared again. The algorithm then recursively sorts parts (1) and (3). The program stops when all elements have been sorted. This occurs when each part has only one element or no element at all. This is the method to divide the array into three parts:

1. Determine the value of the pivot. Suppose the first element is used.
2. Go through the elements using two indexes called `low` and `high`. The initial value of `low` is one higher than the index of the pivot. The initial value of `high` is the largest index of the range being considered.

3. From the left side (i.e., smallest index), if an element is smaller than the pivot, `low` increments. If an element is greater than the pivot, stop changing `low`.
4. From the right side (i.e., the largest index), if an element is greater than the pivot, `high` decrements. If an element is smaller than the pivot, stop changing `high`.
5. Now swap the elements whose indexes are `low` and `high`.
6. Continue steps 3 to 4 until `low` is greater than `high`.
7. Put the pivot between the two parts.

After these steps, the elements are ordered into the three parts. The following figure illustrates the procedure. The pivot is 19, `low` is 1, and `high` is 11.

index	0	1	2	3	4	5	6	7	8	9	10	11
value	19	7	12	23	8	31	6	42	28	16	51	33
variable	pivot	low										high

Because 7 is smaller than 19, `low` increments.

index	0	1	2	3	4	5	6	7	8	9	10	11
value	19	7	12	23	8	31	6	42	28	16	51	33
variable	pivot		low									high

The next value, 12, is also smaller than 19, and `low` increments again. The next value is 23 and it is greater than 19. Thus, `low` stops incrementing.

index	0	1	2	3	4	5	6	7	8	9	10	11
value	19	7	12	23	8	31	6	42	28	16	51	33
variable	pivot			low								high

Now, check the value at the `high` index. The value is 33, greater than the pivot 19, and `high` decrements.

index	0	1	2	3	4	5	6	7	8	9	10	11
value	19	7	12	23	8	31	6	42	28	16	51	33
variable	pivot			low							high	

Since 51 is also greater than 19, `high` decrements again.

index	0	1	2	3	4	5	6	7	8	9	10	11
value	19	7	12	23	8	31	6	42	28	16	51	33
variable	pivot			low						high		

At this moment, the value whose index is `low` is greater than the pivot. The value whose index is `high` is smaller than the pivot. Now we swap these two values.

index	0	1	2	3	4	5	6	7	8	9	10	11
value	19	7	12	16	8	31	6	42	28	23	51	33
variable	pivot			low						high		

Continuing the algorithm, the value of `low` increases because 16 is smaller than 19.

index	0	1	2	3	4	5	6	7	8	9	10	11
value	19	7	12	16	8	31	6	42	28	23	51	33
variable	pivot				low					high		

Because 8 is smaller than 19, `low` increments again.

index	0	1	2	3	4	5	6	7	8	9	10	11
value	19	7	12	16	8	31	6	42	28	23	51	33
variable	pivot					low				high		

Because 31 is greater than 19, `low` stops here. Since 23 is greater than the pivot, `high` decrements.

index	0	1	2	3	4	5	6	7	8	9	10	11
value	19	7	12	16	8	31	6	42	28	23	51	33
variable	pivot					low			high			

The index `high` decrements twice more, and the value at `high` is 6.

index	0	1	2	3	4	5	6	7	8	9	10	11
value	19	7	12	16	8	31	6	42	28	23	51	33
variable	pivot					low	high					

Now the values at `low` and `high` are swapped.

index	0	1	2	3	4	5	6	7	8	9	10	11
value	19	7	12	16	8	6	31	42	28	23	51	33
variable	pivot					low	high					

If `low` increments, it will meet `high`. This means that the array has been divided into three parts: (1) the first element, which is the pivot, (2) the part that is smaller than the pivot, and (3) the part that is greater than the pivot. Now the values at `low` and the pivot are swapped.

index	0	1	2	3	4	5	6	7	8	9	10	11
value	6	7	12	16	8	19	31	42	28	23	51	33
variable						low	high					

The algorithm next sorts the part smaller than the pivot using the same procedure.

index	0	1	2	3	4
value	6	7	12	16	8
variable	pivot	low			high

The algorithm also sorts the part greater than the pivot using the same procedure.

index	6	7	8	9	10	11
value	31	42	28	23	51	33
variable	pivot	low				high

A sample implementation of quick sort is shown below. The function `quickSort` takes only two arguments: the array and its length. The recursive function needs three arguments: the array and the range of indexes to be sorted. Thus, a helper function called `quickSortHelp` is created. This helper function divides the array elements in the specified range into three parts and recursively sorts the first and the third parts.

```c
// CH16:quicksort.c
#include <stdio.h>
#include <stdlib.h>
#include <time.h>
#include <string.h>
#define RANGE      10000
static void swap(int * a, int * b)
{
  int s = * a;
  * a = * b;
  * b = s;
}
static void quickSortHelp(int * arr, int first, int last)
{
  // [first, last]: range of valid indexes (not last - 1)
  if (first >= last) { return; } // no need to sort one or no element
  int pivot = arr[first];
  int low = first + 1;
  int high = last;
  while (low < high)
    {
      while ((low < last) && (arr[low] <= pivot)) // <=, not <
        {
          // <= so that low will increment when arr[low] is the same
          // as pivot, using < will stop incrementing low when
          // arr[low] is the same as pivot and the outer while loop
          // may not stop
          low ++;
        }
      while ((first < high) && (arr[high] > pivot)) // >, not >=
        { high --; }
      if (low < high)
        { swap (& arr[low], & arr[high]);          }
    }
  if (pivot > arr[high]) // move the pivot to the right place
    { swap(& arr[first], & arr[high]); }
  quickSortHelp(arr, first, high - 1);
  quickSortHelp(arr, low, last);
}
void quickSort(int * arr, int len)
{
  quickSortHelp(arr, 0, len - 1);
}
int * arrGen(int size)
// generate an array of integers
{
  if (size <= 0) { return NULL; }
  int * arr = malloc(sizeof(int) * size);
  if (arr == NULL)
    { return NULL; }
```

```
51    int ind;
52    for (ind = 0; ind < size; ind ++)
53       { arr[ind] = rand() % RANGE; }
54    return arr;
55  }
56  void printArray(int * arr, int len)
57  {
58    int ind;
59    int sorted = 1;
60    for (ind = 0; ind < len; ind ++)
61      {
62  #ifdef DEBUG
63        printf("%d ", arr[ind]);
64  #endif
65        if ((ind > 0) && (arr[ind] < arr[ind -1]))
66          { sorted = 0;}
67      }
68    printf("\nsorted = %d\n\n", sorted);
69  }
70  int main(int argc, char * * argv)
71  {
72    if (argc < 2)
73      {
74        printf("need a positive integer\n");
75        return EXIT_FAILURE;
76      }
77    if (argc == 3)
78      { srand(strtol(argv[2], NULL, 10)); }
79    else { srand(time(NULL)); }
80    int num = strtol(argv[1], NULL, 10);
81    if (num <= 0)
82      {
83        printf("need a positive integer\n");
84        return EXIT_FAILURE;
85      }
86    int * arr = arrGen(num);
87    printArray(arr, num);
88    quickSort(arr, num);
89    printArray(arr, num);
90    free (arr);
91    return EXIT_SUCCESS;
92  }
```

This program may appear straightforward. A closer look, however, reveals that some common mistakes may occur. The helper function's second and third arguments specify the range of indexes that are being sorted. This function assumes `last` is a valid index and `quickSort` thus must use `len - 1` at line 42. If this line uses `len`, then the program may access an invalid memory location because `len` is not a valid index. Next, consider line 22 (`arr[low] <= pivot`). If it is rewritten as `arr[low] < pivot`, this small difference may cause problems when some of the array's elements have the same value as the pivot. When this occurs and the line has no =, `low` does not increment. If `arr[high]` is smaller than the pivot, then `high` does not decrement. As a result, neither `low` nor `high` change and the recursive call does not end because `low < high` is always true.

If the original array is already sorted, then the first element is always the smallest and part (1) is empty. As a result, the algorithm does not take advantage of transitivity. Some implementations of quick sort randomly select one array element for the pivot, instead of the first. Using a randomly selected element for the pivot reduces the chance of the pivot being the smallest element.

16.3   Permutations and Combinations

Permutation means selecting distinct objects and the orders matter. Suppose there are four distinct objects: A, B, C, and D. There are four ways to select the first object: A, B, C, or D. After the first object is selected, three objects are available for the second object. Then, two objects are available. After selecting three objects, only one is available. There are $4 \times 3 \times 2 \times 1 = 24$ ways to select four objects as shown in Table 16.1. The first column selects A as the first object; the second column selects B as the first object.

TABLE 16.1:   Twenty four ways to select four objects.

A B C D	B A C D	C A B D	D A B C
A B D C	B A D C	C A D B	D A C B
A C B D	B C A D	C B A D	D B A C
A C D B	B C D A	C B D A	D B C A
A D B C	B D A C	C D A B	D C A B
A D C B	B D C A	C D B A	D C B A

Permutations can be generated using recursion with the following method. Swap the first item with any of the later locations, and then swap the second item with any of the later locations, and so on. The first item, A, may appear in the first, second, third, or fourth location. Every time A moves, it is swapped with the item originally at that location. The second item, B, may also appear in the first, second, third, or fourth column.

```c
// CH16:permute.c
#include <stdio.h>
#include <stdlib.h>
#include <string.h>
void printArray(int * arr, int length)
{
  int ind;
  for (ind = 0; ind < length - 1; ind ++)
    { printf("%c ", arr[ind]); }
  printf("%c\n", arr[length - 1]);
}
void swap(int * a, int * b)
{
  int s = * a;
  * a = * b;
  * b = s;
}
void permuteHelp(int * arr, int ind, int num)
```

```
19   {
20     if (ind == num)
21       {
22         printArray(arr, ind);
23         return;
24       }
25     int loc; // destination of arr[ind]
26     for (loc = ind; loc < num; loc ++)
27       {
28         swap(& arr[ind], & arr[loc]);
29         permuteHelp(arr, ind + 1, num);
30         swap(& arr[ind], & arr[loc]); // swap back
31       }
32   }
33   void permute(int * arr, int num)
34   {
35     permuteHelp(arr, 0, num);
36   }
37   int main(int argc, char * argv[])
38   {
39     if (argc != 2)
40       { return EXIT_FAILURE; }
41     int num = (int) strtol(argv[1], NULL, 10);
42     if (num <= 0)
43       { return EXIT_FAILURE; }
44     int * arr;
45     arr = malloc(sizeof(int) * num);
46     int ind;
47     for (ind = 0; ind < num; ind ++)
48       { arr[ind] = ind + 'A'; } // elements are 'A', 'B', ...
49     permute(arr, num);
50     free (arr);
51     return EXIT_SUCCESS;
52   }
```

Lines 26–31 are the core that generates the permutations. To understand how this works, please check the number of iterations generated. When `ind` is 0, the loop iterates `num` times. When `ind` is 1, the loop iterates `num - 1` times. When `ind` is 2, the loop iterates `num - 2` times. Finally, when `ind` is `num - 1`, the loop iterates only once. This program will iterate $num \times (num - 1) \times (num - 2) \ldots 1 = num!$ times.

TABLE 16.2: Six ways to select two out of four objects. This is a combination problem and the order does not matter: A B is the same as B A.

A B	A C	A D	B C	B D	C D

This is the number of permutations for `num` items. At line 28, `loc` starts at `ind`. When `loc` is `ind`, line 30 keeps the first element at the original location. Without this line, the first element will not stay in the original location. For example, if `A` is the first element, and `loc` starts at `ind + 1`, then `A` is always moved away from the first location, and no generated permutation will begin with A. As a result, the program will fail to generate all possible permutations.

Combination is a related but different problem. Combination selects one or more from a list of distinct objects without considering the orders. Suppose we want to select two objects from A, B, C, and D objects. Selecting A and B is the same as selecting B and A. Table 16.2 shows six ways to select two objects. An array is used to store whether a particular item is selected or not. For example, if arr[0] is 0, A is not selected. If arr[0] is 1, then A is selected. If arr[2] is 0, then C is not selected. If arr[2] is 1, then C is selected.

```c
1   // CH16:combine.c
2   #include <stdio.h>
3   #include <stdlib.h>
4   #include <string.h>
5   void printArray(int * arr, int length)
6   {
7     int ind;
8     for (ind = 0; ind < length; ind ++)
9       {
10        if (arr[ind] == 1)
11          { printf("%c ", ind + 'A'); }
12      }
13    printf("\n");
14  }
15  // arr: array storing whether an element is selected or not
16  // ind: index of the item being decided on whether it is selected
17  // num: the total number of items
18  // toselect: the number of items to be selected
19  // selected: the number of items already selected
20  void combineHelp(int * arr, int ind, int num, int toselect, int selected)
21  {
22    if (selected == toselect) // select enough items
23      {
24        printArray(arr, num);
25        return;
26      }
27    if (ind == num) // end of array, no more item to select
28      { return; }
29    // select this element
30    arr[ind] = 1;
31    combineHelp(arr, ind + 1, num, toselect, selected + 1);
32    // do not select this element
33    arr[ind] = 0;
34    combineHelp(arr, ind + 1, num, toselect, selected);
35  }
36  void combine(int * arr, int len, int toselect)
37  {
38    combineHelp(arr, 0, len, toselect, 0);
39  }
40  int main(int argc, char * argv[])
41  {
42    if (argc != 3)
```

```
43      { return EXIT_FAILURE; } // need two numbers
44    int num = (int) strtol(argv[1], NULL, 10);
45    if (num <= 0)
46      { return EXIT_FAILURE; }
47    int toselect = (int) strtol(argv[2], NULL, 10);
48    if ((toselect <= 0) || (toselect > num))
49      { return EXIT_FAILURE; }
50    int * arr;
51    arr = malloc(sizeof(int) * num);
52    int ind;
53    for (ind = 0; ind < num; ind ++)
54      { arr[ind] = 0; }
55    combine(arr, num, toselect);
56    free (arr);
57    return EXIT_SUCCESS;
58  }
```

When `selected` equals `toselect`, enough items have been selected and the selected items are printed. When `ind` equals `num`, no more items are available for selection. Line 30 selects the item and one is added to `selected` when recursively calling `combineHelp`. Line 33 does not select the item and `selected` is unchanged in the recursive call. Either the item is selected or it is not. The helper function recursively calls itself to determine whether to select the remaining items.

From the examples of permutations and combinations, you can see recursion is a natural way of solving these problems. Recursion is a good approach when the solutions have "branches". In permutation, each element can be in one of many locations. After setting one element to a particular location, the next element also can be in one of many locations. By putting recursive calls inside a loop, the solution naturally solves permutations. For combinations, each element may be selected or not and there are two branches. One reason that makes recursion a better solution is that the number of iterations changes. For both cases, the call stack keeps the values of the array index. The index indicates which array element to consider next. Without using recursion, programmers have to allocate memory for keeping the values of the index.

16.4   Stack Sort

A stack can be used to sort a sequence of numbers, if the sequence satisfies some conditions. A stack can store information based on the "first-in, last-out" rule. The stack sort algorithm is described as follows:

1. Create an empty stack.
2. Read one number from the sequence, call it x.
3. If the stack is empty, push the number x to the stack.
4. If the stack is not empty, we call the number at the top of the stack y.
5. If $y \leq x$, pop y from the stack. Continue steps 4 and 5 until either the stack is empty or top of the stack is greater x.
6. If $y > x$, then push x to the stack.

7. Repeat steps 2 to 6 until finishing the input sequence.
8. If the stack is not empty, then pop all remaining numbers from the stack.
9. The sequence of numbers popped from the stack is sorted if the input sequence is *stack-sortable*, defined below. Stack sort is a theoretically interesting algorithm, because it is fast (faster than quick sort), but works only under particular circumstances.

Consider the first example: the sequence <2, 1>. When 2 is read from the sequence, the stack is empty and 2 is pushed onto the stack (step 3). Next, 1 is read from the sequence, 1 is smaller than the element on top of the stack, and is therefore pushed to the stack (step 6). Now the sequence is finished and we pop the numbers from the stack (step 8) and the result is <1, 2>. Table 16.3 (a) shows the steps.

TABLE 16.3:   Examples of stack sort.

Input	2, 1		1, 2		1, 3, 2			2, 3, 1		
Stack	2 1		1 2		1 3 2			2 3 1		
	2				3			3		
Output	-	1, 2	-	1	1, 2	-	1	1	1, 2, 3	-	2	2	2, 1, 3
	(a)		(b)		(c)			(d)		

The next example considers the sequence $< 1, 2 >$. Table 16.3 (b) shows the steps. The first number 1 is read from the sequence and pushed to the stack. The second number, 2, is read. Since 1 is smaller than 2, 1 is popped from the stack and sent to the output (step 5); 2 is pushed onto the stack (step 3). No more number is available. The only number 2 is popped the result is $< 1, 2 >$.

Table 16.3 (c) shows the third example; the input is the sequence $< 1, 3, 2 >$. The first number, 1, is read from the sequence and pushed onto the stack. The second number, 3, is read. Since 1 is smaller than 3, 1 is popped from the stack and sent to the output; 3 is pushed onto the stack. The third number is smaller than 3, and 2 is pushed to the stack. The numbers are popped and the result is $< 1, 2, 3 >$.

In the fourth example, the input sequence is $< 2, 3, 1 >$. The first number 2 is read and pushed onto the stack. The second number 3 is larger; 2 is popped from the stack and sent to the output. Number 3 is pushed to the stack. The last number is 1 and it is pushed to the stack. Since there is no more number, the stack is popped and the output sequence is $< 2, 1, 3 >$. The numbers are *not* sorted. This process has failed. Stack sort can sort some sequences of numbers but fails to sort the other sequences.

Is there a way to determine whether a sequence of numbers is "stack sortable"? Let M be the largest value of the whole sequence. Without loss of generality, a sequence of numbers can be divided into three parts: $\mathbb{A}$ before M, M, and $\mathbb{B}$ after M. It is possible that the first or third parts (or both) are empty. If M is the first element of the sequence, then $\mathbb{A}$ is empty. If M is the last element of the sequence, then $\mathbb{B}$ is empty. If the entire sequence has only one element, it must be M; both $\mathbb{A}$ and $\mathbb{B}$ are empty. If the largest value M appears multiple times, choose the first one. In other words, M must not appear $\mathbb{A}$ and the numbers in $\mathbb{A}$ must be smaller than M. It is acceptable that M appears in $\mathbb{B}$ (once or multiple times).

$\mathbb{A}$: before M M $\mathbb{B}$: after M

Step 5 of the algorithm pops all the numbers in the stack when M is read. Suppose $M_\mathbb{A}$ is the largest value in $\mathbb{A}$. Of course, $M_\mathbb{A} < M$ because M is the largest value of the entire sequence. Suppose $m_\mathbb{B}$ is the smallest value in $\mathbb{B}$. When M is pushed to the stack, every number in $\mathbb{A}$ must have already been popped. If $m_\mathbb{B} < M_\mathbb{A}$, in the correct output

TABLE 16.4: Stack sort $< 1, 5, 2, 3, 5, 4 >$.

	1	5	2	3	5	4	
Stack		5	5	5	5	5	
						5	
Output	-	$< 1 >$	$< 1 >$	$< 1, 2 >$	$< 1, 2, 3 >$	$< 1, 2, 3 >$	$< 1, 2, 3, 4, 5, 5 >$

m_B should be popped before M_A is popped. However, when M is pushed, M_A has already been popped and there is no chance for m_B to be popped before M_A is popped. As a result, stack sort fails for this sequence. In the last example, <2, 3, 1>, M is 3, M_A is 2, and m_B is 1. The condition $m_B < M_A$ is satisfied so <2, 3, 1> is not stack sortable.

Is this sequence $< 1, 5, 2, 3, 5, 4 >$ stack sortable? Note that the largest value 5 appears twice in this sequence. Table 16.4 shows the steps. Following the procedure described earlier, the first number 1 is pushed to the stack.

The next number 5 is larger than 1 so 1 is popped and 5 is pushed. The output is $< 1 >$. The third number 2 is smaller than 5 and it is pushed. The next number is 3 so 2 is popped from the stack and 3 is pushed. The output is $< 1, 2 >$. The next number is 5 so 3 is popped and 5 is pushed. The output is $< 1, 2 >$. The last number 4 is pushed. Finally, all numbers are popped and the output sequence is $< 1, 2, 3, 4, 5, 5 >$. It is sorted. Thus, $< 1, 5, 2, 3, 5, 4 >$ is stack sortable.

If the same largest value M (5 in this example) appears multiple times, which M should be chosen for breaking the sequence into A, M, and B? Should it be the first M, the second M, the last one, or will any one do? The answer is the first M because we compare only the smallest element in B and do not care about the largest element in B. If we choose an M other than the first, then the first M is in A and M_A must be M. If B contains any number other than M, then m_B must be smaller than M. We would consider the sequence not stack sortable; however, the previous example is stack sortable.

After breaking the sequence into the three parts, the same procedure is applied recursively to A and B to determine whether they are stack sortable. The algorithm for checking stack sortable is described as follows:

1. An empty sequence is stack sortable. This is a base case.
2. Find the largest value in the sequence. If this value appears multiple times in the array, select the first one.
3. Divide the sequence into three parts.
4. If both A and B are empty, then the sequence is stack sortable. The sequence has only one element, i.e., M. This is another base case.
5. If A is empty (B must not be empty), then jump to step 9.
6. If B is empty (A must not be empty), then jump to step 8.
7. Since neither A nor B is empty, find M_A and m_B. If $M_A > m_B$, then the sequence is not stack sortable. This is another base case.
8. Recursively check whether A is stack sortable.
9. Recursively check whether B is stack sortable.

The following implementation checks whether a sequence is stack sortable.

```
// CH16:stacksort.c
int findIndex(int * arr, int first, int last, int maxmin)
// find the index of the largest or smallest element
// the range is expressed by the indexes [first, last]
// maxmin = 1: find largest, maxmin = 0: find smallest
```

```
6   {
7     int ind;
8     int  answer = first;
9     for (ind = first + 1; ind <= last; ind ++)
10      {
11        if (((maxmin == 1) && (arr[answer] < arr[ind])) ||
12            ((maxmin == 0) && (arr[answer] > arr[ind])))
13          { answer = ind; }
14      }
15    return answer;
16  }
17  int findMaxIndex(int * arr, int first, int last)
18  {
19    return findIndex(arr, first, last, 1);
20  }
21  int findMinIndex(int * arr, int first, int last)
22  {
23    return findIndex(arr, first, last, 0);
24  }
25  int isStackSortable(int * arr, int first, int last)
26  // check whether the range of the array is sortable
27  // return 1 if the range of the array is sortable
28  // return 0 if the range of the array is not sortable
29  {
30    if (first >= last) // no or one element is stack sortable
31      { return 1; }
32    int maxIndex = findMaxIndex(arr, first, last);
33    // consider the four cases:
34    // 1. both A and B are empty
35    // Only one element, it is stack sortable already checked earlier
36    // 2. A is empty, B is not empty
37    // check whether B is stack sortable
38    if (first == maxIndex)
39      { return isStackSortable(arr, first + 1, last); }
40    // 3. A is not empty, B is empty
41    // check whether A is stack sortable
42    if (maxIndex == last)
43      { return isStackSortable(arr, first, last - 1); }
44    // 4. neither is empty
45    int maxAIndex = findMaxIndex(arr, first, maxIndex - 1);
46    int minBIndex = findMinIndex(arr, maxIndex + 1, last);
47    if (arr[maxAIndex] > arr[minBIndex]) // not stack sortable
48      { return 0; }
49    int sortA = isStackSortable(arr, first, maxIndex - 1);
50    int sortB = isStackSortable(arr, maxIndex + 1, last);
51    return (sortA && sortB); // return 1 only if both are 1
52  }
```

For an array of n distinct numbers, there are $n!$ permutations. Among them, $\frac{1}{n+1}C_n^{2n}$ are stack sortable. This is called the *Catalan number*. The proof will be given on page 265.

16.5 An Incorrect Recursive Function

Consider the following incorrect implementation of binary search. One line in `binarysearch` is incorrect, as marked by a comment. What is the output of this program?

```
1   // CH16:searchbug.c
2   #include <stdio.h>
3   #include <stdlib.h>
4   #define ARRAYSIZE 10
5   int binarySearchHelp(int * arr, int key, int low, int high)
6   {
7     if (low >= high) // ERROR: should be >, not >=
8       { return -1; }
9     int mid = (low + high) / 2;
10    if (arr[mid] == key)
11      { return mid; }
12    if (arr[mid] > key)
13      { return binarySearchHelp(arr, key, low, mid - 1); }
14    return binarySearchHelp(arr, key, mid + 1, high);
15  }
16  int binarySearch(int * arr, int key, int len)
17  {
18    return binarySearchHelp(arr, key, 0, len - 1);
19  }
20  int main(int argc, char * * argv)
21  {
22    int arr[ARRAYSIZE] = {1, 12, 23, 44, 65, 76, 77, 98, 109, 110};
23    int ind;
24    for (ind = 0; ind < ARRAYSIZE; ind ++)
25      {
26        printf("%d\n", binarySearch(arr, arr[ind], ARRAYSIZE));
27      }
28    return EXIT_SUCCESS;
29  }
```

This is the program's output

```
-1
1
2
-1
4
5
-1
7
8
-1
```

The program searches the array's elements one by one. If `binarySearchHelp` were correct, the program would print: 0, 1, 2, ... 9. When searching for 1, the arguments `low` and `high` change as shown in Table 16.5 (a). The problem occurs when `low` and `high` are both zero and `binarySearchHelp` returns -1 without checking whether `arr[mid]` is the same as `key`. Does this mistake cause `binarySearchHelp` to always return -1? Consider searching for 12, as shown in Table 16.5 (b). The function correctly returns 1.

TABLE 16.5: (a) Incorrect result. (b) Correct result.

low	high	mid	arr[mid]	key	low	high	mid	arr[mid]	key
0	9	4	65	1	0	9	4	65	12
0	3	1	12	1	0	3	1	12	12
0	0	0	1	1					
		(a)					(b)		

As you can see, this program *sometimes* produces correct results and sometimes produces incorrect results. This reinforces the need to have a strategy for testing. It is usually important to automate testing so that you can test many cases easily.

16.6 Problems

16.6.1 Shuffle Cards - 1

Many card games require shuffling cards. The purpose of shuffling cards is to make the result difficult to predict. *Riffle shuffling* is a widely used method for shuffling cards. The method has the following steps: (1) Divide a deck of cards into two groups, called the left deck and right deck (held by the left hand and the right hand). Each group has at least one card. The two groups may have different numbers of cards. This is one reason why the shuffling results are hard to predict. (2) Interleave the cards. Typically, the cards are released by the thumbs of the two hands. It is possible (in fact, likely) that the two thumbs are not perfectly coordinated and multiple cards from one hand are released at once. The order of cards in the left hand does not change: If one card is above another in the left hand, the former is still above the latter after interleaving the cards from the right hand. Similarly, the order of the cards in the right hand does not change.

Consider an example of three cards: A, 2, 3. There are two ways to divide these cards:

1. A in the left hand and 2, 3 in the right hand. For this case, there are three ways to insert A into the deck of 2, 3:

   (a) insert A above 2. The result is A, 2, 3.
   (b) insert A between 2 and 3. The result is 2, A, 3.
   (c) insert A below 3. The result is 2, 3, A.

2. A, 2 in the left hand and 3 in the right hand. For this case, there are three ways to insert 3 into the deck of A, 2:

   (a) insert 3 above A. The result is 3, A, 2.
   (b) insert 3 between A and 2. The result is A, 3, 2.
   (c) insert 3 below 2. The result is A, 2, 3.

Please notice that A, 2, 3 appears twice and 3, 2, A does not appear.

Next, consider four cards: 2, 3, 4, 5. There are three ways to divide these cards:

1. 2 in the left hand and 3, 4, 5 in the right hand. There are four ways inserting 2 into the deck of 3, 4, 5:

   (a) insert 2 above 3. The result is 2, 3, 4, 5.
   (b) insert 2 below 3 and above 4. The result is 3, 2, 4, 5.
   (c) insert 2 below 4 and above 5. The result is 3, 4, 2, 5.
   (d) insert 2 below 5. The result is 3, 4, 5, 2.

2. 2, 3 in the left hand and 4, 5 in the right hand. There are six ways to insert 2, 3 into 4, 5:

   (a) insert 2 and 3 are above 4. The result is 2, 3, 4, 5.
   (b) insert 2 above 4 and insert 3 between 4 and 5. The result is 2, 4, 3, 5.
   (c) insert 2 above 4 and insert 3 below 5. The result is 2, 4, 5, 3.
   (d) insert 2 and 3 between 4 and 5. The result is 4, 2, 3, 5.
   (e) insert 2 between 4 and 5; insert 3 below 5. The result is 4, 2, 5, 3.
   (f) insert 2, 3 below 5. The result is 4, 5, 2, 3.

3. 2, 3, 4 in the left hand and 5 in the right hand. there are four ways inserting 5 into the deck of 2, 3, 4:

   (a) insert 5 above 2. The result is 5, 2, 3, 4.
   (b) insert 5 below 2 and above 3. The result is 2, 5, 3, 4.
   (c) insert 5 below 3 and above 4. The result is 2, 3, 5, 4.
   (d) insert 5 below 4. The result is 2, 3, 4, 5.

There are $4 + 6 + 4 = 14$ possible results. Please notice that the original order 2, 3, 4, 5 appears multiple times and is counted multiple times. There are $4! = 24$ possible ways to arrange 4 cards (equivalent to *permutation*). Shuffling once cannot produce all possible orders of the 4 cards. This question asks you to calculate the number of results using Riffle shuffling to shuffle n cards. If a sequence appears multiple times, count as many times as it appears.

16.6.2 Shuffle Cards - 2

Write a program that take a deck cards and shuffle them once. The program uses `argv[1]` to specify the number of cards; a valid value is between 2 and 13 (for A, 2, 3, ..., 10, J, Q, K).

16.6.3 Shuffle Cards - 3

Modify the program so that the cards can be shuffled more than once.

Part III

Structure

Chapter 17

Programmer-Defined Data Types

We have been using the data types from C, such as `int`, `char`, or `double`. Data types provide valuable information about (1) The amount of memory space needed. For example, `char` is one byte; `int` is (usually) four bytes; `double` is eight bytes. (2) The types of operations. For example, `int` can be used in `switch` but `double` cannot.

C allows programmers to create new types for many reasons. The most obvious reason is to put related data together. For example, a college student has a name (string), year (integer), grade point average (floating-point), and so on.

17.1 Struct and Object

When multiple pieces of data are organized together, it is a *structure*. A structure is a type (similar to `int` or `char`). After creating the structure, the type can be used to create an *object* (borrowing a term from C++ and Java). An object is a specific instance of a type. For example, "bicycle" is a type describing the properties: two wheels, gears, wheel size, etc. Your bicycle is an instance that has these properties. Borrowing another term used in C++ and Java, we call each piece of data an *attribute*. For a bicycle, the wheel size is an attribute. The brand is another attribute. These three terms are further described below:

- *Structure*: A data type so that multiple pieces of data can be organized together. The data may have different types (`int`, `char`, `double`, or even other structures).
- *Object*: A specific instance of a structure. In the example below, `int` and `t` are both types. Suppose `t` is a structure (such as `Bicycle`). Using these types, `x` is a specific instance of integer, and `y` is a specific instance of type `t`.

```
int x;
t y;
```

- *Attribute*: A structure organizes different pieces of data together. Each piece of data is referred to as an attribute. The attributes store the information specific to the particular object (such as the wheel size of a bicycle).

It is important to clearly distinguish these three concepts (structure, object, and attribute). Here are some more examples:

- "Person" is a structure and a type. Individual people are specific instances of Person. Let's call two specific people: "Alice" and "Bob". Their names, ages, heights, and phone numbers are attributes. Alice's attributes have different values from Bob's attributes.
- "Car" is a structure. Every car has some attributes, such as year, brand, license plate number, and color. Your car is a particular instance and it is an object. That means

it has a particular year, brand, and color. My car also has these attributes but the values are different (such as the license plate).

- "Desk" is a structure. Every desk has attributes, such as width, height, number of drawers, weight, material, location, etc. The desk in your office is an instance. It is a particular desk with specific values for those attributes; the values (such as location) are different from the desk at your home.

This is an example that creates a new type for vector. A vector has three attributes: x, y, and z. This new type is called Vector and it puts these attributes together.

```
1   // CH17:vector.h
2   #ifndef VECTOR_H
3   #define VECTOR_H
4   typedef struct
5   {
6       int x;
7       int y;
8       int z;
9   } Vector; // remember ; after the name
10  #endif
```

The type begins with **typedef struct**; this tells **gcc** that a new type is defined here. This type contains multiple attributes and they form a structure. After the closing brace, **Vector** is the name of the new type. In this book, the name of a new type starts with an uppercase letter **V**. It is common to have only one structure in each header file and the file's name is the same as the structure's name, but in lowercase (**vector.h**). The structure **Vector** is defined in the header file **vector.h**. In the following program, **v1** is a **Vector** object. This object has three attributes. To access an attribute, a period is needed after **v1**, such as **v1.x** and **v1.y**.

```
1   // CH17:vector.c
2   #include <stdio.h>
3   #include <stdlib.h>
4   #include <string.h>
5   #include "vector.h" // use " ", not < >
6   int main(int argc, char * argv[])
7   {
8       Vector v1;
9       v1.x = 3;
10      v1.y = 6;
11      v1.z = -2;
12      printf("The vector is (%d, %d, %d).\n", v1.x, v1.y, v1.z);
13      return EXIT_SUCCESS;
14  }
```

The program's output is shown below:

```
The vector is (3, 6, -2).
```

What does line 8 actually do? It creates an object on the call stack. The type `Vector` requires three integers and the call stack stores those three integers. Each attribute is an `int` and occupies 4 bytes. The attributes are not initialized and the values are garbage. Line 9 changes the value at address 100 to 3.

TABLE 17.1: Line 8 creates a `Vector` object called `v1` in the stack memory; the attributes are uninitialized. Line 9 assigns 3 to `v1.x`.

Symbol	Address	Value	Value
v1.z	108	garbage	garbage
v1.y	104	garbage	garbage
v1.x	100	garbage	→ **3**

The address of the object is expressed as `& v1`. This is also the address of the first attribute, i.e., `& v1.x`. They refer to the same memory address but they have different types: `& v1`'s type is `Vector *` and `& v1.x`'s type is `int *`. The address of the second attribute, `& v1.y`, is the address of the first attribute, `& v1.x` plus the size of the first attribute `sizeof(v1.x)`. In general, these two equations are true: (1) The address of the object is the same as the address of the first attribute of the object. (2) The address of the ith attribute is the address of the object plus the sizes of the first, second, ..., $(i-1)^{th}$ attributes.

A `Vector` object can be copied to another `Vector` object, as the following example illustrates:

```
1   // CH17:vector2.c
2   #include <stdio.h>
3   #include <stdlib.h>
4   #include <string.h>
5   #include "vector.h"
6   int main(int argc, char * argv[])
7   {
8     Vector v1;
9     v1.x = 3;
10    v1.y = 6;
11    v1.z = -2;
12    printf("The vector is (%d, %d, %d).\n", v1.x, v1.y, v1.z);
13    Vector v2 = {0};
14    printf("The vector is (%d, %d, %d).\n", v2.x, v2.y, v2.z);
15    v2 = v1; // copy v1's attributes to v2's attributes
16    printf("The vector is (%d, %d, %d).\n", v2.x, v2.y, v2.z);
17    v1.x = -4;
18    v2.y = 5;
19    printf("The vector is (%d, %d, %d).\n", v1.x, v1.y, v1.z);
20    printf("The vector is (%d, %d, %d).\n", v2.x, v2.y, v2.z);
21    return EXIT_SUCCESS;
22  }
```

The program's output is:

```
The vector is (3, 6, -2).
The vector is (0, 0, 0).
The vector is (3, 6, -2).
The vector is (-4, 6, -2).
The vector is (3, 5, -2).
```

Line 13 creates a `Vector` object called `v2` and initializes every attribute to zero. Please remember that C does not initialize the attributes. Attributes must be initialized explicitly. Line 15 copies `v1`'s attributes to `v2`'s attributes. The attributes are copied from `v1` to `v2` one by one. Line 15 is equivalent to

```
v2.x = v1.x;
v2.y = v1.y;
v2.z = v1.z;
```

The values of the two objects' attributes are the same: `v2.x` is 3, `v2.y` is 6, and `v2.z` is -2. Since `v1` and `v2` occupy different addresses in the call stack, changing the attributes of `v1` does not affect the attributes of `v2` and vice versa. Line 17 changes `v1.x`; line 18 changes `v2.y`. The effects are limited to the corresponding addresses. As a result, lines 19 and 20 print different values.

Lines 15, 17, and 18 are analogous to the following example using `int`. Even though `a` and `c` have the same value after `int c = a;`, their values can be modified independently in the subsequent lines.

```
int a = 5;
int c = a;   // c and a have the same value, 5
a = -6;      // a is -6, c is still 5
c = 19;      // c is 19, a is still -6
```

Even though `Vector` is a type and assignment `=` is supported, the type does not have all the properties of built-in types (`int`, `char`, `double`, etc.). For example, we cannot use `==` or `!=` to compare two `Vector` objects:

```
Vector v1;
Vector v2;
v1.x = 1;
v1.y = 2;
v1.z = 3;
v2.x = 0;
v2.y = -1;
v2.z = -2;
if (v1 != v2)
{
    printf("v1 and v2 are different.\n");
}
```

When compiling this function, `gcc` will say:

```
invalid operands to binary !=
```

If we want to compare two `Vector` objects, we have to write a function that compares the attributes, for example,

```
int equalVector(Vector v1, Vector v2)
// return 0 if any attribute is different, 1 if all attributes are equal

{
    if (v1.x != v2.x) { return 0; }
```

```
    if (v1.y != v2.y) { return 0; }
    if (v1.z != v2.z) { return 0; }
    return 1;
}
```

17.2   Objects as Arguments

A `Vector` object can be passed as a function argument. When passing an object as an argument, all attributes are copied to the argument of the called function. This is the same as when passing other types of arguments, such as `int` and `double`: A *copy* of the argument is passed. The following example shows a separate function for printing `Vector` objects:

Frame	Symbol	Address	Value
	v.z	216	−2
	v.y	212	6
printVector	v.x	208	3
	RL	200	line 16
	v1.z	108	−2
main	v1.y	104	6
	v1.x	100	3

```
1   // CH17:vectorarg.c
2   #include <stdio.h>
3   #include <stdlib.h>
4   #include "vector.h"
5   void printVector(Vector v)
6   {
7     printf("The vector is (%d, %d, %d).\n", v.x, v.y, v.z);
8   }
9   int main(int argc, char * argv[])
10  {
11    Vector v1;
12    v1.x = 3;
13    v1.y = 6;
14    v1.z = -2;
15    printVector(v1);
16    return EXIT_SUCCESS;
17  }
```

How do we know that the attributes are copied? In the following program `changeVector` changes the `Vector` object passed to it. However, inside `main`, the attributes of `v1` are unchanged.

```
1   // CH17:vectorarg2.c
2   #include <stdio.h>
3   #include <stdlib.h>
4   #include "vector.h"
5   void printVector(Vector v)
6   {
7     printf("The vector is (%d, %d, %d).\n", v.x, v.y, v.z);
```

```
8    }
9    void changeVector(Vector v)
10   {
11     v.x = 5;
12     v.y = -3;
13     v.z = 7;
14     printVector(v);
15   }
16   int main(int argc, char * argv[])
17   {
18     Vector v1;
19     v1.x = 3;
20     v1.y = 6;
21     v1.z = -2;
22     printVector(v1);
23     changeVector(v1);
24     printVector(v1);
25     return EXIT_SUCCESS;
26   }
```

The output of this program is:

```
The vector is (3, 6, -2).
The vector is (5, -3, 7).
The vector is (3, 6, -2).
```

Calling `changeVector` pushes a new frame to the call stack. The argument is an object that has three attributes. The values are copied from the calling function into the new frame. The function `changeVector` changes the attributes of the object in its own frame. When `changeVector` finishes, the frame is popped and the program resumes at `main`. The attributes of `v1` in `main` are unchanged.

17.3   Objects and Pointers

It is possible to change an object's attributes inside a function and keep the changes even after the function returns. To do this, we need to use pointers. Consider this example.

```
1    // CH17:vectorptr.c
2    #include <stdio.h>
3    #include <stdlib.h>
4    #include "vector.h"
5    void printVector(Vector v)
6    { printf("The vector is (%d, %d, %d).\n", v.x, v.y, v.z); }
7    void changeVector(Vector * p)
8    {
9      p -> x = 5;
10     p -> y = -3;
11     p -> z = 7;
```

```
12    printVector(* p); // need to add * before p
13  }
14  int main(int argc, char * argv[])
15  {
16    Vector v1;
17    v1.x = 3;
18    v1.y = 6;
19    v1.z = -2;
20    printVector(v1);
21    changeVector(& v1); // address of v1
22    printVector(v1);
23    return EXIT_SUCCESS;
24  }
```

The function `changeVector`'s argument is a pointer:

```
void changeVector(Vector * p)
```

This means that `p` is a pointer in the frame of the function `changeVector`. If you refer back to Table 4.4, this way of using `*` makes `p` a pointer. When calling `changeVector` at line 21, `main` provides the address of a `Vector` object, i.e., `& v1`. This can be understood by showing the call stack:

Frame	Symbol	Address	Value	Value	Value	Value
changeVector	p	208	A100			
	RL	200	line 22			
main	v1.z	108	-2			7
	v1.y	104	6		-3	
	v1.x	100	3	5		
				line 9	line 10	line 11

Instead of copying the whole object, attribute by attribute, the argument `p` stores only the address of the object `v1`. This is the address of the first attribute. The `->` symbol (lines 9–11) takes the value at the address, and then gets the corresponding attribute of the object. Pointers are used with structures often and C has this special syntax `->`.

```
p -> x
```

is the same as

```
(*p).x
```

This dereferences `p` first, and then applies `.` for `x`. Dereferencing is another way of using `*` as explained in Table 4.4. If `->` is at the left hand side (LHS) of an assignment, then the attribute is modified (i.e., written). If `->` is at the right hand side (RHS) of an assignment, then the attribute is read.

At line 12, we need to add `*` in front of `p` when `changeVector` calls `printVector`. In `changeVector`, `p` is a pointer. However, `printVector` expects an object because there is no `*` in the line:

```
void printVector(Vector v)
```

In `changeVector`, adding `*` in front of `p` dereferences the pointer, as explained in Table 4.4. Thus, the object stored at addresses 100–112 is copied to the argument of `printVector`. How do we know that the object is copied? In C, arguments are always copied when passed to functions. If the argument is `Vector *`, then the address is copied. If there is no `*` after `Vector` in `printVector`, the argument is an object. As a result, the object is copied. If v's attributes are changed inside `printVector`, then the changes will be lost when the function finishes. The syntax for using objects is:

- If p's value is an address of an object, use `p -> x`. It is allowed to put a space before or after `->` but no space can be added between `-` and `>`.
- If `v` is an object (not an address), use `v.x`.

A function can return a `Vector` object. The following example shows a *constructor* function that creates and initializes a new object:

```
1   // CH17:vectorconstruct.c
2   #include <stdio.h>
3   #include <stdlib.h>
4   #include "vector.h"
5   Vector Vector_construct(int a, int b, int c)
6   {
7     Vector v;
8     v.x = a;
9     v.y = b;
10    v.z = c;
11    return v;
12  }
13  void Vector_print(Vector v)
14  {
15    printf("The vector is (%d, %d, %d).\n", v.x, v.y, v.z);
16  }
17  int main(int argc, char * argv[])
18  {
19    Vector v1 = Vector_construct(3, 6, -2);
20    Vector_print(v1);
21    return EXIT_SUCCESS;
22  }
```

The constructor function has several advantages: It makes a program easier to read. The three arguments remind programmers that a `Vector` object has three attributes. Constructors should guarantee that all attributes are always initialized. Uninitialized variables can make programs behave in surprising ways. Before calling the constructor, v1 is already on the call stack in the frame of the `main` function. When the constructor returns the object, the attributes of `v` (from the constructor) are copied to v1's attributes one by one. Then, the constructor's frame is popped and `v` does not exist anymore.

When the constructor returns, the attributes are copied to the object in the calling function (`main`). If the object has many attributes, this constructor is inefficient because of copying the attributes. One solution is to keep the constructed object in the heap memory without copying the attributes, as shown below.

```
1   // CH17:vectormalloc.c
2   #include <stdio.h>
3   #include <stdlib.h>
4   #include "vector.h"
5   Vector * Vector_construct(int a, int b, int c) // notice *
6   {
7     Vector * v;
8     v = malloc(sizeof(Vector)); // pay attention to sizeof
9     if (v == NULL) // allocation fail
10       {
11         printf("malloc fail\n");
12         return NULL;
13       }
14     v -> x = a;
15     v -> y = b;
16     v -> z = c;
17     return v;
18   }
19   void Vector_destruct(Vector * v)
20   {
21     free (v);
22   }
23   void Vector_print(Vector * v)
24   {
25     printf("The vector is (%d, %d, %d).\n", v -> x, v -> y, v -> z);
26   }
27   int main(int argc, char * argv[])
28   {
29     Vector * v1;
30     v1 = Vector_construct(3, 6, -2);
31     // RL
32     if (v1 == NULL) { return EXIT_FAILURE; }
33     Vector_print(v1);
34     Vector_destruct(v1); // remember to free
35     return EXIT_SUCCESS;
36   }
```

The program creates a `Vector` pointer at line 29. It will be given an address in heap memory returned by `Vector_construct`. Calling `malloc` allocates a piece of memory that is in the heap. The size is sufficient to accommodate three integers. Suppose `malloc` returns A60000. Table 17.2 shows the stack and heap memory.

The pointer's value takes on the address returned by calling `malloc`. Since it is a pointer, the program uses `->` to access the attributes. The statements,

```
v -> x = a;
v -> y = b;
v -> z = c;
```

TABLE 17.2: Vector_construct calls `malloc` to allocate heap memory.

Frame	Symbol	Address	Value	Address	Value
	v	228	A60000	60008	garbage
	c	224	-2	60004	garbage
Vector_construct	b	220	6	60000	garbage
	a	216	3		
	VA	208	A100		
	RL	200	RL		
main	v1	100	garbage		
	stack memory			heap memory	

modify the values at addresses 60000, 60004, and 60008 to 3, 6, and -2 respectively. When Vector_construct returns, v's value is written to the return address 100. Therefore, the call stack becomes:

Frame	Symbol	Address	Value
main	v1	100	A60000

The heap memory must be released by calling `free`. This is the purpose of the destructor Vector_destruct. The concept of constructor and destructor is further explained below.

17.4 Constructors and Destructors

Sometimes objects need to contain pointers that manage dynamically allocated memory. Consider the following example:

```
// CH17:person.h
#ifndef PERSON_H
#define PERSON_H
typedef struct
{
  // date of birth
  int year;
  int month;
  int date;
  char * name; // this is a pointer
} Person;
Person * Person_construct(int y, int m, int d, char * n);
void Person_destruct(Person * p);
void Person_print(Person * p);
#endif
```

Each `Person` object has four attributes, three for the date of birth and one for the name. The name is a pointer because the length of a person's name is unknown. If the name is created with a fixed length, this attribute must use the longest possible name and waste memory when a name is shorter. It is more efficient allocating the length of the name as needed. This is the constructor:

```
1   // CH17:personconstruct.c
2   #include "person.h"
3   #include <stdio.h>
4   #include <string.h>
5   #include <stdlib.h>
6   Person * Person_construct(int y, int m, int d, char * n)
7   {
8     Person * p = NULL;
9     p = malloc(sizeof(Person));
10    if (p == NULL) { return NULL; } // malloc fail
11    p -> year = y;
12    p -> month = m;
13    p -> date = d;
14    p -> name = strdup(n); // malloc + strcpy
15    if ((p -> name) == NULL) // malloc fail
16      {
17        free (p);
18        return NULL;
19      }
20    return p;
21  }
```

Notice how the constructor initializes the attributes in the same order as they are declared in the header file. This is a good programming habit. For the sake of clarity, make things as consistent as possible. This habit prevents accidentally forgetting to initialize an attribute. Below is the destructor:

```
1   // CH17:persondestruct.c
2   #include "person.h"
3   #include <stdlib.h>
4   void Person_destruct(Person * p)
5   {
6     free (p -> name);    // p -> name must be freed before p is freed
7     free (p);
8   }
```

The constructor calls **strdup** and it calls **malloc**. Note that the destructor releases memory in the reverse order that the constructor allocates memory. If the destructor calls free (p) before free (p -> name), then free (p -> name) is invalid. If the destructor does not call free (p -> name), then the program leaks memory. Please remember that every **malloc** must have a corresponding **free**. Below is the implementation of the **Person_print** function:

```
1   // CH17:personprint.c
2   #include "person.h"
3   #include <stdio.h>
4   void Person_print(Person * p)
```

```
5   {
6     printf("Date of Birth: %d/%d/%d\n", p -> year, p -> month, p -> date);
7     printf("Name: %s. ", p -> name);
8   }
```

The following is an example of using the constructor and the destructor:

```
1   // CH17:person1.c
2   #include <stdio.h>
3   #include <stdlib.h>
4   #include <string.h>
5   #include "person.h"
6   int main(int argc, char * argv[])
7   {
8     Person * p1 = Person_construct(1989, 8, 21, "Amy");
9     Person * p2 = Person_construct(1991, 2, 17, "Bob");
10    Person_print(p1);
11    Person_print(p2);
12    Person_destruct(p1);
13    Person_destruct(p2);
14    return EXIT_SUCCESS;
15  }
```

This is the `Makefile` for building the program:

```
1   # CH17:Makefile
2   GCC = gcc
3   CFLAGS = -g -Wall -Wshadow
4   SRCS = person3.c personconstruct.c persondestruct.c personprint.c
5   OBJS = $(SRCS:%.c=%.o)
6   person: $(OBJS)
7           $(GCC) $(CFLAGS) $(OBJS) -o person
8   .c.o:
9           $(GCC) $(CFLAGS) -c $*.c
10  clean:
11          /bin/rm -f *.o person a.out *~ *bak output*
```

Consider the following example. Please notice how **p2** is created.

```
1   // CH17:person2.c
2   #include <stdio.h>
3   #include <stdlib.h>
4   #include <string.h>
5   #include "person.h"
6   void Person_print(Person * p);
7   int main(int argc, char * argv[])
8   {
9     Person * p1 = Person_construct(1989, 8, 21, "Amy");
10    Person * p2 = p1;
```

```
11    Person_print(p1);
12    Person_print(p2);
13    Person_destruct(p1);
14    Person_destruct(p2); // will cause problem
15    return EXIT_SUCCESS;
16  }
```

There is no syntax error in this program, but it contains a serious mistake. To understand the problem, we need to understand what the assignment of line 10 means. This line assigns p1's value to p2. The values of p1 and p2 are the same, i.e., they point to the same memory address. Line 13 calls the destructor and releases the heap memory. This is correct. Line 14 calls the destructor again but the memory has already been released. The same heap memory cannot be released twice.

When p1 and p2 have the same value, changing p1 -> name[0] (the first letter of the name) will also change p2 -> name[0]. The two pointers p1 and p2 store the same heap address. Thus changing p1 -> name[0] also changes p2 -> name[0]. In the next example, both p1 and p2 have distinct values generated by calling Person_construct. Will the following program work?

```
1   // CH17:person3.c
2   #include <stdio.h>
3   #include <stdlib.h>
4   #include <string.h>
5   #include "person.h"
6   int main(int argc, char * argv[])
7   {
8     Person * p1 = Person_construct(1989, 8, 21, "Amy");
9     Person * p2 = Person_construct(1991, 2, 17, "Bob");
10    p2 = p1;  // discard memory for Bob, leak memory
11    Person_print(p1);
12    Person_print(p2);
13    Person_destruct(p1);
14    Person_destruct(p2); // will cause problem
15    return EXIT_SUCCESS;
16  }
```

Line 9 calls the constructor and allocates memory space. However, line 10 still copies p1's value to p2 and the memory assigned to p2 in Line 9 is lost (memory leak). Because p1 and p2 point to the same heap address, Line 14 will still free the same memory the second time. Consider another scenario when the objects are not accessed through pointers:

```
1   // CH17:person4.c
2   #include <stdio.h>
3   #include <stdlib.h>
4   #include <string.h>
5   #include "person.h"
6   int main(int argc, char * argv[])
7   {
8     Person p1; // object, not a pointer
```

TABLE 17.3: Stack and heap memory before p2 = p1; .

Frame	Symbol	Address	Value	Symbol	Address	Value
	p2.name	132	A85000	p2.name[3]	85003	'\0'
	p2.date	128	17	p2.name[2]	85002	'b'
	p2.month	124	2	p2.name[1]	85001	'o'
main	p2.year	120	1991	p2.name[0]	85000	'B'
	p1.name	112	A70000	p1.name[3]	70003	'\0'
	p1.date	108	21	p1.name[2]	70002	'y'
	p1.month	104	8	p1.name[1]	70001	'm'
	p1.year	100	1989	p1.name[0]	70000	'A'
	Stack Memory			Heap Memory		

```
9    Person p2; // object, not a pointer
10   p1.year = 1989;
11   p1.month = 8;
12   p1.date = 21;
13   p1.name = strdup("Amy");
14   p2.year = 1991;
15   p2.month = 2;
16   p2.date = 17;
17   p2.name = strdup("Bob");
18   Person_print(& p1);
19   Person_print(& p2);
20   p2 = p1; // p1 and p2 store the same address
21   Person_print(& p1);
22   Person_print(& p2);
23   free (p1.name);
24   free (p2.name); // free the same memory twice
25   return EXIT_SUCCESS;
26 }
```

This is the program's output:

```
Name: Amy. Date of Birth: 1989/8/21
Name: Bob. Date of Birth: 1991/2/17
Name: Amy. Date of Birth: 1989/8/21
Name: Amy. Date of Birth: 1989/8/21
free(): double free detected
Aborted (core dumped)
```

The program uses **strdup** to copy strings. In this program, both **p1** and **p2** are objects on the call stack, as shown in Table 17.3 What will happen if the program has this line?

```
p2 = p1;
```

The assignment = copies one object's attributes to another object's attributes. After executing this line, the call stack and heap will appear as shown in Table 17.4.

Now, **p1.name** and **p2.name** have the same value (A70000). The heap memory originally pointed to by **p2.name** (allocated by **strdup**) is still in the heap but is no longer accessible

TABLE 17.4: Stack and heap memory after p2 = p1;.

Frame	Symbol	Address	Value	Symbol	Address	Value
	p2.name	132	→ Å70000	-	85003	'\0'
	p2.date	128	17	-	85002	'b'
	p2.month	124	2	-	85001	'o'
main	p2.year	120	1991	-	85000	'B'
	p1.name	112	Å70000	p1.name[3]	70003	'\0'
	p1.date	108	21	p1.name[2]	70002	'y'
	p1.month	104	8	p1.name[1]	70001	'm'
	p1.year	100	1989	p1.name[0]	70000	'A'
	Stack Memory			Heap Memory		

because p2.name is no longer Å85000. This causes memory leaks. Moreover, lines 23 and 24 free the same heap memory at Å70000 twice.

As you can see, if an object's attribute is a pointer, we need to be very careful about how memory is allocated and freed. If we are not careful, then the program may leak memory or release the same memory twice, or both. When an object's attribute is a pointer, that usually indicates the need for four functions.

- *constructor*: Allocates memory for the attribute and assigns the value to the attribute.
- *destructor*: Releases memory for the attribute.
- *copy constructor:* This replaces assignment = by creating a new object from an existing object. This is also referred to as *cloning*. The new object's attribute points to heap memory allocated by calling `malloc`.
- *assignment:* This also replaces = by modifying an object that has already been created by the constructor or the copy constructor. Since the object has already been constructed, the object's attribute stores the address of a heap memory. This memory must be released before allocating new memory.

The first two functions have already been given above. The other two functions are shown below:

```
// CH17:person5.c
#include <stdio.h>
#include <stdlib.h>
#include <string.h>
#include "person.h"
Person * Person_copy(Person * p);
Person * Person_assign(Person * p1, Person * p2);
Person * Person_copy(Person * p)
{
  // create a new object by copying the attributes of p
  return Person_construct(p -> year, p -> month, p -> date, p -> name);
}
Person * Person_assign(Person * p1, Person * p2)
{
  // p1 is already a Person object, make its attribute
  // the same as p2's attributes (deep copy)
  free(p1 -> name); // need to free first because strdup calls malloc
  p1 -> year = p2 -> year;
```

```
19    p1 -> month = p2 -> month;
20    p1 -> date = p2 -> date;
21    p1 -> name = strdup(p2 -> name);
22    return p1;
23  }
24  int main(int argc, char * argv[])
25  {
26    Person * p1 = Person_construct(1989, 8, 21, "Amy");
27    Person * p2 = Person_construct(1991, 2, 17, "Jennifer");
28    Person * p3 = Person_copy(p1); // create p3
29    Person_print(p1);
30    Person_print(p2);
31    Person_print(p3);
32    p3 = Person_assign(p3, p2);
33    Person_print(p3);
34    Person_destruct(p1);
35    Person_destruct(p2);
36    Person_destruct(p3);
37    return EXIT_SUCCESS;
38  }
```

This is the difference between `Person_copy` and `Person_assign`: `Person_copy` creates a new `Person` object by allocating memory. `Person_assign` has to release memory for existing attributes before copying the attributes. The copy constructor allocates separate memory space so that changing one object later does not affect the other. This is called a *deep copy*. The assignment function has to do more work because the object already occupies memory. In our example, the original name in p3 is "Amy". When p2 is copied to p3, p3 `->` name does not have enough memory for the longer name "Jennifer". Thus, the assignment function first releases the memory for p3 `->` name and then allocates memory again by calling `strdup`. The assignment function can check whether p3 `->` name has enough memory. If p3 `->` name has enough memory, it is unnecessary to release p3 `->` name and allocate memory again. The problem is that there is no easy way to know the amount of memory allocated to p3 `->` name earlier. Calling `strlen` does not work because it is possible that p3 `->` name has many unused elements after '\0'.

A deep copy allocates memory so that objects do not share memory. In contrast, a *shallow copy* (e.g., p2 = p1;) allows two objects' attributes to point to the same memory address. Shallow copies can be useful. For example, in a student database, every student has an attribute that points to an object representing the school. This school object contains information about the school, such as its name and address. It is unnecessary for every student to have an individual copy of the school object. There can be one school object shared by every student object. In this scenario sharing makes sense, and the copy constructor and assignment operator should perform a shallow copy of the school attribute. Another reason for using shallow copies is when objects share a very large piece of memory and few objects actually need to modify this shared memory. A copy is made only when an object intends to make changes. This is called *copy on write* and is beyond the scope of this book.

17.5 Structures within Structures

Can a structure's attribute be another structure? Yes. In this example, we move a `Person`'s date of birth from three integers into one `Date` object:

```
// CH17:dateofbirth.h
#ifndef DATEOFBIRTH_H
#define DATEOFBIRTH_H
typedef struct
{
  int year;
  int month;
  int date;
} DateOfBirth;
DateOfBirth DateOfBirth_construct(int y, int m, int d);
void DateOfBirth_print(DateOfBirth d);
#endif
```

This is the file implementing the functions:

```
// CH17:dateofbirth.c
#include "dateofbirth.h"
#include <stdio.h>
DateOfBirth DateOfBirth_construct(int y, int m, int d)
{
  DateOfBirth dob;
  dob.year = y;
  dob.month = m;
  dob.date = d;
  return dob;
}
void DateOfBirth_print(DateOfBirth d)
{
  printf("Date of Birth: %d/%d/%d\n", d.year, d.month, d.date);
}
```

This is the header file for `Person` using `DateofBirth`:

```
// CH17:person6.h
#ifndef PERSON6_H
#define PERSON6_H
typedef struct
{
  char * name;
  DateOfBirth dob;
} Person;
Person * Person_construct(char * n, int y, int m, int d);
void Person_destruct(Person * p);
Person * Person_copy(Person * p);
Person * Person_assign(Person * p1, Person * p2);
```

```
13   void Person_print(Person * p);
14   #endif
```

This is the functions for the Person:

```
1    // CH17:person6.c
2    #include <stdio.h>
3    #include <stdlib.h>
4    #include <string.h>
5    #include "dateofbirth.h"
6    #include "person6.h"
7    int main(int argc, char * argv[])
8    {
9      Person * p1 = Person_construct("Amy", 1989, 8, 21);
10     Person * p2 = Person_construct("Jennifer", 1991, 2, 17);
11     Person * p3 = Person_copy(p1); // create p3
12     Person_print(p1);
13     Person_print(p2);
14     Person_print(p3);
15     p3 = Person_assign(p3, p2); // change p3
16     Person_print(p3);
17     Person_destruct(p1);
18     Person_destruct(p2);
19     Person_destruct(p3);
20     return EXIT_SUCCESS;
21   }
22   Person * Person_construct(char * n, int y, int m, int d)
23   {
24     Person * p;
25     p = malloc(sizeof(Person));
26     if (p == NULL)
27       {
28         printf("malloc fail\n");
29         return NULL;
30       }
31     p -> name = strdup(n);
32     p -> dob = DateOfBirth_construct(y, m, d);
33     return p;
34   }
35   void Person_destruct(Person * p)
36   {
37     // p must be released after p -> name has been released
38     free (p -> name);
39     free (p);
40   }
41   Person * Person_copy(Person * p)
42   {
43     return Person_construct(p -> name, p -> dob.year,
44                             p -> dob.month, p -> dob.date);
45   }
46   Person * Person_assign(Person * p1, Person * p2)
```

```
47  {
48    free(p1 -> name);
49    p1 -> dob = p2 -> dob;
50    p1 -> name = strdup(p2 -> name);
51    return p1;
52  }
53  void Person_print(Person * p)
54  {
55    printf("Name: %s. ", p -> name);
56    DateOfBirth_print(p -> dob);
57  }
```

This program creates a *hierarchy* of structures. A structure contains another structure. `Person_construct` calls `DateOfBirth_construct`. `Person_print` calls `DateOfBirth_print`. This approach has an advantage when the program becomes more complex: such a hierarchy becomes helpful for the organization. Creating one structure that contains everything can be impractical and unclear. Instead, we should put related data together and create a structure, for example, the `DateOfBirth` structure. We can use this structure inside other structures. Each structure should have a constructor to initialize all attributes. If a structure has pointers for dynamically allocated memory, then make sure that there is also a destructor. If deep copy is required (applicable in most cases), remember to write a copy constructor and an assignment function.

17.6 Binary Files and Objects

This section explains how to write an object to a file and how to read an object from a file. This section will talk about both text files and binary files. `Vector` is used as the structure for the examples. The following program contains two write functions and two read functions. `Vector_writet` and `Vector_readt` use text files. `Vector_writeb` and `Vector_readb` use binary files. When using text files, reading and writing objects is as simple as reading and writing one attribute after another. The two functions must process the attributes in the same order. If the orders are different, then the results will be wrong. `Vector_writeb` and `Vector_readb` open files in the binary mode by adding `b` in the second argument when calling `fopen` (i.e., "rb" for reading and "wb" for writing). Some operating systems, including Linux, actually ignore `b`. It is used primarily for compatibility among different systems. Table 17.5 describes the different functions for text and binary files:

TABLE 17.5: Functions for opening, writing to, and reading from text and binary files. Do not mix the functions for text files and for binary files. For example, do not use `fscanf` if a file is created by using `fwrite`.

Operation	Text File	Binary File
open a file	`fopen`	`fopen`
write	`fprintf`	`fwrite`
read	`fgetc`, `fgets`, or `fscanf`	`fread`

This program shows how to read and write text and binary files. The functions for text files, `Vector_writet` and `Vector_readt`, should be easy to understand. The functions for binary files, `Vector_writeb` and `Vector_readb`, use `fwrite` and `fread`.

```c
1   // CH17:vectorfile.c
2   #include <stdio.h>
3   #include <stdlib.h>
4   #include <string.h>
5   #include "vector.h"
6   Vector Vector_construct(int a, int b, int c)
7   {
8     Vector v;
9     v.x = a;
10    v.y = b;
11    v.z = c;
12    return v;
13  }
14  void Vector_print(char * name, Vector v)
15  {
16    printf("%s is (%d, %d, %d).\n", name, v.x, v.y, v.z);
17  }
18  void Vector_writet(char * filename, Vector v) // write to a text file
19  {
20    FILE * fptr;
21    fptr = fopen(filename, "w");
22    if (fptr == NULL)
23      {
24        printf("Vector_writet fopen fail\n");
25        return;
26      }
27    fprintf(fptr, "%d %d %d", v.x, v.y, v.z);
28    fclose (fptr);
29  }
30  Vector Vector_readt(char * filename) // read from a text file
31  {
32    Vector v = Vector_construct(0, 0, 0);
33    FILE * fptr;
34    fptr = fopen(filename, "r");
35    if (fptr == NULL)
36      {
37        printf("Vector_readt fopen fail\n");
38        return v;
39      }
40    if (fscanf(fptr, "%d %d %d", & v.x, & v.y, & v.z) != 3)
41      {
42        printf("fprintf fail\n");
43      }
44    fclose (fptr);
45    return v;
46  }
47  void Vector_writeb(char * filename, Vector v) // write to a binary file
48  {
49    FILE * fptr;
50    fptr = fopen(filename, "w"); // "w" same as "wb" in Linux
```

```
51    if (fptr == NULL)
52      {
53        printf("Vector_writeb fopen fail\n");
54        return;
55      }
56    if (fwrite(& v, sizeof(Vector), 1, fptr) != 1)
57      {
58        printf("fwrite fail\n");
59      }
60    fclose (fptr);
61  }
62  Vector Vector_readb(char * filename) // read from a binary file
63  {
64    FILE * fptr;
65    Vector v; // not initialized
66    fptr = fopen(filename, "r"); // "r" same as "rb" in Linux
67    if (fptr == NULL)
68      {
69        printf("Vector_readb fopen fail\n");
70        return v;
71      }
72    if (fread(& v, sizeof(Vector), 1, fptr) != 1)
73      { printf("fread fail\n"); }
74    return v;
75  }
76  int main(int argc, char * argv[])
77  {
78    Vector v1 = Vector_construct(13, 206, -549);
79    Vector v2 = Vector_construct(-15, 8762, 1897);
80    Vector_print("v1", v1);
81    Vector_print("v2", v2);
82    printf("================================\n");
83    Vector_writet("vectort.dat", v1);
84    v2 = Vector_readt("vectort.dat");
85    Vector_print("v1", v1);
86    Vector_print("v2", v2);
87    v1 = Vector_construct(2089, -3357, 1234);
88    v2 = Vector_construct(7658, 0, 1876);
89    printf("================================\n");
90    Vector_print("v1", v1);
91    Vector_print("v2", v2);
92    Vector_writeb("vectorb.dat", v1);
93    v2 = Vector_readb("vectorb.dat");
94    printf("================================\n");
95    Vector_print("v1", v1);
96    Vector_print("v2", v2);
97    return EXIT_SUCCESS;
98  }
```

To write binary data, `fwrite` is used. This function requires four arguments:

1. The *address* of the object. If it is an object (not a pointer), `&` needs to be added before the object.
2. The size of the object by using `sizeof` to find the size of the object.
3. The number of objects to write. This example writes only one object so the value is 1. If a program writes an array of objects, then this argument is the number of elements in the array.
4. The `FILE` pointer.

The return value of `fwrite` is the number of objects written. This number can be different from the third argument because, for example, the disk may be full and only some elements are written. It is a good programming habit to check whether the return value is the same as the third argument. The data written by `fwrite` needs to be read by `fread`, not `fscanf`. Four arguments are required for `fread` and the order of the arguments is the same as that for `fwrite`.

Text and binary files have advantages and disadvantages. If data are stored in a text file, then it can be read by using the `more` command in the terminal or in a text editor. `Vector_readt` and `Vector_writet` must handle the attributes one by one. The order in `Vector_writet` must be the same as the order in `Vector_readt`. If one more attribute is added to `Vector` (for example, `t` for time), then both `Vector_readt` and `Vector_writet` must be changed. These requirements increase the chances of mistakes: It is easy to change one place and forget to change the other. In contrast, `Vector_writeb` and `Vector_readb` automatically handle the order of attributes. If an attribute is added to `Vector`, there is no need to change `Vector_readb` and `Vector_writeb` because `sizeof` reflects the new size. The disadvantage of binary files is that they cannot be edited and viewed directly. The data files are also specific to the hardware because the size and format of the binary data may change.

17.7 Problems

17.7.1 Structure and Pointer

What is the this program's output?

```
1    // CH17:strptr1.c
2    #include <stdio.h>
3    #include <stdlib.h>
4    #pragma pack(1) // do not to pad any space between attributes
5    typedef struct
6    {
7      char a; // assume 1 byte
8      char b; // assume 1 byte
9      int  c; // assume 4 byte
10     double d; // assume 8 byte
11     int  e; // assume 4 byte
12   } Bag;
13   int main(int argc, char * * argv)
```

```
14  {
15    printf("sizeof(char)   = %ld\n", sizeof(char));
16    printf("sizeof(int)    = %ld\n", sizeof(int));
17    printf("sizeof(double) = %ld\n", sizeof(double));
18    printf("sizeof(Bag)    = %ld\n", sizeof(Bag));
19    Bag barray[10];
20    printf("sizeof(barray) = %ld\n", sizeof(barray));
21    long diff1 = (long) &(barray[1].c) - (long) & (barray[0].b);
22    printf("diff1          = %ld\n", diff1);
23    long diff2 = (long) &(barray[2].d) - (long) & (barray[0].c);
24    printf("diff2          = %ld\n", diff2);
25    // assign values to the attributes
26    int ind;
27    for (ind = 0; ind < 10; ind ++)
28      {
29        barray[ind].a = ind + 'a';
30        barray[ind].b = ind + 'b';
31        barray[ind].c = ind;
32        barray[ind].d = 0.1 * ind;
33        barray[ind].e = ind * 10;
34      }
35    char * chptr = & (barray[0].a);
36    chptr += sizeof(Bag);
37    printf("* chptr = %c\n", * chptr);
38    int * intptr = & (barray[0].c);
39    intptr += 9; // it means 9 * sizeof(int);
40    printf("* intptr = %d\n", * intptr);
41    return EXIT_SUCCESS;
42  }
```

The first four lines of the output are

```
sizeof(char)   = 1
sizeof(int)    = 4
sizeof(double) = 8
sizeof(Bag)    = 18
```

17.7.2   Structure and Attributes' Sizes

What are the outputs?

```
1  // CH17:structsize.c
2  #include <stdio.h>
3  #include <stdlib.h>
4  #pragma pack(1)
5  // tell compiler not to pad any space between
6  // attributes in structure
7  // assume the size of the data types
8  // char:    1 byte
```

```
9    // int:      4 bytes
10   // double:   8 bytes
11   // pointer:  8 bytes
12   #define NUMVECTOR 10
13   typedef struct
14   {
15     int x;
16     int y;
17     int z;
18     double t;
19   } Vector;
20   int main(int argc, char ** argv)
21   {
22     Vector varr[NUMVECTOR];
23     printf("%ld\n", sizeof(varr));
24     Vector * vptr;
25     vptr = & varr[0];
26     printf("%ld\n", sizeof(vptr));
27     int ind;
28     for (ind = 0; ind < NUMVECTOR; ind ++)
29       {
30         varr[ind].x = ind;
31         varr[ind].y = ind * 2;
32         varr[ind].z = ind * 3;
33         varr[ind].t = ind * 4.0;
34       }
35     vptr = malloc(sizeof(Vector) * 100);
36     FILE * fptr = fopen("data", "w");
37     // assume fopen succeeds
38     fwrite(varr, sizeof(Vector), NUMVECTOR, fptr);
39     fclose (fptr);
40     fptr = fopen("data", "r");
41     int rtv = fseek(fptr, 48, SEEK_SET);
42     if (rtv != 0)
43       {
44         fclose (fptr);
45         return EXIT_FAILURE;
46       }
47     // assume fseek succeeds
48     int a = -2019;
49     rtv = fread(& a, sizeof(int), 1, fptr);
50     if (rtv == 0)
51       {
52         fclose (fptr);
53         return EXIT_FAILURE;
54       }
55     printf("%d\n", a);
56     Vector v;
57     v = varr[3];
58     v.x = -264;
```

```
59    printf("%d\n", varr[3].x - v.x);
60    free (vptr);
61    printf("%d\n", (vptr == NULL));
62    // please notice ==, it is not =
63    return EXIT_SUCCESS;
64  }
```

17.7.3 Alternative Ways to Assign Attributes

The following program shows another way to assign attributes in lines 38–41. What are the outputs?

```
1   // CH17:structinit.c
2   #include <stdio.h>
3   #include <stdlib.h>
4   #include <string.h>
5   #pragma pack(1) // tell compiler not to pad any space
6   // assume
7   // sizeof(char) = 1,   sizeof(int) = 4,
8   // sizeof(double) = 8, sizeof(a pointer) = 8
9   typedef struct
10  {
11    int a;
12    int b;
13    int c;
14    int d;
15  } Counter;
16  int func(Counter * cnt, int n)
17  {
18    (cnt -> a) ++;
19    if (n == 0)
20      {
21        (cnt -> b) ++;
22        return 1;
23      }
24    if (n == 1)
25      {
26        (cnt -> c) ++;
27        return 2;
28      }
29    int x = func(cnt, n - 1);
30    int y = func(cnt, n - 2);
31    (cnt -> d) ++;
32    return (x + y);
33  }
34  int main(int argc, char ** argv)
35  {
36    Counter cnt =
37      {
38        .a = 0, // same as cnt.a = 0
```

```
39        .b = 0, // same as cnt.b = 0
40        .c = 0,
41        .d = 0
42      };
43    int v = func(& cnt, 5);
44    printf("cnt = (%d, %d, %d, %d)\n", cnt.a, cnt.b, cnt.c, cnt.d);
45    printf("v = %d\n", v);
46    return EXIT_SUCCESS;
47  }
```

Chapter 18

Programming Problems Using Structure

18.1 Sort a Person Database

This program sorts a database of people. Each person is an object with two attributes: name and age. The program sorts the people by ages or by names. The database is a text file containing two columns: age and name. A few lines of the database are shown below:

```
43 Peter
87 Linda
57 Gregory
61 Larry
```

This is the header file of the `Person` structure and the `PersonDatabase` structure.

```c
// CH18:sort/person.h
#ifndef PERSON_H
#define PERSON_H
typedef struct
{
  int age;
  char * name;
} Person;
typedef struct
{
  int number; // number of persons
  Person * * person; // array of pointers to Person objects
} PersonDatabase;
// read person database from a file
// person is an array of pointers to person objects
// The function returns the pointer of a database or NULL
// The function returns NULL if reading from the file fails
PersonDatabase * Person_read(char * filename);
void Person_sortByName(PersonDatabase * perdb);
void Person_sortByAge(PersonDatabase * perdb);
// save the database in a file.
// return 0 if fail, return 1 if succeed
int Person_write(char * filename, PersonDatabase * perdb);
// write to computer screen
void Person_print(PersonDatabase * perdb);
// release the memory of the database
```

```
27    void Person_destruct(PersonDatabase * perdb);
28    #endif
```

Here are implementations of these functions:

```
1     // CH18:sort/person.c
2     #include "person.h"
3     #include <stdio.h>
4     #include <string.h>
5     #include <stdlib.h>
6     PersonDatabase * Person_read(char * filename)
7     {
8       FILE * fptr = fopen(filename, "r");
9       if (fptr == NULL) { return NULL; }
10      PersonDatabase * perdb = malloc(sizeof(PersonDatabase));
11      if (perdb == NULL)
12        {
13          fclose (fptr);
14          return NULL;
15        }
16      // count the number of people in the file
17      // use the longest name for the size of the buffer
18      int numPerson = 0;
19      int longestName = 0;
20      // longest name, length of buffer to read names
21      while (! feof(fptr))
22        {
23          int age;
24          // find a line that contains a number (age)
25          if (fscanf(fptr, "%d", & age) == 1)
26            {
27              numPerson ++;
28              // the remaning characters are the name
29              int nameLength = 0;
30              while ((!feof (fptr)) && (fgetc(fptr) != '\n'))
31                { nameLength ++; }
32              nameLength ++; // for '\n'
33              if (longestName < nameLength)
34                { longestName = nameLength; }
35            }
36        }
37      // the number of person is known now
38      perdb -> number = numPerson;
39      perdb -> person = malloc(sizeof(Person*) * numPerson);
40      // allocate a buffer to read the names
41      char * name = malloc(sizeof(char) * longestName);
42      int ind = 0;
43      // read the file again and store the data in the database
44      // return to the beginning of the file
45      fseek (fptr, 0, SEEK_SET);
```

```
46    while (! feof(fptr))
47      {
48        int age;
49        if (fscanf(fptr, "%d", & age) == 1)
50          {
51            // remove the space separating age and name
52            fgetc(fptr);
53            fgets(name, longestName, fptr);
54            // remove '\n'
55            char * chptr = strchr(name, '\n');
56            // last line may not have '\n'
57            if (chptr != NULL)
58              { * chptr = '\0'; }
59            perdb -> person[ind] = malloc(sizeof(Person));
60            perdb -> person[ind] -> age = age;
61            perdb -> person[ind] -> name = strdup(name);
62            ind ++;
63          }
64      }
65    free (name);
66    fclose (fptr);
67    return perdb;
68  }
69  static void Person_writeHelp(FILE * fptr, PersonDatabase * perdb)
70  {
71    int ind;
72    for (ind = 0; ind < perdb -> number; ind ++)
73      {
74        // write one person per line
75        fprintf(fptr, "%d %s\n", perdb -> person[ind] -> age,
76                perdb -> person[ind] -> name);
77      }
78  }
79  void Person_print(PersonDatabase * perdb)
80  {
81    printf("---------------------------------------\n");
82    // stdout is a built-in FILE *
83    // stdout: output is sent to the computer screen,
84    // not a file on the disk
85    Person_writeHelp(stdout, perdb);
86  }
87  int Person_write(char * filename, PersonDatabase * perdb)
88  {
89    if (perdb == NULL) { return 0; } // nothing in the database
90    FILE * fptr = fopen(filename, "w");
91    if (fptr == NULL) { return 0; } // cannot open the file
92    Person_writeHelp(fptr, perdb);
93    fclose (fptr);
94    return 1;
95  }
```

```
96   static int comparebyName(const void * p1, const void * p2)
97   {
98     // get addresses of the array elements
99     const Person * * pp1 = (const Person * *) p1;
100    const Person * * pp2 = (const Person * *) p2;
101    // get the elements
102    const Person * pv1 = * pp1;
103    const Person * pv2 = * pp2;
104    // compare the attributes
105    return strcmp((pv1 -> name), (pv2 -> name));
106  }
107  void Person_sortByName(PersonDatabase * perdb)
108  {
109    qsort(perdb -> person, perdb -> number,
110          sizeof(Person *), comparebyName);
111  }
112  static int comparebyAge(const void * p1, const void * p2)
113  {
114    const Person * * pp1 = (const Person * *) p1;
115    const Person * * pp2 = (const Person * *) p2;
116    const Person * pv1 = * pp1;
117    const Person * pv2 = * pp2;
118    return ((pv1 -> age) - (pv2 -> age));
119  }
120  void Person_sortByAge(PersonDatabase * perdb)
121  {
122    qsort(perdb -> person, perdb -> number,
123          sizeof(Person *), comparebyAge);
124  }
125  void Person_destruct(PersonDatabase * perdb)
126  {
127    int ind;
128    for (ind = 0; ind < perdb -> number; ind ++)
129      {
130        free (perdb -> person[ind] -> name);
131        free (perdb -> person[ind]);
132      }
133    free (perdb -> person);
134    free (perdb);
135  }
```

This is the **main** function:

```
1   // CH18:sort/ main.c
2   #include <stdio.h>
3   #include <stdlib.h>
4   #include <string.h>
5   #include "person.h"
6   int main(int argc, char * argv[])
7   {
8     // argv[1]: name of input file
```

```
9    // argv[2]: name of output file (sort by name)
10   // argv[3]: name of output file (sort by age)
11   if (argc < 4) { return EXIT_FAILURE; }
12   PersonDatabase * perdb = Person_read(argv[1]);
13   if (perdb == NULL) { return EXIT_FAILURE; }
14   // Person_print(perdb); // uncomment during debugging
15   Person_sortByName(perdb);
16   // Person_print(perdb); // uncomment during debugging
17   if (Person_write(argv[2], perdb) == 0)
18     {
19       Person_destruct(perdb);
20       return EXIT_FAILURE;
21     }
22   Person_sortByAge(perdb);
23   // Person_print(perdb); // uncomment during debugging
24   if (Person_write(argv[3], perdb) == 0)
25     {
26       Person_destruct(perdb);
27       return EXIT_FAILURE;
28     }
29   Person_destruct(perdb);
30   return EXIT_SUCCESS;
31 }
```

The example introduces a new way to debug a program. The intended output should be saved to a file. The sorted `Person` database can be printed to the computer screen by using a pre-defined `FILE` pointer called `stdout`. It means "standard output". You cannot `fopen` this pre-defined pointer. It already exists when any program runs. Information written to `stdout` will appear on the computer screen. The functions `Person_print` and `Person_write` both call `Person_writeHelp`; it writes the database to `stdout` or a file.

This is an example of the DRY (Don't Repeat Yourself) principle. Here we reuse the same code for saving the data to a file and for printing the same data to the computer screen. If the format of the data needs changes, then only one place needs to be changed. This saves time and reduces the chance of mistakes.

The program calls `qsort`, passing the array of `Person *` pointers—each element of the array is a pointer to a `Person` object. Therefore, each item's size is `sizeof(Person *)`. The two comparison functions, `comparebyName` and `comparebyAge`, need some careful thought. Consider this statement:

```
const Person * * pp1 = (const Person * *) p1;
```

Each argument (p1 and p2) is the address of an array element. Each element is a pointer to a `Person` object, i.e., `Person *`. Thus, the arguments to the comparison functions are pointers to `Person *`, i.e., `Person * *`. One of those `*` simply means it is a pointer. The rest, `Person *`, is what is being pointed to. The two arguments `pp1` and `pp2` in the comparison functions are `Person * *`.

Next, consider

```
const Person * pv1 = * pp1;
```

Inside each function, pv1 and pv2 are the pointers to Person objects, i.e., Person *. Table 4.4 summarizes the different ways of using *. In this comparison function, the first * (after Person) means that pv1 is a pointer. The second * (after =) means dereferencing pp1. Dereferencing a pointer means going to the address stored in pp1, and retrieving the value stored at that address. Since pp1 is the address of another pointer (pp1 is the address of an address), pp1's value is also an address; * pp1 is a pointer and this address is assigned to pv1. For pv1, the names and ages are obtained by using pv1 -> name and pv1 -> age. The comparison function comparebyName compares pv1 -> name with pv2 -> name. The second comparison function compares pv1 -> age with pv2 -> age.

Testing the program needs to compare the answers of the program against the correct answers. We can use the Linux program sort to generate the correct answers. The correct answers are generated as follows: (1) sort -n: sort the first column and treat the column as numbers. Without -n, the first column will be treated as strings and "10" is before "9" because 1 is before 9. (2) sort -k 2: sort by the second column.

This is the Makefile for building and testing the program.

```
1   # CH18:sort/Makefile
2   CFLAGS = -g -Wall -Wshadow
3   GCC = gcc $(CFLAGS)
4   SRCS = person.c main.c
5   OBJS = $(SRCS:%.c=%.o)
6   TEST = ./main database output1 output2
7   VALGRIND = valgrind --tool=memcheck --leak-check=full
8   VALGRIND += --verbose --log-file=logfile
9
10  main: $(OBJS)
11          $(GCC) $(OBJS) -o main
12
13  test: main
14          $(TEST)
15          diff output1 sortbyname
16          diff output2 sortbyage
17          $(VALGRIND) $(TEST)
18
19  memory: main
20          valgrind --leak-check=yes --verbose $(TEST)
21
22  .c.o:
23          $(GCC) $(CFLAGS) -c $*.c
24
25  clean:
26          rm -f *.o *~ a.out main output* logfile
27
```

18.2 Packing Decimal Digits

This problem aims to store two decimal digits per byte. The minimum unit of information in a computer is called a *bit*. One bit can have two possible values: 0 or 1. A sequence of bits can be used to represent a binary number, a number in base 2. This is a *binary system*. We usually think of numbers in base ten, the *decimal system*. In base ten we form numbers with ten different values: 0, 1, 2, 3, 4, 5, 6, 7, 8, 9. What does 2783 mean in the decimal system? Two thousands + seven hundreds + eight tens + three:

$$2 \times 10^3 + 7 \times 10^2 + 8 \times 10 + 3 \times 10^0 \tag{18.1}$$

How does this relate to the binary systems? The number binary 10110 means:

$$1 \times 2^4 + 1 \times 2^2 + 1 \times 2^1 + 0 \times 2^0 \tag{18.2}$$

Another commonly used number system is the hexadecimal system. Hexadecimal numbers are in base sixteen, and thus require sixteen symbols: 0, 1, 2, 3, 4, 5, 6, 7, 8, 9, A, B, C, D, E, F. What does EA29 mean in the hexadecimal system? It means

$$\text{E} \times 16^3 + \text{A} \times 16^2 + 2 \times 16^1 + 9 \times 16^0 \tag{18.3}$$

In C programs, hexadecimal numbers start with 0x (or 0X), for example, 0xAC, 0x9B, and 0x15. Sixteen is the fourth power of two and one hexadecimal digit can express a 4-bit binary number. A decimal number requires four bits. Table 18.1 shows the relationships between the three different number systems: In general, if a number system is base n, n symbols are allowed: zero, one, two, ..., $n - 1$. A number $a_m a_{m-1} a_{m-2}...a_1 a_0$ means

$$a_m \times n^m + a_{m-1} \times n^{m-1} + a_{m-2} \times n^{m-2} + ... + a_1 \times n^1 + a_0 \times n^0 \tag{18.4}$$

How can we convert a number to a different system? If a decimal number is 273, what is the binary representation? $273 = 256 + 16 + 1 = 2^8 + 2^4 + 1 = 1\ 0000\ 0000_b + 1\ 000_b + 1_b$. Therefore, $273_d = 1\ 0001\ 0001_b$. Here, the subscripts d and b indicate the numbers are decimal and binary respectively. Space is added between four binary digits in order to make the numbers easier to read.

In C programs, the minimum size

TABLE 18.1: Different number systems. D: Decimal, **B**: Binary, **H**: Hexadecimal.

D	B	H	D	B	H	D	B	H
0	0	0	8	1000	8	16	10000	10
1	1	1	9	1001	9	17	10001	11
2	10	2	10	1010	A	18	10010	12
3	11	3	11	1011	B	19	10011	13
4	100	4	12	1100	C	20	10100	14
5	101	5	13	1101	D	21	10101	15
6	110	6	14	1110	E	22	10110	16
7	111	7	15	1111	F	23	10111	17

of a variable is one byte (8 bits) and its type is **unsigned char**. The valid decimal values for **unsigned char** are 0 through 255, inclusively. It is not possible to have a one-bit variable in C programs. Also, C does not allow for the expression of binary numbers. For example, $1010\ 0110_b$ is expressed as 0xA6; $1100\ 1011_b$ is expressed as 0xCB. If **gcc** is used, binary numbers may be expressed by adding prefix 0b. For example, 0b1010 is the number 10_d. This is **gcc**'s extension, and may not work in other compilers. Instead, binary numbers should be expressed as hexadecimal numbers. ASCII (American Standard Code for Information Interchange) uses 8 bits (i.e., one byte) to store characters. This is inefficient if only decimal digits (0, 1, 2, ..., 9) are needed. Only 4 bits are necessary for storing a single decimal digit.

This problem asks you to implement a structure called **DecPack**: it packs two decimal digits into one single byte (**unsigned char**). Each **DecPack** object has three attributes:

- **size**: the maximum number of decimal digits that can be stored in a **DecPack** object.
- **used**: the actual number of decimal digits that are stored in a **DecPack** object.

- `data`: an array of `unsigned char`. Each element stores one or two decimal digits. The upper (i.e., left) 4 bits stores one decimal digit and the lower (i.e., right) 4 bits stores another decimal digit. If `size` is an even number, the array has `size / 2` elements. If `size` is an odd number, the array has `(size + 1) / 2` elements.

When inserting a decimal digit using `DecPack_insert`, the function checks whether `data` is full. If it is full, then the size of the `data` array doubles. The old array is copied to the new array and the memory for the old array is released. If a byte has not been used, then the decimal digit uses the upper 4 bits. If the upper 4 bits of a byte are already used, the decimal digit uses the lower 4 bits. When deleting a decimal digit using `DecPack_delete`, the function modifies `used` and returns the most recently inserted decimal digit. The digit's value must be between 0 and 9 (not '0' to '9'). Please be aware that '0' corresponds to value 48 in the ASCII table. For simplicity, `DecPack_delete` does not shrink the `data` array even if `used` is zero. The `DecPack_print` function prints the decimal digits stored in the object. The printed decimal digits should be between '0' and '9'—if the decimal digit is 0, then '0' is printed, if the decimal digit is 1, then '1' is printed. Finally, `DecPack_destroy` releases the memory.

C provides several ways to directly manipulate the bits in a byte. Table 18.2 shows several operators for bit values. The bit-wise AND operation is used between two numbers. If the bits from both numbers are 1, the resultant bit is 1. If one or both bits are zero, then the resultant bit is zero. Sometimes, a program wants to keep some bits while discarding the other bits. For example, if the program wants to keep only the lower (right) four bits of a byte, then the program uses bit-wise AND with 0x0F ($0000\ 1111_b$). Table 18.3 (b) shows this example.

TABLE 18.2: Operators for bits.

operation	operator
bit-wise AND	&
bit-wise OR	|
shift left	<<
shift right	>>
exclusive or (XOR)	∧

TABLE 18.3: (a) The output of AND is 1 only if both bits are 1. (b) Use AND to block or pass bits.

	0	1	1	0	1	0	0	1		-	-	-	-	a	b	c	d
&	1	1	0	1	0	0	1	1	&	0	0	0	0	1	1	1	1
	0	1	0	0	0	0	0	1		0	0	0	0	a	b	c	d
				(a)										(b)			

It does not matter whether - is 0 or 1, the first (higher, left) four bits, the result will always be 0. The other four bits: a, b, c, and d are either 0 or 1 depending on the values of a, b, c, and d. The value 0X0F is called a *mask*. A mask blocks some bits and allows the other bits to pass through. If a program wants to check if the leftmost bit is 1 or 0, then it can use a mask whose binary representation is $1000\ 0000_b$ (0x80 in hexadecimal). The following example checks whether the variable `a`'s leftmost bit is 1 or 0:

```c
unsigned char a = 161;
unsigned char mask = 0x80; // binary 1000 0000
if ((a & mask) != 0) // must not use == 1
{
    // a's leftmost bit is 1
}
else
```

```
{
    // a's leftmost bit is 0
}
```

In this example, `a & mask` is not 0 because 161 is greater than 127 and the leftmost bit must be 1. Please be aware that `!= 0` and `== 1` are different because `a & mask` is actually `0X80` (i.e., 128 in decimal), not 1. The bit-wise AND operator `&` is useful for masking numbers: setting some bits to zero, while leaving the other bits unaffected.

TABLE 18.4: Bit-wise OR operation.

	0	1	1	0	1	0	0	1
|	1	1	0	1	0	0	0	0
	1	1	1	1	1	0	0	1

The second bit-wise operator is OR (`|`) used between two numbers. If the bit from either number is 1, the resultant bit is 1. If both are zero, then the resultant bit is zero.

The third operator is the bit-wise shift left operation $<<$. It moves bits to the left and adds zeros to the right. Table 18.5 (a) shows left-shifting by two. The leftmost two bits are discarded (marked as -) and two zeros are added to the right: 0110 1001_b becomes 1010 0100_b. The bit-wise shift right operation (`>>`) moves bits to the right and adding zeros to the left. Table 18.5 (b) shows an example of shifting right by two. The rightmost two bits are discarded (marked as -) and two zeros are added to the left. 0110 1001_b becomes 0001 1010_b. Shifting right by one is equivalent to division by two. Shifting left by one is equivalent to multiplication with two (ignoring overflow).

TABLE 18.5: (a) Shifting left `<<` adds zero to the right. (b) Shifting right `>>` adds zero the the left. Here, `-` means the bit is discarded.

original	0	1	1	0	1	0	0	1			<< 2
new	-	-	1	0	1	0	0	1	0	0	
						(a)					
original			0	1	1	0	1	0	0	1	>> 2
new	0	0	0	1	1	0	1	0	-	-	
						(b)					

The following program shows how to use bit-wise operations:

```
// CH18:decimal/bits.c
# include <stdio.h>
# include <stdlib.h>
# include <string.h>
int main ( int argc , char * * argv )
{
  unsigned char a = 129;     // decimal 129, hexadecimal 0X81
  unsigned char b = 0XF0;    // decimal 240
  // a = 1000 0001
  // b = 1111 0000
  unsigned char c = a & b;
  // c = 1000 0000
  printf("%d, %X\n", c, c); // decimal 128, hexadecimal 80
  unsigned char d = a | b;
  // d = 1111 0001
  printf("%d, %X\n", d, d); // decimal 241, hexadecomal F1
```

```
17    unsigned char e = d << 3;
18    // e = 1000 1000
19    printf("%d, %X\n", e, e); // decimal 136, hexadecimal 88
20    unsigned char f = d >> 2;
21    // f = 0011 1100
22    printf("%d, %X\n", f, f); // decimal 60, hexadecomal 3C
23    return EXIT_SUCCESS ;
24  }
```

The final bit-wise operation that we consider is the exclusive or operation ($\wedge$), often abbreviated as XOR. The resulting bit is 1 if and only if the two input bits are different. Please note that $\wedge$ means exclusive or (XOR) in C programs. In some other languages, $\wedge$ means exponential. C uses exp for exponential.

TABLE 18.6: Bit-wise XOR operation.

	0	1	1	0	1	0	0	1
$\wedge$	1	1	0	1	0	0	0	0
	1	0	1	1	1	0	0	1

In DecPack, a decimal digital (0 to 9) requires only 4 bits. Thus, to put this digital into the upper 4 bits, it needs to be shifted left by 4: four zeros will be added to the right 4 bits. To retrieve one decimal digit from the upper 4 bits, the byte is shifted right by 4 bits: four zeros will be added to the left 4 bits. To put one decimal digital into the lower 4 bits, it can be added to the byte directly without shifting. To retrieve one decimal digital from the lower 4 bits, a mask 0x0F is used to block the upper 4 bits.

The value of used means the number of digits that have been already inserted. If used is an even number (for example, 8), then the next inserted digit should be the 9th digit. In C programs, array indexes start from 0. The 9th digit uses the 5th byte and the index should be 4. The index is 8 / 2 (integer division). Thus, used / 2 is the correct index. If used is an odd number (for example, 11), then the next inserted digit is the 12th digit. It should be the 6th byte and the index is 5; used / 2 is also the correct index. Thus, used / 2 is the correct index for insertion; used should be incremented after insertion.

When deleting a digit, used should decrement before the retrieval. Aside from being symmetric to insertion, this can be understood by working through some examples. Suppose used is an even number, say 12, then six bytes are used. The last digit is at the 6th byte and the index is 5. If used decrements first, it becomes 11 and used / 2 is 5. If used is an odd number, say 9, then we are using five bytes. The last digit is at the 5th byte and the index is 4. If used decrements first, it becomes 8 and used / 2 is 4. In both cases, used should decrement before deletion. The header file decpack.h is listed below:

```
1   // CH18:decimal/decpack.h
2   #ifndef DECPACK_H
3   #define DECPACK_H
4   typedef struct
5   {
6     int size; // how many digits can be stored
7     int used; // how many digits are actually stored
8     unsigned char * data; // store the digits
9     // size should be 2 * the actually allocated memory because
10    // each byte can store two digits
11  } DecPack;
12  // create a DecPack object with the given size
13  DecPack * DecPack_create(int sz);
```

```
14    // Insert a decimal value into the DecPack object. The new
15    // value is at the end of the array
16    void DecPack_insert(DecPack * dp, int val);
17    // delete and return the last value in the DecPack object
18    // do not shrink the data array even if nothing is stored
19    // The returned value should be between 0 and 9
20    // return -1 if no digit can be deleted
21    int DecPack_delete(DecPack * dp);
22    // print the values stored in the object, the first inserted
23    // value should be printed first
24    // the printed values are between '0' and '9'
25    void DecPack_print(DecPack * dp);
26    // destroy the whole DecPack object, release all memory
27    void DecPack_destroy(DecPack * dp);
28    #endif
```

Here are sample implementations of the functions in `decpack.c`:

```
1     // CH18:decimal/decpack.c
2     # include <stdio.h>
3     # include <stdlib.h>
4     # include <string.h>
5     # include "decpack.h"
6     DecPack * DecPack_create(int sz)
7     {
8       // allocate memory for DecPack
9       DecPack * dp = malloc(sizeof(DecPack));
10      // check whether allocation fails
11      if (dp == NULL) { return NULL; }
12      // initialize size to sz and used to 0
13      dp -> size = sz;
14      dp -> used = 0;
15      // allocate memory for data, should be only sz/2 because
16      // each byte can store two digits
17      // if sz is odd, increment sz by one
18      if ((sz % 2) == 1) { sz ++; }
19      dp -> data = malloc(sizeof(unsigned char) * (sz / 2));
20      // check whether allocation fails
21      if (dp -> data == NULL)
22        {
23          free (dp);
24          return NULL;
25        }
26      // return the allocate memory
27      return dp;
28    }
29    void DecPack_insert(DecPack * dp, int val)
30    {
31      // if the object is empty, do nothing
32      if (dp == NULL) { return; }
33      // if val < 0 or val > 9, ignore and do nothing
```

```
34    if ((val < 0) || (val > 9)) { return; }
35    // If the allocated memory is full, double the size,
36    // allocate memory for the new size, copy the data,
37    // and insert the new value
38    int used = dp -> used;
39    if (used == dp -> size)
40      {
41        unsigned char * newdata = malloc(sizeof(unsigned char) *
42                                   (dp -> size));
43        int iter;
44        for (iter = 0; iter < used; iter ++)
45          { newdata[iter / 2] = dp -> data[iter / 2]; }
46        (dp -> size) *= 2;
47        free (dp -> data);
48        dp -> data = newdata;
49      }
50    // If used is an even number, the inserted value should
51    // use the upper (left) 4 bits.
52    // If used is an odd number, the inserted value should
53    // use the lower (right) 4 bits.
54    //
55    // careful: do not lose the data already stored in DecPack
56    if ((used % 2) == 0)
57      {
58        // shifting left adds zeros for the lower bits
59        dp -> data[used / 2] = (val << 4);
60      }
61    else
62      {
63        // reset the lower four bits, may be left from delete
64        unsigned char upper = dp -> data[used / 2] & 0XF0;
65        dp -> data[used / 2] = upper + val;
66      }
67    (dp -> used) ++;
68  }
69  int DecPack_delete(DecPack * dp)
70  {
71    // if the object is empty, do nothing
72    if (dp == NULL) { return -1; }
73    // return -1 if the DecPack object stores no data
74    if ((dp -> used) == 0) { return -1; }
75    // If used is even, the returned value is the upper (left) 4
76    // bits. Make sure the returned value is between 0 and 9. If used is
77    // odd, the returned value is the lower (right) 4 bits. Make sure
78    // the returned value is between 0 and 9.
79    int val;
80    // decrement the used attribute in the DecPack object
81    (dp -> used) --;
82    int used = dp -> used;
83    if ((used % 2) == 0) { val = dp -> data[used / 2] >> 4; }
```

```
84    else { val = (dp -> data[used / 2]) & OXOF; }
85    // return the value
86    return val;
87  }
88  void DecPack_print(DecPack * dp)
89  {
90    // if the object is empty, do nothing
91    if (dp == NULL) { return; }
92    int iter;
93    int used = dp -> used;
94    // go through every value stored in the data attribute
95    for (iter = 0; iter < used; iter ++)
96      {
97        if ((iter % 2) == 0)
98          { printf("%d", (dp-> data[iter / 2] >> 4));}
99        else { printf("%d", (dp-> data[iter / 2] & OXOF)); }
100     }
101   printf("\n");
102 }
103 void DecPack_destroy(DecPack * dp)
104 {
105   // if the object is empty, do nothing
106   if (dp == NULL) { return; }
107   // release the memory for the data
108   free (dp -> data);
109   // release the memory for the object
110   free (dp);
111 }
```

This is the `main` function:

```
1   // CH18:decimal/main.c
2   #include <stdio.h>
3   #include <stdlib.h>
4   #include "decpack.h"
5   int main ( int argc , char * * argv )
6   {
7     DecPack * dp = DecPack_create(5);
8     int iter;
9     for (iter = 0; iter < 21 ; iter ++)
10      { DecPack_insert(dp, iter % 10); }
11    DecPack_print(dp);
12    for (iter = 0; iter < 7 ; iter ++)
13      {  printf("delete %d\n", DecPack_delete(dp)); }
14    DecPack_print(dp);
15    for (iter = 0; iter < 6 ; iter ++)
16      { DecPack_insert(dp, iter % 10); }
17    DecPack_print(dp);
18    for (iter = 0; iter < 6 ; iter ++)
19      { printf("delete %d\n", DecPack_delete(dp)); }
20    DecPack_print(dp);
```

```
21    DecPack_destroy(dp);
22    return EXIT_SUCCESS ;
23  }
```

This is the `Makefile`

```
1   # CH18:decimal/Makefile
2   GCC = gcc
3   CFLAGS = -g -Wall -Wshadow
4   VALGRIND = valgrind --tool=memcheck --verbose --log-file
5
6   decpack: decpack.c decpack.h main.c
7           $(GCC) $(CFLAGS) decpack.c main.c -o $@
8           $(VALGRIND)=valgrindlog ./decpack
9
10  clean:
11          /bin/rm -f *.o decpack *log
```

18.3   Binary File and Pointer

Section 17.6 describes how to use `fread` and `fwrite` to read and write the attributes of an object. What happens if the object contains one or more pointers? Consider the following example:

```
1   // CH18:fread/array.c
2   #include <stdio.h>
3   #include <stdlib.h>
4   #include <time.h>
5   #pragma pack(1) // tell compiler not to pad any space
6   typedef struct
7   {
8     int length;
9     int * data;
10  } Array;
11  // for simplicity, this program does not check errors
12  int main(int argc, char **argv)
13  {
14    int length = 10;
15    char * filename = "data";
16    Array * aptr1 = NULL;
17    printf("sizeof(aptr1) = %d\n", (int) sizeof(aptr1));
18    aptr1 = malloc(sizeof(Array)); // need to allocate Array first
19    printf("sizeof(aptr1) = %d, sizeof(Array) = %d\n",
20            (int) sizeof(aptr1), (int) sizeof(Array));
21    // allocate memory for the data
22    aptr1 -> length = length;
```

```
23    aptr1 -> data = malloc(sizeof(int) * (aptr1 -> length));
24    printf("sizeof(aptr1): %d, sizeof(aptr1 -> data): %d\n",
25            (int) sizeof(aptr1), (int) sizeof(aptr1 -> data));
26    // initialize the values of the array
27    int ind;
28    for (ind = 0; ind < (aptr1 -> length); ind ++)
29      { aptr1 -> data[ind] = ind; } // 0, 1, 2, ..., 9
30    int sum = 0;
31    for (ind = 0; ind < (aptr1 -> length); ind ++)
32      { sum += aptr1 -> data[ind]; }
33    printf("sum = %d\n", sum);
34    // save the data to a file
35    FILE * fptr = fopen(filename, "w");
36    // write the data to the file
37    if (fwrite(aptr1, sizeof(Array), 1, fptr) != 1)
38      { return EXIT_FAILURE; } // fwrite fail
39    printf("ftell(fptr) = %d\n", (int) ftell(fptr));
40    fclose (fptr);
41    // fill the array with random numbers
42    // ensure the heap contains garbage before releasing it
43    srand(time(NULL)); // set the seed of the random number
44    for (ind = 0; ind < (aptr1 -> length); ind ++)
45      { aptr1 -> data[ind] = rand();  }
46    // read the data from the file
47    Array * aptr2 = NULL;
48    aptr2 = malloc(sizeof(Array));
49    fptr = fopen(filename, "r");
50    if (fread(aptr2, sizeof(Array), 1, fptr) != 1)
51      { return EXIT_FAILURE; } // fread fail
52    // add the data
53    sum = 0;
54    for (ind = 0; ind < (aptr2 -> length); ind ++)
55      { sum += aptr2 -> data[ind]; }
56    printf("sum = %d\n", sum);
57    // release memory
58    free(aptr2);
59    free(aptr1 -> data);
60    free(aptr1);
61    return EXIT_SUCCESS;
62  }
```

The structure **Array** has two attributes: an integer called **length** and an array of integers. Line 29 assigns 0, 1, 2, ..., 9 to the array's elements. Line 37 saves the object to a file using **fwrite**. Line 45 assigns random numbers to the array's elements. Line 50 reads data from the file and saves into the **Array** object. Line 55 adds the array's elements and line 56 prints the sum. The value should be $0 + 1 + 2 + ... + 9 = 45$. Running this program on a 64-bit (8 bytes) machine, here is the output:

```
sizeof(arrptr1) = 8
sizeof(arrptr1) = 8, sizeof(Array) = 12
```

```
sizeof(arrptr1) = 8, sizeof(arrptr1 -> data) = 8
sum = 45
ftell(fptr) = 12
sum = 1289469162
```

The second value of sum may change if the program runs again. The array's elements are set to random values (line 45) after the data has been written to the file. When line 50 reads the data, are the elements set to 0, 1, 2, ..., 9? No. If we run this program with valgrind, it will tell us that the program has an "Invalid read". Why? The reason is that we cannot use fwrite to save an object if an attribute is a pointer. Line 37 saves the value of the attribute and this value is an address provided by malloc. To understand this in a different way, sizeof(Array) is 12 because it includes an integer (4 bytes) and a pointer (8 bytes). Line 37 saves 12 bytes to the file. This is the reason why ftell returns 12 bytes. The array has 10 elements and uses 40 bytes (each integer is 4 bytes). The elements' values are not written to the file. Instead of saving the address, the program should save the data stored at the address. When a structure has a pointer as an attribute, saving the object should take two steps: (1) saving the attributes' values if they are not pointers and (2) saving the data from memory referred to by the pointer, not the addresses in memory.

18.4   Problems

18.4.1   Number Systems

Convert binary number $1010\ 1101_b$ to hexadecimal and decimal.
Convert decimal number 437_d to binary and hexadecimal.

18.4.2   Structure with Pointer-1

Consider the program on Page 235. Does aptr2 -> data points to valid memory? Explain your answer.

18.4.3   Structure with Pointer-2

Modify the program on Page 235 and use fread correctly. Hint: To write the data, the program needs to call fwrite twice. To read the data stored in the file, the program should call fread twice: the first time for the attribute that is not a pointer and the second time for the attribute that is a pointer.

Chapter 19

Linked Lists

This chapter explains how to create a data structure whose size can grow and shrink as needed.

19.1 Dynamic Data Structure

The previous chapters described two common ways to allocate memory: The first scenario is static allocation on the stack memory when the sizes are known. If only stack memory is used, memory leak is not possible and this is an advantage. This is an example using stack memory for an array of 100 integers:

```
int arr[100]; // creates an array with 100 elements.
```

In many cases, however, the size of the needed memory is unknown when the program is written. Instead, the size is known after the program starts running. This is the second scenario. An example is shown below, where the size is given by the user:

```
int * arr;
int length;
printf("Please enter the length of the array: ");
scanf("%d", & length);
arr = malloc(length * sizeof(int));
```

This scenario is often used when reading data from a file following these steps (1) Read the file once to determine how much memory is needed. (2) Allocate the required memory. (3) Call fseek to return to the beginning of the file. (4) Read the file again and store the data in the allocated memory. The following code shows an example:

```
char * data;
fseek(fptr, 0, SEEK_END); // go to the end
int length = (int) ftell (fptr); // get the file's length
data = malloc(sizeof(char) * length);
```

This chapter describes another scenario: it is impossible to know the size of data because the size grows and shrinks. Memory must be allocated as needed. When a piece of memory is no longer needed, it is freed. This is a very common scenario. Imagine that you are creating a social network system. How many users will register? It is possible that there will be millions of users but we have no direct control over who signs up. We cannot have a pre-determined number, say five million users, and reject new registrations after there are already five million users. One solution is to allocate enough memory for everyone on earth but this is wasteful. Moreover, users may come and go. Some users register but forget their

DOI: 10.1201/9781003257981-19

passwords and then create new accounts. Some users may decide not to use this service and delete their accounts. To manage this type of applications, we must be able to allocate memory as needed. Memory usage must grow and shrink as the demands of the applications require. This chapter describes how to use *dynamic structures*.

19.2   Linked Lists

This chapter explains how to create a dynamic data structure, called *linked list*, designed to grow and shrink as needed. This data structure supports the following functions:

- Insert: add new data stored in newly allocated memory.
- Search: determine whether a piece of data has already been inserted.
- Delete: remove one piece of data and free memory.
- Print: print the stored data.
- Destroy: remove all data and free all memory.

A linked list is an example of *container structures*. Container structures may contain different types of data and the code to `insert`, `search`, `delete`, `print`, and `destroy` is quite similar for different types of data.

A linked list is a collection of *nodes* that are linked together by pointers. Each node is an object with at least two *attributes*: (1) A pointer to another node. By convention, this attribute is called `next`. If a given node does not have the next node, then the `next` attribute stores `NULL`. (2) Data. This attribute may be a primitive type such as `int`, `char`, or `double`, an object, or a pointer. Below is an example structure, with two attributes, used as a node in a linked list. For simplicity, the data attribute is an integer.

```
typedef struct listnode
{
  struct listnode * next;
  int value;
} Node; // ; is needed
```

This chapter introduces a *self-referring structure*. Notice that `next` is a pointer to `struct listnode`. This must be a pointer. The C compiler reads source files from top to bottom; thus, it cannot see the type name `Node` yet when `next` is read. Without the knowledge of the entire structure, the compiler does not know the size of the structure. If `next` is a pointer, the compiler knows the size of a pointer (determined by the computer's hardware). We assign a temporary type name: `struct listnode`. This data type can be referred as `struct listnode` or `Node`. It is preferred using `Node` for conciseness. After creating this structure, we can create the first node, by convention, called the `head` of the linked list.

```
Node * head = NULL; // nothing in the list yet
```

The value of this pointer is `NULL`: `NULL` is a special symbol to indicate an invalid memory address. This statement means the linked list does not exist yet.

19.3 Insert Data

To insert data to this linked list, heap memory is allocated and **head** points to this memory address.

```
Node * head = NULL;
head = malloc(sizeof(Node)); // allocate memory
head -> next = NULL; // nothing after this node
head -> value = 917; // store a value
```

TABLE 19.1: Stack and heap memory after creating one Node.

Symbol	Address	Value	Symbol	Address	Value
head	100	A 60000	head -> value	60008	917
			head -> next	60000	NULL
Stack Memory			Heap Memory		

Table 19.1 shows the stack and heap memory after creating the first node in a linked list, and assign a number to the **value** attribute. Calling **malloc** will allocate space in heap memory for the two attributes. Suppose **malloc** returns address 60000, then this value is assigned to the value of **head**. We can create a function **List_insert** that does four things: (1) allocate memory for a new node; (2) initialize the **next** attribute to NULL; (3) assign a value to the **value** attribute; (4) return the first node of the linked list.

```
1   // CH19:listinsert.c
2   #include "list.h"
3   #include <stdio.h>
4   static Node * Node_construct(int val)
5   {
6     Node * nd = malloc(sizeof(Node));
7     nd -> value = val;
8     nd -> next = NULL;
9     return nd;
10  }
11  Node * List_insert(Node * head, int val)
12  {
13    printf("insert %d\n", val);
14    Node * ptr = Node_construct(val);
15    ptr -> next = head; // insert new node before head
16    return ptr;        // return the newly created node
17  }
```

Using this function, we can create a list with two nodes:

```
Node * head = NULL;
head = List_insert(head, 917);
head = List_insert(head, -504);
```

TABLE 19.2:   Stack and heap memory after inserting two
nodes.

Symbol	Address	Value	Symbol	Address	Value
head	100	A80000	value	80008	-504
			next	80000	A60000
			value	60008	917
			next	60000	NULL
Stack Memory			Heap Memory		

Calling `List_insert` with −504 as
the argument creates one more list
node and it is inserted at the beginning
of the list. It is simpler to insert nodes
onto the front of a linked list. Please
note that this means that the value
stored at **head** must change. This is

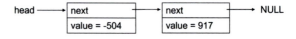

FIGURE 19.1: Illustration of a linked list with
two nodes.

because **head** must be the newly inserted node that we just allocated. Note that there is no
guarantee that when calling **malloc** twice we will obtain consecutive addresses. Table 19.2
shows a gap between the memory allocated to the two list nodes. This is called a linked list
because **head** points to memory address A80000 and it points to A60000. Figure 19.1 is an
illustration of a linked list with two nodes.

This constructor ensures that **next** is always initialized to NULL because NULL indicates
the end of the list. Even though `List_insert` immediately changes **next** after calling
`Node_construct`, it is a good habit to always initialize **next**. In `List_insert`, the newly
constructed node is called **ptr**. Line 15 puts the newly created node in front of the first
node of the old list. Line 16 returns the newly created node. This makes **head** point to the
newly created node. Thus, the most recently added node is at the beginning of the list.
When `List_insert` is called again, a new list node is created and it is the beginning of the
list. The value stored at **head** changes again. Inserting new elements onto the front of the
list is rather like a "stack". The beginning of the list is always the most recently inserted
value. If we always remove from the front (i.e., the **head**), then we indeed meet the property
of a stack: last-in, first-out.

19.4   Search a Linked List

The next function searches a linked list for the node whose value is the same as the given
argument. If the same value appears multiple times, this function returns the first one from
the list's head.

```
1  // CH19:listsearch.c
2  #include "list.h"
3  #include <stdio.h>
4  Node * List_search(Node * head, int val)
5  // head: the head node of the linked list
6  // val: the value to search
7  // If any node stores val, this function returns that node
8  // If multiple nodes store val, this function returns the node
```

```
9    //    closest to the head.
10   // If no node stores val, this function returns NULL
11   {
12     Node * ptr = head;
13     while (ptr != NULL)
14       {
15         if ((ptr -> value) == val)
16           { return ptr;}
17         ptr = ptr -> next;
18       }
19     return ptr;  // must be NULL now
20   }
```

The function starts from the first node in the list. Before the function does anything, the function has to check whether the list is empty. This is the purpose of line 13. If the value is found at line 15, then the function returns the address of this node. Otherwise, `ptr` moves to the next node. If multiple nodes store the value matching the argument `val`, this function returns the first match from `head`. Line 19 should always be `NULL` because that is the reason for getting out of `while`. This example shows the importance of initializing `next` to `NULL` to indicate the end of the list.

19.5   Delete a Node from a Linked List

The `List_delete` function finds and deletes a node that stores a specific value. Figure 19.2 illustrates the process. The first step finds the node *before* the node to be deleted. Suppose q points to the node to be deleted. We need to find the node before q, i.e., p such that `p -> next` is q. The second step changes `p -> next` so that it is linked to the node after q, i.e., `p -> next` is `q -> next`. This is shown in Figure 19.2 (b). The third step frees the memory pointed by q. If the node to delete is the first node of the list (i.e., q and `head` point to the same node), the procedure is slightly different, as shown in Figure 19.2 (d)–(f). In this case, we need to move `head` to point to the second node (i.e., original `head -> next`). The last step frees the memory pointed by q.

```
1    // CH19:listdelete.c
2    #include "list.h"
3    #include <stdio.h>
4    Node * List_delete(Node * head, int val)
5    {
6      printf("delete %d\n", val);
7      Node * q = head;
8      if (q == NULL) // empty list, return NULL
9        { return NULL; }
10     // delete the head node
11     if ((q -> value) == val)
12       {
13         head = head -> next;
```

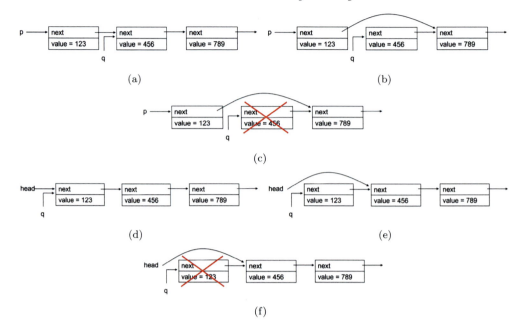

FIGURE 19.2: Procedure to delete the node q.

```
14        free (q);
15        return head;
16    }
17    // not deleting the head node
18    Node * p = head;
19    q = p -> next; // p is before q
20    while ((q != NULL) && ((q -> value) != val))
21      {
22        // check whether q is NULL before checking q -> value
23        p = p -> next;
24        q = q -> next;
25      }
26    if (q != NULL)  // q-> value matches val
27      {
28        // delete the node whose value is val
29        p -> next = q -> next;
30        free (q);
31      }
32    return head;
33 }
```

Lines 20 to 25 find the node whose value is `val`. The `while` loop stops in one of two conditions: either `q` is NULL or `q -> value` is `val`. To avoid a memory error, the function must check the first condition before checking the second condition. If `q` is NULL, then the second condition is not checked. When `q` is NULL, the first part of the logical AND (`&&`) expression is false and the entire logical AND expression is false. The program does not check whether `q -> value` is the same as `val`. This is called *short-circuit* evaluation and

C programs often rely on it. Lines 23 and 24 move p and q to their next nodes. Since q is initialized to p -> next, the code inside the entire block always keeps q and p -> next point to the same node.

If q is NULL at line 26, no node in the linked list stores val and no node needs to be deleted. If q is not NULL, then a node whose value is val has been found. The function changes p -> next to q -> next. This bypasses the node q that is about to be deleted. In this method, q is the node to be deleted and p is the node before q. It is necessary to keep p because it is not possible to go backward from q to p. The function then frees the memory pointed to by q. Using q's value after free(q) will cause segmentation fault. Please be aware that

```
free(q);
```

does not set q's value to NULL. Thus, q's value is still a memory address (not NULL) but this piece of memory is no longer valid after free.

19.6   Print a Linked List

List_print is more straightforward than the previous functions because it does not need to change the list. The function goes through the nodes one-by-one and prints the values.

```
1  // CH19:listprint.c
2  #include "list.h"
3  #include <stdio.h>
4  void List_print(Node * head)
5  {
6    printf("\nPrint the whole list:\n");
7    while (head != NULL)
8      {
9        printf("%d ", head -> value);
10       head = head -> next;
11     }
12   printf("\n");
13 }
```

This function is called at line 11 of listmain.c shown in the next section.

```
11  List_print(head);
```

Please notice that the argument is head, not & head. The List_print function changes head. Will this function lose the list after printing? The answer is No. In this function, head is an argument and it exists in only this function's frame. When this function ends, this head is removed from the stack memory.

19.7   Destroy a Linked List

List_destroy destroys the whole list, releasing the memory for each node. The function keeps a pointer p for the node after the node to be deleted.

```
// CH19:listdestroy.c
#include "list.h"
#include <stdlib.h>
void List_destroy(Node * head)
{
  while (head != NULL)
    {
      Node * p = head -> next;
      free (head);
      head = p;
    }
}
```

The following main function shows how to use the linked list functions we have developed in this chapter.

```
// CH19:listmain.c
#include "list.h"
#include <stdlib.h>
#include <stdio.h>
int main(int argc, char * argv[])
{
  Node * head = NULL; /* must initialize it to NULL */
  head = List_insert(head, 917);
  head = List_insert(head, -504);
  head = List_insert(head, 326);
  List_print(head);
  head = List_delete(head, -504);
  List_print(head);
  head = List_insert(head, 138);
  head = List_insert(head, -64);
  head = List_insert(head, 263);
  List_print(head);
  if (List_search(head, 138) != NULL)
    { printf("138 is in the list\n"); }
  else
    { printf("138 is not in the list\n"); }
  if (List_search(head, 987) != NULL)
    { printf("987 is in the list\n"); }
  else
    { printf("987 is not in the list\n"); }
  head = List_delete(head, 263); // delete the first Node
  List_print(head);
```

```
28    head = List_delete(head, 917); // delete the last Node
29    List_print(head);
30    List_destroy(head);     // delete all Nodes
31    return EXIT_SUCCESS;
32  }
```

This is the `Makefile`

```
# CH18:Makefile
GCC = gcc
CFLAGS = -g -Wall -Wshadow
VALGRIND = valgrind --tool=memcheck --verbose --log-file=valog
SRCS = listdelete.c   listinsert.c  listprint.c
SRCS += listdestroy.c  listmain.c     listsearch.c
OBJS = $(SRCS:%.c=%.o) # OBJS = aredistinct.o main.o

list: $(OBJS)
        $(GCC) $(CFLAGS) $(OBJS) -o $@
        ./list
        $(VALGRIND) ./list
        grep "ERROR SUMMARY" valog

.c.o:
        $(GCC) $(CFLAGS) -c $*.c

clean:
        /bin/rm -f *.o list valog
```

The output of this program is:

```
insert 917
insert -504
insert 326
Print the whole list:
326 -504 917
delete -504
Print the whole list:
326 917
insert 138
insert -64
insert 263
Print the whole list:
263 -64 138 326 917
138 is in the list
987 is not in the list
delete 263
Print the whole list:
-64 138 326 917
delete 917
Print the whole list:
-64 138 326
```

Chapter 20

Programming Problems Using Linked List

20.1 Queues

The function `List_insert` in Section 19.3 always inserts the new value at the beginning of the list. If we always delete nodes from the front of the list, then the linked list is a stack. In this problem, we change the insert function so that (1) the first inserted value is at the beginning of the list and (2) the value inserted most recently is at the end of the list. If we still remove elements from the beginning of the list we have created a *queue*, like a line at a store waiting for service.

```
// CH20:insertqueue.c
Node * List_insert(Node * head, int val)
{
  if (head == NULL)
    { return Node_construct(val); }
  Node * p = head -> next;
  // find the last node
  whie ((p -> next) != NULL) // not (p != NULL)
    { p = p -> next; }
  p -> next = Node_construct(val);
  return head;
}
```

When the `if` condition is true, (i.e., `head` is `NULL`), the list is empty. The inserted node is the first and only node. If `head` is not empty, the function finds the last node. The last node's `next` is `NULL`. Lines 8-9 moves `p` to its `next` until its `next` is `NULL` and this is the last node of the list. Then, line 10 adds the newly created node as `p -> next`. Here are some common mistakes. First, a function using a linked list should *always* check whether the list is empty (line 4) before doing anything else. Second, line 8 should be

```
while ((p -> next) != NULL)
```

The purpose is to find the last node in the list. If `p -> next` is `NULL`, there is nothing after `p` and thus `p` is the last node. It should not be

```
while (p != NULL)
```

In this case, `p` is `NULL` after leaving `while`. As a result, `p -> next` does not exist and line 10 will cause a segmentation fault.

The third common mistake is line 11. It should be

```
11    return head;
```

If it is

```
11    return p;
```

Then only the last two nodes are kept. All the other nodes are lost and this causes memory leak.

20.2   Sort Numbers

This problem modifies `List_insert` so that the values in the list are sorted in ascending order. The function checks whether the list is empty (line 5). If it is empty, the newly created node is returned as the only node. Then, the function checks whether the newly created node's value is smaller than the value of the first node (line 7). If `val` is smaller, the newly created node will become the first node. The original first node becomes the second node (line 9). If the program reaches line 12, the newly created node is not the first node of the list. The function finds the location to insert this newly created node. The function finds a node whose value is equal to or greater than `val`. This node is `r` in the function. The node before `r` is `q`. Thus, the newly created node is between `q` and `r`. Two conditions make the program leave `while` in line 15: (1) when `r` is `NULL` and (2) when (`r -> value`) is no longer smaller than `val`. Condition (1) means `ptr` is the last node of the list. Condition (2) means `ptr` is between `q` and `r`. Lines 21 and 22 can handle both cases. Since the list's first node is unchanged, the function returns `head`.

```
1    // CH20:insertsort.c
2    Node * List_insert(Node * head, int val)
3    {
4      Node * ptr = Node_construct(val);
5      if (head == NULL)
6        { return ptr; }
7      if ((head -> value) > val) // new node becomes the head
8        {
9          ptr -> next = head;
10         return ptr;
11       }
12     // new node is not the head
13     Node * q = head;
14     Node * r = q -> next; // q is always before r
15     while ((r != NULL) && ((r -> value) < val))
16       {
17         r = r -> next;
18         q = q -> next;
19       }
20     // new node is between q and r; it is OK r is NULL
21     q -> next = ptr;
```

```
22    ptr -> next = r;
23    return head;
24  }
```

20.3   Sparse Arrays

Arrays are widely used, but sometimes most of the elements are zeros. These are called *sparse arrays*. Sparse arrays are common when analyzing high-dimensional data. Table 20.1 shows an example. A store keeps records of customers' purchase history. Customer 1 has bought product A 3 times, product E 5 times, and product J 6 times. Customer 3 has bought product B 9 times, product G 7 times, and product I twice. Customer 2 has never bought products A, B, G, H, I, or J from this store.

TABLE 20.1:   A store's record of customer purchase history.

customer	Products									
	A	B	C	D	E	F	G	H	I	J
1	3	0	0	0	5	0	0	2	0	6
2	0	0	1	5	2	1	0	0	0	0
3	0	9	2	0	0	0	7	1	2	5

Such a purchase record can be organized as an array: the customers are the indexes and the purchase history is the array's elements. Storing these elements as typical arrays would waste too much memory because many elements are zeros. A sparse array stores only those elements whose values are non-zero. This problem writes a program managing spare arrays: Each node stores one pair of index and value. The program reads two sparse arrays from two files, merges the arrays, and stores the new array in a file. Merging follows these rules: (1) If an index exists in only one array, then this element is added to the new array. (2) If the same index exists in both arrays, the values are added. If the value is zero, then the element is deleted. The indexes stored in one of the two source file are not necessarily sorted. We can assume that within each input file the indexes are distinct.

TABLE 20.2:   Merge two sparse arrays.

Array 1	index	0		102	315
	value	5		−5	8
Array 2	index		11	102	315
	value		2	5	2
Merged	index	0	11		315
	value	5	2		10

Table 20.2 illustrates what happens when two sparse arrays are merged. The indexes 0 and 11 exist in only one of the original files. Thus, the new list keeps these two indexes and the values. The index 102 exists in both original files. This index is not in the new array because the value becomes zero after the two arrays are merged. The index 315 appears in both arrays with values 8 and 2. The merged array has a value 10. To test this implementation, we want to read sparse arrays from disk. Each line of the file contains two integers: index and value. The two integers are separated by space. The header file is shown below and it declares four functions:

```
1   // CH20:sparse.h
2   #ifndef SPARSE_H
3   #define SPARSE_H
4   typedef struct linked
5   {
6     int index;
7     int value;
8     struct linked * next;
9   } Node;
10  // read a sparse array from a file and return the array
11  // return NULL if reading fails
12  Node * List_read(char * filename);
13  // write a sparse array to a file, return 1 if success, 0 if fail
14  int List_save(char * filename, Node * arr);
15  // merge two sparse arrays
16  // the two input arrays are not changed and the new array
17  // does not share memory with the input arrays
18  Node * List_merge(Node * arr1, Node * arr2);
19  // release all nodes in a sparse array
20  void List_destroy(Node * arr);
21  #endif
```

Below is sample implementation of these four functions. Even though the indexes from input files are not sorted, the new linked list's nodes are sorted by the indexes.

```
1   // sparse.c
2   #include "sparse.h"
3   #include <stdio.h>
4   #include <stdlib.h>
5   static Node * Node_create(int ind, int val);
6   static Node * List_insert(Node * head, int ind, int val);
7   static Node * List_copy(Node * head);
8   Node * List_read(char * filename)
9   {
10    FILE * fptr = fopen(filename, "r");
11    if (fptr == NULL)
12      { return NULL; }
13    int ind;
14    int val;
15    Node * head = NULL;
16    while (fscanf(fptr, "%d %d", & ind, & val) == 2)
17      { head = List_insert(head, ind, val); }
18    fclose (fptr);
19    return head;
20  }
21  int List_save(char * filename, Node * arr)
22  {
23    FILE * fptr = fopen(filename, "w");
24    if (fptr == NULL)
25      { return 0; }
26    while (arr != NULL)
```

```c
27        {
28          fprintf(fptr, "%d %d\n", arr -> index, arr -> value);
29          arr = arr -> next;
30        }
31      fclose (fptr);
32      return 1;
33    }
34    Node * List_merge(Node * arr1, Node * arr2)
35    {
36      Node * arr3 = List_copy(arr1);
37      while (arr2 != NULL)
38        {
39          arr3 = List_insert(arr3, arr2 -> index, arr2 -> value);
40          arr2 = arr2 -> next;
41        }
42      return arr3;
43    }
44    void List_destroy(Node * arr)
45    {
46      if (arr == NULL) { return; }
47      while (arr != NULL)
48        {
49          Node * ptr = arr -> next;
50          free (arr);
51          arr = ptr;
52        }
53    }
54    static Node * Node_create(int ind, int val)
55    {
56      Node * nd = malloc(sizeof(Node));
57      if(nd == NULL) { return NULL; }
58      nd -> index = ind;
59      nd -> value = val;
60      nd -> next = NULL;
61      return nd;
62    }
63    // If the same index appears again, add the value
64    // The returned list is sorted by the index.
65    static Node * List_insert(Node * head, int ind, int val)
66    {
67      if (val == 0)
68        { return head; } // do not insert zero value
69      if (head == NULL) // this is the only node
70        { return Node_create(ind, val); }
71      if ((head -> index) > ind) // insert the new node before the list
72        {
73          Node * ptr = Node_create(ind, val);
74          ptr -> next = head;
75          return ptr;
76        }
```

```
77    if ((head -> index) == ind) // same index, merge the nodes
78      {
79        head -> value += val;
80        if ((head -> value) == 0) // delete this node
81          {
82            Node * ptr = head -> next;
83            free (head);
84            return ptr;
85          }
86        return head;
87      }
88    head -> next = List_insert(head -> next, ind, val);
89    return head;
90  }
91  Node * List_copy(Node * arr)
92  {
93    Node * arr2 = NULL;
94    while (arr != NULL)
95      {
96        arr2 = List_insert(arr2, arr -> index, arr -> value);
97        arr = arr -> next;
98      }
99    return arr2;
100 }
```

Below is a sample `main` function to test the functions.

```
1   // CH20:sparsemain.c
2   #include <stdio.h>
3   #include <stdlib.h>
4   #include "sparse.h"
5   int main(int  argc, char ** argv)
6   {
7     if (argc != 4)
8       { return EXIT_FAILURE; }
9     Node * arr1 = List_read(argv[1]);
10    if (arr1 == NULL)
11      { return EXIT_FAILURE; }
12    Node * arr2 = List_read(argv[2]);
13    if (arr2 == NULL)
14      {
15        List_destroy(arr1);
16        return EXIT_FAILURE;
17      }
18    Node * arr3 = List_merge(arr1, arr2);
19    int ret = List_save(argv[3], arr3);
20    List_destroy(arr1);
21    List_destroy(arr2);
22    List_destroy(arr3);
23    if (ret == 0) { return EXIT_FAILURE; }
```

```
24    return EXIT_SUCCESS;
25  }
```

This is the `Makefile`

```
1   # CH20:Makefile
2   GCC = gcc
3   CFLAGS = -g -Wall -Wshadow
4   LIBS =
5   SOURCES = sparse.c sparsemain.c
6   TARGET = main
7   VALGRIND = valgrind --tool=memcheck --verbose --log-file
8   TEST0 = inputs/input0A inputs/input0B output0
9   TEST1 = inputs/input1A inputs/input1B output1
10
11  sparsemain: $(SOURCES)
12          $(GCC) $(CFLAGS) $(SOURCES) -o $@
13          ./sparsemain $(TEST0)
14          diff -w output0 expected/expected0
15          ./sparsemain $(TEST1)
16          diff -w output1 expected/expected1
17          $(VALGRIND)=valgrindlog0 ./sparsemain $(TEST0)
18          $(VALGRIND)=valgrindlog1 ./sparsemain $(TEST1)
19          grep "ERROR SUMMARY" valgrindlog*
20
21  clean:
22          /bin/rm -f sparsemain *~ output* *log*
```

20.4 Reversing a Linked List

This problem writes a function that reverses a linked list by reversing the individual links between the nodes. The function's input argument is the first node of the original linked list and returns the first node of the reversed linked list. This function should not call `malloc` because calling `malloc` unnecessarily slows down the program. Figure 20.1 (a)(b) show an example list and its reversed form. The GND means the end of the list, i.e., NULL, as shown in some books. Figure 20.1 (c)–(g) show how to reverse a linked list. The first two nodes have already been reversed: `revhead` points to the head of the partially reversed list; `orighead` points to the head of the remaining original list; `origsec` points to the second node of the remaining list. In Figure 20.1 (c), three pointers are used. Figure 20.1 (d) changes `orighead -> next` and makes it point to `revhead`. Figure 20.1 (e) updates `revhead` to the new head of the reversed list. Figure 20.1 (f) updates `orighead` to the new head of the remaining list. Figure 20.1 (g) updates `origsec` to the second node of the remaining list. Below is a sample implementation that reverses a linked list as desired. It essentially implements the four steps depicted in the figure.

```
1   // CH20:listreverse.c
2   #include "list.h"
```

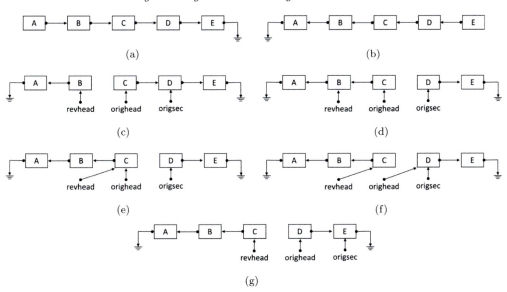

FIGURE 20.1: (a) The original linked list. The list's first points to **A**. (b) The reversed linked list. The list's first points to **E**. (c)–(g) Process to reverse the linked list. The GND symbol (used in some books) indicates the end of the list, i.e., NULL.

```
3   Node * List_reverse(Node * head)
4   {
5     if (head == NULL) { return NULL; } // empty list, nothing to do
6     Node * orighead = head;
7     Node * revhead = NULL; // must initialize to NULL
8     Node * origsec = NULL; // will be updated before using
9     while (orighead != NULL)
10      {
11        origsec = orighead -> next;
12        orighead -> next = revhead;
13        revhead = orighead;
14        orighead = origsec;
15      }
16    return revhead;
17  }
```

The order of the four steps inside **while** is important. Changing the order makes the function incorrect. For example, reversing lines 11 and 12 would lose the remaining list because **orighead** has already been changed and **origsec** is the same as **revhead**. Remember to initialize **revhead** to NULL because it will be the end of the reversed list. It is unnecessary to initialize **origsec** because it is **orighead -> next** before **origsec** is used.

20.5   Doubly Linked List

The linked lists explained in this chapter are uni-directional. It is not possible to go backward. One solution is to create two pointers per node, called `next` and `prev` (meaning previous), as shown in Figure 20.2. This is called a *doubly linked list.* Consider p and q pointing to two adjacent nodes in a doubly linked

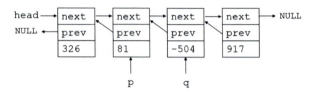

FIGURE 20.2: Doubly linked list.

list. If q and p -> `next` point to the same node, then p and q -> `prev` point to the same node. For the last node of the list, `next` points to NULL. For the first node of the list, `prev` points to NULL. It is common for a doubly linked list to have two pointers: `head` points to the first node and `tail` points to the last node.

This is the structure for doubly linked lists:

```
typedef struct listnode
{
  struct listnode * next;
  struct listnode * prev;
  int value;
} Node; // remember ;
```

Linked lists (including doubly linked lists) have a fundamental drawback: finding a node may need to go through many nodes. A doubly linked list allows going in both directions. However, there is no true advantage using doubly linked list because the fundamental problem (going through many nodes) still exists. Thus linked lists are not widely used. The next chapter describes *binary trees*; binary trees can be much more efficient than linked lists.

Chapter 21

Binary Search Trees

The previous chapters explained linked lists. If we want to find the node where a specific value is stored, we need to start at the first node (usually called the head) and visit the nodes one by one. If no node stores this value, we have to visit every node until the list's end before reaching that conclusion. In a doubly linked list, each node has two links called (`next` and `prev`). A doubly linked list allows for traversing forward using `next` and backward using `prev`. Doubly linked lists still have the same limitations: If the list is long, then finding a particular node may require visiting many nodes. If the node to find is at the middle, a doubly linked list needs to visit half of the entire list to find this node; thus, doubly linked lists are also inefficient. This chapter introduces a new data structure, called *binary tree*; it is more efficient than linked list.

21.1 Binary Tree

Section 16.1 (binary search) provides an example of quickly locating data in an array by skipping large portions of data. The array must be sorted before a binary search can be applied. A sorted array has one major limitation: the size is fixed. Inserting an element in an array needs to allocate a new array with more space, copy data, and free the old array. Linked lists can grow and shrink based on the needs. The memory used by the nodes is unlikely contiguous; hence, it is not possible to skip many nodes in the same way as a sorted array. Instead, it is necessary to follow the links one by one.

It is possible to combine the advantages of both: the flexibility of adding and removing elements (similar to linked lists) and the ability to discard most data quickly (similar to binary search in sorted arrays). This new data type is called *binary search trees*. A binary search tree can discard (almost) half of the data in a single comparison. A binary search tree is one type of binary trees but a binary tree may not necessarily be a binary search tree. Chapter 27 will use binary trees to compress data and these binary trees are not binary search trees.

Similar to a linked list, a binary search tree is composed of nodes that are linked together. Every node in a binary tree has two links called *left* and *right*, as illustrated in Figure 21.1 (a). By convention, a tree is drawn downwards. A binary tree is different from a doubly linked list. In a doubly linked list, if `p -> next` is `q`, then `q -> prev` must be `p`. It is possible to reach `p` from `q` and it is also possible to reach `q` from `p`. In a binary trees, the links are only downwards. It is not possible to go upwards.

The following are some terms used for binary trees. If `q` is `p -> left`, then `q` is called p's *left child*. If `r` is `p -> right`, then `r` is p's *right child*. We call `p` the parent of `q` and `r`. Figure 21.1 (b) shows the relationships of the parent and the children. We also say that `q` and `r` are *siblings*. If a node has no child, then it is called a *leaf node*. All the nodes on the left side of `p` are called p's left *subtree*. All the nodes on the right side of `p` are

DOI: 10.1201/9781003257981-21

called p's right subtree. The top node is called the *root* of the tree; the root can reach every node in the tree.

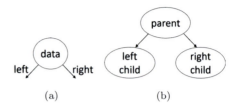

(a)   (b)

FIGURE 21.1: (a) A node has two pointers called left and right. Each node can store one piece of data. (b) The links move from the parent to the children.

Figure 21.2 shows an example of a binary tree. The root stores the value 8. The value 4 is stored in the left child of the root. The nodes storing 1, 4, 5, and 7 are the left subtree of the root. The nodes storing 9, 10, 11, 12, and 15 are the right subtree of the root. The *distance* of a node from the root is the number of links between the root and the node. For example, the distance between the node 7 and the root is 2. The *height* of a binary tree is one plus the longest distance in the tree. The height of the tree above is 4. In a *full* binary tree, each node has either two children or no child. The tree in Figure 21.2 is not full because some nodes (nodes 7, 9, and 12) have only one child each. In a *complete* binary tree, each node, except the nodes just above the leaf nodes, has two children. Figure 21.2 is a complete binary tree. It is possible for a node in a complete binary tree to have only one child, and thus not be a full binary tree. It is also possible that a full binary tree is incomplete. If a binary tree is full and complete and its height is n (i.e., the distance between a leaf node and the root is $n - 1$), then the tree has precisely $2^n - 1$ nodes and 2^{n-1} leaf nodes. In a *balanced* binary tree, the difference between the height of the left subtree and the height of the right subtree is at most one.

We can create tree structures in which each object has three or more links. For example, many computer games take advantage of *octrees* where each node has eight children. In this case, octrees are used to partition three-dimensional space, and are thus useful for indexing the objects in three-dimensional worlds. This book focuses on binary trees because they are useful for many problems.

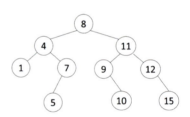

FIGURE 21.2: A binary tree.

A common question is why binary trees are so commonly used but other types of trees (tertiary trees, quaternary trees, or octrees) are not so common. The answer is that two, three, and four have the same expressive capability. More precisely, for any positive value n, it is possible to find k such that $2^k = n$. For example, if n is 4, then k is 2. If n is 16, k is 4. If n is 0.25 (decimal), k is -2. If n is 7, k is $\log_2(7)$ (this is an irrational number). Similarly, it is possible finding numbers p and q such that $3^p = n$ and $4^q = n$. In contrast, one does not have this expressive capability because the power of one is always one, i.e., $1^m = 1$ regardless of the value of m. Thus, two, three, and four have better expressive capability than one. A binary tree is simpler than the other types of trees.

21.2 Binary Search Tree

A binary *search* tree is a binary tree with the following properties. (1) Each node has two links and can store one piece of data. This data can be a primitive type (int, double, char, etc.) or an object. The data (or one part of the data) serves the function of *keys* to distinguish the data stored in different nodes. (2) The key must be distinct. (3) The keys must be *totally ordered*. If a and b are the keys in two different nodes, then either $a < b$ or $a > b$ must be true. Since the keys must be distinct, the case a equal to b does not exist. Transitivity must be satisfied (if $a < b$ and $b < c$, then $a < c$). For example, integers, characters, floating-point numbers, and strings all support total ordering. Complex numbers are not totally ordered and cannot be used as the attributes for binary search trees. (4) For any node with key p, all keys in the entire left subtree must be smaller than p. All keys in the entire right subtree must be greater than p. Figure 21.2 is an example of a binary search tree. Below is the header file for a binary search tree. It shows the structure definition for a tree node and gives function declarations for binary search trees.

```
1   // CH21:tree.h
2   #ifndef TREE_H
3   #define TREE_H
4   #include <stdio.h>
5   typedef struct treenode
6   {
7     struct treenode * left;
8     struct treenode * right;
9     int value;
10  } TreeNode;
11  // insert a value v to a binary search tree, return the new root
12  TreeNode * Tree_insert(TreeNode * root, int v);
13  // search a value in a binary search tree starting with root,
14  // return the node whose value is v, or NULL if no such node exists
15  TreeNode * Tree_search(TreeNode * root, int v);
16  // delete the node whose value is v in a binary search
17  // tree starting with root, return the root of the
18  // remaining tree, or NULL if the tree is empty
19  TreeNode * Tree_delete(TreeNode * root, int v);
20  void Tree_print(TreeNode * root); // print the stored values
21  void Tree_destroy(TreeNode * root); // delete every node
22  #endif
```

A binary search tree has similar functionality to a linked list: both structures support insert, search, and delete. The differences are (1) the internal organization of the data and (2) The efficiency of these operations. A linked list can be considered a special case of a binary tree where every node uses only one link, and the other link is always NULL.

21.3   Insert Data into a Binary Search Tree

```
TreeNode * root = NULL; // good habit to initialize
root = malloc(sizeof(Node));
root -> left = NULL;
root -> right = NULL;
root -> value = 917;
```

This node is called the root because it has no parent. It is also a leaf node because it has no children. It is a good programming habit to *always* set the root to NULL. We have seen many problems when pointers are not correctly initialized because the programmers forget. Some people says, "Unnecessary initialization slows down a program." That is true. The program will be slower by a nanosecond. However, the human time to find and correct such mistakes is much longer.

The Tree_insert function can insert a value to a new (i.e., when root is NULL) or an existing tree (i.e., when root is not NULL). An auxiliary function TreeNode_construct is used to allocate memory and initialize the attributes. Using TreeNode_construct ensures that all attributes (especially, left and right) are properly initialized. When inserting a new value into a binary search tree, a new leaf node is created.

```
// CH21:treeinsert.c
#include "tree.h"
#include <stdlib.h>
static TreeNode * TreeNode_construct(int val)
{
  TreeNode * tn;
  tn = malloc(sizeof(TreeNode));
  tn -> left = NULL; // important: initialize to NULL
  tn -> right = NULL;
  tn -> value = val;
  return tn;
}
TreeNode * Tree_insert(TreeNode * tn, int val)
{
  if (tn == NULL)
    { return TreeNode_construct(val); } // empty, create a node
  if (val == (tn -> value)) // do not insert the same value
    { return tn; }
  if (val < (tn -> value)) // go to the left side
    { tn -> left = Tree_insert(tn -> left, val); }
  else // go to the right side
    { tn -> right = Tree_insert(tn -> right, val); }
  return tn;
}
```

This is an example of calling the Tree_insert function:

```
TreeNode * root = NULL;
root = Tree_insert(root, 917);
root = Tree_insert(root, -504);
```

After inserting two values, the tree has two nodes, as illustrated in Figure 21.3. The Tree_insert function uses recursion. It first checks whether the tree is empty (line 15). If it is empty, a new TreeNode is created and returned. Next, the function checks whether the value is already in the tree. If this value matches the node's value, this value is not inserted. This ensures that all values in the tree are distinct. Line 19 checks whether the value to insert is smaller. If it is, this value should be inserted to the left side of the tree. Otherwise, it should be inserted to the right side of the tree. Please remember to return `tn` at line 23. This ensures that the original tree is intact. Figure 21.4 shows a binary search as values are inserted. The first inserted value is the tree's root.

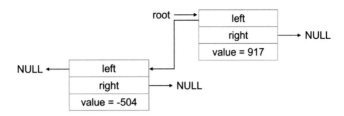

FIGURE 21.3: A binary search tree with two tree node.

21.4 Search a Binary Search Tree

To find whether a given number is stored in a binary search tree, the search function compares the number with the value stored at the root. If the two values are the same, then we know that the value is stored in the tree. If the number is greater than the value stored at the root, then it is impossible to find the value on the left side of the tree. Thus, the entire left subtree is discarded. If the number is smaller than the value stored at the root, then it is impossible to find the value on the right side of the tree. The entire right subtree is discarded. This property is applied recursively until either (1) no node is available to search or (2) the value is found. This is precisely why this structure is called a *binary search tree*: It is a tree that naturally supports searches. In each step, either the left subtree or the right subtree is discarded. In general, searching binary search trees is far more efficient

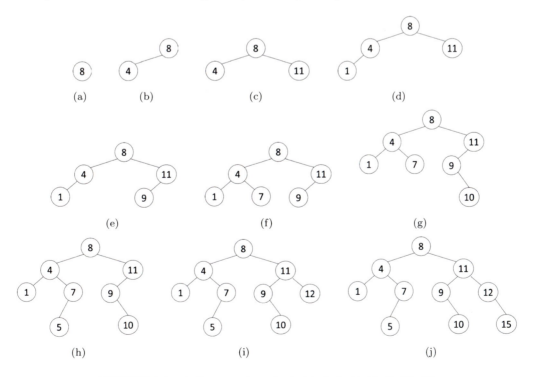

FIGURE 21.4: Insert values 8, 4, 11, 1, 9, 7, 10, 5, 12, 15.

than searching linked lists. It is most efficient when the left side and the right side of each node have the same number of nodes and half of the nodes can be discarded after only one comparison. The following shows how to implement `Tree_search`.

```
// CH21:treesearch.c
#include "tree.h"
TreeNode * Tree_search(TreeNode * tn, int val)
{
  if (tn == NULL) // cannot find
    { return NULL; }
  if (val == (tn -> value)) // found
    { return tn; }
  if (val < (tn -> value)) // search the left side
    { return Tree_search(tn -> left, val); }
  return Tree_search(tn -> right, val);
}
```

Note the similarities to the binary search over an array as described in Section 16.1. A binary search tree is more flexible than a sorted array because a binary search tree supports efficient insertion and deletion.

21.5   Print a Binary Tree

The code listing below shows an example of printing a tree using pre-order, in-order, and post-order traversals.

Visiting every node in a tree is also called *traversing* the tree. Every node is visited once, and only once. Traversing a tree has three steps: (1)

TABLE 21.1: Traversing the three binary search trees in Figure 21.5 (a)–(c).

	(a)	(b)	(c)
pre-order	8 4 11	11 8 4	4 8 11
in-order	4 8 11	4 8 11	4 8 11
post-order	4 11 8	4 8 11	11 8 4

Visiting the node's left side (subtree); (2) Visiting the node's right side; (3) Printing the node's value. There are $3! = 6$ ways to order these three steps but (1) usually precedes (2). The three ways to implement traversing are:

1. Pre-order traversal: The three steps are ordered as $(3) \rightarrow (1) \rightarrow (2)$.
2. In-order traversal: The three steps are ordered as $(1) \rightarrow (3) \rightarrow (2)$. For a binary search tree, in-order will print the values in the ascending order.
3. Post-order traversal: The three steps are ordered as $(1) \rightarrow (2) \rightarrow (3)$.

It is important to understand these three traversal methods because each one is useful in different circumstances, as will become apparent later in this book.

```
// CH21:treeprint.c
#include "tree.h"
static void TreeNode_print(TreeNode *tn)
{ printf("%d ",tn -> value); }
```

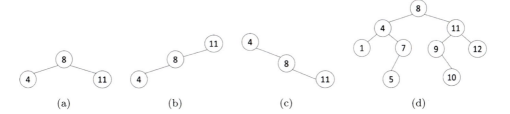

FIGURE 21.5: (a)–(c) Three binary search trees of different shapes. (d) A more complex binary search tree.

```c
static void Tree_printPreorder(TreeNode *tn)
{
  if (tn == NULL)
    { return; }
  TreeNode_print(tn);
  Tree_printPreorder(tn -> left);
  Tree_printPreorder(tn -> right);
}
static void Tree_printInorder(TreeNode *tn)
{
  if (tn == NULL)
    { return; }
  Tree_printInorder(tn -> left);
  TreeNode_print(tn);
  Tree_printInorder(tn -> right);
}
static void Tree_printPostorder(TreeNode *tn)
{
  if (tn == NULL)
    { return; }
  Tree_printPostorder(tn -> left);
  Tree_printPostorder(tn -> right);
  TreeNode_print(tn);
}
void Tree_print(TreeNode *tn)
{
  printf("\n=====Preorder=====\n");
  Tree_printPreorder(tn);
  printf("\n=====Inorder=====\n");
  Tree_printInorder(tn);
  printf("\n=====Postorder=====\n");
  Tree_printPostorder(tn);
  printf("\n");
}
```

Consider the different shapes of binary search trees in Figure 21.5. These three trees store the same values. They have different shapes due to the order of insertion. In (a), 8 is inserted first. In (b), 11 is inserted first. In (c), 4 is inserted first. Table 21.1 shows the outputs of the three traversal methods.

In-order traversal outputs the values in ascending order and has the same outputs for the three different trees. Thus in-order traversal cannot distinguish between different shapes of trees. In contrast, pre-order and post-order traversals can distinguish the different shapes. Next, consider the more complex tree in Figure 21.5 (d). For pre-order, write the value of the root first, followed by the outputs of the left subtree and then the right subtree:

---

8 | pre-order of left subtree | pre-order of right subtree |

The pre-order traversal of the left subtree starts with 4. The pre-order traversal of 4's left subtree is 1 and the pre-order traversal of 4's right subtree is 7 5. The pre-order traversal of the right subtree starts with 11. The pre-order traversal of 11's left subtree is 9 10 and the pre-order traversal of 11's right subtree is 12. Thus, the output is

---

8 | 4   1   7   5 | 11   9   10   12

21.6   Delete from a Binary Search Tree

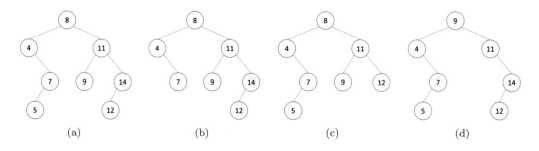

FIGURE 21.6: Delete a node in a binary search tree. (a) Original. (b) Delete 5. (c) Delete 14. (d) Delete 8.

Deleting a node from a binary search tree is more complex than inserting because insertion adds only leaf nodes. Deleting a non-leaf node must maintain the tree's ordering property. When deleting a node, there are three different scenarios: Does the node has no, one, or two children? Figure 21.6 (a) is the original binary search tree. Figure 21.6 (b) deletes node 5 (a leaf node, with no child). This is the first case. The left child of node 7 becomes NULL. Figure 21.6 (c) deletes the node 14. This node has one child. This is the second case. The parent of 14 (node 11) points to 12. Figure 21.6 (d) deletes 8. This node has two children. In order to maintain the properties of a binary search tree, we find the smallest value at the right subtree. The value is 9. Swap these two values. As a result, 9 becomes the root of the tree. Then, node 8 is deleted.

Below is an implementation of the delete function. Lines 8-17 find the node whose value matches val. Lines 19 - 24 handle the first case (no child). Lines 25–36 handle the second case (one child). If the program reaches line 40, this node has two children. Lines 40 and 41 find tn's immediate successor. It is at the right side of tn and hence su starts with tn->right. The immediate successor must also be the leftmost node on tn's right side. The immediate successor may have the right child. It is also possible to use the immediate predecessor but this book uses the successor. Lines 43–44 swap the values. Line 46 deletes the value from the right subtree.

```c
// CH21:treedelete.c
#include "tree.h"
#include <stdlib.h>
TreeNode * Tree_delete(TreeNode * tn, int val)
{
  if (tn == NULL) // no node, cannot delete anything
    { return NULL; }
  if (val < (tn -> value))
    {
      tn -> left = Tree_delete(tn -> left, val);
      return tn;
    }
  if (val > (tn -> value))
    {
      tn -> right = Tree_delete(tn -> right, val);
      return tn;
    }
  // v is the same as tn ->  value
  if (((tn ->  left) == NULL) && ((tn ->  right) == NULL))
    {
      // tn has no child
      free (tn);
      return NULL;
    }
  if ((tn ->  left) == NULL) // tn ->  right must not be NULL
    {
      TreeNode * rc = tn ->  right;
      free (tn);
      return rc;
    }
  if ((tn ->  right) == NULL) // tn ->  left must not be NULL
    {
      TreeNode * lc = tn ->  left;
      free (tn);
      return lc;
    }
  // tn have two children
  // find the immediate successor
  TreeNode * su = tn ->  right; // su must not be NULL
  while ((su -> left) != NULL) // while (su != NULL) is wrong
    { su = su -> left; }
  // su is tn's immediate successor, swap their values
  tn ->  value = su -> value;
  su -> value = val;
  // delete su
  tn ->  right = Tree_delete(tn ->  right, val);
  return tn;
}
```

Here are some common mistakes. Line 40 should use (su -> left) != NULL, not su != NULL. The latter ensures that su is NULL when leaving while. Line 44 will have a problem because su -> value does not exist if su is NULL. A common mistake occurs at line 46 by calling Tree_delete(tn, val). This is wrong because the node to be deleted (node 8) is smaller but it is on the right side (of node 9). Using Tree_delete(tn, val) causes the function to search for (and attempt to delete) 8 from the left side of 9. Node 8 cannot be found on the left side of 9.

21.7   Destroy a Binary Tree

The Tree_destroy function destroys the whole tree by releasing the memory occupied by all the tree nodes. Note that every node must be destroyed once, and only once. Thus it is necessary to traverse the entire tree. Both the left subtree and right subtree must be destroyed before this tree node's memory is released. This is equivalent to post-order traversal.

```
// CH21:treedestroy.c
#include "tree.h"
#include <stdlib.h>
void Tree_destroy(TreeNode * n)
{
   if (n == NULL) { return; }
   Tree_destroy(n -> left);
   Tree_destroy(n -> right);
   free(n); // must be after destroying left and right subtrees
}
```

21.8   Count the Different Shapes of a Binary Tree

How many unique shapes can a binary tree have if the tree has n nodes? First, we need to define shapes. Two binary trees have the same shape if each node has the same number of nodes in the left subtree and the same number of nodes in the right subtree. This rule is applied recursively until reaching leaf nodes. Figure 21.7 shows the different shapes of trees with two or three nodes. Table 21.2 gives the number of uniquely shaped binary trees with 1 through 10 nodes.

Suppose there are $f(n)$ shapes for a binary tree with n nodes. By observation we can tell that $f(1) = 1$ and $f(2) = 2$ We can use them as base cases for a recursive function. If there are k nodes on the left side of the root node, then there must be $n - k - 1$ nodes on the right side of the root node. By definition, the left subtree has $f(k)$ possible shapes and the right side has $f(n - k - 1)$ possible shapes. The shapes on the two sides are independent of each other. This means that for every possible shape in the left subtree, we count every shape in the right subtree. Thus, the number of shapes is $f(k) \times f(n - k - 1)$. The value of k is between 0 and $n - 1$ nodes. The total number of shapes is the sum of all the different

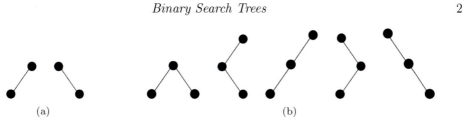

(a)   (b)

FIGURE 21.7: (a) If a binary tree has two nodes, there are two unique shapes. (b) For a binary tree has three nodes, there are five unique shapes.

TABLE 21.2: The numbers of shapes for binary trees of different sizes.

n	1	2	3	4	5	6	7	8	9	10
number of shapes	1	2	5	14	42	132	429	1430	4862	16796

possible values of k.

$$f(n) = \sum_{k=0}^{n-1} f(k) \times f(n-k-1) \qquad (21.1)$$

This is called the *Catalan numbers*. The Catalan numbers also describe the number of sequences that can use stack sort explained in Section 16.4. For example, $f(3) = 5$ meaning that stack sort can sort five sequences of three distinct numbers. Three distinct numbers can have $3! = 6$ sequences (i.e., permutations). Thus, one of them is not stack sortable. Let us consider the six possible sequences of 1, 2, and 3:

1. $< 1, 2, 3 >$
2. $< 1, 3, 2 >$
3. $< 2, 1, 3 >$
4. $< 2, 3, 1 >$
5. $< 3, 1, 2 >$
6. $< 3, 2, 1 >$

Among these six permutations, $< 2, 3, 1 >$ is not stack sortable as shown in Section 16.4. Next, consider binary search trees that store the three numbers shown in Figure 21.8.

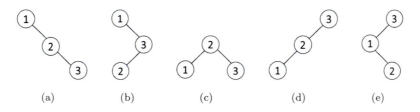

(a)   (b)   (c)   (d)   (e)

FIGURE 21.8: Five different shapes of binary search trees storing 1, 2, and 3.

The five stack sortable sequences are actually the pre-order traversals of the five shapes in Figure 21.8. The sequence e $< 2, 3, 1 >$ is not stack sortable and it is also not a pre-order traversal of the five shapes. This is not a coincidence. Suppose $s(n)$ is the number of possible stack sortable sequences of 1, 2, 3, ..., n. It turns out $s(n)$ is the *Catalan numbers*.

This is a proof that $s(n)$ is the of Catalan numbers. Consider the sequence of numbers $< a_1, a_2, a_3, ... a_n >$ is a particular permutation of 1, 2, ..., n. Suppose the largest value n is a_i $(1 \le i \le n)$. Then the sequence $< a_1, a_2, a_3, ... a_n >$ can be divided into three parts:

$$< a_1, a_2, ..., a_{i-1} > \quad a_i = n \quad < a_{i+1}, a_{i+2}, ..., a_n >$$

What is the condition that makes a sequence stack sortable? Section 16.4 explained that $\max(a_1, a_2, ..., a_{i-1})$ must be smaller than $\min(a_{i+1}, a_{i+2}, ..., a_n)$. Therefore, the first sequence must be a permutation of 1, 2, ..., $i-1$ and the second sequence must be a permutation of i, $i+1$, ..., $n-1$. Moreover, the two sequences $< a_1, a_2, ..., a_{i-1} >$ and $< a_{i+1}, a_{i+2}, ..., a_n >$ must also be stack sortable; otherwise, the entire sequence cannot be stack sortable. Therefore, the entire sequence includes two stack sortable sequences divided by $a_i = n$. By definition, there are $s(i-1)$ stack sortable permutations of the first part, i.e., 1, 2, 3, ..., $i-1$. There are $s(n-i)$ stack sortable permutations of the second part, i, ..., $n-1$. The permutations in these two sequences are independent so there are $s(i-1) \times s(n-i)$ possible permutations of the two sequences. The value of i is between 1 and n. When i is 1, the first value in the sequence is n and this corresponds to the tree in which the root has no left child. When i is n, the last value is n and this corresponds to the tree in which the root has no right child. Thus, the total number of stack sortable permutations is:

$$s(n) = \sum_{i=1}^{n} s(i-1) \times s(n-i) = \sum_{i=0}^{n-1} s(i) \times s(n-i-1). \tag{21.2}$$

This is the Catalan number.

21.9 Problems

21.9.1 Count Nodes

Write a function that counts the number of nodes in a binary tree.

21.9.2 Tree Height

Write a function that reports the height of a binary tree.

21.9.3 Check Binary Search Tree

Write a function that reports whether a binary tree is a binary search tree.

21.9.4 Ancestor-Offspring

Write a function that takes two pointers of `TreeNode` and determines whether one is an ancestor of the other.

21.9.5 Build Binary Tree

Write a program that reads two files: the in-order and post-order traversals. The program outputs the pre-order traversal. Assume the values are distinct.

Consider two input arrays with the outputs of in-order and post-order: (1) in-order: [440, 1425, 4746, 7985, 8168]; (2) post-order: [1425, 440, 8168, 7985, 4746]. From the last value in post-order, 4746 is the root. These two arrays are now divided into two arrays for the left and the right sides of the root: (1) Left: (a) in-order: [440, 1425]; (b) post-order: [1425, 440]. (2) Right: (a) in-order: [7985, 8168]; (b) post-order: [8168, 7985]. For the left side, 440 is the root and 1425 is the right child. Similarly, for the right side, 7985 is the root and 8168 is the right child. The pre-order output is [4746, 440, 1425, 7985, 8168].

Chapter 22

Parallel Programming Using Threads

Multi-core processors are everywhere in desktops, supercomputers, and mobile phones. If a program is written to take advantage of these multiple cores, the program can run faster than on a single core. If a program is written for multiple cores, then the program can be referred to as a *parallel program*. If a program is not written for multiple cores, then it is called a *sequential program*. All programs in this book so far are sequential programs. This chapter provides an introduction to writing parallel programs using *threads*.

22.1 Parallel Programming

There are many ways to write parallel programs. A parallel program performs multiple operations at the same time. Parallel programs are often classified into three categories: (1) SIMD: single instruction, multiple data. This is commonly used in signal processing, such as manipulating data in arrays. When adding two arrays, the same instruction (addition) is applied to all array elements simultaneously. (2) MISD: multiple instructions, single data. Different operations are performed on the same piece of data. As an example, census data is widely studied for various purposes. The same data may be processed simultaneously by different threads of execution, in order to find, for example, the average age and median income of a population. (3) MIMD: multiple instructions, multiple data. This is the most general case. Different operations are performed on different pieces of data. The last type is SISD: single instruction, single data. This is a sequential program. At any moment, the program performs only one operation on one piece of data.

Parallel programs can also run on single-core processors because the operating systems can give the impression of multiple cores. The operating system gives each program a short time interval (usually several milliseconds) so that the program makes some progress. After this interval, the operating system suspends the program, and then allows another program to run. By giving every program a short time interval to make some progress, the operating system gives the impression that every program can make progress. This is called *multi-tasking* and is analogous to several children sharing a slide in a playground. Even though only one person can slide down at any moment (for safety), everyone gets a turn, and everyone enjoys the slide.

In order to improve the overall performance, the operating system may change the lengths of the time intervals depending on what particular programs are doing. For example, when a program wants to read data from a disk, this program has to wait for the disk. During this waiting period, the operating system shortens the program's time interval so that another program can use the processor. If a program waits for a user to enter something on the keyboard, then the operating system also shortens the program's time interval while the program is waiting. Because the lengths of the time intervals can change, it is difficult to predict exactly which program is running at any specific moment of time.

DOI: 10.1201/9781003257981-22

22.2 POSIX Threads

Thread is one way to write MIMD parallel programs. Each thread in a program may execute the code in parallel. A sequential program can be thought of as having a single thread of execution. Parallel programs have two or more threads. This book uses *POSIX threads*, also called *pthread*. POSIX stands for Portable Operating System Interface and it is a standard supported by most operating systems. A typical multi-thread program starts with only one thread, called the main thread or the first thread. The main thread creates one or several threads by calling the `pthread_create` function.

```
#include <pthread.h>
int pthread_create(pthread_t *restrict thread,
                   const pthread_attr_t *restrict attr,
                   void *(*start_routine)(void *),
                   void *restrict arg);
```

This function requires four arguments: (1) An address of a structure called `pthread_t`. This structure is defined in `pthread.h` and it stores information about the newly created thread. You do not need to know what information is stored in `pthread_t`. (2) An address of a structure called `pthread_attr_t`. This specifies optional attributes for initializing a thread. If this argument is `NULL` (commonly used), the thread is initialized with default values. (3) The third is the name of a function. Section 8.2 explains how to use a function as an argument to another function like `qsort`. For `pthread_create`, the function's return type must be `void*` and the function takes precisely one argument. It must be a pointer to the data for this function. By giving different functions to `pthread_create`, different threads can do different things and the program can be MIMD. (4) The fourth is the argument passed to the function specified in the third argument. After calling `pthread_create`, a new thread is created and executes the function specified in the third argument. The main thread and the new thread may now run simultaneously (if there are two or more cores). If the program equally divides its tasks between the first thread and the second thread, then the program can be about twice as fast.

The main thread should call `pthread_join` on the second thread before terminating. This function causes the calling (main) thread to wait until the other thread terminates. After the call to `pthread_join`, there will only be one thread executing. If the main thread does not wait for the second thread to finish, and the main thread terminates first, then the second thread will also be terminated. Below is a simple program creating one thread:

```
1   // CH22:thread.c
2   #include <pthread.h>
3   #include <stdio.h>
4   #include <stdlib.h>
5   void * printHello(void *arg)
6   {
7     int* intptr = (int *) arg;
8     int val = * intptr;
9     printf("Hello World! arg = %d\n", val);
10    return NULL;
11  }
12  int main (int argc, char *argv[])
```

```
13  {
14    pthread_t second;
15    int rtv; // return value of pthread_create
16    int arg = 12345;
17    rtv = pthread_create(& second, NULL, printHello, (void *) & arg);
18    if (rtv != 0)
19      {
20        printf("ERROR; pthread_create() returns %d\n", rtv);
21        return EXIT_FAILURE;
22      }
23    rtv = pthread_join(second, NULL);
24    if (rtv != 0)
25      {
26        printf("ERROR; pthread_join() returns %d\n", rtv);
27        return EXIT_FAILURE;
28      }
29    return EXIT_SUCCESS;
30  }
```

To compile this file into an executable program, we need to add `-lpthread` at the end of the `gcc` command in this way:

```
$ gcc -g -Wall -Wshadow thread.c -o thread -lpthread
```

Adding `-lpthread` links the functions in the *pthread* library. When the program runs, it prints the following output:

```
Hello World! arg = 12345
```

To understand this program, let's start at line 17 where `pthread_create` is called. The first argument is the address of a `pthread_t` object created at line 14. The second argument is `NULL`, and thus the thread is initialized with the default attributes. The third argument is the `printHello` function and the new thread will run the `printHello` function of lines 5 to 11. The function's return type must be `void *`. The function must take one argument and the type must be `void *`. The fourth argument to `pthread_create` is the argument to `printHello` when it is called. In this example, it is the address of an integer. If `pthread_create` succeeds, it returns zero. This indicates that the thread is created normally. Inside `printHello`, the argument is cast to the correct type. Since line 17 uses the address of an integer (`& arg`), the correct type is `int *`. Line 8 reads the integer value at the address. The `printHello` function has no useful information to return so it returns `NULL` at line 10. The main thread calls `pthread_join` to wait for the second thread to finish executing before `main` terminates. If `pthread_join` is not called, the main thread may terminate and destroy the second thread before the second thread gets a chance to print anything to the terminal.

22.3   Subset Sum

The subset sum problem is commonly encountered when studying cryptography. Consider a positive integer k and a set of positive integers $\mathbb{A} = \{a_1, a_2, ..., a_n\}$. Is it possible to find a subset $\mathbb{B} = \{b_1, b_2, ..., b_m\} \subset \mathbb{A}$ such that $k = b_1 + b_2 + ... + b_m$? Note that $\mathbb{B}$ cannot be the empty set because $k > 0$. Since $\mathbb{B}$ is a subset of $\mathbb{A}$, m must be less than or equal to n. Consider this example: $\mathbb{A} = \{19, 10, 2, 9, 8\}$ and $k = 20$. We have $k = 10 + 2 + 8$, and thus there is a solution. Consider another example, $\mathbb{A} = \{3, 5, 1, 2, 6\}$ and $k = 21$. In this case, the sum of all elements in $\mathbb{A}$ is $3 + 5 + 1 + 2 + 6 = 17$, smaller than k. Hence there is no solution. Sometimes multiple solutions are possible. For example, if $\mathbb{A} = \{1, 2, 3, 4, 5\}$ and k is 7. The solutions are $\{1, 2, 4\}$, $\{3, 4\}$, and $\{2, 5\}$.

This problem asks you to write a program that counts the number of subsets whose sums are equal to the value of k. For a set of n elements, there are 2^n subsets. This program restricts the size of sets to 31 so that the number of subsets does not exceed 2^{31}.

One obvious solution to the subset sum problem is to enumerate each subset of $\mathbb{A}$ and then check each to see if the sum of the elements is k. This will take exponential time since a set of size n has 2^n subsets. The number of possible subsets becomes really large. For example, a set of size 400 has 2^{400} subsets; this is more than the number of atoms in the observable universe. There is no known quick solution for the subset sum problem. In computer science, quick usually means that there is a polynomial-time algorithm that solves the problem: an algorithm whose execution time is bounded by a polynomial function of the input size. For example, if we are searching a linked list for a given value, then we may need to traverse the entire list. If the list has n elements then the execution time of the search is bounded by a polynomial function of n. For a polynomial of degree p, the largest term is n^p. The following statement is true:

$$\lim_{n \to \infty} \frac{2^n}{n^p} = \infty. \tag{22.1}$$

This means that the exponential function grows faster than any polynomial. There is always a value of n such that 2^n is larger than n^p, no matter what p is. This can be proved by using the L'Hospital's Rule from calculus. For the subset sum problem, no polynomial-time solution has been discovered. Instead, we have to enumerate all possible solutions and this needs to consider all possible subsets.

TABLE 22.1: Use binary representations to select elements.

Decimal	Binary	Sum	Decimal	Binary	Sum
1	0001	a_1	2	0010	a_2
3	0011	$a_1 + a_2$	4	0100	a_3
5	0101	$a_1 + a_3$	6	0110	$a_2 + a_3$
7	0111	$a_1 + a_2 + a_3$	8	1000	a_4

The program reads the value of k and then the set's elements from a file. After reading the data from the file, the program checks whether the set is valid. The set is invalid if any element is zero or negative, or if two elements have the same value. If the set is invalid, then the program does not attempt to solve the subset sum problem. If the set is valid, then the program generates all possible subsets of the given set. This program first calculates the number of possible subsets. If a set has n elements, then there are 2^n subsets including the empty set. If each subset is given a number, then the subsets are numbers between 0 and $2^n - 1$ inclusively. The empty set is not considered because $k \neq 0$, and thus we only need to consider the subsets labeled 1 to $2^n - 1$. Each number corresponds to a subset, and we check the sum of the numbers in that subset. Table 22.1 explains how the numbers are related to the subset. If the value is $2^n - 1$, every element is included, i.e., $a_1 + a_2 + a_3 + ... + a_n$. Below is a sample implementation of the sequential program.

22.3.1 Sequential Solution

First is the header file:

```
// CH22:subsetsum.h
#ifndef SUBSETSUM_H
#define SUBSETSUM_H
#include <stdio.h>
int subsetEqual(int * setA, int sizeA, int kval, unsigned int code);
// return 1 if the subset expressed by the code sums to kval
// return 0 if the sum is different from kval
int subsetSum(int * setA, int sizeA, int kval);
// the number of subsets in setA equal
int isValidSet(int * setA, int sizeA);
// valid if elements are positive and distinct
// return 1 if valid, 0 if invalid
int countInteger(FILE * fptr);
// how many integers in a file
// fptr must not be NULL, checked by the caller
#endif
```

This `main` function calls several other functions that are declared in this header file. The input file contains a list of integers. The first integer is the value of k and it is not a part of the set.

```
// CH22:main.c
#include <pthread.h>
#include <stdio.h>
#include <stdlib.h>
#include "subsetsum.h"
int main (int argc, char *argv[])
{
  // read the data from a file
  if (argc < 2)
    {
      printf("Need input file name\n");
      return EXIT_FAILURE;
    }
  FILE * fptr = fopen(argv[1], "r");
  if (fptr == NULL)
    {
      printf("fopen fail\n");
      return EXIT_FAILURE;
    }
  int numInt = countInteger(fptr);
  // go back to the beginning of the file
  fseek (fptr, 0, SEEK_SET);
  int kval; // the value equal to the sum
  if (fscanf(fptr, "%d", & kval) != 1)
    {
      printf("fscanf error\n");
```

```
27      fclose(fptr);
28      return EXIT_FAILURE;
29    }
30  numInt --; // kval is not part of the set
31  int * setA = malloc(sizeof(int) * numInt);
32  int ind = 0;
33  for (ind = 0; ind < numInt; ind ++)
34    {
35      int aval;
36      if (fscanf(fptr, "%d", & aval) != 1)
37        {
38          printf("fscanf error\n");
39          fclose(fptr);
40          return EXIT_FAILURE;
41        }
42      setA[ind] = aval;
43    }
44  fclose (fptr);
45  if (isValidSet(setA, numInt) == 1)
46    {
47      printf("There are %d subsets whose sums are %d\n",
48              subsetSum(setA, numInt, kval), kval);
49    }
50  else
51    {
52      printf("Invalid set\n");
53    }
54  free(setA);
55  return EXIT_SUCCESS;
56  }
```

The function `isValid` determines whether a set of integers is valid. A set is invalid if it contains a negative number or zero, or an integer appears more than once.

```
1  // CH22:isvalid.c
2  #include <stdio.h>
3  int isValidSet(int * setA, int sizeA)
4  // valid if every element is positive and distinct
5  // return 1 if valid, 0 if invalid
6  {
7    int ind1;
8    int ind2;
9    for (ind1 = 0; ind1 < sizeA; ind1 ++)
10     {
11       if (setA[ind1] <= 0)
12         { return 0; }
13       for (ind2 = ind1 + 1; ind2 < sizeA; ind2 ++)
14         {
15           if (setA[ind1] == setA[ind2])
16             { return 0; }
17         }
```

```
18        }
19      return 1;
20    }
```

The `countInt` reads integers from a file and counts the number of integers in the file.

```
1    // CH22:countint.c
2    #include <stdio.h>
3    int countInteger(FILE * fptr)
4    {
5      int numInt = 0; // how many integers
6      int value;
7      while (fscanf(fptr, "%d", & value) == 1)
8        { numInt ++; }
9      return numInt;
10   }
```

The function `subsetSum` counts the number of subsets adding to k. In this function, `maxCode` is 2^n and n is the size of the set, i.e., `sizeA`.

```
1    // CH22:sequential.c
2    #include "subsetsum.h"
3    int subsetSum(int * setA, int sizeA, int kval)
4    {
5      unsigned int maxCode = 1;
6      unsigned int ind;
7      for (ind = 0; ind < sizeA; ind ++)
8        { maxCode *= 2; }
9      int total = 0;
10     for (ind = 1; ind < maxCode; ind ++)
11       { total += subsetEqual(setA, sizeA, kval, ind); }
12     return total;
13   }
```

The function `subsetEqual` determines whether a specific subset sums to the value of k:

```
1    // CH22:subsetequal.c
2    #include <stdio.h>
3    int subsetEqual(int * setA, int sizeA, int kval, unsigned int code)
4    {
5      int sum = 0;
6      int ind = 0;
7      unsigned int origcode = code;
8      while ((ind < sizeA) && (code > 0))
9        {
10         if ((code % 2) == 1)
11           { sum += setA[ind]; }
12         ind ++;
```

```
13        code >>= 1; // shift right by 1 means divided by 2
14      }
15    if (sum == kval)
16      {
17        printf("equal: sum = %d, code = %X\n", sum, origcode);
18        return 1;
19      }
20    return 0;
21  }
```

22.3.2 Multiple-Threads Solution

To parallelize[1] the sequential program, we need to determine how to distribute the work evenly across several threads. Each thread can be responsible for checking the sums of some of the subsets. Suppose a set has n elements and t threads are used to solve the subset sum problem (excluding the main thread). The first thread checks the subsets between 1 and $\lfloor \frac{2^n}{t} \rfloor$. Here, $\lfloor x \rfloor$ is the *floor* function. It is the largest integer equals to x (when x is an integer) or smaller than x (when x is not an integer). For example, $\lfloor 9 \rfloor = 9$ and $\lfloor 4.7 \rfloor = 4$. The second thread checks the subsets between $\lfloor \frac{2^n}{t} \rfloor + 1$ and $2 \times \lfloor \frac{2^n}{t} \rfloor$. It is important to handle the last thread with caution. If t is not a factor of 2^n, then the program must ensure that the thread includes the last set (value is $2^n - 1$).

The parallel program contains three steps:

1. Create an object as the argument to each thread. Each object specifies (a) the range of the subsets to be examined, (b) the set, (c) the set's size, (d) the value of k, and (e) the number of subsets whose sums are equal to k. It is necessary to give each thread all relevant information because sharing variables will be incorrect, as explained later in Section 22.4.
2. Create the threads. Each thread checks some subsets and computes the number of subsets whose sums equal to k.
3. The main thread waits for every thread to complete and then adds the number reported by each thread.

The **checkRange** function is used by each thread, and is an argument of **pthread_create**. Different threads check different ranges. This is a SIMD program because the same function is used in every thread.

This header file defines the structure needed for each thread.

```
1  // CH22:threaddata.h
2  #ifndef THREADDATA_H
3  #define THREADDATA_H
4  typedef struct
5  {
6    unsigned int minval; // min and max specify the range to check
7    unsigned int maxval;
```

---

[1]Note that being able to parallelize a solution requires a CPU with parallel capabilities. Virtually all modern CPUs provide support for multiple execution cores, including those from Intel, AMD, and ARM. Note also that the threading interfaces covered here do not support GPGPUs (General Purpose Graphics Processing Units), which are beyond the scope of this book.

```
8    int numSol;            // number of solutions
9    int * setA;            // shared array, not changed by threads
10   int sizeA;             // number of elements in the set
11   int kval;
12 } ThreadData;
13 #endif
```

Below is the code listing for the **subsetSum** function using threads:

```
1  // CH22:parallel.c
2  #include <pthread.h>
3  #include <stdio.h>
4  #include <stdlib.h>
5  #include "threaddata.h"
6  #include "subsetsum.h"
7  #define NUMBER_THREAD 16
8  void * checkRange(void * range)
9  {
10   ThreadData * thd = (ThreadData *) range;
11   unsigned int minval = thd -> minval;
12   unsigned int maxval = thd -> maxval;
13   // printf("minval = %d, maxval = %d\n", minval, maxval);
14   unsigned int ind;
15   // caution: need to use <= for max
16   int numsol = 0;
17   for (ind = minval; ind <= maxval; ind ++)
18     {
19        numsol += subsetEqual(thd -> setA, thd -> sizeA, thd -> kval, ind);
20     }
21   thd -> numSol = numsol;
22   return NULL;
23 }
24 int subsetSum(int * setA, int sizeA, int kval)
25 // This function does not allocate memory (malloc)
26 // No need to free memory if failure occurs
27 {
28   pthread_t tid[NUMBER_THREAD];
29   ThreadData thd[NUMBER_THREAD];
30   // set the values for the thread data
31   unsigned int maxCode = 1;
32   unsigned int ind;
33   for (ind = 0; ind < sizeA; ind ++) { maxCode *= 2; }
34   int total = 0;
35   unsigned int minval = 1;
36   unsigned int size = maxCode / NUMBER_THREAD;
37   unsigned int maxval = size;
38   // prepare the data for each threadf
39   for (ind = 0; ind < NUMBER_THREAD - 1; ind ++)
40     {
41        thd[ind].minval = minval;
```

```
42        thd[ind].maxval = maxval;
43        thd[ind].numSol = 0;
44        thd[ind].setA = setA;
45        thd[ind].sizeA = sizeA;
46        thd[ind].kval = kval;
47        minval = maxval + 1;
48        maxval += size;
49      }
50    // handle the last thread differently because
51    // maxCode may not be a multiple of NUMBER_THREAD
52    thd[ind].minval = minval;
53    thd[ind].maxval = maxCode - 1; // remember -1
54    thd[ind].numSol = 0;
55    thd[ind].setA = setA;
56    thd[ind].sizeA = sizeA;
57    thd[ind].kval = kval;
58    // create the threads
59    for (ind = 0; ind < NUMBER_THREAD; ind ++)
60      {
61        int rtv;
62        rtv = pthread_create(& tid[ind], NULL,
63                        checkRange, (void *) & thd[ind]);
64        if (rtv != 0) { printf("ERROR: pthread_crate() fail\n");}
65      }
66    // wait for the threads to complete
67    for (ind = 0; ind < NUMBER_THREAD; ind ++)
68      {
69        int rtv;
70        rtv = pthread_join(tid[ind], NULL);
71        if (rtv != 0)
72          {
73            printf("ERROR; pthread_join() returns %d\n", rtv);
74            return EXIT_FAILURE;
75          }
76        total += thd[ind].numSol; // add the number of solutions
77      }
78    return total;
79  }
```

A few details are worth noting. First, the ranges checked by the threads must be mutually exclusive. If one subset is checked by two or more threads and this subset's sum happens to equal to k, then this subset is counted multiple times and the total is wrong. Second, the threads combined should check all subsets (excluding the empty set). Also, checkRange needs to be consistent with the ranges assigned in subsetSum. In particular, if checkRange uses <= maxval, then the maximum value checked by the last thread must be maxCode - 1, not maxCode. The threads' attribute setA is a pointer to an array. This means that every thread uses the same piece of memory. This is acceptable because the threads do not modify the array. The other attributes are not shared because attributes are int and unsigned int (i.e., not pointer).

This is the `Makefile` for testing the parallel and sequential program:

```
1   # CH22:Makefile
2   SHELL = /bin/bash
3   GCC = gcc
4   CFLAGS = -g -Wall -Wshadow
5   LIBS = -lpthread
6   OBJS = countint.o isvalid.o subsetequal.o main.o
7
8   thread: thread.c
9           $(GCC) $(CFLAGS) thread.c -o thread $(LIBS)
10          ./run-valgrind.sh ./thread
11
12  sequential: sequential.c $(OBJS)
13          $(GCC) $(CFLAGS) sequential.c $(OBJS) -o sequential
14
15  parallel: parallel.c $(OBJS)
16          $(GCC) $(CFLAGS) parallel.c $(OBJS) -o parallel $(LIBS)
17
18  sync: sync.c
19          $(GCC) $(CFLAGS) sync.c -o sync $(LIBS)
20          ./sync
21
22  outsync: outsync.c
23          $(GCC) $(CFLAGS) outsync.c -o outsync $(LIBS)
24          ./outsync
25
26  testall: parallel sequential testgen
27          /bin/rm -f -r outputs
28          mkdir outputs
29          # go through all test cases stored in inputs/
30          for case in inputs/*; do \
31                  # echo $$case; \
32                  # dirname $$case; \
33                  filename=$$(basename $$case); \
34                  # echo $$filename; \
35                  ./parallel $$case | sort > outputs/$$filename.p; \
36                  ./sequential $$case | sort > outputs/$$filename.s; \
37                  diff outputs/$$filename.p outputs/$$filename.s; \
38          done
39
40  testgen: testgen.c
41          $(GCC) $(CFLAGS) testgen.c -o testgen
42          /bin/rm -f -r inputs
43          mkdir inputs
44          # 1 1: valid input, subset sum: yes
45          # 1 0: valid input, subset sum: no
46          # 0 0: invalid input
47          for case in 5 10 15 20 ; do \
48          ./testgen  $$case 1 1 > inputs/validyes$$case; \
49          ./testgen  $$case 1 0 > inputs/validno$$case; \
```

```
50          ./testgen   $$case 0 0 > inputs/invalid$$case; \
51          done
52
53  .c.o:
54          $(GCC) $(CFLAGS) -c $*.c
55
56  clean:
57          /bin/rm -f thread seqout* parallel
58          /bin/rm -f sequential log* testgen *.o
59          /bin/rm -f -r outputs sync outsync inputs
```

Lines 40–51 generate different test cases: valid inputs or invalid inputs. For valid inputs, the test cases are further divided into whether the subset sum has a solution (yes) or not (no). Lines 26–38 test the parallel and sequential programs using all test cases. Line 30 goes through all test cases stored in the **inputs** directory. This is a **shell** program. Line 32 uses **dirname** to extract the name of the directory (should be **inputs**). Line 33 uses **basename** to obtain the file name without the **inputs** directory. Lines 35–36 execute the parallel and sequential versions of the subset sum programs. Their outputs should be sorted before comparison (line 37) because the parallel version has multiple threads. When a thread discovers a solution, the thread prints the subset. Since the threads may interleave, the order of their outputs may be different from the order of the sequential program's outputs. Using the **sort** program ensures the outputs from the parallel program match the order of the sequential program.

22.4   Interleave the Execution of Threads

The threads in the subset sum program share a common array **setA**. An advantage of threads is the ability to share memory. For this example, the array's elements can be shared. In the subset sum case, the threads never modify the shared memory (i.e., **setA**), but only read the elements from the array. Sharing data can be problematic sometimes. The only memory that the threads modify is the attribute **numSol**, and each thread has a unique copy of this variable. The main thread calls **pthread_join** on each thread and waits until all the threads have completed. Then the main thread adds the **numSol** values. What could happen if threads share memory that may be read and modified? The following listing is a simple and instructive example:

```
1   // CH22:outsync.c
2   // multiple threads read and modify a shared variable
3   #include <pthread.h>
4   #include <stdio.h>
5   #include <stdlib.h>
6   #define NUMBER_THREAD 16
7   void * tfunc(void *intarg)
8   {
9     int * intptr = (int *) intarg;
10    while (1)
11      {
```

```
12        (* intptr) ++;
13        (* intptr) --;
14        if ((* intptr) != 0)
15          {
16            printf("value is %d\n", * intptr);
17            return NULL;
18          }
19        }
20      return NULL;
21  }
22  int main (int argc, char *argv[])
23  {
24    pthread_t tid[NUMBER_THREAD];
25    int rtv; // return value of pthread_create
26    int ind;
27    int intarg = 0;
28    for (ind = 0; ind < NUMBER_THREAD; ind ++)
29      {
30        rtv = pthread_create(& tid[ind], NULL, tfunc, (void *) & intarg);
31        if (rtv != 0)
32          {
33            printf("pthread_create() fail %d\n", rtv);
34            return EXIT_FAILURE;
35          }
36      }
37    for (ind = 0; ind < NUMBER_THREAD; ind ++)
38      {
39        rtv = pthread_join(tid[ind], NULL);
40        if (rtv != 0)
41          {
42            printf("pthread_join() fail %d\n", rtv);
43            return EXIT_FAILURE;
44          }
45      }
46    return EXIT_SUCCESS;
47  }
```

This program creates 16 threads that share the address of the same integer variable (intarg in main). Each thread increments and decrements the value stored at that address (i.e., the integer). If a thread finds that the value is not zero, then it prints a message and terminates. Otherwise, the thread will continue indefinitely. The value of intarg starts with zero. Each thread increments and decrements the value in these two lines:

```
12  (* intptr) ++;
13  (* intptr) --;
```

Then, each thread checks whether the value is zero:

```
14  if ((* intptr) != 0)
```

Will the threads ever print anything? Is it possible that any thread returns NULL and terminates? Yes, it is possible. When we execute this program, the program may print 1, −1, and 0. How can this be possible? If a thread increments and decrements the value before checking, how can it be possible that the value be different from zero? It can be even more surprising when we see the output that includes: `value is 0`. This makes no sense because the program should print the message only if the value is non-zero, based on the condition at line 14. What is wrong with this program?

If a computer has multiple cores, these threads may run simultaneously. It is also possible that one or several threads wait because there are insufficient number of cores. The operating system controls the execution of threads by giving each thread a short time interval. After each time interval ends, the thread suspends execution so that another thread can execute and make progress. There is no guarantee when a thread is suspended and how much progress a thread has made. The operating system needs to manage all programs and threads so that no single program or thread can occupy the processor for too long. It is possible that one thread is executing line 12, while another thread is executing line 13. How can `* intptr` be anything other than zero after the increment and decrement operations?

What happens when the program executes this statement `(* intptr)++`? Because `intptr` stores `intarg`'s address, this statement increments the value stored in `intarg`. To execute this statement, the computer must do three things: (1) read the value of `* intarg`; (2) increment the value; and (3) write the new value to `* intarg`. Please notice that we want to modify `* intarg` (an integer), not `intarg` (an address). Line 13 is also composed of three steps: (1) read the value of `* intarg`; (2) decrement the value; and (3) write the new value to `* intarg`. The operating system may suspend a thread anywhere in these steps. The value of `intarg` changes only at the last step. During the first and the second steps, the value is stored in a temporary location (called *register*) inside the processor. Threads may share memory space but they do not share registers.

Table 22.2 shows one possible interleaving of the execution orders of two threads. The table divides each of lines 12 and 13 into the three steps mentioned above. In this table, time progresses downwards. We use - to indicate that a thread is suspended. If thread 1 is suspended right after the value has incremented, then the value is 1 when thread 2 reads it. Thread 2 increments the value and it becomes 2. Then, thread 2 is suspended and thread 1 resumes. Thread 1 reads the value and it is 2. Thread 1 decrements the value to 1, checks whether it is zero, and prints 1.

TABLE 22.2: Interleaving threads 1 and 2. The program prints value 1.

time	Thread 1			Thread 2			intarg
	line	step	operation	line	step	operation	
0	line 12	(1)	read	-	-	-	0
1	line 12	(2)	increment	-	-	-	0
2	line 12	(3)	write	-	-	-	1
3	-	-	-	line 12	(1)	read	1
4	-	-	-	line 12	(2)	increment	1
5	-	-	-	line 12	(3)	write	2
6	line 13	(1)	read	-	-	-	2
7	line 13	(2)	decrement	-	-	-	2
8	line 13	(3)	write	-	-	-	1
9	line 14		compare with 0	-	-	-	1
10	line 16		print	-	-	-	1

If we change the ordering, Table 22.3 shows why it is possible to see the value 0 printed. Thread 1 is suspended after it checks `intarg`'s value: it is one and the condition is true. Then thread 2 decrements the value to zero. When thread 1 resumes and reads the value, it

TABLE 22.3:   Interleaving threads 1 and 2. The program prints value 0.

time	Thread 1 line	step	operation	Thread 2 line	step	operation	intarg
0	line 12	(1)	read	-	-	-	0
1	line 12	(2)	increment	-	-	-	0
2	line 12	(3)	write	-	-	-	1
3	-	-	-	line 12	(1)	read	1
4	-	-	-	line 12	(2)	increment	1
5	-	-	-	line 12	(3)	write	2
6	line 13	(1)	read	-	-	-	2
7	line 13	(2)	decrement	-	-	-	2
8	line 13	(3)	write	-	-	-	1
9	line 14		compare with 0	-	-	-	1
10	-	-	-	line 13	(1)	read	1
11	-	-	-	line 13	(2)	decrement	1
12	-	-	-	line 13	(3)	write	0
13	line 16		print	-	-	-	0

is zero and 0 is printed. In other words, it is possible that `intarg`'s value is nonzero when the condition is checked and is 0 when the value is printed.

How could the designers of threads allow such interleaving to happen? First, it is not a flaw in the specification of threads. The source of the problem is that there is no simple way to predict the order in which multiple threads execute their code. Thus it allows operating systems to manage the computer resources more efficiently.

Is this a contrived example? Do scenarios like this happen when solving real-world problems? It actually happens quite often. For example, when several people try to purchase tickets for the same flight, the shared variable is the total number of tickets sold. If only one seat is available and several people buy the ticket simultaneously, then the flight is overbooked. Airlines do this on purpose because some people buy tickets but never board their flights. In the unlikely scenario that everyone actually checks in for the flight, airlines give vouchers to volunteers for taking later flights.

22.5   Thread Synchronization

The previous section described a problem in multi-threaded programs. The problem occurs because there is no good way to predict the order in which multiple threads may read and modify the same shared variable. There is no problem when threads do not share data. There is no problem when they share read-only data. For the subset sum problem, the threads share the array but no thread modifies the array; thus, no problem occurs.

One solution is to prevent interleaving of the threads. This defeats the purpose of threads because the threads cannot run in parallel. Another solution prevents undesirable interleaving when shared variables are read or written. This solution uses *atomic operations*. Each atomic operation contains multiple steps together as a whole and the operation cannot be divided into individual steps. Atom comes from the Greek word *atomon*, meaning uncuttable. Modern physics tells us that an atom can actually be divided to electrons, neutrons, and protons. Nevertheless, an "atomic operation" still means multiple steps as a whole and cannot be divided.

Threads can specify which operations must be atomic. An atomic operation is called a *critical section*. In the previous example, the critical section should include the code where the variable is read or written. If the threads take turns to increment and decrement the variable atomically, then the value will always remain zero. Thus, the question becomes how to ensure that the threads take turns executing the critical sections. Only one thread can start a critical section at a time. After a critical section starts, no other thread can enter the critical section until it finishes. In other words, The threads must be *synchronized*. *Synchronization* restricts how threads' operations may interleave. This is achieved by using a *mutually exclusive lock*, also called *mutex lock* or *mutex* for short.

Consider an analogy of a shared library study room with the following rules: (1) The room has a lock and only one key. (2) Before a student enters the room, the student must obtain the key from the library's reception desk. (3) Only one student can enter the room and must keep the key inside the room. (4) After the student enters the room, the student must immediately lock the door. (5) When the student leaves the room, the door is unlocked and the key is returned to the library's reception desk. (6) If a student wants to use the room without the key, the student has to wait.

A mutex comes with a pair of lock and unlock statements. The code between this pair of statements is the *critical section*. A mutex lock is similar to the lock of the library's study room: (1) Each critical section has a lock and the operating system keeps the key. (2) Before a thread enters the critical section, the thread must obtain the key from the operating system. (3) Only one thread can enter the critical section. The thread keeps the key while running the code in the critical section. (4) After a thread enters the critical section, the operating system locks the critical section and no other thread can enter. (5) When the thread leaves the critical section, the thread unlocks the critical section and returns the key to the operating system. (6) If a thread wants to enter the critical section without the key, then the thread has to wait.

The following example shows how to use a critical section.

```
1   // CH22:sync.c
2   // mutex lock protects a shared variable
3   #include <pthread.h>
4   #include <stdio.h>
5   #include <stdlib.h>
6   #define NUMBER_THREAD 16
7   typedef struct
8   {
9     int * intptr;            // pointer to shared memory
10    pthread_mutex_t * mlock; // lock of the critical section
11  } ThreadData;
12  void * tfunc(void *tharg)
13  {
14    ThreadData * td = (ThreadData *) tharg;
15    int * intptr = td -> intptr;
16    pthread_mutex_t * mlock = td -> mlock;
17    while (1)
18      {
19        int rtv;
20        rtv = pthread_mutex_lock(mlock); // lock
21        // beginning critical section
22        if (rtv != 0)
23          {
```

```
24              printf("mutex_lock fail\n");
25              return NULL;
26            }
27          (* intptr) ++;
28          (* intptr) --;
29          if ((* intptr) != 0)
30            {
31              printf("value is %d\n", * intptr);
32              return NULL;
33            }
34          // end critical section
35          rtv = pthread_mutex_unlock(mlock); // unlock
36          if (rtv != 0)
37            {
38              printf("mutex_unlock fail\n");
39              return NULL;
40            }
41        }
42    return NULL;
43  }
44  int main (int argc, char *argv[])
45  {
46    pthread_mutex_t mlock;                  // create the lock
47    pthread_mutex_init(& mlock, NULL);     // initialize the lock
48    int val = 0;
49    ThreadData tharg;
50    tharg.intptr = & val;                  // share memory address
51    tharg.mlock  = & mlock;                // all threads share the same lock
52    pthread_t tid[NUMBER_THREAD];
53    int rtv; // return value of pthread_create
54    int ind;
55    for (ind = 0; ind < NUMBER_THREAD; ind ++)
56      {
57        rtv = pthread_create(& tid[ind], NULL, tfunc, (void *) & tharg);
58        if (rtv != 0)
59          {
60            printf("pthread_create() fail %d\n", rtv);
61            return EXIT_FAILURE;
62          }
63      }
64    for (ind = 0; ind < NUMBER_THREAD; ind ++)
65      {
66        rtv = pthread_join(tid[ind], NULL);
67        if (rtv != 0)
68          {
69            printf("pthread_join() fail %d\n", rtv);
70            return EXIT_FAILURE;
71          }
72      }
73    pthread_mutex_destroy(& mlock);
```

```
74      return EXIT_SUCCESS;
75    }
```

The program has a structure `ThreadData` that includes two pointers: one for the integer's address (i.e., the shared memory) and the other for the mutex's address (the lock). For a critical section to work as intended, all the threads must attempt to lock and unlock the same mutex (equivalent to the same study room). A pointer to the mutex is passed in `ThreadData` at line 51. If each thread has its own mutex, then this is equivalent to multiple study rooms in the library; as a result, threads can run simultaneously. The critical section includes the code that reads and writes the shared variable. Each thread obtains the key by calling `pthread_mutex_lock` right after entering the `while` block. If the thread cannot lock the mutex (because another thread is in the critical section), then this thread will wait at `pthread_mutex_lock` until the thread can obtain a key. The key is returned to the operating system by calling `pthread_mutex_unlock` at the end of the `while` block.

The `main` function creates a single `ThreadData` object shared by all threads. Before calling `pthread_mutex_lock` or `pthread_mutex_unlock`, the lock must be initialized by calling `pthread_mutex_init`. This is done in the `main` function. What is the output of this program? Nothing. The `if` condition in `threadfunc` is never true and nothing is printed. This means that all threads keep running indefinitely.

This chapter introduces parallel programming using threads. Writing correct multi-threaded programs can be challenging, and developing better tools and programming languages for this purpose is an ongoing topic of research. When writing multi-threaded programs, it is important to identify critical sections and make them atomic. Failure to do so can result in surprising results.

22.6   Amdahl's Law

A typical multi-thread program starts with one thread (the main thread, often the sequential part of a computation). This thread may do some work (such as reading data from a sequential file) before creating more threads. Then, multiple threads are created for computing the results in parallel, provided there are multiple execution cores (a reasonable assumption on modern CPUs). The results from multiple threads are later combined into the final result. If a program is structured this way, then there is an obvious problem: The initialization and the finalization steps are sequential and can become the bottleneck.

Consider the following scenario. A sequential (single-threaded) program takes 100 seconds. The program runs on a computer with an infinite number of cores. The initialization and the finalization steps account for 1% of the execution time (i.e., 1 second). The remaining 99% of execution time is divided between two threads. What is the performance improvement of the two-threads solution? The new execution time is $1 + \frac{99}{2} = 50.5$ seconds, reduction of 49.5 seconds (almost half of the original 100 seconds). Suppose that the 99% of execution time is divided among three threads. The execution time becomes $1 + \frac{99}{3} = 34$ seconds. What is the execution time when 99 threads are used? It is $1 + \frac{99}{99} = 2$ seconds. How about 990 threads? It is $1 + \frac{99}{990} = 1.1$ seconds. The reduction in execution time is only 0.9 seconds after increasing the number of threads from 99 threads to 990 threads. This is called the *diminishing return*. If the program uses an infinite number of threads, the execution is still greater than one second. The initialization and the finalization steps seem like a small portion (1 %) of the total execution time for the single-thread program. As more threads are used, initialization and finalization steps become a bigger portion of the total execution time.

The mathematical model for this situation is called the *Amdahl's Law*. The model says that adding more threads has diminishing returns. To further reduce execution time, it will be necessary to reduce the time spent on the initialization and the finalization. We now take a look at the theory behind Amdahl's Law.

22.6.1 Speedup vs. Efficiency

We want to use parallelism to compute answers more quickly. How much more quickly? To understand this, we introduce two important topics when it comes to understanding the benefits of parallelism:

We define speedup as

$$S = \frac{T_1}{T_n}$$

where T_1 is defined as the execution time of the sequential algorithm for the problem on a single processor, and T_n is the execution time of the parallel algorithm on n processors. Notice several things:

- T_n should be smaller than T_1, since the parallel algorithm should run faster than the sequential algorithm.

- The larger the value of S, the better.

- T_1 is supposed to be the run time of the best possible sequential algorithm, but in general, the best possible algorithm is an unknown quantity. Thus, it is often the case that T_1 is simply a version of the parallel program that is run sequentially.

- We define linear speedup as:
$$S = \frac{T_1}{T_n} = n$$

We would expect that speedup cannot be better (larger) than linear and indeed should be smaller. If the entire work of the sequential program could be evenly divided among the n processors, they could all complete in $1/n$ the time. But it is unlikely that the work could be divided evenly; programs tend to have a sequential part, such as initialization or reading data from or writing results to sequential files. If the sequential part can only be done on a single machine, then only the rest can be run in parallel. We will examine this in more detail when we discuss Amdahl's law. Even if the program could be evenly divided among n processors, the processors would probably have to coordinate their work with each other, which would require extra instruction executions beyond the sequential program. Therefore, T_n may be $\frac{1}{n}$ of a larger value than T_1.

Moreover, T_1 is supposed to be the best-known sequential algorithm. If the parallel algorithm runs faster on a single machine, it would be a better sequential algorithm, and therefore, you'd use it. So you can expect the algorithm T_1 to be at least as good as the algorithm for T_n. You cannot expect any help from differences in the algorithms in achieving even linear speedup.

However, in practice, super-linear speedup is sometimes observed. There are several reasons for this:

$$S > n$$

- The hardware is different. The parallel machine has more processors, and hence more cache memory, for one thing. Better locality and pipelining can also play a role.

- The algorithm is different. For example, a depth-first search on a sequential machine might be translated into a collection of depth-first searches on the nodes of a parallel computer, but the parallel depth-first searches would have an element of a breadth-first search. A single depth-first search might spend a large amount of time on one fruitless branch, whereas with several searches, it is likely that another path might find the solution more quickly.

Efficiency is defined as

$$E = \frac{S}{n} = \frac{T_1}{nT_n} = \frac{T_1/n}{T_n}$$

The formula shows two ways to think about efficiency. Suppose you were to run the parallel program on a serial machine. The serial machine would have to execute all the parallel processes. If there are n processes, then the serial execution should not take more than about nT_n (assuming that the time to swap the processor from one process to another is negligible). Efficiency, then, would measure the ratio of the actual sequential time to the worst expected time to execute the n processes sequentially.

Suppose that, on the other hand, you calculate how long you would expect it to take to run the sequential algorithm on n processors, assuming linear speedup. That gives you $\frac{T_1}{n}$.

The efficiency would be the ratio of execution time with linear speedup to observed execution time. If speedup is no greater than linear, efficiency will be less than or equal to 1.

22.6.2 Understanding Amdahl's Law

Amdahl's law does not really deserve the title of law, as it is not a law in the scientific sense. It is merely a back-of-the-envelope attempt (or conjecture) to prove that there are severe limits to the speedup that can be achieved by a parallel program. Amdahl's law asserts that there is a serial part of any parallel program that must be executed sequentially, and the time required for this part will be a lower limit on the time the program takes to execute. Consider a serial program that executes in time T. Let's calculate the best speedup we could achieve if a fraction f of the execution time is taken up by sequential execution. If you divide the parallel execution time into the serial and parallel parts, you get speedup with an upper bound of

$$E = \frac{T}{fT + \frac{(1-f)T}{n}}$$

We get this equation by taking the definition of speedup and breaking down Tn into the time taken by the serial fraction fT and the time taken by the parallel fraction $(1-f)T$. We divide the parallel fraction by n to calculate the best we could expect from a linear speedup.

T appears as a factor in both the numerator and the denominator. Thus, it can be removed, which leads to an equation not involving T, or

$$S = \frac{1}{f + \frac{(1-f)}{n}}$$

As n approaches infinity (i.e., the number of processors is increased), we arrive at the folllowing limit:

$$\lim_{x \to \infty} S = \lim_{x \to \infty} \frac{1}{f + \frac{(1-f)}{n}} = \frac{1}{f}$$

22.6.3   The Limit's of Amdahl's Law

A flaw in the reasoning behind Amdahl's Law (first described by Gustafson and Barsis in `https://dl.acm.org/doi/10.1145/42411.42415`) is that it deals with fixed-sized problems and questions how much faster they can be run. This is not, however, the way massively parallel processors are used. Take the example of weather forecasting. The calculations are made by superimposing a mesh onto the atmosphere and calculating pressure, temperature, humidity, etc., at each mesh point, repeatedly using the values at the surrounding points at small time intervals. The more numerous the mesh points and the smaller the time intervals, the better the forecast. But the more calculations that are required, the slower the program runs. And for weather forecasting, if the calculation takes too long, it loses all value. When presented with a faster machine, weather forecasters will use more grid points and a smaller step size. They increase the problem size to the largest possible value that allows the answer to be reached in the same amount of time.

Let's rephrase the calculation, starting with a parallel program with serial fraction g that runs in time R on n processors. If we ran the calculation on a single processor, how long would it take? The answer is

$$T = gR + n(1 - g)R$$

This equation follows since the serial fraction will still take the same time gR and the n parts of the parallel fraction $(1 - g)R$ would have to be interleaved.

This results in the speedup calculation

$$S = \frac{gR + n(1 - g)R}{R} = g + n(1 - g)$$

a linear speedup with slope $(1 \times g)$. The efficiency is

$$E = 1 - g\frac{n - 1}{n}$$

which approaches the parallel fraction as the number of processors increases. In this formulation, there is no theoretical limit on speedup. As long as we scale the problem size to the size of the machine, we will not run into limits.

Another aspect of this argument against Amdahl's law is that, as the problem size increases, the serial fraction may decrease. Consider a program that reads in two N-by-N matrices, multiplies them, and writes out the result. The serial I/O time grows as N^2, while the multiplication, which is highly parallelizable, grows as N^3.

22.7   Problems

22.7.1   Interleaving of Threads

Is it possible for the program in Section 22.4 to print 2? Draw a table similar to Table 22.2 to explain.

22.7.2   Interleaving of Threads

Explain why the program in Section 22.4 may print -1. Draw a table similar to Table 22.2 to explain.

Chapter 23

Unit Test

Testing is an essential part of software development. Testing can be classified into *unit test* and *integration test*. A unit test may test a function, a structure, or a file. An integration test, as the name suggests, tests when multiple units are put together. This chapter explains how to develop unit tests using the GoogleTest framework. The examples use *rational numbers*.

23.1 Google Test Framework

Before we explain how to use the *Google Test* framework, please ensure that you have the tools installed using this command on Linux:

```
sudo apt-get install libgtest-dev
```

Google Test is designed for C++, not C. The program's extension is `.cpp` for C++, not `.c` for C. This chapter writes unit tests in GoogleTest by using macros that generate C++ code for the unit tests. It is not necessary to know C++ for writing your tests. The `TEST()` macro creates a class (the C++ version of struct, with additional features such as data protection and inheritance). This is a very simple function to calculate the square of a number:

```cpp
// CH23:square.cpp
double square (const double val)
{
  return (val * val);
}
```

This is a program to test the `square` function. Section 3.4 explains the need to separate the code to be tested (production code) from the testing code.

```cpp
// CH23:testsquare.cpp
#include <gtest/gtest.h>
double square (const double val);
TEST(SquareTest, PositiveNumbers)
{
    EXPECT_EQ (324, square (18.0));
    EXPECT_EQ (625, square (25));
    EXPECT_EQ (49,  square (7.0));
    // EXPECT_EQ (52,  square (6.3)); // fail
}
TEST(SquareTest, NegativeNumbers)
{
```

```
13      EXPECT_EQ (64, square (-8.0));
14      EXPECT_EQ (841, square (-29));
15      EXPECT_EQ (49,  square (-7.0));
16      // EXPECT_EQ (133,  square (-9.4)); // fail
17    }
18    int main(int argc, char ** argv)
19    {
20      testing::InitGoogleTest(& argc, argv);
21      return RUN_ALL_TESTS();
22    }
```

At the top of this program, we need to include `<gtest/gtest.h>`. This header defines some macros needed for testing. The `main` function starts with `testing::InitGoogleTest(& argc, argv);` to initialize the testing framework. The `main` function can simply `return RUN_ALL_TESTS();` and the testing framework will do all the remaining work. Tests are conducted in the two `TEST` macros. Each macro has two inputs. The first is the name of a *test suite* and the second is the name of a *test*. Usually, a test suite includes several tests. In this example, the test suite `SquareTest` has two tests called `PositiveNumbers` and `NegativeNumbers`. Each test has three `EXPECT_EQ` statements. Each statement has two arguments and the tests check whether the first argument equals the second argument.

We need to use `g++`, not `gcc` to build the executable. The following is a `Makefile` for building and testing the program.

```
1    # CH23:Makefile1
2    # Makefile for testsquare
3    GPP = g++ -g
4    LIBS = -lgtest -pthread
5    test: testsquare.cpp
6            $(GPP) square.cpp testsquare.cpp -o testsquare $(LIBS)
7            ./testsquare
8    clean:
9            /bin/rm -f *.o a.out testsquare
```

It is important to add `-lgtest -pthread` because Google Test needs these two libraries. Chapter 22 has explained the *pthread* library. This is the program's output:

```
[==========] Running 2 tests from 1 test suite.
[----------] Global test environment set-up.
[----------] 2 tests from SquareTest
[ RUN      ] SquareTest.PositiveNumbers
[       OK ] SquareTest.PositiveNumbers (0 ms)
[ RUN      ] SquareTest.NegativeNumbers
[       OK ] SquareTest.NegativeNumbers (0 ms)
[----------] 2 tests from SquareTest (0 ms total)

[----------] Global test environment tear-down
[==========] 2 tests from 1 test suite ran. (0 ms total)
[  PASSED  ] 2 tests.
```

If we take lines 9 and 16 out from comments, this is the execution result:

```
[==========] Running 2 tests from 1 test suite.
[----------] Global test environment set-up.
[----------] 2 tests from SquareTest
[ RUN      ] SquareTest.PositiveNumbers
testsquare.cpp:9: Failure
Expected equality of these values:
  52
  square (6.3)
    Which is: 39.69
[  FAILED  ] SquareTest.PositiveNumbers (0 ms)
[ RUN      ] SquareTest.NegativeNumbers
testsquare.cpp:16: Failure
Expected equality of these values:
  133
  square (-9.4)
    Which is: 88.36
[  FAILED  ] SquareTest.NegativeNumbers (0 ms)
[----------] 2 tests from SquareTest (0 ms total)


[----------] Global test environment tear-down
[==========] 2 tests from 1 test suite ran. (0 ms total)
[  PASSED  ] 0 tests.
[  FAILED  ] 2 tests, listed below:
[  FAILED  ] SquareTest.PositiveNumbers
[  FAILED  ] SquareTest.NegativeNumbers

 2 FAILED TESTS
```

The test clearly shows that lines 9 and lines 16 fail. Moreover, the test shows the values: Line 9 expects 52 (first number) and receives 39.69 (second number). Line 16 expects 133 (first number) and receives 88.36 (second number).

This simple example explains several important concepts in tests: First, the program to test (the `square` function) and the test (`testsquare.cpp`) should be in two different files. This ensures that the test does not interfere with the tested function. Second, the test has expected values and the values from the function's result. To write a good test, it is necessary to know the expected result. Third, the tests can be organized into a suite.

Even though this book is about C programming, this chapter uses Google Test and it is designed for C++. Most valid C programs are also valid C++ programs. However, *some* valid C programs are invalid C++ programs because C++ has more *reserved words* than C. For example, a C program may use `class` as a variable name because `class` is not a reserved word in C. This valid C program is not a valid C++ program because `class` is a reserved word in C++. Similarly, `new`, `delete`, `public`, `private`, `protected`, `operator` are reserved words in C++ but not in C.

Here are some commonly used terms in the context of software tests. (1) *Assertions.* In all unit testing frameworks, a key building block is assertion. Assertion checks whether something is true. The result of an assertion is success or failure. When a failure occurs, the program stops. Google Test can continue even if an assertion has failed. The previous example reported two failures. As explained in Section 3.5, you should not put `assert` in production code. (2) *Test Suite.* A test suite contains one or multiple unit tests for a particular part of a program. In the earlier example, the tests for `square` form one test suite. A large program will likely need many test suites for different parts of the programs. Writing unit tests is an essential skill for software developers. This chapter uses operations of rational numbers as examples and takes advantage of the `GoogleTest` framework.

23.2 Rational Numbers

A rational number can be written as the quotient $\frac{p}{q}$ of two integers p and q. Examples of rational numbers include $\frac{-3}{11}$, $\frac{9}{17}$, and $\frac{26}{125}$. Rational numbers are a subset of *real numbers*. Some real numbers are irrational, such as π, $\sqrt{7}$, and e. Most computer programs can handle *floating-point numbers* with *finite precisions*. Some rational numbers, for example $\frac{1}{3}$, need infinite precisions. Thus, we want to keep the format of a quotient. A rational number can be defined by the following C struct, `Rational` in the file `rational.h`:

```
6   typedef struct
7   {
8     long num;   // numerator
9     long den;   // denominator
10    bool valid; // false if denominator is zero or overflow
11  } Rational;
```

The `Rational` structure is an *abstract data type*. Each `Rational` object has a numerator (long integer) and denominator (long integer). In addition, the `valid` attribute indicates whether the rational representation is valid. Two reasons can make a rational number invalid: (1) The denominator is zero. (2) The operation to compute a new rational number results in an *overflow*. Overflow means that an arithmetic operation (such as addition or multiplication) generates a number that is too large for the memory used to store the value. For example,

```
unsigned char a = 240;
unsigned char b = 152;
unsigned char c = a + b;
```

Each `unsigned char` has 8 bits and can store up to 255. The result of `a + b` is 392 and it exceeds 255. Thus, `c` does not have enough memory to store 392 and this is an example of overflow. We will come back to the topic of overflow and explain how to handle it.

Let's consider how rational numbers work. Suppose we want to add two rational numbers $\frac{1}{2}$ and $\frac{3}{4}$. To perform this operation, we first convert $\frac{1}{2}$ to $\frac{2}{4}$ so that both numbers have a common denominator. Then the two numbers are added: $\frac{2}{4} + \frac{3}{4} = \frac{5}{4}$. A general solution adding two ration numbers $\frac{n_1}{d_1} + \frac{n_2}{d_2}$ needs to make them have the same denominator first.

$$\frac{n_1}{d_1} + \frac{n_2}{d_2} = \frac{n_1 d_2}{d_1 d_2} + \frac{n_2 d_1}{d_1 d_2} = \frac{n_1 d_2 + n_2 d_1}{d_1 d_2}. \tag{23.1}$$

Similarly, we can obtain the general solution for subtraction:

$$\frac{n_1}{d_1} - \frac{n_2}{d_2} = \frac{n_1 d_2}{d_1 d_2} - \frac{n_2 d_1}{d_1 d_2} = \frac{n_1 d_2 - n_2 d_1}{d_1 d_2}. \tag{23.2}$$

After the calculation, we often need to divide the numerator and the denominator by the greatest common divisor (GCD), if the GCD is greater than one. For example, $\frac{1}{4} + \frac{1}{6} = \frac{6}{24} + \frac{4}{24} = \frac{10}{24} = \frac{5}{12}$. Dividing the numerator and the denominator by their GCD is important preventing the numerator and the denominator from becoming too large and exceeding the values that can be stored in `long`.

Multiplication of rational numbers is defined as

$$\frac{n_1}{d_1} \times \frac{n_2}{d_2} = \frac{n_1 n_2}{d_1 d_2}. \tag{23.3}$$

Division is defined as

$$\frac{n_1}{d_1} \div \frac{n_2}{d_2} = \frac{\frac{n_1}{d_1}}{\frac{n_2}{d_2}} = \frac{n_1 d_2}{d_1 n_2}. \tag{23.4}$$

The `Rational` structure can handle rational numbers that require infinite precisions (such as $\frac{1}{3}$) but the numerator and the denominator are `long` and still have finite lengths. It is still possible to have overflow and we need a plan to handle overflow. We can use `cling` to show the smallest and the largest values for `long`; `cling` is a tool that can run C code interactively. To install `cling`, please type the following commands:

```
/bin/bash -c "$(curl -fsSL
↪   https://raw.githubusercontent.com/Homebrew/install/HEAD/install.sh)"
echo '# Set PATH, MANPATH, etc., for Homebrew.' >> /home/yunglu/.profile
echo 'eval "$(/home/linuxbrew/.linuxbrew/bin/brew shellenv)"' >>
↪   /home/yunglu/.profile
eval "$(/home/linuxbrew/.linuxbrew/bin/brew shellenv)"
brew install cling
```

```
1  $ cling
2
3  ***************** CLING ******************
4  * Type C++ code and press enter to run it *
5  *            Type .q to exit              *
6  *******************************************
7
8  [cling]$ #include <limits.h>
9  [cling]$ long a
10 [cling]$ a = LONG_MAX
11 (long) 9223372036854775807
12 [cling]$ a++
13 (long) 9223372036854775807
14 [cling]$ a
15 (long) -9223372036854775808
16 [cling]$ long b
17 [cling]$ b = LONG_MIN
18 (long) -9223372036854775808
19 [cling]$ b
20 (long) -9223372036854775808
21 [cling]$ b-1
22 (long) 9223372036854775807
23 [cling]$
```

Line 10 assigns a's value to LONG_MAX. This is the largest valid value for long. Incrementing a (line 12) changes the value to a negative number (line 15). Line 17 assigns b's value to LONG_MIN. This is a negative number. Line 21 subtracts 1 and the value becomes 9223372036854775807; this is a positive number. The example shows the importance of understanding and preventing overflow. Some C compilers (such as gcc) provide built-in functions for testing whether an arithmetic operation will overflow. See https://gcc.gnu.org/onlinedocs/gcc/Integer-Overflow-Builtins.html for additional details. Here are the built-in functions for handling overflow operations:

```
bool __builtin_saddl_overflow (long int a, long int b, long int *res)
bool __builtin_smull_overflow (long int a, long int b, long int *res)
bool __builtin_ssubl_overflow (long int a, long int b, long int *res)
bool __builtin_uadd_overflow (unsigned int a, unsigned int b, unsigned int
↪  *res)
```

The first two arguments are the inputs. The third argument (a pointer) is the output. If overflow occurs, these functions return true. If overflow does not occur, these functions return false. Consider the letters between builtin and overflow. They have the *n-op-t* pattern. The first part *n* can be s or u: s means signed numbers and u means unsigned numbers. Either s or u is followed by the operations: add, mul, and sub mean addition, multiplication, and subtraction respectively. The third part *t* is the data type. The ending l means long int. This can be verified by using cling:

```
1   $ cling
2
3   ***************** CLING *****************
4   * Type C++ code and press enter to run it *
5   *              Type .q to exit            *
6   ******************************************
7
8   [cling]$ long a, b, c;
9   [cling]$ bool result;
10  [cling]$ #include <limits.h>
11  [cling]$ a = LONG_MAX
12  (long) 9223372036854775807
13  [cling]$ b = 0
14  (long) 0
15  [cling]$ result = __builtin_saddl_overflow(a, b, &c)
16  (bool) false
17  [cling]$ c
18  (long) 9223372036854775807
19  [cling]$ b = 1
20  (long) 1
21  [cling]$ result = __builtin_saddl_overflow(a, b, &c)
22  [cling]$ c
23  (long) -9223372036854775808
24  (bool) true
```

Line 15 adds 0 to a. This does not cause overflow and the function returns false (line 16). Line 19 changes b to 1. Adding 1 to a causes overflow and the function returns true (line 24).

23.3   Rational Numbers and Operations

23.3.1   Create `Ratoinal` Object

The data type `Rational` is organized to support the following operations:

- Initialize a `Rational` object. Please refer to page 195 about the concept of objects.
- Retrieve the numerator and the denominator values.
- Perform arithmetic operations (add, subtract, multiply, and divide) and relational operations (equal, greater).
- Negate a `Rational` object.
- Print a `Rational` object.

We can create a `Rational` object in several ways by (1) specifying the numerator and the denominator, (2) using an existing `Rational` object, (3) using only one number as the numerator and setting the denominator as one. A `Rational` number is invalid if the denominator is zero. Later, we will check whether an arithmetic operation leads to overflow. If overflow occurs, the rational number is also invalid. These functions are listed in the `rational.h` file:

```
12   void rational_init(Rational *number, long num, long den);
13   void rational_from_rational(Rational *dest, const Rational *src);
14   void rational_from_long(Rational *number, long num);
15   long rational_numerator(Rational *number);
16   long rational_denominator(Rational *number);
17   void rational_print(const Rational *number, FILE *stream);
18   void rational_add(const Rational *n1, const Rational *n2,
19                     Rational *result);
20   void rational_subtract(const Rational *n1, const Rational *n2,
21                         Rational *result);
22   void rational_multiply(const Rational *n1, const Rational *n2,
23                         Rational *result);
24   void rational_divide(const Rational *n1, const Rational *n2,
25                       Rational *result);
26   void rational_compare(const Rational *n1, const Rational *n2,
27                        int *result);
28   bool long_add(long a, long b, long *c);
29   bool long_multiply(long a, long b, long *c);
30   bool long_subtract(long a, long b, long *c);
31   #endif
```

The program offers three ways to create a new `Rational` object: `rational_init`, `rational_from_rational` and `rational_from_long`. The first creates a `Rational` object by the numerator and the denominator. The second starts with another `Rational` object. The third starts with the numerator by setting the denominator to one.

```
16   static void reduce_fraction(Rational *number)
17   {
18     long common_divisor = long_gcd(number->num, number->den);
19     if ((common_divisor) == 0)
```

```
20      { return; }
21      // neither denominator nor numerator is zero
22      number->num /= common_divisor;
23      number->den /= common_divisor;
24      if ((number->den) < 0)
25        {
26          number->den = - number->den;
27          number->num = - number->num;
28        }
29    }
30    static void rational_internal_init(Rational *number,
31                                       long num, long den)
32    {
33      number->num = num;
34      number->den = den;
35      if (den == 0)
36        {
37          number -> valid = false;
38          return;
39        }
40      else
41        { number -> valid = true; }
42      reduce_fraction(number);
43    }
44    void rational_init(Rational *number, long num, long den)
45    {
46      rational_internal_init(number, num, den);
47    }
48    void rational_from_rational(Rational *dest, const Rational *src)
49    {
50      rational_internal_init(dest, src->num, src->den);
51    }
52    void rational_from_long(Rational *number, long den)
53    {
54      rational_internal_init(number, den, 1L);
55    }
```

A static function `rational_internal_init` is used by the three functions for creating a `Rational` object. This static function checks whether the denominator is zero and decides whether this `Rational` object is valid. If the denominator is zero, this is not a valid rational number. The `rational_internal_init` function will ensure that the rational number is represented as a reduced fraction. The function calls `reduce_fraction()` and it finds the greatest common divisor (GCD) of the numerator and the denominator.

```
7     static long long_gcd(long a, long b)
8     {
9       if ((a == 0) && (b == 0))
10        { return 0; }
11      if (b == 0)
12        { return labs(a); }
```

```
13    else
14      { return long_gcd(b, a % b); }
15  }
```

Two functions can retrieve the denominator and numerator:

```
56  long rational_numerator(Rational *number)
57  {
58    return number->num;
59  }
60  long rational_denominator(Rational *number)
61  {
62    return number->den;
63  }
```

If we want to see the values of a `Rational` object, we can use the `rational_print` function. It also prints whether the object is valid or not. C does not have a way to print `true` or `false` directly. Thus, the attribute `valid` is printed using `%d` (as an integer). This function prints to a file (second argument). If the intended output is the computer screen, the second argument can be `stdout`. This is a pre-defined file pointer for the computer screen.

```
64  void rational_print(const Rational *number, FILE *stream)
65  {
66    fprintf(stream, "%ld/%ld (valid=%d)\n",
67            number->num, number->den, number->valid);
68  }
```

23.3.2 Arithmetic Operations

After creating `Rational` objects, we can perform arithmetic operations: addition, subtraction, multiplication, and division. Three functions use the builtin functions to determine whether overflow occurs:

```
69  bool long_add(long a, long b, long *c)
70  {
71    return __builtin_saddl_overflow(a, b, c); // true: overflow
72  }
73  bool long_multiply(long a, long b, long *c)
74  {
75    return __builtin_smull_overflow(a, b, c); // true: overflow
76  }
77  bool long_subtract(long a, long b, long *c)
78  {
79    return __builtin_ssubl_overflow(a, b, c); // true: overflow
80  }
```

Both `rational_add` and `rational_subtract` can use `rational_add_sub`.

```c
static void rational_add_sub(const Rational *n1, const Rational *n2,
                             Rational * result, bool addition)
{
    // used by both add and sub
    // addition: true; subtraction: false
    /*
        n1->num      n2->num
       ---------- +- ---------- =
        n1->den      n2->den


        (n1->num) * (n2->den) +- (n2->num) * (n1->den)
       ------------------------------------------------
                      (n1->den) * (n2->den)
    */
    /*
       The result is invalid, if
       either n1 or n2 is invalid, or
       the numerator or the denominator overflows.
    */
    if (((n1->valid) == false) || ((n2->valid) == false))
      {
        result->valid = false;
        return;
      }
    long den1den2; // (n1->den) * (n2->den)
    long num1den2; // (n1->num) * (n2->den)
    long num2den1; // (n2->num) * (n1->den)
    long num;      // (n1->num) * (n2->den) +- (n2->num) * (n1->den)
    bool overflow1, overflow2, overflow3, overflow4;
    overflow1 = long_multiply(n1->den, n2->den, & den1den2);
    overflow2 = long_multiply(n1->num, n2->den, & num1den2);
    overflow3 = long_multiply(n2->num, n1->den, & num2den1);
    if (addition == true)
      { overflow4 = long_add(num1den2, num2den1, & num); }
    else
      { overflow4 = long_subtract(num1den2, num2den1, & num); }
    bool overflow = overflow1 || overflow2 || overflow3 || overflow4;
    if (overflow == true)
      {
        result->valid = false;
        return;
      }
    rational_internal_init(result, num, den1den2);
}
```

The fourth argument of `rational_add_sub` determines whether addition or subtraction is used. This function checks whether overflow occurs for multiplication, addition, or subtraction. If overflow occurs, the result is invalid. With this function, addition and subtraction functions can be implemented:

```
125  void rational_add(const Rational *n1, const Rational *n2,
126                    Rational *result)
127  {
128    rational_add_sub(n1, n2, result, true);
129  }
130  void rational_subtract(const Rational *n1, const Rational *n2,
131                         Rational *result)
132  {
133    rational_add_sub(n1, n2, result, false);
134  }
```

Multiplication and division can be implemented based on the definitions:

```
135  void rational_multiply(const Rational *n1, const Rational *n2,
136                         Rational *result)
137  {
138    if (((n1->valid) == false) || ((n2->valid) == false))
139      {
140        result->valid = false;
141        return;
142      }
143    long den1den2;
144    long num1num2;
145    bool overflow1, overflow2;
146    overflow1 = long_multiply(n1->num, n2->num, &num1num2);
147    overflow2 = long_multiply(n1->den, n2->den, &den1den2);
148    if ((overflow1 == true) || (overflow2 == true))
149      {
150        result->valid = false;
151        return;
152      }
153    rational_internal_init(result, num1num2, den1den2);
154  }
155  void rational_divide(const Rational *n1, const Rational *n2,
156                       Rational *result)
157  {
158    if (((n1->valid) == false) || ((n2->valid) == false) ||
159        ((n2->num) == 0))
160      {
161        result->valid = false;
162        return;
163      }
164    long num1den2, den1num2;
165    bool overflow1, overflow2;
166    overflow1 = long_multiply(n1->num, n2->den, &num1den2);
167    overflow2 = long_multiply(n2->num, n1->den, &den1num2);
168    if ((overflow1 == true) || (overflow2 == true))
169      {
170        result->valid = false;
171        return;
```

```
172        }
173      rational_internal_init(result, num1den2, den1num2);
174    }
```

Finally, a function compares two **Rational** objects:

```
175    void rational_compare(const Rational *n1, const Rational *n2,
176                          int *result)
177    {
178      // result = -1 if (n1) < (n2)
179      // result = 0 if (n1) == (n2)
180      // result = 1 if (n1) > (n2)
181      // result = 2 if either n1 or n2 is invalid or overflow
182      Rational diff;
183      rational_subtract(n1, n2, & diff);
184      if ((diff.valid) == false)
185        {
186          * result = 2;
187          return;
188        }
189      if ((diff.num) < 0)
190        {
191          * result = -1;
192          return;
193        }
194      if ((diff.num) == 0)
195        {
196          * result = 0;
197          return;
198        }
199      * result = 1;
200    }
```

23.4   Use and Test Rational Numbers

This section presents two programs using the rational numbers. The first program demonstrates how to use the **Rational** structure and the functions. The second program uses the Google Test framework.

23.4.1   Use Rational Numbers

The first part of this program creates several **Rational** objects and prints the values.

```
1    // demo.cpp
2    // demonstrate how to use rational numbers
3    #include <stdio.h>
```

```c
#include <stdlib.h>
#include "rational.h"
int main(int argc, char *argv[])
{
  Rational r1, r2, r3, result;
  rational_init(&r1, 25, 0); // this should be invalid
  printf("r1 = ");
  rational_print(&r1, stdout);
  rational_init(&r1, 25, 75); // should be reduced to 1/3
  printf("r1 = ");
  rational_print(&r1, stdout);
  rational_init(&r2, -100, 200); // should be reduced to -1/2
  printf("r2 = ");
  rational_print(&r2, stdout);
  rational_init(&r3, -100, -200); // should be reduced to 1/2
  printf("r3 = ");
  rational_print(&r3, stdout);
  rational_init(&r3, 0, 25); // should be reduced to 0/1
  printf("r3 = ");
  rational_print(&r3, stdout);
  // test arithmetic operations
  printf("r1 + r2 = ");
  rational_add(&r1, &r2, &result); // 1/3 + (-1/2) = -1/6
  rational_print(&result, stdout);
  printf("r1 - r2 = ");
  rational_subtract(&r1, &r2, &result); // 1/3 - (-1/2) = 5/6
  rational_print(&result, stdout);
  printf("r1 * r2 = ");
  rational_multiply(&r1, &r2, &result); // (1/3) * -( 1/2) = -1/6
  rational_print(&result, stdout);
  printf("r1 / r2 = ");
  rational_divide(&r1, &r2, &result); // (1/3) / (-1/2) = - 2/3
  rational_print(&result, stdout);
  rational_init(&result, 1, 1);
  // exponent until it is no longer valid, r1 = 1/3
  int pwd = 1;
  while (result.valid)
    {
      // 1/3, 1/9, 1/27 ...
      rational_multiply(&result, &r1, &result);
      printf("r1^%d = ", pwd);
      if (result.valid)
        { rational_print(&result, stdout); }
      else
        {
          printf("[overflow]: ");
          rational_print(&result, stdout);
        }
      pwd ++;
    }
```

```
54      rational_init(&result, 1, 1);
55      // multiply until it is no longer valid, r1 = 1/3, r2 = 1/2
56      pwd = 2;
57      while (result.valid)
58        {
59          rational_multiply(&r1, &r1, &r1); // square of r1
60          rational_multiply(&r2, &r2, &r2); // square of r2
61          printf("r1^%d = ", pwd);
62          rational_print(&r1, stdout);
63          printf("r2^%d = ", pwd);
64          rational_print(&r2, stdout);
65          rational_add(&r1, &r2, &result);
66          printf("result = ");
67          if (result.valid)
68            { rational_print(&result, stdout); }
69          else
70            {
71              printf("[overflow]: ");
72              rational_print(&result, stdout);
73            }
74          pwd *= 2;
75        }
76      return EXIT_SUCCESS;
77    }
```

Line 9 tests whether a rational number with zero in the denominator will be correctly marked as invalid. The program also tests whether the denominators and numerators will be reduced by their greatest common divider (GCD). For example, r2 is $\frac{25}{75}$ and should be reduced to $\frac{1}{3}$. This is the program's output.

```
r1 = 25/0 (valid=0)
r1 = 1/3 (valid=1)
r2 = -1/2 (valid=1)
r3 = 1/2 (valid=1)
r3 = 0/1 (valid=1)
```

Next, the program performs arithmetic operations, including addition, subtraction, multiplication, and division. This is the program's output.

```
r1 + r2 = -1/6 (valid=1)
r1 - r2 = 5/6 (valid=1)
r1 * r2 = -1/6 (valid=1)
r1 / r2 = -2/3 (valid=1)
```

The next part of the program tests a rational number's exponents until it becomes invalid due to overflow. This is the program's output (the first and the last three lines):

```
r1^1 = 1/3 (valid=1)
r1^2 = 1/9 (valid=1)
r1^3 = 1/27 (valid=1)
...
```

```
r1^38 = 1/1350851717672992089 (valid=1)
r1^39 = 1/4052555153018976267 (valid=1)
r1^40 = [overflow]: 1/4052555153018976267 (valid=0)
```

The last part of the program adds two rational numbers' exponents until the sum becomes invalid due to overflow. This is the program's output.

```
r1^2 = 1/9 (valid=1)
r2^2 = 1/4 (valid=1)
result = 13/36 (valid=1)
r1^4 = 1/81 (valid=1)
r2^4 = 1/16 (valid=1)
result = 97/1296 (valid=1)
r1^8 = 1/6561 (valid=1)
r2^8 = 1/256 (valid=1)
result = 6817/1679616 (valid=1)
r1^16 = 1/43046721 (valid=1)
r2^16 = 1/65536 (valid=1)
result = 43112257/2821109907456 (valid=1)
r1^32 = 1/1853020188851841 (valid=1)
r2^32 = 1/4294967296 (valid=1)
result = [overflow]: 43112257/2821109907456 (valid=0)
```

These results suggest that the implementation of rational numbers' operations are correct. Next, we will use Google Test to perform unit tests.

23.4.2   Test Rational Numbers

The following is the testing program. Let's start with the `main` function: it initilizes the testing framework and leaves the work to the framework:

```
117  int main(int argc, char **argv)
118  {
119    testing::InitGoogleTest(&argc, argv);
120    return RUN_ALL_TESTS();
121  }
```

The tests are organized into a suite and several tests. The suite is called `RationalTest`. The tests are organized as `Initialization`, `Compare`, `Add`, `Subtract`, and so on. Before testing rational numbers, we can also test the functions that detect overflow. This is called `Long` test in the test suite.

```
5   TEST(RationalTest, Long)
6   {
7     long a, b, c, success;
8     // LONG_MAX: add and subtract
9     a = LONG_MAX;
10    b = 1;
11    ASSERT_TRUE(long_add(a, b, &c));        // overflow
12    ASSERT_FALSE(long_subtract(a, b, &c)); // no overflow
13    ASSERT_FALSE(long_multiply(a, b, &c)); // no overflow
14    // LONG_MIN: add and subtract
```

```
15    a = LONG_MIN;
16    ASSERT_TRUE(long_subtract(a, b, &c));   // underflow
17    ASSERT_FALSE(long_add(a, b, &c));       // no underflow
18    ASSERT_FALSE(long_multiply(a, b, &c));  // no underflow
19    // multiply
20    a = LONG_MAX;
21    b = 2;
22    EXPECT_TRUE(long_multiply(a, b, &c)); // overflow
23    a = LONG_MIN;
24    EXPECT_TRUE(long_multiply(a, b, &c)); // underflow
25    // small numbers
26    a = 25;
27    b = 35;
28    // The following test will fail, should not overflow (thus, false)
29    // EXPECT_TRUE(long_add(a, b, &c));
30    // EXPECT_TRUE(long_subtract(a, b, &c));
31    // EXPECT_TRUE(long_multiply(a, b, &c));
32  }
```

These tests evaluate whether overflow or underflow may occur. Adding one to the maximum value (line 11) will cause overflow. Subtracting one from the maximum value (line 12) will not cause overflow. Lines 29-31 will not cause overflow. Thus, long_add, long_subtract, and long_multiple will return false. EXPECT_TRUE will fail in these cases.

This test uses both ASSERT and EXPECT. When ASSERT fails, the program immediately stops. This can be applied when the remaining tests are no longer meaningful. When EXPECT fails, the program continues running the other tests. If you are not sure which one to use, use EXPECT because it allows you to discover multiple test failures at once.

Next, let's consider the Initialization test. It checks whether $\frac{300}{400}$ is correctly reduced to $\frac{3}{4}$ (lines 40 and 41) by using rational_numerator and rational_denominator. Lines 46 and 47 will fail because the correct result should be equal EQ but the test uses NE (not equal).

```
33  TEST(RationalTest, Initialization)
34  {
35    Rational r1, r2, r3;
36    rational_init(&r1, 1, 2);
37    rational_init(&r2, 300, 400);
38    EXPECT_EQ(rational_numerator(&r1), 1L);
39    EXPECT_EQ(rational_denominator(&r1), 2L);
40    EXPECT_EQ(rational_numerator(&r2), 3L);
41    EXPECT_EQ(rational_denominator(&r2), 4L);
42    rational_from_rational(&r3, &r1);
43    EXPECT_EQ(rational_numerator(&r3), 1L);
44    EXPECT_EQ(rational_denominator(&r3), 2L);
45    rational_from_long(&r3, 4L);
46    // EXPECT_NE(rational_numerator(&r3), 4L); // should be EQ
47    // EXPECT_NE(rational_denominator(&r3), 1L); // should be EQ
48  }
```

The next test evaluates the rational_compare function. This function determines whether one rational number is less than, equal to, or greater than another rational number. These conditions correspond to $-1, 0$, and 1 stored in the result. If either number is invalid, the result is invalid. The `rational_compare` function uses `rational_subtract`; hence, if `rational_subtract` produces an invalid result, `rational_compare`'s result is also invalid. When the result is invalid, the `result` is 2.

```
49  TEST(RationalTest, Compare)
50  {
51    Rational r1, r2, r3;
52    rational_init(&r1, 1, 2);
53    rational_init(&r2, 300, 400);
54    rational_init(&r3, 3, 4);
55    int result;
56    rational_compare(&r1, &r2, &result); // 1/2 < 3/4, result is -1
57    EXPECT_LT(result, 0);
58    rational_compare(&r3, &r2, &result); // result is -1
59    EXPECT_EQ(result, 0);
60    rational_init(&r2, 3, 0); // invalid
61    rational_compare(&r3, &r2, &result); // result is 2
62    EXPECT_GT(result, 1);
63    rational_from_rational(&r2, &r3); // r2 same as r3, result is 0
64    rational_compare(&r3, &r2, &result);
65    // The following should fail
66    // EXPECT_EQ(result, 1);
67  }
```

The remaining tests have similar structures. This is the rest of the test suite:

```
68  TEST(RationalTest, Add)
69  {
70    Rational r1, r2, expected, result;
71    int comparison;
72    rational_init(&r1, 1, 2);
73    rational_init(&r2, -1, 4);
74    rational_init(&expected, 1, 4);
75    rational_add(&r1, &r2, &result); // 1/2 + (-1/4) = 1/4
76    rational_compare(&result, &expected, &comparison);
77    EXPECT_EQ(comparison, 0);
78    rational_init(&r1, LONG_MAX, 2);
79    rational_init(&r2, 1, 2);
80    rational_add(&r1, &r2, &result);
81    rational_compare(&result, &expected, &comparison);
82    EXPECT_EQ(comparison, 2);
83  }
84  TEST(RationalTest, Subtract)
85  {
86    Rational r1, r2, expected, result;
87    int comparison;
88    rational_init(&r1, 2, 3);
89    rational_init(&r2, -1, 6);
90    rational_init(&expected, 5, 6);
91    rational_subtract(&r1, &r2, &result);
92    rational_compare(&result, &expected, &comparison);
93    EXPECT_EQ(comparison, 0);
```

```
94   }
95   TEST(RationalTest, Multiply)
96   {
97     Rational r1, r2, expected, result;
98     int comparison;
99     rational_init(&r1, 2, 3);
100    rational_init(&r2, -30, -20);
101    rational_init(&expected, 1, 1);
102    rational_multiply(&r1, &r2, &result);
103    rational_compare(&result, &expected, &comparison);
104    EXPECT_EQ(comparison, 0);
105  }
106  TEST(RationalTest, Divide)
107  {
108    Rational r1, r2, expected, result;
109    int comparison;
110    rational_init(&r1, -2, 3);
111    rational_init(&r2, 2000, -3000);
112    rational_init(&expected, 1, 1);
113    rational_divide(&r1, &r2, &result);
114    rational_compare(&result, &expected, &comparison);
115    EXPECT_EQ(comparison, 0);
116  }
```

This is the Makefile:

```
1    # CH23:Makefile
2    # Makefile for testing rational numbers
3    GPP = g++ -g
4    LIBS = -lgtest -pthread
5    demo: demo.cpp rational.cpp rational.h
6            $(GPP) demo.cpp rational.cpp -o demo
7            ./demo
8    test: rational_test.cpp rational.cpp rational.h
9            $(GPP) rational_test.cpp rational.cpp -o rational_test $(LIBS)
10           ./rational_test
11   clean:
12           /bin/rm -f *.o a.out rational_test demo
```

This is the program's output:

```
[==========] Running 7 tests from 1 test suite.
[----------] Global test environment set-up.
[----------] 7 tests from RationalTest
[ RUN      ] RationalTest.Long
[       OK ] RationalTest.Long (0 ms)
[ RUN      ] RationalTest.Initialization
[       OK ] RationalTest.Initialization (0 ms)
[ RUN      ] RationalTest.Compare
[       OK ] RationalTest.Compare (0 ms)
[ RUN      ] RationalTest.Add
[       OK ] RationalTest.Add (0 ms)
```

```
[ RUN      ] RationalTest.Subtract
[       OK ] RationalTest.Subtract (0 ms)
[ RUN      ] RationalTest.Multiply
[       OK ] RationalTest.Multiply (0 ms)
[ RUN      ] RationalTest.Divide
[       OK ] RationalTest.Divide (0 ms)
[----------] 7 tests from RationalTest (0 ms total)

[----------] Global test environment tear-down
[==========] 7 tests from 1 test suite ran. (0 ms total)
[  PASSED  ] 7 tests.
```

If lines 29, 30, 31, 46, 47, and 66 are taken out from comments, this is the result:

```
[==========] Running 7 tests from 1 test suite.
[----------] Global test environment set-up.
[----------] 7 tests from RationalTest
[ RUN      ] RationalTest.Long
rational_test.cpp:29: Failure
Value of: long_add(a, b, &c)
  Actual: false
Expected: true
rational_test.cpp:30: Failure
Value of: long_subtract(a, b, &c)
  Actual: false
Expected: true
rational_test.cpp:31: Failure
Value of: long_multiply(a, b, &c)
  Actual: false
Expected: true
[  FAILED  ] RationalTest.Long (0 ms)
[ RUN      ] RationalTest.Initialization
rational_test.cpp:46: Failure
Expected: (rational_numerator(&r3)) != (4L), actual: 4 vs 4
rational_test.cpp:47: Failure
Expected: (rational_denominator(&r3)) != (1L), actual: 1 vs 1
[  FAILED  ] RationalTest.Initialization (0 ms)
[ RUN      ] RationalTest.Compare
rational_test.cpp:66: Failure
Expected equality of these values:
  result
    Which is: 0
  1
[  FAILED  ] RationalTest.Compare (0 ms)
[ RUN      ] RationalTest.Add
[       OK ] RationalTest.Add (0 ms)
[ RUN      ] RationalTest.Subtract
[       OK ] RationalTest.Subtract (0 ms)
[ RUN      ] RationalTest.Multiply
[       OK ] RationalTest.Multiply (0 ms)
[ RUN      ] RationalTest.Divide
```

```
[       OK ] RationalTest.Divide (0 ms)
[----------] 7 tests from RationalTest (0 ms total)

[----------] Global test environment tear-down
[==========] 7 tests from 1 test suite ran. (0 ms total)
[  PASSED  ] 4 tests.
[  FAILED  ] 3 tests, listed below:
[  FAILED  ] RationalTest.Long
[  FAILED  ] RationalTest.Initialization
[  FAILED  ] RationalTest.Compare

 3 FAILED TESTS
```

This section explains how to use Google Test to evaluate the functions that implement the arithmetic operations for `Rational`.

23.5   Testing Strategies

This chapter focuses on testing a simple library for rational numbers as an abstract data type. Writing tests for this simple data type appears straightforward but writing good tests for complex data types can require much more thinking. The following suggestions can be helpful when testing complex software:

- It is important to separate tests from the "production code", as shown in Figure 3.1. Do not mix testing code from production code.
- Tests should be independent of one another and not rely on passing in a certain order. This is important for multiple reasons: (1) If a test depends on another test, it can be difficult to understand what causes a test to fail. (2) Many testing frameworks may run tests in parallel on available CPU cores. (3) A testing framework may create different objects to isolate a test from other tests.
- Tests should be organized into groups. In this example, the tests are groups for arithmetic, comparisons, and initialization functions. Such an organization can help think more carefully about what the program should do and whether there are sufficient tests for the different categories.
- Tests should be available across different hardware and software environments. The `GoogleTest` framework is designed for different operating systems or toolchains. When writing tests, it is advisable to avoid writing hardware-specific tests. In case you encounter the situation when you need to write tests for specific hardware or operating systems, please enclose these parts by `#ifdef ... #endif` (conditionally compilation) so that these parts are used only when the conditions are true.
- Tests should make failures clear by giving proper names. Do not test too many things at once. Most testing frameworks will run a test until it fails but will still run all of the other tests that precede or follow it in the source code. Most unit testing frameworks, including Google Test, will tell you the total number of successes and the total number of failures. The sum of the number of successes and failures is equal to the number of testing functions.
- Unit tests should be simple and fast, especially in large projects. Software developers can write and run unit tests quickly after adding new functions to the programs.

- It is possible that testing code itself is buggy, even though the program to be tested is correct. For example, to create rational numbers, a test may unintentionally cause overflow. Thus, it is important to keep tests simple. If a test fails, it is easy to determine whether the test is wrong, or the tested code is wrong.

This chapter introduces *unit tests*. After testing each unit, these units should be integrated to solve problems. The next part of this book uses several applications to explain how to integrate multiple parts of programs.

Part IV

Applications

Chapter 24

Find the Exit of a Maze

The following chapters use problems and reference solutions to integrate the materials covered in multiple previous chapters.

24.1 Maze File Format

The first problem is to develop a computer program that finds a way to get out of a maze. Imagine that you are an adventurer looking for hidden treasure in caves in the remnants of a lost civilization. Unfortunately, you become trapped in an underground maze. Only walls are visible, and you must develop a strategy to find the exit. You need to write a program that finds the path from your current location to the exit. A maze can be described by a file like the example shown below.

```
bbbbbbbbbEbbbbbbbbbbb
b         b   b   b b
b bbbbbbb b b b b b b
b b   sb b b b b b b b
b b b b bbb b b b b b
b b b b   b b b b b b
b b b b b b b b b b b
b b b b b b b b b b b
b b b b b b b b b b b
b   b   b   b   b   b
bbbbbbbbbbbbbbbbbbbbb
```

The characters represent:

- 'b': brick
- ' ': (space) corridor
- 'E': exit, i.e., the destination
- 's': starting location

The maze is divided into cells. Each cell is represented by a coordinate: (row, column). Rows move up or down vertically and columns move left or right horizontally. The top left corner is (0, 0). After moving right one step, the coordinate becomes (0, 1). From (0, 1), moving down one step reaches coordinate (1, 1). Figure 24.1 shows the coordinates. In the example, the starting coordinate is (3, 5) and the exit is at (0, 9). The maze is very dark and you can see only one step in front of you. You do not know if a corridor is a dead end until you reach the end. After discovering a dead end, you need to move backward, find a different option, and search again.

DOI: 10.1201/9781003257981-24

This chapter provides an opportunity using several topics covered in this book so far: (1) read a maze from a file; (2) allocate memory to store the maze cells; and (3) use recursion to move around the maze and find the exit.

A structure can be defined to store relevant information about a maze. This structure stores the maze's size (number of rows and number of columns), the starting location, the exit location, and the current location during movement. The structure also has a two-dimensional array to store the information for each cell in the maze. A constructor function creates and initializes the maze object by reading a file. The destructor function releases the memory used in the maze object, and is called before the program ends.

$(0,0)$ $(0,1)$ $(0,2)$

$(1,0)$ $(1,1)$ $(1,2)$

$(2,0)$

$(3,0)$

FIGURE 24.1: Coordinates of maze cells.

```c
// CH24:maze.h
#ifndef MAZE_H
#define MAZE_H
#include <stdbool.h>
typedef struct
{
  int * * cells;
  int numrow;
  int numcol;
  int startrow;
  int startcol;
} Maze;
bool readMaze(const char * filename, Maze * * maz);
void printMaze(Maze * maz);
void freeMaze(Maze * maz);
void findDistance(Maze * maz); // shortest distance of reachable cells
#endif
```

24.2   Strategy to Find Exit

Suppose it is possible to leave marks in the cells. The following is a strategy to find the exit. (1) Inside a corridor, go as far as possible, as shown in Figure 24.2 (a). (2) If the bricks

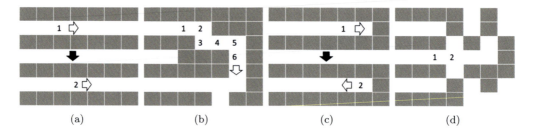

    (a)   (b)   (c)   (d)

FIGURE 24.2: Strategy to find the exit. The blocks are bricks.

force a turn, turn and keep moving forward, as shown in Figure 24.2 (b). (3) If a corridor reaches a dead end, turn around, and move backward along the same corridor, as shown in Figure 24.2 (c).

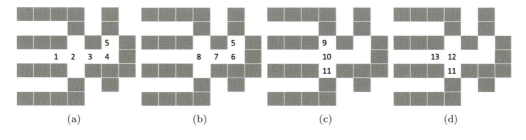

(a) (b) (c) (d)

FIGURE 24.3: Strategy at an intersection.

Next, we consider the strategy to handle intersections. An intersection means a cell with multiple options to choose, as shown at cell 2 in Figure 24.2 (d). At this cell, it is possible to go right, up, or down. We do not know which one is the best choose because we cannot foresee whether one particular option can lead to the exit. Suppose our first choice is to go right and move to cell 3, as shown in Figure 24.3 (a). We want to keep moving forward if it is possible. Thus, the next step moves to cell 4 and then 5, as shown in Figure 24.3(a) At cell 5, a dead end is detected. As a result, we move background to cell 8 (earlier it was cell 2), shown in Figure 24.3(b). This time we choose to go up and move to cell 9. Another dead end is discovered. Thus, we move down to cell 10 (it was cell 8 earlier). We can keep moving down and enter cell 11, shown in Figure 24.3(c). At the moment, we reach the conclusion that we have to move backward. We move to cell 12 (earlier it was cell 10) and cell 13 (earlier it was cell 1).

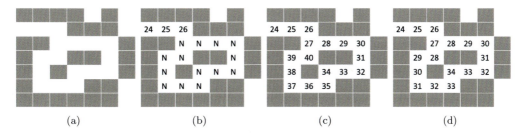

(a) (b) (c) (d)

FIGURE 24.4: Handle multiple paths.

What happens if there are multiple paths between two cells? Figure 24.4 (a) shows an example. Since we are allowed to mark the visited cells, we can mark the starting point as zero. When we move to the next cell, it is marked as one, then two, then three. These numbers are the distances from the starting point. Consider the situation when we come to these cells from the upper left with the distances marked 24, 25, and 26. If a cell has not been visited, it has no mark and we use "N" to indicate the unvisited cells, as shown in Figure 24.4 (b). As we move forward, we mark the cells by increasing numbers, until we reach the cell 40, shown in Figure 24.4 (c). If we move forward, we will mark the next cell as 41. However, this cell was earlier marked 27. That means this cell was visited before and the distance from the started point is shorter. Thus, we should not move forward anymore. Instead, we should treat this situation like reaching a dead end and go back to the previous intersection. We will go backward to cell 27. The cell 27 must be an intersection: that is the reason why it can be reached through two paths. From the cell 27, we can choose another option, going down this time, and mark the cells of the distances from the starting point as 28, 29, ... as shown in Figure 24.4 (d). Continue going forward until the cell 34. If we go any further, we will mark the next cell as 35 but it was already marked 33. Thus, we should not go any further. This is treated as a dead end again.

24.3   Implement the Strategy

How can such a strategy be implemented in C? We will explain step by step. First, we define some symbols:

```c
// CH24:maze.c
#include <stdio.h>
#include <stdlib.h>
#include "maze.h"
// directions, ORIGIN marks the starting point
enum {ORIGIN, EAST, SOUTH, WEST, NORTH};
// move forward or backward
enum {FORWARD, BACKWARD};
```

This `readMaze` function reads the maze from a file:

```c
bool readMaze(const char * filename, Maze ** maz)
{
  FILE * fptr = fopen(filename, "r");
  if (fptr == NULL)
    { return false; }
    int linelen = 0;
  int maxlinelen = 0;
  int numline = 0;
  int onech;
  while (! feof(fptr))
    {
      onech = fgetc(fptr);
      if (onech != EOF)
        {
          if (onech == '\n') // end of a line
            {
              numline ++;
              if (maxlinelen < linelen)
                { maxlinelen = linelen; }
              linelen = 0;
            }
      else
        { linelen ++; }
        }
    }
  if (numline <= 2) // invalid maze
    {
```

```
36       fclose (fptr);
37       return false;
38     }
39   Maze * mz = malloc(sizeof(Maze));
40   * maz = mz;
41   mz -> numrow = numline;
42   mz -> numcol = maxlinelen;
43   mz -> cells = malloc(sizeof(int *) * numline);
44   int indrow = 0;
45   int indcol = 0;
46   for (indrow = 0; indrow < numline; indrow ++)
47     {
48       (mz -> cells)[indrow] = malloc(sizeof(int) * maxlinelen);
49       // assume this malloc succeeds, do not check
50       for (indcol = 0; indcol < maxlinelen; indcol ++)
51         {
52           // set every cell to -1 (not reachable)
53           (mz -> cells)[indrow][indcol] = -1;
54         }
55     }
56   // return to the beginning of the file
57   fseek(fptr, 0, SEEK_SET);
58   indrow = 0;
59   indcol = 0;
60   int maxlength = 2 * numline * maxlinelen + 1;
61   while (indrow < numline)
62     {
63       bool breakline = false;
64       while (breakline == false)
65         {
66           onech = fgetc(fptr);
67           if (onech == EOF)
68             { return false; } // should not happen
69           switch (onech)
70             {
71             case ' ': // corridor
72             case 'E': // exit
73               // possibly reachable
74               // make the value large enough and they must be reduced
75               // if the value does not reduce, it is not reachable
76               mz -> cells[indrow][indcol] = maxlength;
77               break;
78             case 's': // starting point
79               mz -> cells[indrow][indcol] = 0; // distance is 0
80               mz -> startrow = indrow;
81               mz -> startcol = indcol;
82               break;
83             case '\n':
84               breakline = true;
85               break;
```

```
86              case 'b': // brick
87                  mz -> cells[indrow][indcol] = -1; // unreachable
88              }
89              indcol ++;
90          }
91          indrow ++;
92          indcol = 0;
93      }
94      fclose (fptr);
95      return true;
96  }
```

The shortest distance from the starting point is zero (the starting point itself). A negative number can be used to mark bricks because the strategy described above does not enter a cell if the cell's value is smaller. The `readMaze` function initializes every cell to -1 (line 53). Then, the exit or the corridor cell is marked by a number larger than the largest possible distance (line 76). This program uses 2 × width × height plus 1 as the largest possible distance. For the starting point, the distance is marked 0 (line 79).

The next function prints the maze's cells. This can ensure that the maze has been read correctly.

```
97  void printMaze(Maze * maz)
98  {
99    if (maz == NULL)
100       {
101           return;
102       }
103   int indrow;
104   int indcol;
105   for (indrow = 0; indrow < (maz -> numrow); indrow ++)
106       {
107           for (indcol = 0; indcol < (maz -> numcol); indcol ++)
108             { printf("%4d ", (maz -> cells)[indrow][indcol]); }
109           printf("\n");
110       }
111 }
```

Before the program ends, the memory allocated for the maze should be freed:

```
112 void freeMaze(Maze * maz)
113 {
114   int indrow;
115   for (indrow = 0; indrow < (maz -> numrow); indrow ++)
116       {
117           free ((maz -> cells)[indrow]);
118       }
119   free (maz -> cells);
120   free (maz);
121 }
```

The next function is `nextDistance`. Before the program enters a cell, this function is called. The function takes four arguments: a pointer to the maze, the current row, the current column, and the intended direction. If the intended direction is north, the row decrements by one. If the intended direction is east, the column increments by one. Lines 133–136 check whether the row and the column are valid. If either is invalid, this function returns −1 to indicate this move is invalid. The bricks are already marked −1 earlier. If the cell is valid, the function returns the value stored at the cell. If this is not a brick, it is a current distance from the starting point. If a cell has not been visited, the value is 2 × width × height plus 1.

```
122   static int nextDistance(Maze * maz, int row, int col, int dir)
123   {
124     /* (row, col) is the current location */
125     switch (dir)
126       {
127       case NORTH: row --; break;
128       case SOUTH: row ++; break;
129       case WEST:  col --; break;
130       case EAST:  col ++; break;
131       }
132     // check invalid index, -1 means cannot enter the cell
133     if (row < 0) { return -1; }
134     if (row >= (maz -> numrow)) { return -1; }
135     if (col < 0) { return -1; }
136     if (col >= (maz -> numcol)) { return -1; }
137     // valid index, check the cell
138     return (maz->cells)[row][col];
139   }
```

Next, let's consider the `move` function. This function finds the shortest distance of each reachable cell. This is a recursive function and it takes advantage of the stack memory for function calls. When this function enters a cell, it marks the distance (line 148). Then, the function checks whether it is possible to move to neighbor cells. This function calls `nextDistance` to obtain the current distance of a neighbor cell and store the result in `dest`. If `dest` is greater than this cell's distance plus one, entering the neighbor cell can shorten the distance and this function enters the neighbor cell by calling itself. Please notice how `row`, `col`, and `distance` change in the call. If it is impossible to enter any neighbor cell and shorten the neighbor's distance, this cell has reached a dead end. The function does not call itself and the function goes back (by popping the top frames).

```
140   static void move(Maze * maz, int row, int col, int distance)
141   {
142     int dest; // the distance from this cell to the starting point
143     if (distance == -1)
144       {
145         fprintf(stderr, "WRONG. Enter a brick.\n");
146         return;
147       }
148     (maz -> cells)[row][col] = distance;
149     // move if the a neighbor's distance is larger
150     // than the current distance + 1
151     dest = nextDistance(maz, row, col, EAST);
152     if (dest > (distance + 1)) // move can shorten the distance
```

```
153        { move(maz, row, col + 1, distance + 1); }
154      dest = nextDistance(maz, row, col, WEST);
155      if (dest > (distance + 1))
156        { move(maz, row, col - 1, distance + 1); }
157      dest = nextDistance(maz, row, col, NORTH);
158      if (dest > (distance + 1))
159        { move(maz, row - 1, col, distance + 1); }
160      dest = nextDistance(maz, row, col, SOUTH);
161      if (dest > (distance + 1))
162        { move(maz, row + 1, col, distance + 1); }
163    }
```

The `findDistance` function finds the shortest distance of each cell from the starting cell if the cell is reachable from the starting cell. This function calls the `move` function explained earlier from the starting cell with distance zero. This `move` function will visit the reachable cells. Then, the `findDistance` performs post-processing by assigning -1 (i.e., unreachable) to the cells whose distances are too long.

```
164  void findDistance(Maze * maz)
165  {
166    if (maz == NULL) { return; }
167    move(maz, maz -> startrow, maz -> startcol, 0);
168    // mark unreachable cells as -1
169    int row, col;
170    int maxlength = 2 * (maz -> numrow) * (maz -> numcol) + 1;
171    for (row = 0; row < (maz -> numrow); row ++)
172      {
173        for (col = 0; col < (maz -> numcol); col ++)
174          {
175            if ((maz -> cells[row][col]) == maxlength)
176              { maz -> cells[row][col] = -1; }
177          }
178      }
179  }
```

The `main` function is shown below:

```
1   // CH24: main.c
2   #include <stdio.h>
3   #include <stdlib.h>
4   #include <stdbool.h>
5   #include "maze.h"
6   int main(int argc, char * * argv)
7   {
8     // argv[1]: input
9     // output uses printf
10    if (argc < 2)  { return EXIT_FAILURE; }
11    Maze * maz;
12    bool rtv;
13    rtv = readMaze(argv[1], & maz);
14    if (rtv == false)  { return EXIT_FAILURE;  }
```

```
15    findDistance(maz);
16    printMaze(maz);
17    freeMaze(maz);
18    return EXIT_SUCCESS;
19  }
```

The problem is a good example of using recursion because the same strategy is applied to different cells. Moreover, each intersection has multiple options (i.e., branches). As explained on page 184, recursion is particularly helpful in handling branches.

24.4   Problems

24.4.1   Mark of Bricks

Explain why assigning -1 can prevent entering a cell filled by a brick? Can any other negative value serve the same purpose (prevent entering a brick)? Can zero also serve the same purpose?

24.4.2   Multiple Exits

Can this method be used to handle a maze with multiple exits?

24.4.3   Order of Directions

The move function checks whether it is possible to go the east neighbor first. If it checks the east neighbor last (after west, north, and south), will the output be different?

24.4.4   Change `if` Conditions

The move function has the following conditions:

```
if (dest > (distance + 1))
```

If it is replaced by

```
if (dest >= (distance + 1)) // change > to >=
```

is the program still correct? Explain your reason.

Chapter 25

Sudoku

25.1 Sudoku Game

Sudoku is a number game with a 9×9 board (81 cells) of numbers. Each row (of 9 cells) has numbers of 1, 2, ..., 9. Each column (also 9 cells) has numbers of 1, 2, ..., 9. Figure 25.1 (a) shows an example of a solution of Sudoku. The following are the three rules: Each number between 1 and 9 appears exactly once in the 9 cells of

1. Each column shown in Figure 25.1 (a).
2. Each row Figure 25.1 (b).
3. Each 3×3 block shown in Figure 25.1 (c).

The 81 cells are divided into nine 3×3 blocks, as shown by the thick lines in Figure 25.2 (a). A Sudoku puzzle has some of the cells empty and the problem is to fill these cells. Figure 25.2 (b) shows a Sudoku puzzle. It marks the rows as 1, 2, 3, ..., 9 and the columns as A, B, C, ..., I. We will refer to a cell by its (row, column). For example, (1, C) has value 3 and (9, B) has value 7. Let's consider column A first. Seven of the nine cells have already been filled and the only two missing numbers are 6 and 7 for rows 3 and 4. Row 4 already has 6 (in column E). Thus cell (3, A) must be 6 and cell (4, A) must be 7. Next, let's consider row 2. Three numbers are missing in this row: 1, 2, and 7 for cells (2, B), (2, C), and (2, H). Block (1, A) - (3, C) already has 1 at (1, A). Thus, 1 cannot be used for (2, B) or (2, C). Cell (2, H) must be 1. Cell (2, B) must not use 7 because (9, B) already has 7. Thus, (2, B) must be 2 and (2, C) must be 7. The partially filled Sudoku puzzle is shown in Figure 25.2 (c).

Next, let's consider the block (1, G) - (3, I). Numbers 2 and 7 are missing. Column G already has 2 at cell (6, G). Thus, number 2 must be used at cell (3, H); cell (3, G) has

1	8	3	2	7	6	5	4	9
5	2	7	4	9	8	3	1	6
6	4	9	1	3	5	7	2	8
7	9	1	5	6	2	8	3	4
2	3	8	7	4	9	6	5	1
4	5	6	3	8	1	2	9	7
8	1	2	9	5	7	4	6	3
9	6	4	8	2	3	1	7	5
3	7	5	6	1	4	9	8	2

(a)

1	8	3	2	7	6	5	4	9
5	2	7	4	9	8	3	1	6
6	4	9	1	3	5	7	2	8
7	9	1	5	6	2	8	3	4
2	3	8	7	4	9	6	5	1
4	5	6	3	8	1	2	9	7
8	1	2	9	5	7	4	6	3
9	6	4	8	2	3	1	7	5
3	7	5	6	1	4	9	8	2

(b)

1	8	3	2	7	6	5	4	9
5	2	7	4	9	8	3	1	6
6	4	9	1	3	5	7	2	8
7	9	1	5	6	2	8	3	4
2	3	8	7	4	9	6	5	1
4	5	6	3	8	1	2	9	7
8	1	2	9	5	7	4	6	3
9	6	4	8	2	3	1	7	5
3	7	5	6	1	4	9	8	2

(c)

FIGURE 25.1: An example of Sudoku. This example is from the book "Sudoku Collection, Volume 124 by Kappa Books".

DOI: 10.1201/9781003257981-25

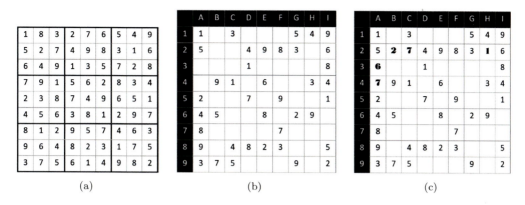

FIGURE 25.2: (a) The 81 cells are divide into nine 3×3 blocks. (b) A Sudoku puzzle has some unfilled cells. (c) Row 2 and column A are filled.

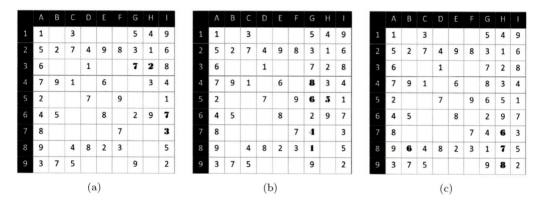

FIGURE 25.3: More cells are filled.

only one choice: 7. Column I needs to fill numbers 3 and 7 to cells (6, I) and (7, I). Row 7 already has 7 so number 7 must be used for (6, I) and number 3 is used for (7, I). This partial result is shown in Figure 25.3 (a). Three numbers, 5, 6, and 8, are missing in the block (4, G) - (6, I). The unfilled cells are (4, G), (5, G), and (5, H). Column G already has 5 at (1, G) and 5 must be used in (5, H). Row 4 already has number 6 at (4, E) and 6 must be used in (5, G). The only unfilled cell is 8 and it must be used at (4, G). Column G has only two unfilled cells now: (7, G) and (8, G). The unused numbers are 1 and 4. Row 8 already has 4 at (8, C) so 4 must be used at (7, G). The remaining number 1 is used at (8, G). The partially filled puzzle is shown Figure 25.3 (b). Row 8 has two missing numbers: 6 and 7 for (8, B) and (8, H). Column B already has 7 at (9, B) so (8, H) must be 7 and (8, B) must be 6. Column H has two missing numbers: 6 and 8 for (7, H) and (9, H). Number 8 appears at (7, A) so (9, H) must be 8; (7, H) must be 6. The result is shown Figure 25.3 (c).

25.2 Recursive Solution

For easy Sudoku games like the ones above, the unique values in the unfilled cells can be determined by repetitively checking the three rules on page 322. More difficult Sudoku games need to consider the values in several cells simultaneously. Figure 25.4 shows an example. Some cells have several options and a player needs to guess the values in some cells first. After more and more cells are filled, the player can determine whether the earlier guesses are correct. If the guesses are correct (so far), the player fills more cells. If the guesses are wrong and lead to violating one or multiple rules, the player has to change the guessed values. This guess-correct method is similar to the recursive solution described in Section 24.2 for finding the exit of a maze: both methods use *depth-first* with *backtrack*. Let's use Figure 25.4 to explain how this method works.

Before applying the recursive solution for Sudoku, we can apply the three rules to fill as many cells as possible. Consider cell (8, I). This cell's value cannot be 1, 2, 3, or 5 because all of them have already been used in row 8. The cell cannot be 6, 7, or 9 because they have been used by column I. Also, value 8 is used in the same block by cell (9, G). The only allowed value for (8, I) is 4. After filling (8, I), cell (7, I) can be filled. It must not be 2, 3, 7, or 8 because all of them have been used by row 7. This cell cannot use 6, 7, or 9 because all of them have been used by column I. Values 4, 5, and 8 are used in the same block. Thus, the only allowed value for (7, I) is 1. After filling (8, I) and (7, I), cell (9, I) has only one option: 3. The reason is that 1, 2, 4, 5, and 8 have been taken by the same block. Column 9 already uses 6, 7, and 9. The only value left is 3.

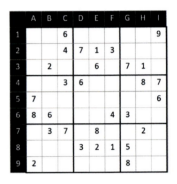

FIGURE 25.4: A more difficult Sudoku puzzle.

Next, consider a cell whose value cannot be decided by the three rules directly. It is necessary to guess a value and fill in some other cells before concluding whether this guess is valid or not. Cell (1, A) has three options: 1, 3, and 5 because 2, 4, and 6 are already used in the same block. The first row uses 6 in (1, C) and 9 in (1, I) so these two values cannot be used again in (1, A). Column A uses 7 and 8 and they cannot be used in (1, A), either. Among the three remaining options (1, 3, and 5), we can pick any as our first guess. Let's pick 1 for now. Figure 25.5 (a) shows the current state; the gray background of (1, A) indicates that this is a guess and the value is not fixed yet.

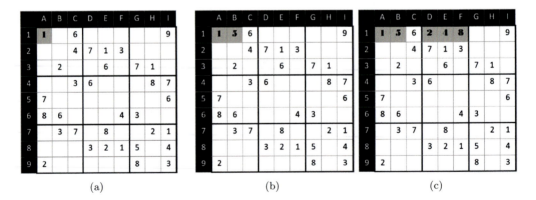

(a)   (b)   (c)

FIGURE 25.5: (a) Cell (1, A) is temporarily marked as 1. (b) Cell (1, B) is temporarily marked as 5. (c) Cell (1, D) is temporarily marked as 2.

Before guessing 1 for (1, A), cell (1, B) has options 1, 3, 7, and 8. Since 1 is already used by (1, A), cell (1, B) can choose one from 3, 7, or 8. Please be aware that (1, A) is only temporarily set to 1. It is possible that (1, A) should be 3 or 5. If (1, A) is not 1, then

(1, B) may choose 1. Figure 25.5 (b) shows the state after both (1, A) and (1, B) have been filled; the gray background indicates that both are guesses. Cell (1, C) is already filled by 6. The next unfilled cell is (1, D) and the options are 2, 4, 5, and 8. It is temporarily set to 2. This process continues for (1, E) and (1, F), as shown in Figure 25.5 (c).

At this point, cell (1, G) has no solution. Row 1 has already used 1, 2, 4, 5, 6, 8, and 9. Column G already has 3, 7, and 8. To find a solution for (1, G), we go back (i.e., *backtrack*) and check the most recently filled cell (1, F). Cell (1, F) has no other solution, either. We go further back to (1, E) and it has no other solution unless (1, B) is changed. Our earlier guess for (1, B) is incorrect. It is necessary to go back (again, backtrack) and modify the guess for (1, B). The next option for (1, B) is 7. After selecting 7 for (1, B), (1, D) can select 2 again; (1, E) can select 4; (1, F) can select 5. Again, (1, G) has no solution. This means one (or possibly more than one) earlier guess is wrong. It is necessary to backtrack and change the guess. Suppose (1, F) chooses 8. Now, (1, G) can choose 4 and (1, H) can choose 3. This process continues until finding a solution (when all cells are filled and the numbers meet the three rules) or concluding that there is no solution. This guess-backtrack is very similar to the solution for the maze. For the maze, at an intersection, we guess a direction and move forward to that cell. We go as far as possible. If a dead end is encountered, we move back to the intersection and choose a different option. For Sudoku, we guess the number of a cell and move forward to fill as many cells as possible. If we encounter the situation when a cell has no solution, we move backward and change our earlier guesses.

25.3   Implement the Solution

This is a sample input file. If a cell is unfilled, it is marked as 0.

```
1    082400370
2    043267089
3    090385000
4    005003060
5    301020507
6    020500800
7    000654030
8    430892750
9    058001690
```

The implementation uses a structure called *Sudoku*. It has three attributes: (1) `filled` stores the number of cells that have the final values; (2) `cells` stores the values of the cells; and (3) `allow` stores the list of allowed values for each cell. If value `n` is allowed at `cell[r][c]`, then `allowed[r][c][n]` is `true`; otherwise, it is `false`. Initially, each cell allows all possible values from 1, 2, ..., 9.

```
1    // sudoku.h
2    #ifndef SUDOKU_H
3    #define SUDOKU_H
4    #include <stdbool.h>
5    typedef struct
6    {
7       int filled; // how many cells' values are final
```

```
8    char cells[9][9]; // cells' values
9    bool allowed[9][9][10]; // allowed value in a cell; [][][0] not used
10 } Sudoku;
11 bool readSudoku(char * filename, Sudoku * sud);
12 void printSudoku(Sudoku * sud);
13 void saveSudoku(char * filename, Sudoku * sud);
14 void solveSudoku(Sudoku * sud);
15 bool networkSudoku(char * ipaddr, int port, Sudoku * sud, int * servsock);
16 void sendSudoku(int servsock, Sudoku * sud);
17 #endif
```

The program provides the following functions:

1. readSudoku: read an unsolved Sudoku from a file
2. solveSudoku: fill the cells of Sudoku
3. printSudoku: print the status of Sudoku
4. saveSudoku: save the solved Sudoku to a file

Two functions networkSudoku and sendSudoku allow the program to obtain a puzzle from the Internet. More details about network programming will be explained in Section 25.5. The readSudoku function opens a file, reads one character at a time using fgetc (line 27) and stores the value in a one-dimensional array called numbers (line 28). This program uses this one-dimensional array so that it can take advantage of the one million Sudoku problems on https://www.kaggle.com/bryanpark/sudoku. Section 25.5 will provide more details about the one million Sudoku problems. The readSudoku function skips '\n' at the end of each line (line 31).

```
16 bool readSudoku(char * filename, Sudoku * sud)
17 {
18   FILE * fptr = fopen(filename, "r");
19   if (fptr == NULL) { return false; }
20   char numbers[81];
21   int cnt = 0;
22   for (int row  = 0; row < 9; row ++)
23     {
24       int ch;
25       for (int col = 0; col < 9; col ++)
26         {
27           ch = fgetc(fptr);
28           numbers[cnt] = ch;
29           cnt ++;
30         }
31       ch = fgetc(fptr); // remove '\n'
32     }
33   fclose(fptr);
34   createSudoku(numbers, sud);
35   return true;
36 }
```

The `createSudoku` function takes the one-dimensional array and fills a Sudoku structure. This function calls `initSudoku` to initialize the Sudoku's attributes. Line 90 assigns a value to a cell. Please be aware that `ch` may be `'0'`, meaning that the value is unknown. If the value is between `'1'` and `'9'`, this cell's value is finalized. Line 94 sets all elements of the `allowed` array to `false` because this cell's value is already fixed. The `removeUsed` function uses the numbers in the known cell to eliminate the options of unfilled cells in the same row, the same column, and the same block. The `printAllow` function shows the allowed options of each unfilled cell. For debugging purposes, lines 101 and 102 print the current status and the values allowed in each unfilled cell.

```
81   static void createSudoku(char * numbers, Sudoku *sud)
82   {
83     initSudoku(sud);
84     int cnt = 0;
85     for (int row = 0; row < 9; row ++)
86       {
87         for (int col = 0; col < 9; col ++)
88           {
89             char ch = numbers[cnt];
90             sud-> cells[row][col] = ch;
91             if ((ch >= '1') && (ch <= '9'))
92               {
93                 for (int allow = 1; allow <= 9; allow ++)
94                   { sud -> allowed[row][col][allow] = false; }
95                 removeUsed(sud, row, col, ch);
96                 (sud -> filled) ++;
97               }
98             cnt ++;
99           }
100      }
101    // printSudoku(sud);
102    // printAllow(sud);
103  }
```

Let's examine the `initSudoku` function next. It assigns 0 to the `filled` attribute since no cell has been filled yet. For each cell, the `allowed` attribute is an array to indicate which number is allowed. The first element (index 0) is not used. The other 9 elements indicate whether the numbers are allowed. In the initial stage, all 9 numbers are allowed. Hence, line 113 assigns `true` to the attribute.

```
104  static void initSudoku(Sudoku * sud)
105  {
106    sud -> filled = 0;
107    for (int row = 0; row < 9; row ++)
108      {
109        for (int col = 0; col < 9; col ++)
110          {
111            sud -> allowed[row][col][0] = false;
112            for (int allow = 1; allow <= 9; allow ++) // start from 1
113              { sud -> allowed[row][col][allow] = true; }
```

```
114                    }
115                 }
116           }
```

The `removeUsed` function is called when a cell's value is fixed. The arguments include this cell's row, column, and value. This function goes through the column, the row, and the block of this cell and removes this value from the options.

```
117   static void removeUsed(Sudoku * sud, int row, int col, char val)
118   {
119     // remove this value from the row
120     for (int colcnt = 0; colcnt < 9; colcnt ++)
121       { sud -> allowed[row][colcnt][val - '0'] = false; }
122     // remove this value from the column
123     for (int rowcnt = 0; rowcnt < 9; rowcnt ++)
124       { sud -> allowed[rowcnt][col][val - '0'] = false; }
125     // remove this value from the 3 x 3 block
126     int rowstart = (row / 3) * 3;
127     int colstart = (col / 3) * 3;
128     for (int rowcnt = rowstart; rowcnt < rowstart + 3; rowcnt ++)
129       {
130         for (int colcnt = colstart; colcnt < colstart + 3; colcnt ++)
131           { sud -> allowed[rowcnt][colcnt][val - '0'] = false; }
132       }
133   }
```

The `printSudoku` prints the cells' values. To help debugging, this function also prints the column labels (A to I) and the row labels (1 to 9). To make the unfilled cells easier to see, this function uses - instead of 0.

```
37   void printSudoku(Sudoku * sud)
38   {
39     if (sud == NULL) { return; }
40     printf("   ");
41     for (int row = 0; row < 9; row ++) { printf("%c", row + 'A'); }
42     printf("\n");
43     for (int row = 0; row < 9; row ++)
44       {
45         printf("%d: ", row + 1);
46         for (int col = 0; col < 9; col ++)
47           {
48             char val = sud->cells[row][col];
49             if ((val >= '1') && (val <= '9')) { printf("%c", val); }
50             else { printf("-"); }
51           }
52         printf("\n");
53       }
54   }
```

This shows an example of the output of the `printSudoku` function:

```
   ABCDEFGHI
1: 859472613
2: 624153879
3: 173986245
4: 987321456
5: 362845197
6: 415697382
7: 548239761
8: 736518924
9: 291764538
```

The `printAllow` function is used for debugging. This function prints the options for each cell. If a cell's value is already determined by the input, it is unnecessary to print the options for this cell. This function first decides whether a cell has any option (lines 142–147). If this cell has at least one option (checked at line 148), this function prints the list of allowed values.

```
134  void printAllow(Sudoku * sud)
135  {
136    for (int row = 0; row < 9; row ++)
137      {
138        for (int col = 0; col < 9; col ++)
139          {
140            bool skip = true;
141            int allow = 1;
142            while ((allow <= 9) && (skip == true))
143              {
144                if (sud -> allowed[row][col][allow] == true)
145                  { skip = false; }
146                allow ++;
147              }
148            if (skip == false)
149              {
150                printf("Allow at [%d][%c]: ", row + 1, col + 'A');
151                for (allow = 1; allow <= 9; allow ++)
152                  {
153                    if (sud -> allowed[row][col][allow] == true)
154                      { printf("%d ", allow); }
155                  }
156                printf("\n");
157              }
158          }
159      }
160  }
```

The following shows examples of the output of `printAllow`:

```
Allow at [5][F]: 1 2 6
Allow at [5][G]: 1 4 6 8
```

```
Allow at [5][H]: 1 4 6
Allow at [6][A]: 1 5 8
Allow at [6][B]: 5
Allow at [6][D]: 1 4 8
Allow at [6][E]: 1 3 4 7 8
Allow at [6][F]: 1 3 7
Allow at [6][I]: 1 7 8
```

As can be seen, the cell (6, B) has only one option. When we start solving the Sudoku puzzle, this cell will be filled soon. The other cells have more options. The next function to examine is saveSudoku. It opens a file for writing (line 57), saves the values in the cells (line 62), adds a newline character after 9 numbers (line 63), and closes the file (line 65).

```
55  void saveSudoku(char * filename, Sudoku * sud)
56  {
57    FILE * fptr = fopen(filename, "w");
58    if (fptr == NULL) { return; }
59    for (int row = 0; row < 9; row ++)
60      {
61        for (int col = 0; col < 9; col ++)
62          { fprintf(fptr, "%c", sud -> cells[row][col]); }
63        fprintf(fptr, "\n");
64      }
65    fclose(fptr);
66  }
```

Now we are ready to explain the solveSudoku function. This function has two parts: without recursion (lines 69-75) and with recursion (lines 79). In the first part, solveSudoku calls fillSudoku to find a cell that has only one allowed number. If such a cell is found, the number is assigned and sud -> filled increases. The first part continues as long as more cells can be filled. When no more cells can be filled, the first part ends. If all 81 cells have been filled (line 76), the function stops. If any cell is still unfilled, the function enters the second part by calling guessFill using recursion to solve the Sudoku.

```
67  void solveSudoku(Sudoku * sud)
68  {
69    bool progress = true;
70    while (progress) // stop if cannot fill any more cell
71      {
72        int filled = sud -> filled;
73        fillSudoku(sud);
74        if (filled == (sud -> filled)) { progress = false; }
75      }
76    if ((sud -> filled) == 81) { return; } // solved
77    // printf("need recursion\n");
78    // printSudoku(sud);
79    guessFill(sud);    // need to guess
80  }
```

The `fillSudoku` function goes through every cell and finds any cell that has only one allowed number. If such a cell is found (line 177), this cell is assigned the only allowed number. Next, `removeUsed` is called to remove this number from the allowed arrays of the cells of the same row, the same column, and the same block.

```
161  static void fillSudoku(Sudoku * sud)
162  {
163    for (int row = 0; row < 9; row ++)
164      {
165        for (int col = 0; col < 9; col ++)
166          {
167            int numallowed = 0;
168            char allowval = '0';
169            for (int allow = 1; allow <= 9; allow ++)
170              {
171                if ((sud -> allowed[row][col][allow]) == true)
172                  {
173                    numallowed ++;
174                    allowval = '0' + allow;
175                  }
176              }
177            if (numallowed == 1)
178              {
179                sud -> cells[row][col] = allowval;
180                (sud -> filled) ++;
181                removeUsed(sud, row, col, allowval);
182              }
183          }
184      }
185  }
```

The recursive solution uses the `guessFill` function but it immediately calls the `guessFillHelper` function. The latter has two additional arguments for the row and the column of a cell. The `guessFill` function calls the `guessFillHelper` function by starting from the upper left corner.

```
186  static void guessFill(Sudoku * sud)
187  {
188    guessFillHelper(sud, 0, 0);
189  }
```

The `guessFillHelper` function first finds an unfilled cell (lines 195 - 208). If no such cell can be found (line 209), this Sudoku is solved and the function stops. Otherwise, the function selects a value from the list of allowed values (line 214). At line 219, the `isValidFill` (to be shown later) is called to determine whether selecting this value violates any of the three rules (for the same row, the same column, and the same block). If no rule is violated, the `guessFillHelper` function calls itself to fill the next cell (line 222). If line 222 returns `false`, the value assigned to this cell leads to a violation in the future and a different value is selected from the list of allowed values. If no value can be selected for this cell, the function reaches line 228 because an earlier guess was wrong. The function returns false so that an earlier cell can select a different value. Do you notice that lines 214–227 have a similar structure as the move function on page 320? The move function calls the nextDistance function to determine whether entering a neighbor cell can shorten the neighbor's distance to the starting point. The guessFillHelper function calls isValidFill to determine whether filling this cell violates any rule.

```
190  static bool guessFillHelper(Sudoku * sud, int row, int col)
191  {
192    bool foundCell = false;
193    int findrow = row;
194    int findcol = col;
195    while ((foundCell == false) && (findrow < 9) && (findcol < 9))
196      {
197        if ((sud -> cells[findrow][findcol]) == '0') // not assigned
198          { foundCell = true; }
199        else
200          {
201            findcol ++;
202            if (findcol == 9)
203              {
204                findrow ++;
205                findcol = 0;
206              }
207          }
208      }
209    if (foundCell == false) // all cells filled
210      {
211        sud -> filled = 81;
212        return true;
213      }
214    for (int allow = 1; allow <= 9; allow ++)
215      {
216        if ((sud -> allowed[findrow][findcol][allow]) == true)
217          {
218            char val = allow + '0';
219            if (isValidFill(sud, findrow, findcol, val) == true)
220              {
221                sud -> cells[findrow][findcol] = val;
222                if (guessFillHelper(sud, findrow, findcol) == true)
223                  { return true; }
224                sud -> cells[findrow][findcol] = '0'; // guess wrong, reset
225              }
226          }
227      }
228    return false;
229  }
```

The isValidFill function is relatively straightforward. The function checks whether the same value has been used in the same row, the same column, or the same block. If the value has already been used, this function returns `false`. If this value has not been used, this function returns `true` at the end.

```
230   static bool isValidFill(Sudoku * sud, int row, int col, char val)
231   {
232     for (int colcnt = 0; colcnt < 9; colcnt ++)
233       {
234         if (colcnt != col)
235           {
236             if (sud-> cells[row][colcnt] == val) // already used
237               { return false; }
238           }
239       }
240     for (int rowcnt = 0; rowcnt < 9; rowcnt ++)
241       {
242         if (rowcnt != row)
243           {
244             if (sud -> cells[rowcnt][col] == val)
245               { return false; }
246           }
247       }
248     int rowstart = (row / 3) * 3;
249     int colstart = (col / 3) * 3;
250     for (int rowcnt = rowstart; rowcnt < rowstart + 3; rowcnt ++)
251       {
252         for (int colcnt = colstart; colcnt < colstart + 3; colcnt ++)
253           {
254             if ((rowcnt != row) && (colcnt != col))
255               {
256                 if (sud -> cells[rowcnt][colcnt] == val)
257                   { return false; }
258               }
259           }
260       }
261     return true;
262   }
```

Sudoku is another example where recursion can be used "naturally". Sudoku meets the three essential properties of recursion explained in Chapter 13. Sudoku has recurring patterns because each cell has to follow the same rules. The changes occur because the cells are filled gradually. The stop condition is met when all cells are filled.

25.4   Design Decisions

This section explains the thinking process so that readers understand the factors considered in this solution. This chapter explains why the sample solution is written in this way. Readers are encouraged to review these reasons and judge whether the authors have made reasonable decisions.

The decision is to choose clarity over efficiency. The program performs many redundant computations. For example, `fillSudoku` calls `removeUsed` after each cell is filled. It is more efficient, if `removeUsed` is called only once after all known values are filled. This sample solution instead calls `removeUsed` multiple times because we believe doing so improves clarity. Readers can follow the changes of the options in the other cells after one cell is filled.

When writing the solution for Sudoku, an important question is how to keep track of the state of progress. The minimum amount of data needed is the numbers stored at the 81 cells. Thus, the only needed attribute is a 9 × 9 array of numbers, called `cells`. It is possible to create another 9 × 9 array of `true` or `false` to indicate whether a cell's value has been determined. The presented solution does not use the second array; instead, the solution uses zero to indicate that a cell's value has not been assigned. The reason is that a valid solution can use only numbers between 1 and 9. Thus, it is easy to choose an invalid value (i.e., 0) to indicate whether a cell has not been assigned. If another array is used, the program needs to update both arrays when assigning a value to a cell. When two attributes are related, it is important to keep them consistent. Since it is possible to use one attribute (value zero or 1 to 9) to generate the other (`false` or `true`), we decide not to create an array of `false` or `true` for the purpose of preventing inconsistency. Please notice that saving memory is not a factor of consideration because an array of 81 `false` or `true` needs a tiny piece of memory.

If the 9 × 9 array is the only needed data for tracking progress, it is not even necessary to create the structure `Sudoku`. The reference solution creates the `Sudoku` because it has additional attributes: `filled` and `allowed`. Both of them can be derived from `cells`. Why does the solution have these two additional attributes? The values of these two attributes change as more cells are filled. If `Sudoku` does not have these two attributes, their values need to be calculated many times and such calculation can slow down the program noticeably. However, we already said efficiency is not a main concern. There is a more important reason than efficiency: these two attributes can be used to keep track of the program's progress. If `filled` is 81, all cells are filled and the program can stop. The array's elements in `allowed` can be used to determine which values are available for each cell. These two attributes can also help readers track the progress of the program. Thus, these two attributes can used in the program, even though they can be derived from `cells`.

The `Sudoku` structure has two 9 × 9 arrays for `cells` and `allowed`. Each element of `cells` is an integer between '0' and '9' ('0' means unassigned). Each element of `allowed` is an array indicating whether the numbers between 1 and 9 are used. Is it better to create another structure called `Cell` and make the `Sudoku` contain 9 × 9 `Cell`? Why does the sample solution not create the `Cell` structure? Each `Cell` object has only two attributes (the value if it is already determined and an array storing the allowed values). The advantage of creating the `Cell` structure is not strong. The list of allowed values depends on the values stored in the other cells of the same row, same column, and same block. Thus, the list of allowed numbers depends on multiple cells and should be an attribute of `Sudoku`, not `Cell`. If a `Cell` object has only one attribute for storing an integer, there is no need to create the `Cell` structure.

When are the attributes updated? Obviously, `cells` should be updated when reading the input from the file. The other attributes are used for the solution. They can be updated at the beginning of the solution. They can also be updated in the `createSudoku` function, as shown in the program. This program updates `filled` and `allow` in the `createSudoku` function for several reasons. First, updating these two attributes needs to go through the cells. The `createSudoku` function already goes through the cells. Second, updating `filled` and `allowed` in `createSudoku` reflects the initial state so that these two attributes are consistent with `cells`. Updating `filled` and `allowed` is to prepare for solving the game.

Readers may discover that `filled` and `allowed` are not updated in the recursive solution in `guessFillHelper`. As explained earlier, `filled` and `allowed` can be derived from `cells`. When `cells` is updated in `guessFillHelper` (lines 221 and 224), it is necessary to update `filled` and `allowed` for consistency. Updating them requires additional code and makes the program more complex. More important, `filled` is used to terminate recursion (lines 209-213) and `allowed` is used to control which values are considered (lines 214–227). If `allowed` is updated while it is also used, confusion (to the computer and to readers) arises. The recursive solution needs to increase `filled` when the solution guesses some cells. If any of the guesses is incorrect, the solution needs to decrease `filled`. Keeping `filled` consistent during recursion is unnecessarily complex. Thus, `guessFillHelper` does not update `filled` or `allowed`.

25.5 Network Communication

This section explains how to take advantage of the one million Sudoku puzzles from `https://www.kaggle.com/bryanpark/sudoku`. The puzzles are stored in one single file of more than 150MB. Instead of saving them in one million files, we will keep them in the original file. Moreover, instead of sharing this large file, we will create a program that can select and send one of the puzzles over the Internet. Another computer program reads the puzzle, solves it, and sends the result over the Internet.

The Internet has fundamentally changed our everyday life. Through the Internet, one can shop, share photographs, read news, watch movies, and do many more. The Internet can be thought of as a telephone system. The Internet is complex with many components talking to each other using specific *protocols* for different purposes. For the Internet, a protocol can be considered as a "language" (like

TABLE 25.1: Analogy between computer network and telephone network.

Computer Network	Telephone
Protocol	Language
Host name (or IP address)	Phone number
Port	Extension
Server	Receptionist
Socket	Phone

English, French, Japanese, Korean, Italian, Chinese, Arabic, or Spanish). Two machines can communicate if they use the same protocol, similar to the situation when two people speak the same language. A protocol can specify what type of data can be exchanged (such as text, photograph, video, and sound), the formats, the purpose, and the operations performed on the data. The Internet is built in layers. At the very bottom, electrical signals travel through wires or wireless channels. These signals can be considered as phonetic symbols like /k/ or /a/. The signals are converted to bits (i.e., zeros or ones), similar to the way phonetic symbols form the sounds. The bits are put together to give basic meanings expressed in bytes. The equivalent in language is that sounds form words.

This section uses *socket* to exchange information. It is relatively basic and allows more flexibility. A socket is simply a stream of bytes and there is no structure in the data. Programmers need to define the meaning of the data. This section uses the protocol called *TCP/IP*. Actually, this is two protocols: TCP means Transmission Control Protocol and IP means Internet Protocol. IP is the foundation of TCP and TCP uses the functions provided by IP. The details of the differences between TCP and IP are beyond the scope of this book.

For two machines to communicate, they must know each other. The network identity of a machine is often expressed as a *host name* or an *IP address*. For example, the website of Purdue University is `https://www.purdue.edu/`; this is the *host name* of the web server. The IP address is `128.210.7.200`. *Domain name servers (DNS)* provide a mapping between IP addresses and host names. A host name (or an IP address) can be thought of as a telephone number. If a machine wants to communicate with another machine, the first machine must connect to the correct IP address (similar to dialing the correct phone number). Each machine has many *ports*, similar to the extensions of the same phone number. Valid port numbers are between 0 and 65535. The ports between 0 and 1023 are reserved for specific protocols, for example, port 80 for Hypertext Transfer Protocol (HTTP) used in the World Wide Web. Port 25 is reserved for the Simple Mail Transfer Protocol (SMTP) needed to deliver email. In Linux, the `ifconfig` command can find the machine's IP address.

On the Internet, machines are often configured as *servers* or *clients*. When a person visits a website, this person's web browser is a client; the website is hosted on a server. We can think of a server as a receptionist, waiting for a client to start a phone call. A server and a client communicate through *sockets*; we can think of a socket as a telephone. To start a network server, it must have a phone (socket), a phone number (hostname or IP address), and an extension (port number). They must also speak the same language (protocol).

25.5.1 Server

This section creates a server that provides Sudoku puzzles through networks. A client requests a Sudoku puzzle and sends the solution. The server checks the solution and informs the client whether the solution is correct. The one million Sudoku puzzles at `www.kaggle.com` are stored in a single CSV (comma-separated value) file. Each line has two columns storing one puzzle and the solution. The unfilled cells are marked as 0. There are 164 characters in each line: 81 characters for a puzzle, one character for a comma, 81 characters for the solution, and one new line `'\n'`.

Let's first consider how the one million Sudoku puzzles can be read. The program needs one input argument (`argv[1]`) as the name of the file. Each line has 164 characters (line 18). The program goes to the end of the file using `fseek` (line 19) and finds the size of the file by calling `ftell` (line 20). The number of lines is the ratio of the file's length and each line's length (line 21).

```
13  int main(int argc , char **argv)
14  {
15    if (argc != 2) { return EXIT_FAILURE; }
16    FILE * fptr = fopen(argv[1], "r");
17    if (fptr == NULL) { return EXIT_FAILURE; }
18    int width = 164; // puzzle (81) + common + answer (81) + '\n'
19    fseek(fptr, 0, SEEK_END);
20    long loc = ftell(fptr);
21    int numline = loc / width;
```

Next, the program prepares to receive network connections. The program first gets a network socket (line 23); calling a socket is analogous to getting a telephone set. The `socket` function has three arguments to specify the types of communication. The first argument selects a *communication domain*. For this example, `AF_INET` means using version 4 of the

Internet Protocol (IPv4). The second argument specifies the *communication semantics*; here SOCK_STREAM means reliable, two-way, connection. When the third argument is zero, only one protocol is used. There are many possible options for these arguments. Due to the limited space of this book, we will not elaborate all the possibilities. The socket function returns an integer as a descriptor. If calling socket fails, the descriptor is −1.

```
22  int descptr;
23  descptr = socket(AF_INET , SOCK_STREAM , 0); // IPv4, reliable, single
24  if (descptr == -1) { return EXIT_FAILURE; }
```

The next step connects this socket to a particular *port* by calling the bind function. This is analogous to giving a telephone number to the telephone set. The bind function needs three arguments. The first is the descriptor from the socket. The second is a structure sockaddr. The third is the size of the second argument. This example uses zero for server.sin_port. This tells the bind function to find an available port. If server.sin_port's value is not zero, we intend to use a specific port number. If this port is already used by another program, bind fails.

```
25  struct sockaddr_in server;
26  server.sin_family = AF_INET;
27  server.sin_addr.s_addr = INADDR_ANY;
28  server.sin_port = 0; // system assigns an available port
29  int rtv = bind (descptr, (struct sockaddr *) & server , sizeof(server));
30  if (rtv < 0) { return EXIT_FAILURE; }
```

We need to get this server's IP address and the port number so that a client program can connect to. This is composed of the following steps: (1) calling getsockname to obtain this machine's name; (2) calling uname to obtain the information about this machine's operating system; (3) calling gethostbyname to obtain the machine's IP address. The program has to call inet_ntoa and ntohs to convert the byte orders of this machine and the byte orders of the Internet. Here, nto means "network-to". Calling these functions is necessary because some machines adopt *big endian* (including the Internet protocols) and the others use *little endian* (such as Intel's i386 family). The difference is explained in Figure 27.7. Calling these two functions ensure that the byte orders are consistent.

```
31  // get IP address and port
32  struct sockaddr_in serv_addr;
33  socklen_t servlen = sizeof(serv_addr);
34  rtv = getsockname(descptr, (struct sockaddr *) &serv_addr, & servlen);
35  if (rtv < 0) { return EXIT_FAILURE; }
36  struct utsname unamestruct;
37  uname(& unamestruct);
38  struct hostent hostentry;
39  struct hostent * hostptr = & hostentry;
40  hostptr = gethostbyname(unamestruct.nodename);
41  char * hostip = inet_ntoa(*((struct in_addr*)
42                              hostptr -> h_addr_list[0]));
43  printf("host IP = %s\n", hostip);
44  printf("port number %d\n", ntohs(serv_addr.sin_port));
```

At this moment, the server is ready. It calls `listen` and waits for clients' connections. Calling `listen` is analogous to sitting next to a telephone waiting for its ringing. The second argument (3 in this example) is the length of the waiting queue, meaning the number of clients allowed to wait for connections.

```
45    listen(descptr, 3);
46    printf("Server ready\n");
```

The next few lines creates the variables needed to respond to clients' connections.

```
47    struct sockaddr_in client;
48    char message[1024];
49    int client_sock;
50    int client_size;
51    client_size = sizeof(struct sockaddr_in);
52    srand(time(NULL));
53    bool keeprun = true;
54    int whichline;
55    char oneline[256];
```

The server's function runs continuously in the following steps:

1. Wait for a client's connection. After the server calls `listen` (line 45), the server is ready. When a client intends to connect, the `accept` function (line 58) informs the server. We can think of the `accept` as a ringing telephone.
2. Randomly choose a line in the CSV file (line 61).
3. Read this line from the file. Line 62 goes to the beginning of this line; line 63 reads this line from the file.
4. Use `write` to send the first 81 characters to the client (line 64). The `write` function has three arguments: the socket, an array of data, and the number of bytes to send.
5. Use `recv` to receive the response from the client (line 65). The `recv` function needs four arguments: The first three arguments are the socket, an array of data, and the length of the data. The fourth argument is a flag. When the flag's value is zero, `recv` is the same as the `read` function.
6. Compare the response with the correct answer. Lines 67-68 set the end (`'\0'`) of the two character arrays so that we can use `strcmp` to compare them (line 69). Please remember that `oneline` contains both the puzzle and the correct answer. The answer starts at the index of 82 (after 81 characters for the puzzle and a comma).
7. Inform the client whether the answer is correct (line 73).

```
56    while (keeprun)
57      {
58        client_sock = accept(descptr, (struct sockaddr *) &client,
59                             (socklen_t*) &client_size);
60        if (client_sock < 0) { return EXIT_FAILURE; }
61        whichline = rand() % numline;
62        fseek(fptr, whichline * width, SEEK_SET);
63        fgets(oneline, 164, fptr);
```

```
64        write(client_sock, oneline, 81);
65        int recvlen = recv(client_sock , message , 1024 , 0);
66        if (recvlen < 0) { return EXIT_FAILURE; }
67        message[recvlen] = '\0'; // end the string
68        oneline[163] = '\0';      // replace '\n' by '\0'
69        if (strcmp(message, & oneline[82]) == 0)
70          { strcpy(oneline, "Correct"); }
71        else
72          { strcpy(oneline, "Wrong"); }
73        write(client_sock, oneline, strlen(oneline));
74        printf("receive %s\nresult %s\n", message, oneline);
75      }
76    return EXIT_SUCCESS;
77  }
```

25.5.2   Client

It is time to examine how to write a client program to receive a Sudoku problem and send the answer. It starts by creating a socket (line 266). It connects to a server by using the server's IP address and the port number (line 272). The program uses the **recv** function to obtain 81 characters from the server as the Sudoku problem.

```
263  bool networkSudoku(char * ipaddr, int port, Sudoku * sud, int * servsock)
264  {
265    int sock;
266    sock = socket(AF_INET , SOCK_STREAM , 0);
267    if (sock == -1) { return false; }
268    struct sockaddr_in server;
269    server.sin_addr.s_addr = inet_addr(ipaddr);
270    server.sin_family = AF_INET;
271    server.sin_port = htons(port);
272    int rtv = connect(sock , (struct sockaddr *) &server , sizeof(server));
273    if (rtv < 0) { return false; }
274    char message[1024]; // more than necessary
275    int msglen = recv(sock, message, 1024, 0);
276    if (msglen != 81) { return false; }
277    createSudoku(message, sud);
278    * servsock = sock;
279    return true;
280  }
```

After the Sudoku problem is solved, the **sendSudoku** function sends the result to the server. Lines 285–292 take the two-dimensional attributes **cells** and convert the values into a one-dimensional array. This array is sent to the server (line 293). The program uses the **recv** function to obtain the result, either "Correct" or "Wrong".

```
281  void sendSudoku(int servsock, Sudoku * sud)
282  {
```

```
283    char message[1024];
284    int cnt = 0;
285    for (int row = 0; row < 9; row ++)
286      {
287        for (int col = 0; col < 9; col ++)
288          {
289            message[cnt] = sud -> cells[row][col];
290            cnt ++;
291          }
292      }
293    write(servsock, message, 81);
294    int msglen = recv(servsock , message , 1024 , 0);
295    if (msglen < 0) { return; }
296    message[msglen] = '\0';
297    printf("%s\n", message);
298    close(servsock);
```

This is the `main` function. It allows two ways to obtain a Sudoku problem: by a file or by network. This is controlled by `argv[1]`. If it is "f", the problem is from a file. If it is "n", the problem is from a network server. The program calls `solveSudoku` (line 31). The result is either saved to a file or sent to the server.

```
1     // CH25:main.c
2     #include <stdio.h>
3     #include <stdlib.h>
4     #include <stdbool.h>
5     #include <string.h>
6     #include "sudoku.h"
7     int main(int argc, char * * argv)
8     {
9       // argv[1]: "f"- input from a file, "n"- from network
10      // argv[2]: if argv[1] is "f"- input file name
11      //          if argv[1] is "n"- host name of network
12      // argv[3]: if argv[1] is "f"- output file name
13      //          if argv[1] is "n"- network port
14      if (argc < 4)  { return EXIT_FAILURE; }
15      if ((strcmp(argv[1], "f") != 0) && (strcmp(argv[1], "n") != 0))
16        { return EXIT_FAILURE; }
17      Sudoku sud;
18      bool rtv = false;
19      int servsock;
20      if (strcmp(argv[1], "f") == 0)
21        { rtv = readSudoku(argv[2], & sud); }
22      else
23        {
24          if (strcmp(argv[1], "n") == 0)
25            {
26              int port = strtol(argv[3], NULL, 10);
27              rtv = networkSudoku(argv[2], port, & sud, & servsock);
28            }
```

```
29        else { return EXIT_FAILURE; } // neither "f" nor "n"
30      }
31    if (rtv == false) { return EXIT_FAILURE; }
32    solveSudoku(& sud);
33    // printSudoku(& sud);
34    if (strcmp(argv[1], "f") == 0)
35      { saveSudoku(argv[3], & sud); }
36    else
37      { sendSudoku(servsock, & sud); }
38    return EXIT_SUCCESS;
39  }
```

This section provides a simplified example of a server-client pair showing how to communicate through the Internet. Writing good network programs can be very complex because network programs may fail in many different ways. For example, calling socket, bind, accept, and connect may fail due to wrong arguments, network disconnected, or network congestion. The simple example does not handle errors. Instead, when any error is detected, the program exits.

Here are several additional factors good network programs should consider. First, the server and the client know in advance that a Sudoku is described by 81 letters. In most cases, network programs do not know the size of data in advance. Thus, they need to communicate about the sizes. Second, the sample programs assume that the write function sends all data successfully and the recv function receives all data at once. In reality, it is possible that write/recv does not send/receive all data at once, especially when large amounts of data are sent or received. This is normal in network programs and not a mistake. The returned value of write/recv is the number of bytes actually sent/received. The server program shown has another serious problem: it can talk to only one client at any moment. For this example, the Sudoku solver (the client) is quite fast and communication between the server and the client ends quickly. If a client may take a long time, this restriction of the server can create serious problems. A common solution is for the server to create a thread for each new connection from a client. Multiple threads allow the server to communicate with multiple clients simultaneously.

25.6 Problems

25.6.1 Check Sudoku

Write a C program to check whether 81 numbers (organized by 9 lines, each with 9 numbers) is a valid solution for Sudoku.

25.6.2 Transfer Large File

Write a pair of server-client programs to transfer a large file. The client sends a large file to the server. The server saves the data in a file. Before sending the file, the client sends 8 bytes as the length of the file. It is necessary to check whether write sends all bytes and whether recv (or use read) receives all bytes.

Chapter 26

Image Processing

The rapid growth of digital photography is one of the most important technological changes in the past decades. Cameras are now standard on mobile phones, tablets, and laptops. There is also a proliferation of webcams and surveillance cameras. All of these digital images need computer programs to analyze and understand the data. For example, social media websites use facial recognition to make it easier to find your friends in photographs. Computer vision is able to determine what people are doing in images. This chapter introduces some basics of image processing. The main goal is to explain how to read and write images, as well as how to modify the colors in the image pixels. For simplicity, this chapter considers only one image format: *bitmap* (BMP). BMP files are not normally compressed and the pixels are independently stored. A more commonly used format is called Joint Photographic Experts Group, also known as *JPEG*. JPEG files are compressed using the discrete cosine transform (DCT). This compression algorithm is beyond the scope of this book.

26.1 Structure for Image

An image includes many *pixels*; each pixel has one single color. The colors of the pixels are called the "data" of the image. The pixels are what human eyes see. In addition to the colors, an image has additional information about the image, such as the date when the photo was taken, where the photo was taken, the exposure time, the focal length, and the brand of the camera. This additional information is called "metadata". Metadata means the description of the data. A bitmap image file has two parts. The first part is the metadata (also called *header* of the file, this is not the header file `.h`). The second part is the data (i.e., colors of the pixels). The header is 54 bytes in length and the size of the data depends on the number of pixels. The header is defined as:

```
1   // CH26:bmpheader.h
2   #ifndef _BMPHEADER_H_
3   #define _BMPHEADER_H_
4   #include <stdint.h>
5   // tell compiler not to add space between the attributes
6   #pragma pack(1)
7   // A BMP file has a header (54 bytes) and data
8   typedef struct
9   {
10      uint16_t type;          // Magic identifier
11      uint32_t size;          // File size in bytes
12      uint16_t reserved1;     // Not used
13      uint16_t reserved2;     // Not used
```

DOI: 10.1201/9781003257981-26

```
14   uint32_t offset;              //
15   uint32_t header_size;         // Header size in bytes
16   uint32_t width;               // Width of the image
17   uint32_t height;              // Height of image
18   uint16_t planes;              // Number of color planes
19   uint16_t bits;                // Bits per pixel
20   uint32_t compression;         // Compression type
21   uint32_t imagesize;           // Image size in bytes
22   uint32_t xresolution;         // Pixels per meter
23   uint32_t yresolution;         // Pixels per meter
24   uint32_t ncolours;            // Number of colors
25   uint32_t importantcolours;    // Important colors
26   } BMP_Header;
27   #endif
```

This header file introduces several new concepts. Line 6 tells the compiler not to add any padding between the attributes of a structure. This ensures that the size of a header object is precisely 54 bytes. Without this line, the compiler may align the attributes for better performance (execution speed). This header file includes `<stdint.h>`. It contains definitions of integer types that are guaranteed to have the same sizes on different machines. The `int` type on one machine may have a different size from the `int` type on another machine. When reading a 54-byte header from a file, we need to use the same size for the header regardless of the machine. These types defined in `<stdint.h>` all have `int` in them, followed by the number of bits, and `_t` (to indicate this is a data type). Thus, a 32-bit integer is `int32_t`. If the type is unsigned, then it is prefixed with a u. An unsigned 16-bit integer is `uint16_t`.

TABLE 26.1: Sizes (bytes) of the attributes of the header. All together, the header uses 54 bytes.

Attribute	Type	Size	Attribute	Type	Size
type	uint16_t	2	size	uint32_t	4
reserved1	uint16_t	2	reserved2	uint16_t	2
offset	uint32_t	4	header_size	uint32_t	4
width	uint32_t	4	height	uint32_t	4
planes	uint16_t	2	bits	uint16_t	2
compression	uint32_t	4	imagesize	uint32_t	4
xresolution	uint32_t	4	yresolution	uint32_t	4
ncolours	uint32_t	4	importantcolours	uint32_t	4

In the bitmap header structure, some attributes are 16 bits and the others are 32 bits. They are all unsigned because none of the attributes can take negative values. The order of the attributes is important because the order must meet the bitmap specification. Reordering the attributes will cause errors. The size of the header is calculated in Table 26.1. The header provides information about the size of the image. The number of pixels changes based on the image's width and height. To store the pixels in memory, we need to use another structure, called `BMP_Image` shown below.

```
1   // CH26:bmpimage.h
2   #ifndef _BMPIMAGE_H
3   #define _BMPIMAGE_H
4   #include "bmpheader.h"
5   typedef struct
```

```
6   {
7     BMP_Header header; // not a pointer
8     unsigned int data_size;
9     unsigned int width;
10    unsigned int height;
11    unsigned int bytes_per_pixel;
12    unsigned char * data; // a pointer
13  } BMP_Image;
14  #endif
```

A `BMP_Image` includes the header, `data_size`, width and height (duplicated from the header), the number of bytes per pixel, and a pointer to the pixel data. The `data_size` is the `size` of the file after subtracting the size of the header, i.e., `sizeof(BMP_Header)`. Even though `sizeof(BMP_Header)` is 54, it is bad to write 54 directly. The size can be derived from `sizeof(BMP_Header)`. Few people can understand what 54 means, but most C programmers can understand `sizeof(BMP_Header)`.

```
1   // CH26:bmpfile.h
2   #ifndef _BMPFILE_H_
3   #define _BMPFILE_H_
4   #include "bmpimage.h"
5   // open a BMP image given a filename
6   // return a pointer to a BMP image if success
7   // returns NULL if failure.
8   BMP_Image *BMP_open(const char *filename);
9   // save a BMP image to the given a filename
10  // return 0 if failure
11  // return 1 if success
12  int BMP_save(const BMP_Image *image, const char *filename);
13  // release the memory of a BMP image structure
14  void BMP_destroy(BMP_Image *image);
15  #endif
```

The header has a "magic number" whose value must be 0X4D42. This is a way to check whether or not the file is a valid BMP file (similar to the MD5 checksum). If the value is not 0X4D42, then it is not a valid BMP file. Using the magic number is a quick, but imperfect, solution for determining whether it is a BMP file. The `size` attribute in the header is the size of the entire file, including the header. Each pixel has three color values: red, green, and blue. Each color uses one byte. Thus, the value of `bits` is 24 bits per pixel. The images considered in this chapter have only one image plane and compression is not used. The correct value for `planes` should be 1; the correct value for `compression` should be 0. The following program reads a BMP image and checks whether it is valid. Reading an image takes the following steps: (1) read the header (line 41); (2) calculate the size of needed heap memory (line 47); (3) allocate memory (line 51); (4) read the pixels (line 53). Saving an image to a file also needs to save the header (line 72) and the pixels (line 79) separately. Please notice the symmetry of `BMP_open` and `BMP_save`.

```
1   // CH26:bmpfile.c
2   #include <stdio.h>
3   #include <stdlib.h>
4   #include "bmpfile.h"
```

```
5   // correct values for the header
6   #define MAGIC_VALUE    0X4D42
7   #define BITS_PER_PIXEL 24
8   #define NUM_PLANE      1
9   #define COMPRESSION    0
10  #define BITS_PER_BYTE  8
11  // return 0 if the header is invalid, 1 if the header is valid
12  static int checkHeader(BMP_Header * hdr)
13  {
14    if ((hdr -> type) != MAGIC_VALUE) { return 0; }
15    if ((hdr -> bits) != BITS_PER_PIXEL) { return 0; }
16    if ((hdr -> planes) != NUM_PLANE)    { return 0; }
17    if ((hdr -> compression) != COMPRESSION) { return 0; }
18    return 1;
19  }
20  // close opened file and release memory
21  BMP_Image * cleanUp(FILE * fptr, BMP_Image * img)
22  {
23    if (fptr != NULL) { fclose (fptr); }
24    if (img != NULL)
25      {
26        if (img -> data != NULL) { free (img -> data); }
27        free (img);
28      }
29    return NULL;
30  }
31  // read a BMP file from a file
32  BMP_Image *BMP_open(const char *filename)
33  {
34    FILE * fptr     = NULL;
35    BMP_Image *img = NULL;
36    fptr = fopen(filename, "r"); // "rb" unnecessary in Linux
37    if (fptr == NULL) { return cleanUp(fptr, img); }
38    img = malloc(sizeof(BMP_Image));
39    if (img == NULL)  { return cleanUp(fptr, img); }
40    // read the header
41    if (fread(& (img -> header), sizeof(BMP_Header), 1, fptr) != 1)
42      {
43        // fread fails
44        return cleanUp(fptr, img);
45      }
46    if (checkHeader(& (img -> header)) == 0) { return cleanUp(fptr, img); }
47    img -> data_size = (img -> header).size - sizeof(BMP_Header);
48    img -> width     = (img -> header).width;
49    img -> height    = (img -> header).height;
50    img -> bytes_per_pixel = (img -> header).bits / BITS_PER_BYTE;
51    img -> data =  malloc(sizeof(unsigned char) * (img -> data_size));
52    if ((img -> data) == NULL) { return cleanUp(fptr, img); } // malloc fail
53    if (fread(img -> data, sizeof(char),
54              img -> data_size, fptr) != (img -> data_size))
```

```
55        { return cleanUp(fptr, img); } // fread fails
56     char onebyte;
57     if (fread(& onebyte, sizeof(char), 1, fptr) != 0)
58        {
59          // the file still has data, something is wrong
60          return cleanUp(fptr, img);
61        }
62     // everything successful
63     fclose (fptr);
64     return img;
65   }
66   // save an image to a file
67   int BMP_save(const BMP_Image *img, const char *filename)
68   {
69     FILE * fptr    = NULL;
70     fptr = fopen(filename, "w");
71     if (fptr == NULL) { return 0; }
72     // write the header first
73     if (fwrite(& (img -> header), sizeof(BMP_Header), 1, fptr) != 1)
74        {
75          // fwrite fails
76          fclose (fptr);
77          return 0;
78        }
79     if (fwrite(img -> data, sizeof(char), img -> data_size,
80                fptr) != (img -> data_size))
81        {
82          // fwrite fails
83          fclose (fptr);
84          return 0;
85        }
86     // everything successful
87     fclose (fptr);
88     return 1;
89   }
90   void BMP_destroy(BMP_Image *img)
91   {
92     free (img -> data);
93     free (img);
94   }
```

Section 18.3 describes a structure that has a pointer as an attribute. That section explained the need to call **fread** or **fwrite** twice: once for the attributes that are not pointers and the second time for the pointer attribute. The functions BMP_open and BMP_save show how to handle an attribute (**data**) that is a pointer.

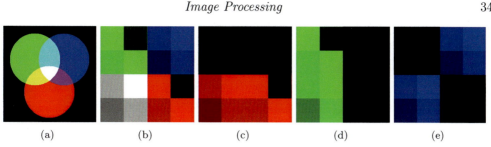

$$(a) \qquad (b) \qquad (c) \qquad (d) \qquad (e)$$

FIGURE 26.1: (a) The RGB color space, showing the primary colors and their mixtures. White is produced by mixing all three primary colors together. Color filters: (b) original images, (c) red only, (d) green only, and (e) blue only.

26.2 Image Pixels and Colors

In this BMP file format, each pixel uses three bytes representing the three primary colors of the visible spectrum: red, green, and blue. This is commonly referred to as the RGB color space. Other color spaces exist and are used for various purposes. Another common color space is HSV (hue, saturation, and value) and it is useful for some types of image analysis. BMP images store their pixels in the RGB color space. RGB is an *additive* color space: red and green is yellow; red and blue is magenta; green and blue is cyan. White is generated by combining all three colors. This section explains several methods for processing BMP images. Figures 26.1 to 26.5 are in the color insert.

The image's colors are stored in the `data` attribute. Every pixel uses three consecutive bytes. For example, the first pixel uses the first three bytes: `data[0]`, `data[1]`, and `data[2]`. The second pixel uses `data[3]`, `data[4]`, and `data[5]`. Among the three elements, the first byte represents blue, the second represents green, and the third represents red. Thus, the order is actually BGR, starting from the smaller index. Each `data` element is a byte and has a value between 0 and 255 (inclusive). Larger values mean brighter colors. If a given pixel is pure blue, then the first element (among the three-element group for a pixel) is non-zero and the other two elements are zero. If a given pixel is pure red, then the red element is non-zero and the other two elements are both zero. If all three elements are 255, then the pixel is the brightest white. If all three elements are 0, then the pixel is black. If the three elements have the same value that is neither 0 nor 255, the pixel is gray. A smaller value makes a darker gray.

Even though an image is two-dimensional, `data` stores the pixels in a one-dimensional array because managing one-dimensional arrays is usually simpler than managing two-dimensional arrays. Each pixel has an (x, y) coordinate. The origin $(0, 0)$ is at the top left corner of the image. The X coordinate increases to the right and the Y coordinate increases downward. This is the same coordinate system as shown in Figure 24.1. In this coordinate system, we can access the color values of pixels (x, y) by calculating their index in `data`. The formula is:

$$\text{Blue: } 3 \times (y \times \text{width} + x) \qquad (26.1)$$

$$\text{Green: } 3 \times (y \times \text{width} + x) + 1 \qquad (26.2)$$

$$\text{Red: } 3 \times (y \times \text{width} + x) + 2 \qquad (26.3)$$

The following listing is a header file that declares the functions we will consider in the rest of this chapter.

```
1   // CH26:bmpfunc.h
2   #ifndef _BMPFUNC_H_
3   #define _BMPFUNC_H_
4   #include "bmpimage.h"
5   // keep only one color,
6   // clr = 2, keep red; clr = 1, keep green; clr = 0, keep blue
7   void BMP_color(BMP_Image *image, int clr);
8   // Invert all of the image data in a BMP image: (value = 255 - value)
9   void BMP_invert(BMP_Image *image);
10  // calculate vertical edges using the given threshold value
11  void BMP_edge(BMP_Image *image, int thrshd);
12  // convert an RGB image to a gray-level image
13  void BMP_gray(BMP_Image *image);
14  // calculate the histogram of each color
15  void BMP_histogram(BMP_Image *image);
16  // make a checkerboard
17  void BMP_checker(BMP_Image *image);
18  // mix the colors
19  void BMP_mix(BMP_Image *image);
20  // equalize by making the darkest to and brightest to 255
21  void BMP_equalize(BMP_Image *image);
22  #endif
```

26.3   Color Filter

The first processing function is the color filter BMP_Color. The method takes a BMP image and an integer between 0 and 2. The integer indicates which color will be selected. If a color is not selected, it is set to zero.

```
1   // CH26:bmpcolor.c
2   #include "bmpfunc.h"
3   void BMP_color(BMP_Image *img, int clr) // clr: 0- blue, 1- green, 2- red
4   // selected color is kept, the other two colors are set to zero
5   {
6     int pxl;
7     for (pxl = clr; pxl < (img -> data_size); pxl ++)
8       {
9         // set the other color components to zero
10        if ((pxl % 3) != clr) { img -> data[pxl] = 0; }
11      }
12  }
```

Figure 26.1 (b)–(d) select one color and set the other two colors to zeros, revealing the contribution of the selected color. If the selected color is zero in the original image, then the resultant pixel becomes black. For example, the upper left of Figure 26.1 (b) is green. If red or blue is selected, then the upper left pixels become black, as shown in Figure 26.1 (c) and (e). Similarly, the upper right pixels of Figure 26.1 (b) are pure blue. This means that these pixels become black if red or green is selected, as shown in Figure 26.1 (c) and

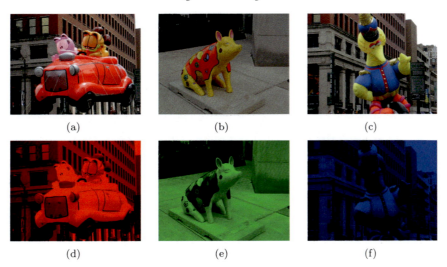

(a)   (b)   (c)

(d)   (e)   (f)

FIGURE 26.2: Color filters: (a)–(c) original images, (d) red only, (e) green only, and (f) blue only.

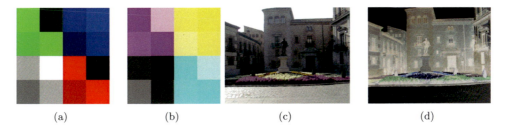

(a)   (b)   (c)   (d)

FIGURE 26.3: Color inversion. (a),(c): original; (b),(d): inverted.

(d). In most images, for example, Figure 26.2, each pixel is a mixture of all three colors. After applying a color filter, the corresponding color stands out while the other two colors are removed.

26.4   Invert Colors

The next method inverts the color of each pixel. Figure 26.3 shows the result. If a pixel is originally red, the pixel becomes cyan (green and blue). If a pixel is originally blue, the pixel becomes yellow (green and red).

```
1  // bmpinvert.c
2  #include "bmpfunc.h"
3  void BMP_invert(BMP_Image *img)
4  {
5    int pxl;
```

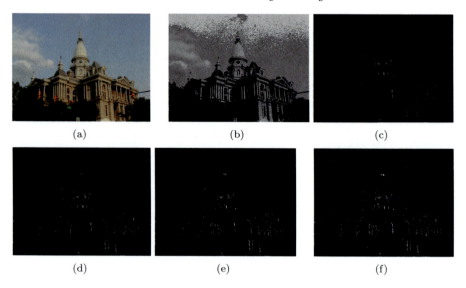

FIGURE 26.4: Detecting vertical edges. (a) The original image. (b) Gray-scale image. The detected edges use different threshold values. (c) 120. (d) 100. (e) 80. (f) 60. Many vertical edges are not detected when the threshold is too high. When the threshold is too low, there are many false-positive edges (like the sky).

```
6    for (pxl = 0; pxl < (img -> data_size); pxl ++)
7      { img -> data[pxl] = 255 - (img -> data[pxl]); }
8    }
```

26.5   Detect Edges

An edge can be defined as a sudden change of colors. This book describes a simple algorithm for detecting edges. The algorithm includes the following steps: (1) Convert the RGB values to gray levels. This is the formula for converting an RGB value to its corresponding gray level: $0.2989 \times$ red + $0.5870 \times$ green + $0.1140 \times$ blue. (2) Find the difference in the gray levels between two adjacent pixels. (3) If the difference is greater than a threshold value, then an edge has been detected. Selecting the correct threshold depends on many factors. As shown in Figure 26.4, if the threshold is too high, then some edges are not detected. If the threshold is too low, then the detection is sensitive to noise. The code below gives the function for detecting vertical edges using this method. If a pixel belongs to an edge, this pixel becomes white. If a pixel does not belong to an edge, the pixel is set to black.

```
1    // CH26:bmpedge.c
2    #include "bmpfunc.h"
3    #include <stdlib.h>
4    static int RGB2Gray(char red, char green, char blue)
```

```
5   {
6       // this is a commonly used formula
7       double gray = 0.2989 * red + 0.5870 * green + 0.1140 * blue;
8       return (int) gray;
9   }
10  void BMP_edge(BMP_Image *img, int thrshd)
11  {
12      // create a two-dimension array for the gray level
13      int width  = img -> width;
14      int height = img -> height;
15      char * * twoDGray = malloc(sizeof(char *) * height);
16      int row;
17      int col;
18      for (row = 0; row < height; row ++)
19        { twoDGray[row] = malloc(sizeof(char *) * width); }
20      // convert RGB to gray
21      int pxl = 0;
22      for (row = 0; row < height; row ++)
23        {
24          for (col = 0; col < width; col ++)
25            {
26              twoDGray[row][col] = RGB2Gray(img -> data[pxl + 2],
27                                            img -> data[pxl + 1],
28                                            img -> data[pxl]);
29              pxl += 3;
30            }
31        }
32      // detect edges and save the edges in the image
33      pxl = 0;
34      for (row = 0; row < height; row ++)
35        {
36          pxl += 3; // skip the first pixel in each row
37          for (col = 1; col < width; col ++)
38            {
39              int diff = twoDGray[row][col] -
40                twoDGray[row][col - 1]; // horizontally adjacent pixels
41              if (diff < 0) { diff = - diff; } // take the absolute value
42              if (diff > thrshd) // an edge, set color to white
43                {
44                  img -> data[pxl + 2] = 255;
45                  img -> data[pxl + 1] = 255;
46                  img -> data[pxl]     = 255;
47                }
48              else // not an edge, set color to black
49                {
50                  img -> data[pxl + 2] = 0;
51                  img -> data[pxl + 1] = 0;
52                  img -> data[pxl]     = 0;
53                }
54              pxl += 3;
```

```
55              }
56          }
57      for (row = 0; row < height; row ++) { free(twoDGray[row]); }
58      free (twoDGray);
59  }
```

26.6 Equalize Colors

Sometimes an image is over-exposed (too bright) or under-exposed (too dark). The image can usually be enhanced by using *color equalization* with the following steps: (1) Find the maximum and the minimum values of the colors. (2) If the maximum and the minimum values are different, scale the maximum value to 255 and the minimum value to 0. (3) Scale the color based on a formula. There are many ways to scale the pixel's colors. One simple method is called *linear scaling*: using a linear equation to express the relationship between the original color and the new color. Let x and y be the old and the new colors, then a linear equation has two coefficients: a and b.

$$y = ax + b \tag{26.4}$$

Suppose M and m are the original maximum and minimum values. They should become 0 and 255 after the scaling. The following two equations are used to determine the correct values for a and b.

$$\begin{aligned} 0 &= am + b \\ 255 &= aM + b \end{aligned} \tag{26.5}$$

$$a = \frac{255}{M - m} \text{ and } b = -\frac{255m}{M - m} \tag{26.6}$$

The code listing below implements this color equalization method.

```
1   // CH26:bmpequalize.c
2   #include "bmpfunc.h"
3   void BMP_equalize(BMP_Image *img)
4   {
5       int pxl;
6       unsigned char redmin   = 255;
7       unsigned char redmax   = 0;
8       unsigned char greenmin = 255;
9       unsigned char greenmax = 0;
10      unsigned char bluemin  = 255;
11      unsigned char bluemax  = 0;
12      // find the maximum and the minimum values of each color
13      for (pxl = 0; pxl < (img -> data_size); pxl += 3)
14          {
15              unsigned char red   = img -> data[pxl + 2];
16              unsigned char green = img -> data[pxl + 1];
17              unsigned char blue  = img -> data[pxl];
```

```
18      if (redmin > red) { redmin = red; }
19      if (redmax < red) { redmax = red; }
20      if (greenmin > green) { greenmin = green; }
21      if (greenmax < green) { greenmax = green; }
22      if (bluemin > blue) { bluemin = blue; }
23      if (bluemax < blue) { bluemax = blue; }
24    }
25  // calculate the scaling factors, max and min must be different
26  // to prevent divided by zero error
27  double redscale   = 1.0;
28  double greenscale = 1.0;
29  double bluescale  = 1.0;
30  // do not divide by zero
31  if (redmax > redmin)
32    { redscale = 255.0 / (redmax - redmin); }
33  if (greenmax > greenmin)
34    { greenscale = 255.0 / (greenmax - greenmin); }
35  if (bluemax > bluemin)
36    { bluescale = 255.0 / (bluemax - bluemin);    }
37  // equalize the pixels
38  for (pxl = 0; pxl < (img -> data_size); pxl += 3)
39    {
40      if (redmax > redmin)
41        {
42          img -> data[pxl + 2] =
43            (int) (redscale * (img -> data[pxl + 2] - redmin));
44        }
45      if (greenmax > greenmin)
46        {
47          img -> data[pxl + 1] =
48            (int) (greenscale * (img -> data[pxl + 1] - greenmin));
49        }
50      if (bluemax > bluemin)
51        {
52          img -> data[pxl] =
53            (int) (bluescale * (img -> data[pxl] - bluemin));
54        }
55    }
56 }
```

Figures 26.5 and 26.6 show examples of equalization.

26.7   main Function

This **main** function can select different functions for image processing. It takes three arguments: (1) argv[1] is the input image's name, (2) argv[2] is the function (such as red

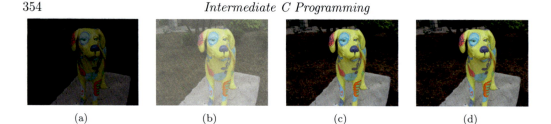

(a)   (b)   (c)   (d)

FIGURE 26.5: Equalization. (a),(b): original images; (c),(d): processed images.

(a)   (b)   (c)   (d)

FIGURE 26.6: Equalization. (a),(b): original images; (c),(d): processed images.

to keep only the red color, or `equalize` to equalize the colors), (3) `argv[3]` is the output image's name.

```c
// CH26:main.c
#include <stdio.h>
#include <stdlib.h>
#include <string.h>
#include "bmpimage.h"
#include "bmpfile.h"
#include "bmpfunc.h"
#define THRESHOLD 140
int main(int argc, char **argv)
{
  // Check arguments
  if (argc < 4)
    {
      printf("Usage: image <input> <function> <output>\n");
      return EXIT_FAILURE;
    }

  // open the input file
  BMP_Image *img = BMP_open(argv[1]);
  if (img == NULL)  { return EXIT_FAILURE; }
  if (strcmp(argv[2], "invert") == 0)  { BMP_invert(img); }
  if (strcmp(argv[2], "red") == 0)      { BMP_color(img, 2); }
  if (strcmp(argv[2], "green") == 0) { BMP_color(img, 1); }
  if (strcmp(argv[2], "blue") == 0)    { BMP_color(img, 0); }
  if (strcmp(argv[2], "edge") == 0)  { BMP_edge(img, THRESHOLD); }
  if (strcmp(argv[2], "gray") == 0)  {  BMP_gray(img);  }
  if (strcmp(argv[2], "equalize") == 0) { BMP_equalize(img); }
  if (strcmp(argv[2], "checker") == 0)  { BMP_checker(img);  }
```

```
29   if (strcmp(argv[2], "mix") == 0) {  BMP_mix(img);  }
30   // Save the file
31   if (BMP_save(img, argv[3]) == 0)
32     {
33       printf("Output file invalid!\n");
34       BMP_destroy(img);
35       return EXIT_FAILURE;
36     }
37   // Destroy the BMP image
38   BMP_destroy(img);
39   return EXIT_SUCCESS;
40 }
```

This chapter gives a starting point for image processing. Image processing is a rich subject and there are many books on the topic and related topics.

26.8   Problems

26.8.1   Color Histogram

Write a program to read an image and calculate the *histogram* of each color. A histogram is the distribution of values. More specifically, a histogram counts the occurrence of each value. The program's input is a BMP file. The output is $255 \times 3 = 765$ numbers. If an image is reddish, the histogram should have high values in the red component.

26.8.2   Color Space

Write a program to create the image shown in Figure 26.1 (a).

26.8.3   Gradient

Section 26.5 takes an image and outputs the edge pixels. Modify the program and output the *gradient* of the input image. The gradient image shows the changes in adjacent pixels. The gradient is calculated by taking the difference of adjacent pixels. The output image shows the absolute value of the difference. If two adjacent pixels are the same, the output pixel is black. If two adjacent pixels are black and white, the output pixel is white.

26.8.4   Vertical Mirror

Write a program that takes an input image and output the vertical mirror image.

Chapter 27

Huffman Compression

Section 20.5 introduced binary trees through the example of binary search trees. This chapter describes another way to use binary trees in a popular compression method called *Huffman Compression* or *Huffman Coding*. Huffman Coding was developed by David Huffman in the early 1950s. After several decades, the method is still widely used as one of the best compression algorithms.

27.1 Variable-Length Coding

The American Standard Code for Information Interchange (ASCII) is a fixed-length representation using 8 bits for each letter, even though some letters (such as e and s) are more common than some others (such as q and z). In contrast, Huffman Compression uses variable-length representations. If a letter appears often, then it uses fewer bits. If a letter appears rarely, then more bits are used. The average length of all letters is shorter and the information is compressed. Huffman Coding is *lossless compression* because the original data can be fully recovered. *Lossy compression* means the original data cannot be fully recovered. Lossy compression may achieve higher *compression ratios* than lossless compression and is useful when full recovery of the original data is unnecessary. Lossy compression is commonly used to compress images because the loss may be subtle and cannot be detected by human eyes. JPEG is an example of lossy compression. The compression ratio is defined as:

$$\frac{\text{Size of uncompressed file}}{\text{Size of compressed file}} \tag{27.1}$$

This chapter uses Huffman Coding to compress articles written in English. Given a set of letters (or symbols or numbers) and their occurrences, Huffman Coding is optimal because Huffman Coding uses the fewest bits on average.

Huffman compression uses variable-length coding of letters with the following principles: (1) If a letter does not appear in the data, no code is created for this letter. (2) Suppose x and y are two letters; c_x and c_y are the codes for x and y. If x occurs more often than y, then $|c_x| \leq |c_y|$, meaning that the length of c_x is no greater than the length of c_y. Please notice that it is possible their codes have the same length, i.e., $|c_x| = |c_y|$; $|c_x| = |c_y|$ does not imply that the two letters have the same occurrences. Moreover, $|c_x| < |c_y|$ does not imply that x occurs more often than y (they may have the same occurrences). (3) No code is a *prefix* of another code. This is the definition of prefix: Suppose $c_1 = a_1 a_2 ... a_m$ and $c_2 = b_1 b_2 ... b_n$ are two codes. If c_1 is a prefix of c_2, then $m \leq n$ and $a_1 = b_1$, $a_2 = b_2$, ... $a_m = b_m$. In variable-length codes, a prefix is not allowed; otherwise, ambiguity occurs.

Consider a file with only eight letters: a, b, c, d, e, f, g, and h. To encode these letters, only 3 bits are sufficient because $2^3 = 8$. That means that each character can be assigned to a unique 3-bit sequence. Next consider the situation when the letters' occurrences are quite

DOI: 10.1201/9781003257981-27

different, as shown in Table 27.1 (a) The table also shows the codes (bit sequences) for the characters. The average number of bits is $2\times22.50\%+4\times8.75\%+4\times7.50\%+3\times10.00\%+2\times26.25\%+4\times5.00\%+3\times11.25\%+4\times8.75\% = 2.8125$ bits per letter. This is $1-\frac{2.8125}{3} = 6.25\%$ reduction in the length over using 3-bit codes. This saving is modest because the occurrences are somewhat close. Next, consider the example in Table 27.1 (b). The average number of bits is $2\times29.0\%+5\times3.0\%+5\times5.0\%+5\times4.0\%+1\times40.0\%+4\times9.0\%+5\times3.0\%+4\times7.0\% = 2.37$. The reduction is $1-\frac{2.37}{3} = 21\%$. This is more noticeable. We will explain how to generate these codes (called a "code book") in the next section.

TABLE 27.1:   Occurrences and codes of the eight letters.

Letter	Occurrence	Code	Length	Occurrence	Code	Length
a	54 (22.50%)	01	2	116 (29.0%)	10	2
b	21 (8.75%)	1111	4	12 (3.0%)	11000	5
c	18 (7.50%)	1101	4	20 (5.0%)	11101	5
d	24 (10.00%)	000	3	16 (4.0%)	11100	5
e	63 (26.25%)	10	2	160 (40.0%)	0	1
f	12 (5.00%)	1100	4	36 (9.0%)	1111	4
g	27 (11.25%)	001	3	12 (3.0%)	11001	5
h	21 (8.75%)	1110	4	28 (7.0%)	1101	4
average length	2.8125			2.37		
	(a)			(b)		

27.2   Compress

To compress a file, the following steps are needed: (1) Count the occurrences of the characters. (2) Sort the characters by occurrences in the ascending order. (3) Build a tree based on the occurrences. (4) Convert the tree to the code book. (5) Replace the letters in the original file by their corresponding codes. The chapter uses "encode" and "compress" interchangeably. Similarly, "decode" and "decompress" are used interchangeably. Also, "letter" and "character" are used interchangeably.

27.2.1   Count and Sort Occurrences

The first step of Huffman Coding is to determine the occurrence of each letter in the document being compressed. We use a structure for this purpose. Each object has two attributes: the ASCII code and the occurrence of this code.

```
1   // CH27:occur.h
2   // count the number of occurrences of the characters in a file
3   #ifndef OCCUR_H
4   #define OCCUR_H
5   #include <stdio.h>
6   #define NUMCHAR 256
7   typedef struct
8   {
9     unsigned char ascii; // ASCII value
10    int occur; // how many times does this ASCII value occurs
11  } CharOccur;
12  // count the occurrencies of the characters
```

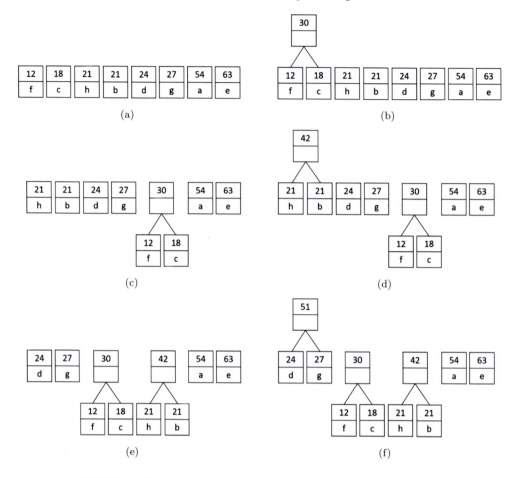

FIGURE 27.1: Process to create the Huffman compression tree.

```
13    // return the total number of characters in the file
14    // return 0 if cannot read from the file
15    // occur is an array whose elements store the characters and occurrences
16    int countOccur(char * filename, CharOccur * occur, int length);
17    void printOccur(CharOccur * occur, int length, FILE * pfptr);
18    int compareOccur(const void * p1, const void * p2);
19    #endif
```

The countOccur function reads the file one character at a time and counts how many times the character occurs. Lines 23–24 use the character's ASCII code as the array index.

```
5     int countOccur(char * filename, CharOccur * occur, int length)
6     {
7       FILE * fptr = fopen(filename, "r");
8       int count = 0;
9       if (fptr == NULL) { return 0; } // fopen fail
10      // initialize the array elements
11      int ind;
```

```
12    for (ind = 0; ind < length; ind ++)
13      {
14        occur[ind].ascii = -1;
15        occur[ind].occur = 0;
16      }
17    while (! feof (fptr))
18      {
19        int onechar = fgetc(fptr);
20        if ((onechar >= 0) && (onechar < length))
21          {
22            count ++;
23            occur[onechar].ascii = (char) onechar;
24            occur[onechar].occur ++;
25          }
26      }
27    fclose (fptr);
28    return count;
29  }
```

Sorting the array by the occurrence can be accomplished by calling **qsort**:

```
34  qsort(chararr, NUMCHAR, sizeof(CharOccur), compareOccur);
```

This is the comparison function:

```
42  int compareOccur(const void * p1, const void * p2)
43  {
44    const CharOccur * ip1 = (const CharOccur *) p1;
45    const CharOccur * ip2 = (const CharOccur *) p2;
46    const int iv1 = ip1 -> occur;
47    const int iv2 = ip2 -> occur;
48    if (iv1 != iv2)
49      { return (iv1 - iv2); }
50    // if same occurrences, ordered by the ASCII values
51    const char cv1 = ip1 -> ascii;
52    const char cv2 = ip2 -> ascii;
53    return (cv1 - cv2);
54  }
```

27.2.2 Build the Code Tree

Let's consider how to create the codes in Table 27.1 (a). Figure 27.1 illustrates the process of creating the Huffman compression tree. The process is explained below:

1. The letters are sorted by the occurrences in the ascending order. The occurrence of each letter is marked above the letter, as shown in Figure 27.1 (a). Each box is actually a binary tree node. If two letters have the same number of occurrences, it does not matter which is the first: The order will affect the codes but will not change the average number of bits per letter.

2. Create a binary tree node as the parent of the first two letters (the smallest two occurrences). This parent node's occurrence is the sum of the occurrences of the two children. as shown in Figure 27.1 (b). This parent node does not store any letter.

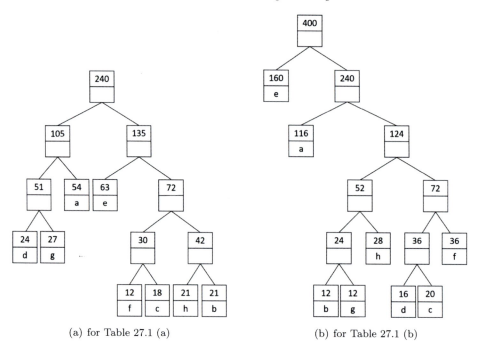

(a) for Table 27.1 (a)   (b) for Table 27.1 (b)

FIGURE 27.2: Code trees. The process stops when all letters belong to the same tree.

3. Insert the newly created binary tree back and maintain the ascending order, as illustrated in Figure 27.1 (c).
4. Figure 27.1 (d) repeats the second step by creating a binary tree node as the parent of the first two nodes.
5. Figure 27.1 (e) repeats the third step by inserting the newly creating back and maintaining the ascending order.
6. Figure 27.1 (f) repeats the second step again by creating a binary tree node as the parent of the first two nodes. This newly created tree node is inserted while maintaining the ascending order.

The final result is a tree shown in Figure 27.2 (a). The letters are stored in the leaf nodes. Starting from the tree's root, moving left adds 0 to the code and moving right adds 1 to the code. The code for e is 10 because, from the root, the path moves right first (adding 1) and then moves left (adding 0). The code for g is 001 because the path from the root moves left twice (adding 00) and then moves right once (adding 1). Please verify the codes in the tree are the same codes in Table 27.1 (a). This tree has the following properties, matching the rules on page 356. The tree's leaf nodes store the eight letters. Only the leaf nodes store the letters. If a node is not a leaf node, it doesnot

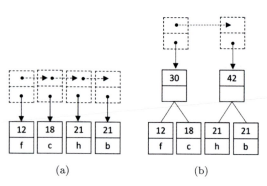

(a)   (b)

FIGURE 27.3: Tree nodes (solid lines) are connected by list nodes (dash lines).

store any letter. If a letter (such as g) occurs more often than another letter (such as c), the code for g (length 3) is no longer than the code for c (length 4). From the root, a parent node is the prefix of its child nodes. If a node is not a leaf node, this node must have both children because the method to build the tree creates a non-leaf node by taking the first two nodes as the children. Of course, a leaf node has no child. Figure 27.2 (b) shows the tree for Table 27.1 (b). Figure 27.3 shows how the nodes are organized: a linked list connects the binary tree nodes.

27.2.3 Create Code Book and Compress Data

Table 27.1 (a) shows how to encode data. If letter a appears in the original data, replace it by 01. If letter h appears in the original data, replace it by 1110. Figure 27.4 shows how the code book is structured. The code book is a two-dimensional array: the number of rows is the number of leaf nodes in the tree. The first column stores the letters. In this example, the longest code needs four zero or one. We use -1 to indicate the end of the code. The number of columns is two plus the length of the longest code; it is equivalent to the tree's height plus one. Three rows have zero in their first code (i.e., column 1); this is the number of leaf nodes of the root's left subtree. Five rows have one in their first code; this is the number of leaf nodes of the root's right subtree.

27.2.4 Describe the Coding Tree

The tree in Figure 27.2 depends on the input file. Thus, it is necessary to describe the tree for each compressed file because different files may have different trees. The description must reproduce exactly the same tree. Problem 21.9.5 describes a way to specify a binary tree by using the in-order and post-order outputs.

Due to the properties of Huffman compression trees, a tree can be uniquely described by using post-order only with some additional information. It is not necessary to also use in-order. In this post-order description, if a leaf node is encountered, the node is printed using two letters: 1 followed by the letter stored in this node. If a non-leaf node is encountered, print 0. A final 0 is added after the root to

	Column					
Row	0	1	2	3	4	5
0	d	0	0	0	-1	-1
1	g	0	0	1	-1	-1
2	a	0	1	-1	-1	-1
3	e	1	0	-1	-1	-1
4	f	1	1	0	0	-1
5	c	1	1	0	1	-1
6	h	1	1	1	0	-1
7	b	1	1	1	1	-1

Rows 0–2: 3 rows. Rows 3–7: 5 rows.

FIGURE 27.4: The codebook is a two-dimensional array. This is the codebook for Table 27.1 (a). Unused array elements are filled with -1.

indicate that the tree's description is complete. There should be the same number of 1 and 0. Consider the tree in Figure 27.2(a). A pair of parentheses is used for each node. If the node is a leaf node, inside each pair starts with $\mathbb{L}$, followed by the occurrence and the letter. If the node is not a leaf node, inside each pair starts with $\mathbb{N}$, followed by the sum of the occurrences of the children. The post-order description of Figure 27.2(a) is ($\mathbb{L}$24 d) ($\mathbb{L}$27 g) ($\mathbb{N}$51) ($\mathbb{L}$54 a) ($\mathbb{N}$105) ($\mathbb{L}$63 e) ($\mathbb{L}$12 f) ($\mathbb{L}$18 c) ($\mathbb{N}$30) ($\mathbb{L}$21 h) ($\mathbb{L}$21 b) ($\mathbb{N}$42) ($\mathbb{N}$72) ($\mathbb{N}$135) ($\mathbb{N}$240). The occurrences are not needed when describing the tree. The tree is described (with the additional ending 0) as

```
1d1g01a01e1f1c01h1b00000
```

The compressed file for Figure 27.2 (a) includes three parts:

1. Post-order description of the tree: `1d1g01a01e1f1c01h1b00000`.
2. Length of the original file: 240. The binary representation is 1111 0000.
3. Codes for the letters; replacing a by 01, b by 1111, c by 1101, etc. If the first four letters in the original file are abcd, they will become 01 1111 1101 0000. Space is added for better readability.

The beginning of the compressed file will be

```
1d1g01a01e1f1c01h1b00000
1111 0000
01 1111 1101 0000
```

27.2.5   Use Bits

To compress a file, the codes in Table 27.1 are actually bits. In other words, letter e in Table 27.1 (b) is replaced by a single bit 0. In the original file, letter e is expressed by one byte. Thus, this compression can reduce the data size by $1 - \frac{1}{8} = 87.5\%$. This is a significant reduction. Even for d and u, the reduction is 50% (from one byte to four bits). When saving the tree, the 1 in front of a letter should use only one bit; one bit 0 is used to indicate a non-leaf node. These bits (either 0 or 1) are called *control bits*. Each letter still uses one byte (8 bits); this is called a *data byte*. Let's consider the example above. Table 27.2 marks the tree description as control bits (C) or data bytes (D). Most programming languages (including C) have no data types for bits. In C programs, the smallest unit is one-byte using `unsigned char`.

TABLE 27.2:   Mark the tree description as control (C) or data (D) for Figure 27.2 (a).

1	d	1	g	0	1	a	0	1	e	1	f	1	c	0	1	h	1	b	0	0	0	0
C	D	C	D	C	C	D	C	C	D	C	D	C	D	C	C	D	C	D	C	C	C	C

description	1	d	1	g	0	1	a	0
bits	1	0110 0100	1	0100 0111	0	1	0110 0001	0
remove boundary	1	0110 0100	1	0100 0111	0	1	0110 0001	0
arrange as bytes	1	0110 0100	1	0100 0111	0	1	0110 0001	0

FIGURE 27.5: Use bits to describe the tree.

Figure 27.5 shows how to handle the bits. The first row shows the beginning of the tree's post-order description. The second row replaces each data byte by the ASCII value. The ASCII value for d is 100 in decimal, 64 in hexadecimal, or 0110 0100 in binary. The ASCII value for g is 103 in decimal, 67 in hexadecimal, 0110 0111 in binary. The third row removes the boundaries of control bits and data bytes. The fourth row inserts boundaries between bytes. The first bit of the first byte is always used for a control bit. As a result, only seven bits are available. The last bit of d has to move to the first bit of the second byte. The next bit is a control bit. Two bits in the second bytes have been used and only six bits are available for letter g. The last two bits of g use the first two bits of the third byte. The next two bits are both control bits. Only four bits are available for a. Thus, the last four bits of a have to move to the fourth bytes. This example shows that the locations of the control bits change and it is necessary to keep track of the changes.

The first bit of the first byte is the control bit 1. It can be created by using the hexadecimal value 0X80. This bit is followed by the first seven bits of d; these bits can be obtained by shifting the letter right by one. The shift operations were explained in Section 18.2. The first bit of the second byte is the last bit of d. This can be created by shifting the letter left by seven (seven bits of zero will be inserted to the right side). It should be apparent that the amounts of shifts (one and seven) should add up to eight because each byte has eight bits.

As explained earlier, a compressed file has three parts: (1) the compression tree using the post-order description, (2) the length of the original file, and (3) the codes. The length will be a four-byte integer (32 bits). This is sufficient for an article with more than four billion letters because $2^{32} = 4,294,967,296$. If a novel has 1,000 pages, it has approximately 500,000 words (500 words per page). Suppose the average length of a word is 10 letters, this novel has 5,000,000 letters. Thus, a 4-byte integer is more than sufficient to encode a novel of 1,000 pages. For (1) and (3), if the last byte is not fully used, zero bits are added to complete the last byte of each part (this is called *padding* zeros). Finally, a newline character '\n' is added to the end of (1) and (2).

Consider an input file composed of 11 # followed by 15 /. The original file is

###########///////////////

The compression file in the text format is

1#1/00
26
00000000000111111111111111

The code for symbol # is 0; the code for is 1. Please notice that the length uses 4 bytes. More details about the methods to arrange the 4 bytes are available below.

description	1	#		1	/		0	0	\n
bits	1	0010 0011		1	0010 1111		0	0	0000 1010
remove boundary	1	0010 0011	1		0010 1111	0	0		0000 1010
arrange as bytes	10010001	11001011			11000000				0000 1010

FIGURE 27.6: Use bits to describe the tree of a file composed of 10 # followed by 15 /.

To convert this text format into the binary format, first consider the tree description. Figure 27.6 shows the compression tree in bits. The ASCII value of # is 35 (decimal), 23 (hexadecimal), and 0010 0011 (binary). The first seven bits of # is 001 0001. Adding the leading control bit 1, the first byte is 1001 0001. The last bit of # is 1 and it becomes the first bit of the second byte. The second control bit is 1 and it becomes the second bit of the second byte. The ASCII value of / is 47 (decimal), 2F (hexadecimal), and 0010 1111 (binary). The first six bits of / is 00 1011. Together with the earlier two bits, the second byte is 1100 1011. The remaining two bits from / become the first two bits of the third byte. The next two control bits are both zeros. Only four bits of the third byte are used and the last four bits are padded at the end. Thus, the third byte is 1100 0000. The next byte is the new line character '\n' and its ASCII value is 10 (decimal) or 0000 1010 (binary).

The next four bytes are an integer of 26 (decimal) or 0001 1010 (binary). If it is written using four bytes, the leading three bytes are zeros. Thus, the four-byte representation of 26 is

Address	Little Endian Value	Big Endian Value
A+24	0X12	0X78
A+16	0X34	0X56
A+8	0X56	0X34
A	0X78	0X12

Address	A	A+8	A+16	A+24
Little Endian	0X78	0X56	0X34	0X12
Big Endian	0X12	0X34	0X56	0X78

(a)   (b)

FIGURE 27.7: Big endian and little endian are different formats to store data 0X12345678.

0000 0000 0000 0000 0000 0000 0001 1010. When this number is stored inside a computer file, the rightmost byte (0001 1010) is stored first and the leftmost byte (0000 0000) is stored last. This is called *little endian* and is used in Intel processors. This program is tested on an Intel processor; thus, the program's output uses little endian. In contrast, *big endian* stores the leftmost byte first and the rightmost byte last. Big endian is used by some other processors, such as the Motorola 68 family. Consider a larger number 0X12345678 (hexadecimal). If it is stored in the little endian format, the four bytes are ordered as 0X78 0X56 0X34 0X12 in the increasing addresses. If it is stored in the big endian format, the four bytes are ordered as 0X12 0X34 0X56 0X78. These two data formats can be explained in Figure 27.7. Figure 27.7 (a) shows the addresses vertically in the descending order from bottom to top. In little endian, 0X12 (the leftmost byte) appears on the top and 0X78 (the rightmost byte) appears at the bottom. Figure 27.7 (b) rearranges the addresses horizontally and the rightmost byte 0X78 appears first in little endian. As a reminder, page 337 mentioned that `ntohs` can be used to handle the differences between big and little endian.

For the compressed file, after the post-order description of the tree, the next four bytes are the original file's length without padding. After the length is a new line character '\n'. The next five bytes are

```
0001 1010 0000 0000   0000 0000 0000 0000 0000 1010
```

Space is added for better readability. The first byte 0001 1010 is 26, the length of the original file. The next three bytes are zeros. The fifth byte is the new line character 0000 1010. After the length and the new line, there are 11 zeros (for 11 #), followed by 15 ones (for 15 /). Only 26 bits are used and 6 zeros are padded at the end (to make the codes a multiple of 8). These are the codes for the data:

```
0000 0000 0001 1111 1111 1111 1100 0000
```

Now, we can put all bytes together:

```
1001 0001 1100 1011 1100 0000 0000 1010
0001 1010 0000 0000 0000 0000 0000 0000 0000 1010
0000 0000 0001 1111 1111 1111 1100 0000
```

This binary file cannot be read or modified by typical text editors. Instead, we need tools that can convert the bits into characters (i.e., '0' or '1') for humans. In Linux `xxd` is a tool showing the bits in a binary file. This is the output of `xxd -b` when reading the compressed file.

```
00000000: 10010001 11001011 11000000 00001010 00011010 00000000   ......
00000006: 00000000 00000000 00001010 00000000 00011111 11111111   ......
0000000c: 11000000
```

Each row has seven columns. The first column shows the addresses. The remaining six columns show the content.

27.3 Decompress

Decompression is the reverse of compression. The decompression program needs to separate the three parts in the compressed file: (1) the description of the tree, (2) the length of the original file, and (3) the letters expressed in the codes. The decompression program does not need to count the occurrences of letters. Instead, it can read the compression tree directly. The compression tree is described by the post-order rule: (1) a leaf node is printed by adding 1 in front of a letter; (2) a non-leaf node is printed as 0. Thus, when 1 is seen, a letter should follow and this creates a tree node for the letter. When 0 is seen, it is a non-leaf node as the parent of the most recent two nodes. Consider this description of the tree on page 361.

`1d1g01a01e1f1c01h1b00000`

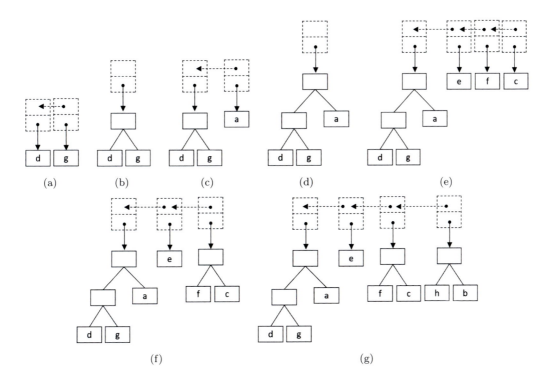

FIGURE 27.8: The process to create the compression tree from post-order description. The most recently added nodes are at the beginning of the linked list; thus, the direction of the links is the opposite of Figure 27.3. Solid lines are tree nodes; dash lines are list nodes.

Let's rebuild the tree from this description. After reading `1d1g`, two tree nodes are added and they are connected by two list nodes, as shown in Figure 27.8 (a). Next, 0 is read and the two tree nodes share the same parent, as shown in Figure 27.8 (b). At this moment, there is only one list node. Reading `1a` adds another tree node, shown in Figure 27.8 (c). The next `0` makes the two most recent tree nodes siblings shown in Figure 27.8 (d). After reading `1e1f1c`, the list nodes and tree nodes are shown in Figure 27.8 (e). The next `0` creates a tree node and makes the most recent two tree nodes siblings, shown in Figure 27.8 (f). Figure 27.8 (g) shows the tree after reading `1h1b0`. The remaining `0` will build the tree like Figure 27.2 (a). After reading the tree, the decompression program reads an integer as the length of the original file.

After rebuilding the tree and reading the length, the decompression program reads the codes to obtain the original data. This process follows the following steps: (1) Start from the root; (2) Read one bit from the compressed file; (3) If the bit is 0, move to the left child. If the bit is 1, move to the right child. (4) When a leaf node is encountered, print the letter stored at this node. Move back to the root. These four steps are repeated until enough letters are printed (based on the length of the original file).

27.4   Implementation

27.4.1   Test Case Generator

This is the most complex program in this book. We will spend some time explaining how the program is written and tested. Let's start with the test cases. This is the case in Table 27.1 (a). The first column is the letters. The second column is the occurrences.

```
1    a 54
2    b 21
3    c 18
4    d 24
5    e 63
6    f 12
7    g 27
8    h 21
```

A program converts these test cases to letters. This is the converted result.

```
aaaaaaaaaaaaaaaaaaaaaaaaaaaaaaaaaaaaaaaaaaaaaaaaaaaaaabbbbbbbbbbbbbbbbbbbbb
cccccccccccccccccdddddddddddddddddddddddddeeeeeeeeeeeeeeeeeeeeeeeeeeeeeeeeee
eeeeeeeeeeeeeeeeeeeeeeeeeeeffffffffffffggggggggggggggggggggggggggghhhhhhh
hhhhhhhhhhhhhhhh
```

This is the case in Table 27.1 (b).

```
1    a 116
2    b 12
3    c 20
4    d 16
5    e 160
6    f 36
7    g 12
8    h 28
```

This is the converted result for Table 27.1 (b).

```
aaaaaaaaaaaaaaaaaaaaaaaaaaaaaaaaaaaaaaaaaaaaaaaaaaaaaaaaaaaaaaaaaaaaaaaaa
aaaaaaaaaaaaaaaaaaaaaaaaaaaaaaaaaaaaaaaaaaabbbbbbbbbbbbbcccccccccccccccccccccdd
ddddddddddddddddeeeeeeeeeeeeeeeeeeeeeeeeeeeeeeeeeeeeeeeeeeeeeeeeeeeeeeeeeeee
eeeeeeeeeeeeeeeeeeeeeeeeeeeeeeeeeeeeeeeeeeeeeeeeeeeeeeeeeeeeeeeeeeeeeeeeeeee
eeeeeeeeeeeeeeeeeeeeeeefffffffffffffffffffffffffffffffffffffffffgggggggggggggghhh
hhhhhhhhhhhhhhhhhhhhhhhhhhh
```

This is the conversion program:

```c
// CH27:testgen.c
// convert a test case from letter-occurrence pairs to print the letters
// for example, if input is a 23, this program prints a 23 times
#include <stdio.h>
#include <stdlib.h>
#define NUMCHAR 256
int main(int argc, char * * argv)
{
  if (argc != 3) { return EXIT_FAILURE; }
  FILE * inptr = fopen(argv[1], "r");
  if (inptr == NULL) { return EXIT_FAILURE; }
  int occur[NUMCHAR] = {0};
  char val;
  int count;
  while (fscanf(inptr, "%c %d\n", & val, & count) == 2)
    {
      // printf("%c %d\n", val, count);
      if (occur[(int) val] != 0)
        { printf("Repeated character %c\n", val); }
      occur[(int) val] = count;
    }
  fclose(inptr);
  FILE * outptr = fopen(argv[2], "w");
  int ind;
  for (ind = 0; ind < NUMCHAR; ind ++)
    {
      for (count = 0; count < occur[ind]; count ++)
        {
          fprintf(outptr, "%c", ind);
        }
    }
  fclose(outptr);
  return EXIT_SUCCESS;
}
```

27.4.2 main **Function**

This is the main function:

```
1   // CH27:main.c
2   #include <stdio.h>
3   #include <stdlib.h>
4   #include <string.h>
5   #include "compress.h"
6   #include "decompress.h"
7   int main(int argc, char * * argv)
8   {
9     if (argc != 5) { return EXIT_FAILURE; }
10    // argv[1]: "c"- compress, "d"- decompress
11    // argv[2]: input file path (including directory and file name)
12    // argv[3]: output file directory (without file name)
13    // argv[4]: input file name (without directory)
14    int func = 0; // 0: invalid, 1: compress, 2: decompress
15    if (strcmp(argv[1], "c") == 0) { func = 1; }
16    if (strcmp(argv[1], "d") == 0) { func = 2; }
17    if (func == 0) { return EXIT_FAILURE;}
18    // The output is stored in the file with name argv[4]/argv[3].out
19    // This program save progress in argv[4]/argv[3].progress
20    int namelength = strlen(argv[3]) + strlen(argv[4]);
21    char * outputname = malloc(sizeof(char) * (namelength + 10));
22    char * progressname = malloc(sizeof(char) * (namelength + 10));
23    strcpy(outputname, argv[3]);
24    strcat(outputname, argv[4]);
25    strcpy(progressname, outputname);
26    strcat(progressname, ".progress");
27    int rtv; // return value
28    if (func == 1)
29      {
30        strcat(outputname, ".cmp"); // compressed file
31        rtv = compress(argv[2], outputname, progressname);
32      }
33    if (func == 2)
34      {
35        strcat(outputname, ".res"); // restored text file
36        rtv = decompress(argv[2], outputname, progressname);
37      }
38    free (outputname);
39    free (progressname);
40    if (rtv == 0) { return EXIT_FAILURE; }
41    return EXIT_SUCCESS;
42  }
```

The function takes five arguments: `argv[1]` specifies whether the program should compress or decompress the input file. The input file's name is `argv[2]`. This name is expected to include a directory, for example, `original/input1`. The next two arguments specify the output directory (for example, `output/`) and the file's name without the directory (for example, `input1`). By adding the output directory as an argument, the program separates the input files from the output files in different directories. This `main` also creates the name of a file, with `.progress` as the extension (line 26), recording the program's progress. The compressed file has `.cmp` as the extension (line 30). The decompressed file has `.res` (meaning restored) extension.

27.4.3 Makefile

The `main` function is designed to be tested by this `Makefile`:

```
1   # CH27: Makefile
2   WARNING = -Wall -Wshadow --pedantic
3   ERROR = -Wvla -Werror
4   GCC = gcc -std=c99 -g $(WARNING) $(ERROR)
5   VAL = valgrind --tool=memcheck --log-file=vlog --leak-check=full --verbose
6   SRCS = main.c occur.c compress.c list.c tree.c bits.c decompress.c
7   OBJS = $(SRCS:%.c=%.o)
8
9   huffman: $(OBJS)
10          $(GCC) $(OBJS) -o huffman
11
12  compress: testgen huffman
13          rm -f -r compressed
14          mkdir compressed
15          for origpath in original/*; do \
16          filename=$$(basename $$origpath); \
17          ./huffman c $$origpath compressed/ $$filename; \
18          done
19
20  decompress: compress
21          rm -f -r restored
22          mkdir restored
23          for comppath in compressed/*cmp; do \
24          filename=$$(basename $$comppath); \
25          echo $$filename; \
26          ./huffman d $$comppath restored/ $$filename; \
27          done
28          # compare the original with the decompressed files
29          for origpath in original/*; do \
30          filename=$$(basename $$origpath); \
31          echo $$filename; \
32          diff $$origpath restored/$$filename.cmp.res; \
33          done
34
35  testgen: testgen.c
36          $(GCC) testgen.c -o testgen
37          for num in 1 2 3 4 5 6 7 8; do \
38          ./testgen cases/case$$num original/input$$num; \
39          done
40
41  memory1: huffman
42          $(VAL) ./huffman c original/King1963 compressed/ King1963
43
44  memory2: huffman
```

```
45              $(VAL) ./huffman d compressed/King1963.cmp restored/ King1963.cmp
46
47    .c.o:
48              $(GCC) $(TESTFALGS) -c $*.c
49
50    clean: # remove all machine generated files
51              rm -f huffman occur testgen *.o *~ vallog
52              rm -f -r original/input*
53              rm -f -r compressed restored vlog
```

It has several sections. The `testgen` section starts at line 35 and converts the letter-occurrence pairs to an input file. The `huffman` section builds the executable. The most important sections are `compress` and `decompress`. The `compress` section goes through every file in the `original` directory and compresses the file. The compressed file and the progress report are stored in the `compressed` directory. The `decompress` section also compares the decompressed file with the original file (line 32). This `Makefile` can greatly reduce the effort for testing and debugging.

27.4.4 Compression

27.4.4.1 `compress` Function

The `compress` function implements the five steps described in Section 27.2.

```c
17    int compress(char * infile, char * outfile, char * progressfile)
18    {
19      // steps:
20      // 1. count the occurrences of the letters
21      // 2. sort in the ascending order
22      // 3. build the tree
23      // 4. convert the tree into the code book
24      // 5. replace the letters by the codes
25      // step 1:
26      CharOccur chararr [NUMCHAR];
27      FILE * pfptr = fopen(progressfile, "w");
28      if (pfptr == NULL) // fopen fail
29        { return 0; }
30      int total = countOccur(infile, chararr, NUMCHAR);
31      if (total == 0) // nothing in the file
32        { return 0; }
33      // step 2:
34      qsort(chararr, NUMCHAR, sizeof(CharOccur), compareOccur);
35      // save the progress to a file
36      printOccur(chararr, NUMCHAR, pfptr);
37      // step 3:
38      TreeNode * tree = buildCodeTree(chararr, NUMCHAR, pfptr);
39      if (tree == NULL)
40        { return EXIT_FAILURE; }
41      // step 4:
42      CodeBook * cbook = malloc(sizeof(CodeBook));
43      buildCodeBook(tree, cbook);
```

```
44      printCodeBook(cbook, pfptr);
45      // step 5:
46      encodeFile(infile, outfile, cbook, tree);
47      Tree_destroy(tree);
48      destroyCodeBook(cbook);
49      return total;
50  }
```

The countOccur function has already been explained in Section 27.2.1. The next sections explains the buildCodeTree, buildCodeBook, and encodeFile functions.

27.4.4.2 buildCodeTree Function

The buildCodeTree function closely reflects the procedure described in Figure 27.1.

```
7   TreeNode * buildCodeTree(CharOccur * chararr, int length, FILE * pfptr)
8   {
9       ListNode * head = NULL;
10      int ind;
11      // build the list with ascending order
12      for (ind = 0; ind < length; ind ++)
13          {
14              CharOccur * optr = & chararr[ind];
15              if ((optr -> occur) != 0)
16                  {
17                      head = List_insertChar(head, optr -> ascii, optr -> occur);
18                  }
19          }
20      List_print(head, pfptr);
21      // merge the nodes and build the tree
22      while ((head -> next) != NULL)
23          {
24              TreeNode * tree1 = head -> tnptr;
25              TreeNode * tree2 = (head -> next) -> tnptr;
26              TreeNode * tp  = Tree_merge(tree1, tree2);
27              ListNode * p = head;
28              ListNode * q = head -> next;
29              head = List_insertTree(q -> next, tp, true);
30              free (p);
31              free (q);
32          }
33      List_print(head, pfptr);
34      TreeNode * tree = head -> tnptr;
35      free (head); // list no longer needed
36      return tree;
37  }
```

27.4.4.3 List_insertTree Function

The List_insertTree function is used for both compression and decompression. For compression, the list nodes should keep the ascending order of the occurrences. For decompression, the nodes follow the post-order description of the tree. The function's third argument, `order`, determines whether to sort the nodes. If `order` is `true`, the nodes are sorted by ascending order, as shown in Figure 27.1. If `order` is `false`, the newly inserted node is always at the beginning of the list (line 20), as shown in Figure 27.8.

```
11  ListNode * List_insertTree(ListNode * head, TreeNode * tn, bool order)
12  // if order is true, insert in ascending order
13  // if order is false, insert at the beginning
14  {
15    ListNode * ln = ListNode_create(tn);
16    if (head == NULL) // empty list, create first list node
17      { return ln; }
18    // insert in the ascending order
19    int occur = tn -> occur;
20    if ((order == false) ||
21        (occur < ((head -> tnptr) -> occur))) // at the beginning
22      {
23        ln -> next = head;
24        return ln;
25      }
26    // p is always before q
27    ListNode * p = head;
28    ListNode * q = p -> next;
29    // find where to insert, ascending order
30    while ((q != NULL) && ((q -> tnptr) -> occur) < occur)
31      {
32        p = p -> next;
33        q = q -> next;
34      }
35    // does not matter whether q is NULL or not
36    p -> next = ln;
37    ln -> next = q;
38    return head;
39  }
```

27.4.4.4   `buildCodeBook` **Function**

The code book uses a structure

```
1   // CH27:codebook.h
2   #ifndef COODBOOK_H
3   #define COODBOOK_H
4   typedef struct
5   {
6     int * * codes;
7     int numRow;
8     int numCol;
9   } CodeBook;
10  #endif
```

The first attribute `codes` is a two-dimensional array shown in Figure 27.4. The other two attributes store the sizes of the array. The `buildCodeBook` function finds the number of leaf nodes (line 86); this is the number of rows for the two-dimensional array. Next, the function finds the tree's height (line 87). The number of columns is one plus the height (line 88). Lines 90–101 allocate memory for the two-dimensional array. All elements are initialized to −1 (line 100). The `buildCodeBook` function calls the `buildCodeBookHelper` to fill the two-dimensional array.

```
84  static void buildCodeBook(TreeNode * root, CodeBook * cbook)
85  {
86    int numRow = Tree_leaf(root);
87    int numCol = Tree_height(root);
88    numCol ++; // to accommodate the ending -1
89    // column start at 1 because [0] stores the character
90    cbook -> numRow = numRow;
91    cbook -> numCol = numCol;
92    cbook -> codes = malloc(sizeof(int*) * numRow);
93    int row;
94    for (row = 0; row < numRow; row ++)
95      {
96        cbook -> codes[row] = malloc(sizeof(int) * numCol);
97        int col;
98        // initialize to -1
99        for (col = 0; col < numCol; col ++)
100          { cbook-> codes[row][col] = -1; }
101      }
102    row = 0;
103    buildCodeBookHelper(root, cbook, & row, 1);
104  }
```

The `buildCodeBookHelper` visits the tree's nodes. If a leaf node is encountered (line 59), the node's ASCII value is stored at the first column (index is 0). Then the function moves to the next row. If the tree node is not a leaf node, the function visits the left subtree (lines 66-74) and the right subtree (lines 75–82). When visiting the left subtree, the function finds the number of leaf node of the subtree and fills the zero to the number of rows (line 72). Then the function visits the left child (line 73) by calling itself. Visiting the right subtree follows a similar procedure.

```
51  static void buildCodeBookHelper(TreeNode * tn, CodeBook * cbook,
52                                  int * row, int col)
53  {
54    if (tn == NULL) // nothing to do
55      { return; }
56    // is it a leaf node?
57    TreeNode * lc = tn -> left;
58    TreeNode * rc = tn -> right;
59    if ((lc == NULL) && (rc == NULL))
60      {
61        // finish one code
62        cbook -> codes[*row][0] = tn -> ascii;
63        (* row) ++;
```

```
64        return;
65      }
66    if (lc != NULL)
67      {
68        // populate this column of the entire subtree
69        int numRow = Tree_leaf(lc);
70        int ind;
71        for (ind = * row; ind < (* row) + numRow; ind ++)
72          { cbook -> codes[ind][col] = 0; }
73        buildCodeBookHelper(lc, cbook, row, col + 1);
74      }
75    if (rc != NULL)
76      {
77        int numRow = Tree_leaf(rc);
78        int ind;
79        for (ind = * row; ind < (* row) + numRow; ind ++)
80          { cbook -> codes[ind][col] = 1; }
81        buildCodeBookHelper(rc, cbook, row, col + 1);
82      }
83  }
```

27.4.4.5   encodeFile **Function**

At this moment, the code book is ready and the program can encode (i.e., compress) the file by calling the encodeFile function.

```
131  static void encodeFile(char * infile, char * outfile,
132                         CodeBook * cbook, TreeNode * tree)
133  {
134    FILE * inptr = fopen(infile, "r");
135    if (inptr == NULL)
136      { return; }
137    FILE * outptr = fopen(outfile, "w");
138    if (outptr == NULL)
139      { return; }
140    // save the tree in the output file
141    Tree_save(tree, outptr);
142    // find the length of the file
143    fseek(inptr, 0, SEEK_END);
144    int length = ftell(inptr);
145    // save the file length in the output file
146    fwrite(& length, sizeof(int), 1, outptr);
147    unsigned char newline = '\n';
148    fwrite(& newline, sizeof(unsigned char), 1, outptr);
149    // find each ASCII's index in the code book
150    int ASCII2code[NUMCHAR] = {-1};
151    int numRow = cbook -> numRow;
152    int row;
153    for (row = 0; row < numRow; row ++)
154      {
```

```
155        int ascii = cbook -> codes[row][0];
156        ASCII2code[ascii] = row;
157      }
158    // convert the letters from the input and save in the output file
159    fseek(inptr, 0, SEEK_SET); // go back to the beginning of the file
160    int count = 0;
161    unsigned char whichbit = 0;
162    unsigned char curbyte  = 0;
163    while (! feof(inptr))
164      {
165        int ch = fgetc(inptr);
166        if (ch != EOF)
167          {
168            row = ASCII2code[ch];
169            int col = 1;
170            while (cbook -> codes[row][col] != -1)
171              {
172                writeBit(outptr, cbook -> codes[row][col],
173                         & whichbit, & curbyte);
174                col ++;
175              }
176            count ++;
177          }
178      }
179    if (count != length)
180      { printf("count = %d, length = %d\n", count, length); }
181    padZero(outptr, & whichbit, & curbyte);
182    fclose (inptr);
183    fclose (outptr);
184  }
```

The function saves the tree first. The `Tree_saveHelper` function is the post-order description of the tree. When a leaf node is encountered (line 108), a bit of 1 is saved first (line 110) and then the letter is saved (line 111). If a non-leaf node is encountered, a bit of 0 is saved (line 113).

```
99   static void Tree_saveHelper(TreeNode * tree, FILE * fptr,
100                              unsigned char * whichbit,
101                              unsigned char * curbyte)
102  {
103    if (tree == NULL) { return; }
104    TreeNode * lc = tree -> left;  // left child
105    TreeNode * rc = tree -> right; // right child
106    Tree_saveHelper(lc, fptr, whichbit, curbyte);
107    Tree_saveHelper(rc, fptr, whichbit, curbyte);
108    if ((lc == NULL) && (rc == NULL)) // leaf node
109      {
110        writeBit(fptr, 1, whichbit, curbyte);
111        writeByte(fptr, tree -> ascii, whichbit, curbyte);
112      }
113    else { writeBit(fptr, 0, whichbit, curbyte); }
```

```
114   }
115   void Tree_save(TreeNode * tree, FILE * fptr)
116   {
117     if (tree == NULL) { return; }
118     unsigned char whichbit = 0;
119     unsigned char curbyte = 0;
120     Tree_saveHelper(tree, fptr, & whichbit, & curbyte);
121     writeBit(fptr, 0, & whichbit, & curbyte);
122     padZero(fptr, & whichbit, & curbyte);
123     writeByte(fptr, '\n', & whichbit, & curbyte);
124   }
```

After saving the tree, the original file's length is saved. This is achieved in `encodeFile` by calling `fseek` (line 143) to set to the end of the file. Line 144 uses `ftell` to obtain the file's length. The original file's length is saved by using `fwrite` (line 146). Lines 150–157 create a mapping table from the ASCII values to the code book's rows. For example, the first row of the table in Figure 27.4 is the letter d. The array `ASCII2code` uses d's ASCII value (100 in decimal) as the index. The array element at this index stores 0. This means when letter d is seen, the program uses the code stored at row 0 in the code book. Lines 163–178 reads the letters from the original file and replace the letters by their codes stored in the code book.

27.4.4.6   `writeBit` and `writeByte` Functions

The `writeBit` function is called when saving only one bit to a file.

```
3   int writeBit(FILE * fptr, unsigned char bit,
4                   unsigned char * whichbit, unsigned char * curbyte)
5   // * whichbit indicates which bit this is written to
6   // (0 means leftmost, 7 means rightmost) curbyte is the current byte
7   // When * whichbit is zero, curbyte is reset
8   // When * whichbit is 7, this byte is written to the file
9   // The function returns 1 if a byte is written to the file
10  // returns 0 if no byte is written, -1 if fwrite fails
11  {
12    if ((* whichbit) == 0) { * curbyte = 0; } // reset the byte
13    // shift the bit to the correct location
14    unsigned char temp = bit << (7 - (* whichbit));
15    * curbyte |= temp; // store the data
16    int value = 0;
17    if ((* whichbit) == 7)
18      {
19        int ret;
20        ret = fwrite(curbyte, sizeof(unsigned char), 1, fptr);
21        // printByte(* curbyte); // for debugging
22        if (ret == 1) { value = 1; }
23        else { value = -1; }
24      }
25    * whichbit = ((* whichbit) + 1) % 8;
26    return value;
27  }
```

```
28  int writeByte(FILE * fptr, unsigned char onebyte,
29                  unsigned char * whichbit, unsigned char * curbyte)
30  {
31    int iter;
32    for (iter = 0; iter < 8; iter ++)
33      {
34        unsigned char bit = ((onebyte & 0X80) != 0);
35        if (writeBit(fptr, bit, whichbit, curbyte) == -1) { return -1; }
36        onebyte <<= 1;
37      }
38    return 1;
39  }
```

The `writeByte` function writes one byte to the compressed file. This is used for the letters and the newlines.

27.4.4.7 padZero **Function**

This function fills the unused bits by zeros. The function writes 0 (one bit) until all bits of the current byte are used.

```
40  int padZero(FILE * fptr, unsigned char * whichbit,
41                  unsigned char * curbyte)
42  {
43    int rtv;
44    while ((* whichbit) != 0)
45      {
46        rtv = writeBit(fptr, 0, whichbit, curbyte);
47        if (rtv == -1) { return -1; }
48      }
49    return rtv;
50  }
```

27.4.5   Decompression

The process to decompress a file follows the description in Section 27.3.

27.4.5.1   decompress **Function**

The `decompress` function follows three steps: (1) reads the tree, (2) reads the original file's length, and (3) replaces the codes by the letters.

```
8   int decompress(char * infile, char * outfile, char * progressfile)
9   {
10    // steps:
11    // 1. read the tree
12    // 2. read the length
13    // 3. convert the codes to the letters
14    FILE * pfptr = fopen(progressfile, "w");
15    if (pfptr == NULL) // fopen fail
16      { return 0; }
```

```
17    FILE * infptr = fopen(infile, "r");
18    if (infptr == NULL)
19      { return 0; }
20    TreeNode * tree = restoreCodeTree(infptr, pfptr);
21    Tree_print(tree, 0, pfptr);
22    int length;
23    if (fread(& length, sizeof(int), 1, infptr) != 1)
24      { fprintf(pfptr, "wrong format\n"); }
25    fprintf(pfptr, "%d\n", length);
26    unsigned char newline;
27    if (fread(& newline, sizeof(unsigned char), 1, infptr) != 1)
28      { fprintf(pfptr, "wrong format\n"); }
29    if (newline != '\n')
30      { fprintf(pfptr, "wrong format\n"); }
31    decodeFile(infptr, outfile, length, tree);
32    fclose(infptr);
33    fclose(pfptr);
34    Tree_destroy(tree);
35    return length;
36  }
```

27.4.5.2 `restoreCodeTree` Function

This function follows the explanation in Figure 27.8. It reads one bit from the compressed file (line 137). If this bit is one, the function reads one byte as the letter. A new tree node is created (line 143) to store this letter. This tree node is added to the list (line 145). The third argument of `List_insertTree` is `false` and this node is inserted at the beginning (i.e., not sorted). If the bit is 0 (line 147), the function takes the most recently added two nodes (lines 154 and 155) and makes them share the same parent (line 156). When the same numbers of bit 1 and bit 0 are read (lines 164–165), the tree is fully built. If the last byte has unused bits, the function removes these unused bits (line 164). The next byte should be newline (line 171).

```
125  TreeNode * restoreCodeTree(FILE * infptr, FILE * pfptr)
126  {
127    bool finishedtree = false;
128    int numOne  = 0;
129    int numZero = 0;
130    unsigned char bit;
131    unsigned char byte;
132    unsigned char whichbit = 0;
133    unsigned char curbyte  = 0;
134    ListNode * head = NULL;
135    while (finishedtree == false)
136      {
137        readBit(infptr, & bit, & whichbit, & curbyte);
138        if (bit == 1)
139          {
140            numOne ++;
141            readByte(infptr, & byte, & whichbit, & curbyte);
```

```
142              // printf("1%c\n", byte);
143              TreeNode * tn = Tree_create(byte, -1); // occur does not matter
144              fprintf(pfptr, "1%c", byte);
145              head = List_insertTree(head, tn, false);
146          }
147       if (bit == 0)
148          {
149              numZero ++;
150              fprintf(pfptr, "0");
151              if ((head != NULL) && ((head -> next) != NULL))
152                 {
153                     // merge the most recent two tree nodes
154                     TreeNode * tree1 = head -> tnptr;
155                     TreeNode * tree2 = (head -> next) -> tnptr;
156                     TreeNode * tp  = Tree_merge(tree2, tree1); // note the order
157                     ListNode * p = head;
158                     ListNode * q = head -> next;
159                     head = List_insertTree(q -> next, tp, false);
160                     free (p);
161                     free (q);
162                 }
163             }
164        if (numOne == numZero)
165           { finishedtree = true; }
166      }
167   TreeNode * tree = head -> tnptr;
168   free (head);
169   removePad(infptr, & whichbit, & curbyte);
170   readByte(infptr, & byte, & whichbit, & curbyte); // should be '\n'
171   if (byte != '\n')
172     { printf("wrong format\n"); }
173   fprintf(pfptr, "\n");
174   return tree;
175 }
```

27.4.5.3 `readBit` and `readByte` Functions

The `readBit` and `readByte` functions are similar to the `writeBit` and `writeByte` functions. If the bit is the first bit in a byte (line 55), one byte is read from the file (line 58). Otherwise, the function reuses the byte that has already been read and is stored in `curbyte`. The function shifts the byte by the correct amount to obtain the bit (line 62). The `readByte` function reads eight bits to obtain one byte.

```
51 int readBit(FILE * fptr, unsigned char * bit,
52             unsigned char * whichbit, unsigned char * curbyte)
53 {
54   int ret = 1;
55   if ((* whichbit) == 0)
56      {
57        // read a byte from the file
```

```
58        ret = fread(curbyte, sizeof(unsigned char), 1, fptr);
59      }
60    if (ret != 1) { return -1; } // read fail
61    // shift the bit to the correct location
62    unsigned char temp = (* curbyte) >> (7 - (* whichbit));
63    temp = temp & 0X01; // get only 1 bit, ignore the others
64    * whichbit = ((* whichbit) + 1) % 8; // increase by 1 for the next bit
65    * bit = temp;
66    return 1;
67  }
68  int readByte(FILE * fptr, unsigned char * onebyte,
69                unsigned char * whichbit, unsigned char * curbyte)
70  {
71    int iter;
72    unsigned char byte = 0;
73    unsigned char bit;
74    for (iter = 0; iter < 8; iter ++)
75      {
76        if (readBit(fptr, & bit, whichbit, curbyte) == -1) { return -1; }
77        byte <<= 1;
78        byte = byte | bit;
79      }
80    * onebyte = byte;
81    return 1;
82  }
```

27.4.5.4 removePad Function

This function removes the remaining bits in a byte.

```
83  int removePad(FILE * fptr, unsigned char * whichbit,
84                unsigned char * curbyte)
85  {
86    int rtv;
87    unsigned char bit;
88    while ((* whichbit) != 0)
89      {
90        rtv = readBit(fptr, & bit, whichbit, curbyte);
91        if (rtv == -1) { return -1; }
92      }
93    return rtv;
94  }
```

27.4.5.5 decodeFile Function

The function reads the bits from the compressed file. If the bit is 0, it goes to the left child. If the bit is 1, it goes to the right child. If a leaf node is encountered (line 51), the letter is printed to the output file.

```
37  static void decodeFile(FILE * infptr, char * outfile,
38                         int length, TreeNode * tree)
39  {
40    FILE * outfptr = fopen(outfile, "w");
41    if (outfptr == NULL) { return; }
42    unsigned char bit;
43    unsigned char whichbit = 0;
44    unsigned char curbyte  = 0;
45    TreeNode * tn = tree;
46    while (length > 0)
47      {
48        readBit(infptr, & bit, & whichbit, & curbyte);
49        if (bit == 0) { tn = tn -> left; }
50        if (bit == 1) { tn = tn -> right; }
51        if ((tn -> left) == NULL) // leaf node
52          {
53            fprintf(outfptr, "%c", tn -> ascii);
54            tn = tree; // return to the top
55            length --;
56          }
57      }
58    fclose (outfptr);
59  }
```

27.4.6 Compression Ratios

What compression ratio can be achieved by this method? Let's consider the Latex source for Chapter 13 (this book uses Latex; it is a text formatting program). The original Latex file has 47,964 bytes. The compressed file has 29,573 bytes. The compression ratio is 1.62 ($\frac{47964}{29573} = 1.62$). The Nobel Lecture by Dr. Marie Curie in 1911 has 26,476 bytes. The compressed file has 14,660 bytes. The compression ratio is 1.80. The most frequently used letter is space and it occurs 3,938 times. The least used letters include *, X, U, and J. Each appears only once. The shortest code has 3 bits; the longest code has 15 bits.

27.5 Problems

27.5.1 Compression Tree

A file has 20 a followed by 20 b. Write down the post-order description of the compression tree in the text format.

27.5.2 Compressed File

Continue the previous problem. Write down the entire compressed file (including the tree, the length, the codes) in the text format.

27.5.3 Compressed File

Continue the previous problem. What is the output of xxd -b when the input is the binary format of the compressed file?

27.5.4 One-Letter Input

If the input file has only one letter $ and it repeats 100 times. What is compressed file in the text format?

27.5.5 Compressed File

Continue the previous problem. What is the output of xxd -b when the input is the binary format of the compressed file?

27.5.6 Number of Leaf Nodes

Is it possible that the tree has an odd number of leaf nodes?

27.5.7 Compression Ratio

If an input file has 100 letter $ (i.e., $ repeats 100 times), what is the compression ratio using the binary format?

If an input file has 10,000 letter X followed by 10,000 letter Y, what is the compression ratio using the binary format?

27.5.8 Tree Description

If the compression tree is

```
1a1$1X01%1Z1Y001@0000
```

What is the code for X? What is the code for Y?

27.5.9 Highest Possible Compression Ratio

Using the compression method described in this chapter, what is the highest possible compression ratio?

27.5.10 Lowest Possible Compression Ratio

Using the compression method described in this chapter, what is the lowest possible compression ratio?

Index

Epilogue: The Computer Engineer as Tool-User

James C. Davis, PhD

If you've made it this far, congratulations! You now have a reasonable command of C programming, and are ready to apply it in advanced courses and in the workplace. You were also introduced to many software engineering tools that can be applied to C programming and in other software contexts. The purpose of this epilogue is to help you integrate your understanding of the C programming language and the accompanying software tools, leading to a more robust understanding of *software engineering*.

Engineering Tools

As tool users, humans are nearly unique in the animal kingdom. Humans have certainly developed the widest range of tools of all species. Engineers are no exception.

Engineers develop and use tools to make our work more efficient. Digging dirt with a stick is difficult—a shovel makes things go more quickly. If a large amount of dirt must be moved quickly, a more advanced tool can be employed, such as an excavator. Similarly, joining together two pieces of wood is difficult without tools. If a carpenter wants to do this more quickly, they may use a hammer and nails, or clamps and glue.

As we use tools, we must not give up our responsibility as engineers. There is an old saying that "Only bad craftspeople blame their tools". Tools can make engineers more efficient, but tools can also introduce defects into engineered products. For example, if you are trying to join together two pieces of wood, you might glue them together. Yet suppose you are in Antarctica: the glue may fail in extreme cold. An engineer must understand the context in which the product will be used in order to decide which tools to use. Tools must be used properly; the engineer is responsible for the product regardless of the chosen tools.

Tools thus benefit engineers, but they also require engineers to take responsibility for using them properly. The Software Engineering Code of Ethics was published jointly by the two major professional societies for computing, the Association of Computing Machinery (ACM) and the Institute of Electrical and Electronics Engineers (IEEE). This code is focused on software *products* and software *engineers*. It makes no mention of the tools used to build a product. The responsibility for a high-quality product lies with the software engineering team that produces the product. The software engineers must select and use their tools skillfully, keeping costs low (better efficiency) while promoting high quality of the product (responsibility).

Using Tools in Software Engineering, Efficiently and Responsibly

In the previous section, we argued that software engineers are tool-users, and that this interpretation carries with it the characteristics of *efficiency* and *responsibility*. We illustrate this viewpoint by examining some tools that might be used while performing different software engineering tasks.

When Writing Software

As you completed the exercises in this book, you may have needed to refer to external resources to better understand the task or the errors you encountered. I think of these external resources as knowledge tools. For example, you might have referred to the Linux manual for bash or for some of the APIs you used, such as library calls (e.g., malloc and free) or system calls (e.g., open, read, write, and close). Alternatively, you might have sought a resource on the Internet and found a pertinent Question and Answer on a discussion forum such as Stack Overflow. These tools have different characteristics for efficiency and responsibility.

Reading a manual is slow going. On my MacBook, the programming manuals for open, read, write, and close[1] total 3,548 words, or a little over 7 single-spaced pages. I suppose it would take over 10 minutes to read all of them, even supposing they are simple and easy to digest (they are not!). Meanwhile, I find that many of my questions about reading and writing files can be answered in about 20 seconds on Stack Overflow. Clearly, Stack Overflow provides large efficiency gains.

Let us now consider responsibility. I have seen students complete entire programming assignments by dint of repeated recourse to Stack Overflow. They copy code to address each error, and the code compiles. But they end up with a Franken-solution that they don't fully understand, and so when it doesn't quite pass all of the test cases they struggle to debug and repair it. In contrast, students who study the manuals may take longer to finish the assignment, but they will make steady progress instead of having to make many revisions.

As engineers, we want both—we want our products to be efficient, and yet responsibly-made. Tools such as Stack Overflow are valuable because they help us skip right to the part of a manual that is pertinent. I am not advising you to ignore that. But I do advise you to use Stack Overflow and similar knowledge resources responsibly. When I use Stack Overflow, I ask myself four questions:

1. "Do I have enough expertise to understand whether the advice is sound?" If I do, splendid. But if not, your time might be better spent developing your expertise.

2. "Will I be able to debug this code snippet when it breaks?" Most Stack Overflow posts need to be tailored to your context, and many have subtle errors because they are intended as illustrations. You should never take code from someone else without knowing how it works.

3. "How critical is it that I fully understand this problem and its solution?" In engineering work, some knowledge is critical and other knowledge is not. Most engineers don't need a deep mastery of date-time formats or the RFC defining valid email addresses. Internet resources are a great way to find suitable code snippets for such tasks, which you can then bury within a friendly API in a utility library. But if you are working

---

[1] I typed "man 2 open | wc -w" to count the number of words

on code for critical business processes (or the key algorithm in your school project), step carefully.

4. "How long have I been looking for a solution to my problem?" Personally, I use a "5 minutes" rule. If I have been looking for a solution for more than 5 minutes, this is usually a signal that there's something wrong with my question. That means I should switch to studying and developing my understanding of the problem and the tools I am using. An alternative explanation is that my problem is sufficiently obscure that I am one of the first people to try to solve it—so I'd better focus on solving it!

When Debugging Software

As you completed the exercises in this book, you probably found that your software code was often incorrect. One approach for debugging, or finding the errors in your code, is to carefully read the code and see if you can spot the error. This approach is nearly tool-less, not counting the tool you are using to read the code. In Chapter 3.3, we talked about two tools that can be used for debugging. One tool was printf, which enables the strategy called *logging*: a program is instrumented with printf statements that report its dynamic behavior to the engineer. Another tool is called a debugger, such as gdb (command-line) or ddd (a graphical interface for gdb). These tools have different characteristics for efficiency and responsibility.

It is hard to say whether logging or debugging is a more efficient approach. Depending on the nature of the bug, a single log statement might help you find it; or a long session with a debugger might be necessary to truly understand a defect that lies in the interplay of two components. There is plenty of research that shows, however, that either of these tools will be more efficient than trying to understand an error somewhere in hundreds of lines of code.

This brings us to the matter of responsibility. Here we must tread carefully. When you study software carefully (the tool-less approach), you end up with a deep knowledge of its behaviors and assumptions. After you identify the bug, you will likely be able to repair it without compromising existing behaviors or assumptions. In contrast, I have observed many students whose use of loggers or debuggers accelerates their *discovery* of a bug, but who then take shortcuts in repairing it because they have not truly understood the bug in its context.

My point is not that you should never use a logger or a debugger. These tools make you more efficient at their goal—locating the defect. However, you must use them responsibly. Once you have located the defect, you must then study the code to ensure that your repair does not break something else.

When Delegating Software Engineering Work

The computing field is always changing. One major recent change has been the advent of Generative Artificial Intelligence tools (GenAI) such as OpenAI's ChatGPT tool, Google's Bard tool, and GitHub's CoPilot tool. Some of these tools are structured as question-answering systems similar to Stack Overflow. Others are more closely integrated with the software engineering process, such as the auto-complete functionality offered by CoPilot. Both of these styles of GenAI differ from prior software engineering tools in that they are interactive. Previous tools, whether debuggers, code generators, or knowledge collectors, were static and required you to adapt whatever they produced to fit your particular context. These new GenAI tools are dynamic; if you have additional requirements, you can ask them to refine their proposals to your special case.

Since GenAI tools were developed by software companies, they are particularly good at software-related tasks. You can ask them to implement common data structures, explain errors in your code, write documentation, and generate "boilerplate" material such as implementing a web client using a particular library. Because GenAI tools are interactive, I think of them less as a question-answering tool like Stack Overflow, and more as a kind of engineering assistant to whom I can delegate some of my work.

I strongly encourage you to work with GenAI tools. The software engineers who learn to use these tools well will find themselves vastly more productive than those who refuse or use them inexpertly. This should come as no surprise, of course, because engineers are tool users and GenAI is just another kind of tool. But like all tools, using GenAI will require you to balance efficiency against responsibility. Like all tools, you should use GenAI only to the limit of your own competence. If you will not be able to assess the result of the tool, then you should not use the tool.

I have two specific recommendations when working with the current generation of GenAI tools. *First*, you should fully understand the specification of the software you are trying to create. GenAI tools are great at providing a first draft of software, but they will struggle to catch all of the edge cases—and filling in those edge cases via prompts may be less efficient than simply editing the first draft proposed by the tool. *Second*, you (the engineer) will have to do the work of design. The current generation of GenAI is great at filling out a template, or implementing individual functions, but it struggles when asked to come up with the template or to decompose a problem into individual functions.

Although you must exercise your engineering judgment, even the current generation of GenAI allows you to access expertise that might otherwise be expensive to acquire. For example, you might be developing software to run on a particular hardware platform like ARM64. You might know, conceptually, that ARM64 includes optimized instructions such as Single-Instruction-Multiple-Data (SIMD) to apply the same operation to an entire vector of data. This reduces the time to transform the vector, as well as the energy cost of doing so; both latency and energy efficiency are reasons to draw on these capabilities. However, you might not know the specific incantation to employ SIMD in your context, nor the preferred libraries for doing so. George Thiruvathukal, one of the authors of this book, was in exactly this situation. He worked with ChatGPT-3.5 to develop a working program tailored to ARM64, and what would have taken days (from reading manuals) or hours (from scouring the Internet) took him minutes instead. GenAI tools gave George a substantial efficiency boost, and because George had the conceptual mastery of SIMD he was able to responsibly assess (and revise) the proposals of ChatGPT. Engineering expertise and engineering judgment will allow you to ask the right questions of GenAI, assess the quality of the results, and revise them as needed. Or, in other words, you need your engineering expertise and your engineering judgment to use GenAI both efficiently and responsibly.

I ultimately view GenAI as an assistant to a software engineer. The engineer remains responsible both for the design as well as the implementation. The GenAI tool makes the creation of the implementation more efficient, but the engineer remains responsible for ensuring that the result is well designed and fully solves the problem at hand. The software engineer will not be replaced; don't worry that your job will be automated away. But to perform well in that job, you should use all of the tools at your disposal, and that includes GenAI.

Concluding Remarks

Computing is an exciting field to enter. Modern society runs on computers, and computers obey their software and hardware. Computer engineering (whether focused in software or hardware) is truly the profession of the 21st century. One characteristic of computing is that nothing stays the same. Like Moore's Law, it seems that every 2-3 years, a groundbreaking technology or tool is introduced to improve the productivity of computer engineers. As a future computer engineer, you are responsible for learning these new tools—otherwise you are doing yourself, your employer, and your customers a disservice. You must always use these tools efficiently and responsibly. Use your judgment, and have fun.

This book has the most comprehensive coverage of programming concepts I have seen during my time in college. It effectively breaks down the concepts, making it easier to comprehend programming development practices and their practical applications. I also enjoyed how simple and not overly complex the coding examples were in illustrating the concepts, which greatly aids in avoiding overwhelming the reader. Learning new programming concepts can be daunting, but this book successfully presents them in manageable portions, making them more accessible. The concepts and problems described in this book are commonly used in the industry, thereby cultivating critical thinking skills essential for engineers and programmers. It was a game changer when I had the book in college!

Damini Rijhwani

Every programmer should go out and read through this book right now! Each page explains fundamental concepts in a novel way that teaches through example, practical application, and a debugging perspective. It shines where other programming books fall short through its exploration of programming concepts from a multitude of angles- providing a comprehensive view for readers. It helps readers avoid common pitfalls experienced by all programmers and sets a strong foundation for readers to continue to build on top of. I have met many aspiring software engineers and existing software engineers who struggle to progress past the beginner/intermediate level of programming because they lack the training and mindset that this book highlights. I personally have experienced rapid improvement on my own programming capabilities after employing the programming methodology demonstrated in this book. It truly provides the most holistic view of Intermediate C Programming that I've seen and I hope everyone with any interest in programming has the privilege of learning from it.

Tiffany Chen

Intermediate C Programming second edition is a well-structured and comprehensive guide that serves as an excellent resource for programmers looking to expand their knowledge of the C programming language. With its focus on intermediate-level concepts, this book bridges the gap between beginner-level tutorials and more advanced programming texts. This book takes a systematic approach to presenting the material to ensure that readers have a solid foundation before moving on to more intermediate-level concepts. Each topic of programming is explained in detail, with relevant code snippets and practical examples that are applicable to real-world scenarios. This comprehensive coverage is a valuable resource for programmers looking to enhance their programming skills and as well as coding quality.

Ashley Kim

Printed in the United States
by Baker & Taylor Publisher Services